INFANTS
AND
TODDLERS

INFANTS
AND
TODDLERS

RICK A. CAULFIELD
University of Hawaii

Prentice
Hall

Upper Saddle River, New Jersey 07458

Library of Congress Cataloging-in-Publication Data

Caulfield, Rick (Rick A.)
  Infants and toddlers / Rick Caulfield.
    p.   cm.
  Includes bibliographical references and index.
  ISBN 0-13-014583-1 (alk. paper)
    1. Infants—Development. 2. Infant psychology. 3. Infants—Care. 4. Child development.
  5. Toddlers—Psychology. 6. Toddlers—Care. I. Title.

HQ774.C38 2001
305.232—dc21

00–46953

VP/Editorial Director: Laura Pearson
Senior Acquisitions Editor: Jennifer Gilliland
Editorial Assistant: Nicole Girrbach
AVP/Director of Manufacturing and Production: Barbara Kittle
Managing Editor: Mary Rottino
Production Editor: Lisa M. Guidone
Prepress and Manufacturing Manager: Nick Sklitsis
Prepress and Manufacturing Buyer: Tricia Kenny
Cover Designer: Bruce Kenselaar
Cover Art: Barbara Campbell, Liaison Agency, Inc.
Art Manager: Guy Ruggiero
Line Art Coordinator: Mirella Signoretto
Director, Image Resource Center: Melinda Lee Reo
Manager, Rights & Permissions: Kay Dellosa
Interior Image Specialist: Beth Boyd
Director of Marketing: Beth Gillett Mejia
Senior Marketing Manager: Sharon Cosgrove
Copyeditor: Kathy Pruno
Proofreader: Rainbow Graphics
Indexer: Niels Buessem, Andover Publishing Services

This book was set in 10/12 New Baskerville by Pine Tree Composition, Inc., and was printed and bound by R.R. Donnelley and Sons. The cover was printed by Phoenix Color Corp.

© 2001 by Prentice-Hall, Inc.
A Division of Pearson Education
Upper Saddle River, New Jersey 07458

Printed in the United States of America
10 8 8 7 6 5 4 3 2 1

ISBN: 0-13-014583-1

Prentice-Hall International (UK) Limited, *London*
Prentice-Hall of Australia Pty. Limited, *Sydney*
Prentice-Hall Canada Inc., *Toronto*
Prentice-Hall Hispanoamericana, S.A., *Mexico*
Prentice-Hall of India Private Limited, *New Delhi*
Prentice-Hall of Japan, Inc., *Tokyo*
Pearson Education Asia Pte. Ltd., *Singapore*
Editora Prentice-Hall do Brasil, Ltda., *Rio de Janeiro*

**DEDICATED TO
MY WIFE, DIANE,
AND OUR TWO CHILDREN,
ERIN AND KEVIN**

BRIEF CONTENTS

CONTENTS

PART III DEVELOPMENTAL FOUNDATIONS

7 PHYSICAL GROWTH AND DEVELOPMENT 133

8 COGNITIVE DEVELOPMENT 161

PART IV SUPPLEMENTAL TOPICS

11 HEALTH AND NUTRITION   238

PREFACE

This book covers an exciting period in the human lifespan from conception to the end of age 3. It is a remarkable story of physical, cognitive, and psychosocial transformations. Infants enter a distinctly social world at birth. Families provide the first contact with the outside world. At the same time, infants live in a uniquely cultural context. The expectations and traditions of cultures across the world shape child-rearing attitudes and practices with direct consequences on development.

RECURRENT THEMES IN BOOK

Four important themes recur throughout this book: uniqueness of each infant and toddler, importance of families, interdependent relationship between young children and caregivers, and sociocultural context of development. Each contributes to a richly varied picture of infants and toddlers:

- **Uniqueness of each infant and toddler.** Each child is a unique being. While this book primarily focuses on typical development, parents and professional caregivers must adapt their styles to meet the individual needs of each child.

- **Importance of family.** The family is the cornerstone of every society. In a time of instant communication and global interconnection, it still remains the primary source of sustenance and nurturance in the early years of life.

- **Interdependent relationship between young children and caregivers.** The interaction between children and their caregivers is a two-way street. Adults exert a profound influence, but infants also play an active role in engaging with their physical and social world.

- **Sociocultural context of development.** Culture is an important aspect of development. It not only shapes parents' expectations about children's abilities but also influences their caregiving patterns.

COMPREHENSIVE COVERAGE

This book follows a topical approach. It is organized into four major parts: Part 1 examines past views of infants and toddlers, different theories of development, and research methods. Part 2 discusses conception, prenatal development, childbirth, and the first month after birth. Part 3 covers physical, cognitive, language, and psychosocial development during the first 3 years. Part 4 addresses issues of health and nutrition and guidance and early education.

The topics in Part 4 can be linked with specific chapters in Part 3. For example, Chapter 11 on health and nutrition can be covered after a discussion of physical growth and development in Chapter 7. As children start to crawl and walk, safety must be addressed to minimize injuries while maximizing opportunities to explore. Likewise, proper nutrition is tied to optimal physical growth. Chapter 12 examines caregivers' role in encouraging socially appropriate behavior as children begin to exhibit increasing independence and engage in extended social contacts, topics discussed in Chapter 10. Lastly, the second half of Chapter 12 weaves the different strands of development in Part 3 into a composite picture of appropriate practices that meet the needs of infants and toddlers in out-of-home programs.

SPECIFIC FEATURES

This book incorporates a number of unique features. Each is designed to stimulate and broaden students' interest in the reading material:

- **Parenting issues and sociocultural influences.** To bride theory and research, in each chapter, special boxes highlight issues of concern to parents and underscore the impact of culture on all aspects of development.

- **Historical voices.** Interspersed throughout each chapter are historical voices, providing interesting insights into the prevailing views and beliefs of infants and toddlers at the time.

- **Special boxes.** Other topics of interest are covered in special boxes to expand on information presented in the text.

- **Infants with special needs.** At the end of each chapter in Part 3, special needs are discussed with a particular focus on early identification and intervention.

ACKNOWLEDGMENTS

Every book is a collaborative effort. It requires the involvement of countless individuals. I especially want to thank my dedicated students enrolling in my courses at the University of Hawaii at Manoa. They have provided a living laboratory to explore together the wondrous journey of development during the first few years. I have noticed an increasing number of men who have been taking my courses and entering fields traditionally associated with women. Men can make enormous contributions to the development of infants and toddlers, whether as parents or professional caregivers.

I also wish to acknowledge colleagues and reviewers who provided constructive criticisms and helpful suggestions on drafts of this book. Special thanks go to the superb editorial staff at Prentice Hall, particularly Senior Acquisitions Editor Jennifer Gilliland and Senior Production Editor Lisa M. Guidone, for their support in making this book a reality.

Finally, my immediate family deserves the greatest thanks. The unconditional love of my wife, Diane, and our two wonderful children, Erin and Kevin, shaped not only my own personal growth and development but also the scope and content of this book.

Rick A. Caulfield

INTRODUCTION AND HISTORICAL PERSPECTIVES

The well-being of the adult is intimately connected with the kind of life that he had when he was a child.

Maria Montessori, *The Secret of Childhood*

The first smile. The first steps. The first words. Infancy marks a period of rapid changes, both physically and psychologically. Has it always been thought of as an important period in life, as many people believe today? Or did society's views of infants change throughout history? Chapter 1 explores infancy's place in the lifespan, the impact of sociocultural factors on development, and historical views of infants.

A myriad of images comes to mind when people think of infants. The birth of a baby marks a special moment in the lives of parents. To some, it brings awe and wonder; to others, responsibility and uncertainty. The major milestones of the infant's first few years of life usually elicit universal emotions among adults. In different parts of the world, parents view their infants as a bridge to both the past and future. A new member added to the family often brings a sense of continuity as well as possibility.

Infancy has received considerable attention from the media. Hundreds of parenting articles and books have been written on the subject. The scientific study of infants has played an influential role in shaping caregiving practices. Until the 20th century, parents relied on their own intuition or cultural tradition about the proper care of infants. However, as a result of contemporary research in diverse fields, the image of infants has evolved from one of helpless creatures to that of competent social beings from the moment of birth.

IMPORTANCE OF INFANCY IN HUMAN LIFESPAN

Infancy can be seen as the first step in a remarkable journey of human development. It has been portrayed in a number of ways—the first chapter in a book or act in a play, one of four seasons during the year, or the first rung on a ladder. It is derived from *infans,* a Latin word meaning "without speech." Perhaps the ancient Romans thought that the period of infancy ended when a person began to speak, although in reality, infants actually start to acquire language long before they utter their first word. Today, infancy usually involves the first year of life, whereas toddlerhood refers to children from 1 to 3 years of age.

Across the world, people generally agree that infancy is a separate, distinct period in life. Questions are frequently asked about infancy's importance because of its place in human development. Is it a critical time in life? Do the circumstances of the first 2 years of life irreversibly affect later development? Philosophers throughout history have debated the importance of infancy. However, it was not until the late 19th century that systematic observations of infants were conducted. In the early 20th century, scientific theories explaining human behavior began to emerge.

Sigmund Freud had a profound impact on the study of infants during the first half of the 20th century. His psychoanalytic theory supported the view of infancy as a **critical period** in life, *a time of vulnerability with long-lasting, irreversible consequences.* The early years of life, he believed, determined the eventual personality of adults. In particular, he theorized that unexplained fears, or neuroses, developed as a result of real or imagined traumatic experiences a person encountered in infancy or early childhood (Freud, 1920).

Two studies are often cited in support of the view of infancy as a critical period. Spitz (1945) concluded that institutionalized infants showed severe developmental delays and depressed, withdrawn behavior because of maternal deprivation, or the lack of emotional contact with a caring adult. Although a trained staff provided adequate custodial care, the infants did not receive attentive, individualized care from adults. Goldfarb (1945) had reached a similar conclusion in his own study of institutionalized infants. However, critics argued that Spitz and Goldfarb failed to follow their subjects' progress to determine whether infants' initial experiences had irreversible consequences. In other words, did the effects persist even when the infants moved into a more enriched environment?

Other studies attempted to examine the effects of changing or modifying the environment of institutionalized infants. Skodak and Skeels (1945) placed deprived infants with severe delays in an institution with mentally retarded adults. They found that the institutionalized adults eagerly welcomed the infants into their wards. The average IQ of the infants at the time of the transfer fell into the mildly retarded range, but after 1 to 2 years with the adults, the infants scored dramatic gains. In another study, Skodak and Skeels (1949) compared adopted infants with a group that remained in the institution and found that the adopted infants clearly benefited from the improved quality of care. After 2 years, the infants' performance revealed an average IQ.

Skodak and Skeels' studies showed that infants can overcome the negative effects of deprived conditions if they receive appropriate enrichment at an early age. Other studies since then seem to support the view of infancy as a **sensitive period** in life, *a time of vulnerability with long-lasting but not necessarily irreversible consequences.* Skodak and Skeel have been severely criticized because of their study's methodological flaws (Longstreth, 1981). However, other researchers have verified that deprived infants are able to make significant gains if the quality of their lives is significantly improved (Dennis, 1973; Kagan & Klein, 1973).

For example, in their cross-cultural study, Kagan and Klein (1973) observed infants who spent the first year of life in windowless huts in an isolated Guatemalan village. During the first year, mothers took care of their infants in the huts' dark interior. Infants were rarely talked to or played with. They left the huts only when they began to walk at about 15 months. Although initially showing motor delays compared with their European American counterparts, Guatemalan infants made remarkable gains later. In fact, Guatemalan preadolescents matched their European American peers on cognitive tasks at 11 to 12 years of age. Other studies have reported similar results of infants who have overcome insurmountable odds (Werner, 1995).

Taken together, the view of infancy as a critical period has been overstated. Infants show a remarkable resiliency, or ability to recover from deprived conditions (Bateson & Hinde, 1987; Bornstein, 1989). On the other hand, the notion of infancy as a sensitive period has been gaining increasing acceptance, not only because it emphasizes the importance of the first few years of life, but also because it acknowledges infants' capacity to change. If there is a critical period, it occurs in prenatal development. Because the brain and other major organs develop rapidly during the second to eighth weeks of gestation, any environmental insult may result in long-lasting and often irreversible effects on the developing child. Examples include excessive maternal intake of alcohol and drugs or malnutrition during pregnancy.

SOCIOCULTURAL CONTEXT OF INFANCY

Infants do not develop in isolation. From the moment of birth, they take an active role in exploring the physical world and shaping their interaction with others. Infants elicit and maintain the attention of their caregivers with a variety of behavioral responses. Although infants rely primarily on involuntary reflexes during the initial weeks and months of life, they begin to interact with their caregivers in increasingly purposeful ways. Take crying, for example. At first, it is an automatic response to an internal state— hunger or pain—or external stimuli—a loud noise. It typically elicits an immediate reaction from most caregivers. When adults respond to their cries consistently, infants gradually learn to trust the world, forming secure relationships with others.

The care of infants generally takes place in the context of the family, the basic unit of every society. The family is defined as a group of persons who are committed to one an-

Each infant is a unique being from the moment of birth.
Photo courtesy of Tami Dawson, Photo Resource Hawaii.

other in an intimate, interpersonal relationship (Rice, 1998). Because infants require an extended period of development before they reach a sufficient level of independence and productivity in life, they need the responsive care and attention of adults, particularly their parents, to survive. The family provides the initial contact with the physical and social world. The kinds of experiences they receive depend on the cultural beliefs and traditions of adults.

Major sources of socialization include adults providing the primary care, the composition of the family, and cultural factors. The interdependent relationship between the infant and the other socializing agents is shown in Figure 1–1. Each component has a bidirectional impact on one another signified with arrows. Further, the model is divided into two parts. The first part deals with the immediate social context of the infant's relationship with his or her primary caregivers. It centers on *the mutual accommodation, or continual adjustment, between infants and their caregivers,* referred to as **reciprocity**. The second

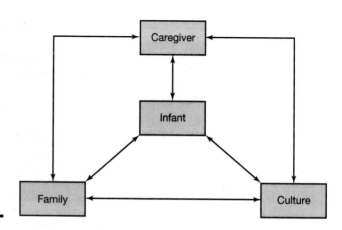

FIGURE 1–1 Sociocultural Model of Infancy

part involves the extended social context of the infant's relationship with others. Specifically, the family and culture play equally major roles in influencing not only the quality but also the quantity of interaction between the infant and his or her primary caregivers (Caulfield, 1995).

The sociocultural model consists of four interdependent components: infant, caregiver, family, and culture. The relevant variables of each one are shown in Table 1–1.

INFANT

Infants are active participants in their environment. Relevant variables influencing infants' interaction with others include their age, sex, developmental history, and **temperament**, or *their individual behavioral style and characteristic way of responding to different situations or people.*

Knowingly or unknowingly, parents and other caregivers behave in ways reflecting their expectations based on the infant's age. In the United States and other industrialized nations, experienced and educated adults generally respond to the infant's crying during the first weeks and months after birth. However, later during the second year, adults usually accept and even encourage infant's increased independence. At the same time, the infant's gender may also shape adults' expectations. Based on adults' cultural beliefs and traditions, infants may be channeled into gender-specific activities. For example, both boys and girls might be given different types of toys or encouraged to engage in stereotypical tasks.

The developmental or medical history and behavioral style of infants play an important role. Unforeseen factors, such as low birth weight or prematurity, may limit their contact with adults. In addition, infants' unique way of exploring the world and

TABLE 1–1	SOCIOCULTURAL CONTEXT OF INFANCY
Component	**Relevant Variables**
Infant	Age
	Sex
	Developmental or medical history
	Behavioral style or temperament
Caregiver	Knowledge of infants' development
	Level of education and experience
	Method of discipline
	Behavioral style or temperament
Family	Composition
	Size
	Educational and economic level
	Social network
Culture	Expectations of infants' abilities
	Beliefs about child-rearing practices

interacting with people reflects their distinctive individuality. Their genetic inheritance contributes to their personality and shapes the quality of emotional contact they experience with their caregivers.

CAREGIVER

A caregiver refers to a person who is able to meet the physical and psychological needs of infants. Relevant variables that affect caregivers' relationship with infants include knowledge of development, level of experience and education, method of discipline, and behavioral style.

Caregivers' knowledge of development is closely related to their own level of experience and education. Experienced parents or professional caregivers working with infants and toddlers tend to provide a more responsive environment. Further, caring adults generally understand the developmental tasks of infancy. Adults' method of discipline may have a direct impact on the quality of their relationship with infants.

PARENTING ISSUES

NONPARENTAL CARE

The issue of nonparental care in infancy has received considerable attention in recent years. Concerns have been raised about the long-term consequences of out-of-home care on infants' emotional attachment during the first year of life (Egeland & Hiester, 1995; Scarr & Eisenberg, 1993).

The number of single parents and working mothers has risen sharply in the last half of the 20th century. Belsky (1986, 1987) concluded that babies who spent at least 20 hours a week in out-of-home care demonstrated insecure patterns of attachment with their parents. He was particularly worried about the long-term impact of out-of-home care on children's aggressiveness later in preschool. However, others have questioned his conclusions (Clarke-Stewart, 1989; Phillips et al., 1987).

The issue depends not on the infants' age at the time of entry or length of care but instead the kind and quality of care they receive. One study examined the effects of maternal employment on 1-year-old infants' attachment (Chase-Lansdale & Owen, 1987). The investigators did not find any significant difference between infants whose mothers stayed at home or went back to work. Other more recent studies have found similar results (Clarke-Stewart, Gruber, & Fitzgerald, 1994; Roggman et al., 1994).

Although the debate continues, countless parents are faced each day with the reality of having to put their infants in the care of others. To minimize the possible negative effects of nonparental care, minimum licensing standards are required to ensure that the basic needs of infants are met. Still, custodial care is not the only factor. The quality of emotional contact between adults and infants is an important ingredient (Caruso, 1996).

FAMILY

In all societies, families generally provide the care that infants need to survive. Parents and relatives play an important role in instilling the values of their culture and modeling acceptable behavior. The composition of families varies considerably from one to two parents to an extended household with other relatives who live in the household. Other important factors include the socioeconomic level of families, such as their ability to provide food and shelter, and their social network with the community at large (Knox & Schacht, 1997).

Ethnicity sometimes determines the size, structure, and composition of families. The "typical" family in the United States is not necessarily composed of two parents and children. Minorities generally live in large, extended families. African Americans, Hispanic Americans, and Asian Americans, in particular, have historically lived in multigenerational families. Grandparents are likely to be directly involved in child-rearing responsibilities. For example, in African American families, grandmothers have played an active role in caring for grandchildren (Wakschlag, Chase-Lansdale, & Brooks-Gunn, 1996). The involvement of grandparents seems to provide numerous benefits. In single-parent households, which account for about half of African American families, grandparents bring a wealth of experience in modeling parenting skills (Chase–Lansdale, Brooks-Gunn, & Zamsky, 1994).

CULTURE

The cultural context of the caregiving environment exerts a profound influence in shaping development. It consists of a set of beliefs and expectations about the infant's abilities and about child-rearing practices affecting the way the caregiver interacts with the infant from the moment of birth. The cultural group varies considerably in size from a small hunting and gathering group to a large, industrialized nation. Whatever its size, the cultural group influences social behavior, although individual variability may occur among its members (Brislin, 1997; Lonner & Malpass, 1994).

Cultural variations in child-rearing practices exist across the world. For example, distinct cultural differences between Japanese and European Americans were found in terms of maternal responsiveness (Bornstein, Azuma, Tamis-LeMonda, & Ogino, 1990; Bornstein, Toda, Azuma, Tamis-LeMonda, & Ogino, 1990). Japanese mothers typically respond to their infants' social orientation, whereas European American mothers usually attempt to direct their infants' attention to objects in the environment. Both engage in activities their respective cultures value. Japanese mothers organize their interactions with their infants to strengthen the emotional bond between them. On the other hand, European American mothers often structure their interactions to foster independence in their infants.

RECURRENT THEMES IN INFANCY

The developmental progression of infants is a complex, yet remarkable, process. Parents and other adults who come into contact with infants marvel at infants' presumed helplessness at birth and later emerging independence in such a short time. Recurrent themes emerge in any discussion of human development. The major themes resemble a woven fabric. Each thread in it represents an important part of the whole. Separately, each one tells only a part of the story; together, they form a complete picture:

■ **Interdependent relationships among major developmental domains.** Subsequent chapters focus on infants' development from conception to 3 years. Three major areas are covered: physical, cognitive, and psychosocial development (see Table 1–2). Each area is closely tied to the others. When infants make progress in one area of development, advances typically occur in another. There are numerous examples. When infants begin to crawl and walk, they enter a new chapter in their development. The achievement of independent locomotion increases their opportunities to explore the physical world which, in turn, fosters their cognitive ability to learn about the physical properties of objects. As infants master emerging physical and cognitive skills, they develop a sense of competence, which plays an important role in infants' psychosocial development. Therefore, although each developmental area is discussed separately, in reality, the four major areas are interconnected with each another. Infants are not a collection of parts but an integrated whole.

■ **Influence of heredity and environment.** The contribution of heredity and environment to development has been debated for hundreds of years. The debate intensified in the 20th century as scientists attempted to answer the following question: Do genes determine development or does the environment shape the outcome? In fact, both play an important role. Heredity is sometimes referred to as **nature**, or *the biological and genetic factors that influence development,* and environment as **nurture**, or *the influence of environment and experience on development.* Numerous examples illustrating the interaction between heredity and environment abound. Of course, infants inherit their genes from their biological parents at the moment of conception. Their genetic inheritance influences the rate and extent of physical growth. At the same time, the environment exerts a profound effect. Poor diet or illness is likely to affect infants' eventual physical size (Morgan, 1990). Likewise, a nonstimulating environment takes a toll on infants' ability to learn about the world. Exposure to a nonstimulating environment limits the realization of infants' genetic potentiality, whereas a stimulating one fosters optimal development of the brain (Ricciuti, 1993).

TABLE 1–2 MAJOR DOMAINS OF DEVELOPMENT	
Domain	**Description**
Physical	Physical development entails changes in the growth of the body, the brain, sensory capacities, and motor skills. It exerts an influence on both cognitive and psychosocial development.
Cognitive	Cognitive development refers to changes that occur in mental abilities, including thinking, learning, solving problems, and communicating. It is closely tied to both physical and psychosocial development.
Psychosocial	Psychosocial development refers to the development of the personality and emotions and the formation of relationships with others. It affects the physical and cognitive aspects of development.

■ **Norms and individual differences.** Development generally unfolds in a predictable manner. Genetic factors largely determine **maturation**, *the orderly sequence of changes*, although the environment provides opportunities to practice emerging skills. No one teaches infants to roll over, sit, crawl, and walk, but social praise from others rewards their accomplishment and encourages similar attempts in the future. **Norms**, on the other hand, refer to *the average ages that typical skills are achieved.* Based on repeated observations of a large sample of infants, norms serve an important function in providing caregivers with some guidelines in gauging infants' progress. Although norms may play an important role, they do not supersede the importance of recognizing the individuality of each infant.

■ **Reciprocal nature of development.** In the past, researchers have focused on the direct influence of adults on infants. However, in recent years, researchers have increasingly recognized the influence of infants on their caregivers (Scarr, 1992). Infants do actively shape their environment. For example, parents tend to respond positively to "easygoing" infants who smile frequently and behave predictably. On the other hand, "difficult" infants usually elicit a different response from their parents,

PARENTING ISSUES

NATURE–NURTURE CONTROVERSY

Is nature or nurture the most important factor in shaping human behavior and development? It is an age-old question. Judith Harris renewed interest in a debate stretching back to Plato and other ancient philosophers. In *The Nurture Assumption,* she argues that parents contribute their genes and play a minimal role thereafter (Harris, 1998). Peers, not parents, have a profound influence on development. Children eventually discard their parents' values "like a dorky sweater" once they come into contact with peers. Studies of twins appear to support Harris's claims. Identical twins separated in infancy and reared in different homes are no more different than twins raised in the same home. The same thing applies to siblings. Harris's analysis of research indicates that parents do not have any long-term effect on their children's behavior.

Of course, other experts disagree with Harris. They worry about the impact of her thesis on the way parents raise their children. Will it encourage parental neglect or abuse? Will it send the wrong message to parents who may feel that they do not have to pay attention to their children because "it does not matter"? The answer seems to be that peers do make a difference, but so do parents. In one study, researchers have found that the quality of teens' relationship with their parents is the key ingredient in determining whether they will become involved in alcohol, sex, tobacco, and violence (Begley, 1998). So, both nature and nurture play a major role in shaping the course of development. Parents' influence continues to be felt in the choices children make long after they begin to exercise their own judgment of right and wrong.

perhaps hostility or rejection. Therefore, infants can and do influence the direction and outcome of their own development.

■ **Cultural differences. Cultures** differ across the world. They provide *a set of attitudes and beliefs transmitted from one generation to another within a particular group of people.* For example, Mayan infants sleep in their mothers' beds until age 2, whereas in the United States, European American infants typically do not (Morelli et al., 1992). Whereas Mayan parents emphasize the value of closeness with infants, European American parents in general stress the importance of independence. In both cases, cultural beliefs about infants may affect the kinds of experiences they receive. Other studies of infants and their parents in other cultures have led to similar conclusions. **Cross-cultural studies**, *the comparison of a culture with one or more other cultures,* provide information on the similarities or differences between cultures. The discussion of cultural differences is woven into each subsequent chapter in order to gain an appreciation of cultural contributions on development.

■ **Continuity and discontinuity of development.** Two divergent notions of development have emerged in recent years. Some developmentalists emphasize the **continuity of development**, *the belief that development involves gradual, continuous changes.* The slow, steady growth of an acorn represents their view. On the other hand, others stress the **discontinuity of development**, *the belief that development consists of a series of distinct stages.* The metamorphosis of a caterpillar as it changes into a butterfly ascribes the other view. Developmentalists who ally themselves with either continuous or discontinuous development highlight the importance of environmental influences or the role of heredity on the process of development, respectively. Neither extreme view tells the whole story. In reality, different aspects of development show evidence of both. For example, infants' first words, although a seemingly abrupt, discontinuous event, is actually the result of months of growth and practice. The important point is that human growth and development begin at conception and continue until death. The stage of infancy in the human lifespan, including the prenatal period before birth, marks the first step in a long journey.

HISTORICAL PERSPECTIVES

Throughout history, infants have been raised in families. In Western societies, families have traditionally adhered to the following common set of beliefs: families consisted of a married couple, their children, and other relatives who lived in a common household; marriage was seen as a lifelong commitment; and fathers were expected to be the breadwinners (Mintz & Kellogg, 1988). However, during the last half of the 20th century, the traditional concept of families has been challenged in the United States and other industrialized nations. Among the contributing factors are the changing views of marriage and the role of women in society today (Cheal, 1993). Yet, one thing has not changed. The role of families has always been to serve as the primary socializing agent in the lives of infants. The important factor is not the composition of families but the quality of emotional contact between caregivers and infants.

This section first focuses on early views of families and their functions during the Roman and medieval periods of Western history, a span of about 2,000 years. Then it traces the evolving role and diversity of families in the United States during the past three centuries.

ANCIENT ROMANS

The ancient Romans left a lasting legacy to Western civilization. The family was the cornerstone of their society. The term itself is based on the Latin root *familia* referring to a group of people living in the same household. It included not only parents and their children but also slaves (Dixon, 1992).

The Roman family fulfilled a variety of important functions. It served as the foundation of economic production. Each succeeding generation of children were trained to meet a specific economic task such as farming. It also fulfilled a socializing role. Parents, particularly fathers, instilled moral values, particularly *pietas* (piety), the acknowledgment of ties to the family, and *gravitas* (gravity), the character or demeanor of the person (Rawson, 1991).

Until the Punic Wars in the second and third centuries B.C., the Roman father wielded considerable power. He had the right to reject or abandon an infant (Rawson, 1986). However, the father's power of life and death gradually diminished while the rights of the mother increased. The Roman family demonstrated a remarkable ability to adapt to changing circumstances.

MEDIEVAL PERIOD AND RENAISSANCE

The medieval period in Western Europe spanned a period of almost 1,000 years after the fall of the Roman Empire in fifth century A. D. During the middle ages, families lived primarily in villages. There they toiled in the field and home, and married and raised children. People shared a common purpose and sense of community (Gies & Gies, 1990).

In medieval English villages, the family was a bulwark of continuity in a sea of change. Its size fluctuated during its generational cycle as the young couple married and settled

---

HISTORICALLY SPEAKING

MEDIEVAL PERIOD

Bartholomew, English Franciscan
De Proprietatibus Rerum, 13th century A.D.
The child cometh of the substance of father and mother, and taketh of them feeding and nourishing, and profiteth not, neither liveth, without help from them.

Source: Bartholomew (1924), pp. 58–59.

into a life with children (Gies & Gies, 1987). Babies were born at home with the help of midwives. The newborn was baptized immediately at birth, lest it die in a state of original sin (Hanawalt, 1988). The midwife then carried the child to the church. The priest blessed the child and read a passage from the Bible (Owst, 1926/1965; Gottlieb, 1993).

Medieval parents had been accused of cruelty to their children. Evidence of harsh discipline can be found (Aries, 1960/1962; deMause, 1974). However, in general, the lives of children were valued. The records of coroners captured the anguish of parents who lost a child as the result of an accident. They yielded rare glimpses of a baby in a cradle at a fireplace, children at work and play, little boys following their fathers to the field or mill, or little girls helping their mothers at home. A sermon focused on a child's imagination as he played with "small bits of wood, to build a chamber, buttery, and hall, to make a white horse of a wand, a sailing ship of broken bread . . ." (Owst, 1961, p. 34).

The Middle Ages ended in the 14th century as a spirit of artistic and intellectual revival emerged in Italy and swept through western Europe. The Renaissance, as it is now called, resulted from a renewed interest in the civilizations of the ancient Greeks and Romans (Hale, 1994; Palmer & Colton, 1995).

ENLIGHTENMENT: LOCKE AND ROUSSEAU

Whereas scholars of the 15th and 16th centuries assumed that the classical works provided a reliable source of knowledge, thinkers of the 17th century onward rejected obeisant acceptance of authority and resolved to rely instead on their own intellects. They lived in an enlightened age because they challenged traditional notions of the world. They believed that natural, not supernatural, forces governed the universe and that rigorous scientific methods advanced human knowledge in all areas of inquiry. Two influential minds of the Enlightenment, Locke and Rousseau, applied the same skepticism to the study of human behavior and, in the process, revised western European conceptions of childhood.

John Locke (1632–1704) founded the English empiricist tradition. He postulated that knowledge originated from experience and rejected the concept of original sin (Locke, 1690/1894). He compared the mind to *a blank tablet*, **tabula rasa**, at birth. "[T]he souls of the newly-born," he wrote, "are just empty tablets afterwards to be filled in by observation and reasoning . . ." (Locke, 1958, p. 137).

Likewise, French philosopher Jean Jacques Rousseau (1712–1778) made a significant contribution to western European thought during the 18th century. He believed in the preservation of humankind's natural goodness. In his view, the fundamental aim of education was to protect children from society's evils. His basic premises about the goodness of nature and the corrupting influence of society were summarized in an oft-quoted passage of *Emile*:

> God makes all things good; man meddles with them and they become evil. He forces one soil to yield the products of another, one tree to bear another's fruit. (Rousseau, 1762/1911, p. 5)

In *Emile*, Rousseau described the development of a fictitious child, "an orphan," living in accordance with nature. The book itself was organized into four separate **stages**, or *periods of development with distinct qualitative changes,* of the child's life. They included infancy (birth to 2) and childhood (2 to 12). Rousseau affirmed, as Locke did, the primary role of the senses in the formation of the mind and acquisition of knowledge from the moment of birth:

> We are born capable of learning, but knowing nothing, perceiving nothing. The mind, bound up within imperfect and half grown organs, is not even aware of its own existence. (Rousseau, 1762/1911, p. 28)

Rousseau exerted a profound influence on child-rearing and educational practices in western Europe during the 19th and 20th centuries. Johann Heinrich Pestalozzi, Johann Friedrich Herbart, Friedrich Froebel, and Maria Montessori incorporated Rousseau's ideas into their teaching methods. Their approaches in turn influenced educational innovations in the United States such as Montessori's emphasis on treating children with dignity and respect and providing developmentally appropriate materials and activities to meet their individual needs. Even the developmental theories of the 20th century reflected Rousseau's recognition of infancy as a distinct period and use of sequential stages in describing children's development.

The western European influence found its way to the early settlements of the North American continent in the early 17th century. During the subsequent course of American history, culturally diverse groups from other corners of the world contributed immensely to the diversity and quality of life in the United States.

UNITED STATES

The American family is a not a single entity. It is a product of historical, demographic, and economic changes over nearly four centuries. Even before western Europeans settled on the eastern seaboard, the native Americans, the original inhabitants of the continent, developed their own distinctive forms of kinship. Therefore, a discussion of native American families provides an appropriate starting point.

Native Americans. The establishment of western European settlements in North America resulted in the eventual displacement of an entirely different social and economic system. Native American societies generally lacked the private ownership of land and natural resources that formed the basis of western European organization (Coontz, 1988).

In native American societies, the reciprocity of resources was a matter of survival. John Heckewelder, a missionary, wrote of the Iroquois' concept:

> Whatever liveth on the land, whatsoever groweth out of the earth, and all that is in the rivers and waters flowing through the same, was given jointly to all, and every one is entitled to his share. (Morgan, 1881/1965, p. 49)

Two broad systems of kinship prevailed in native American societies of North America. The foraging groups of the northern woods and the Great Basin were based on bilateral descent. In other words, a person's heritage was traced to his or her father and mother. On the other hand, farming groups with plentiful resources usually followed a unilateral system of one side of the family or the other.

In both systems, the nuclear family did not stand alone. In foraging and hunting societies, families spent part of the year on their own but coalesced into large groups during the summer at social ceremonies. In the south, densely populated villages centered on the cultivation of crops during the summer but later divided into small hunting units during the fall and winter. The constant flux created a flexible organization facilitating mutual dependence between individuals and different groups within the tribe. Further, a variety of practices allowed a group to expand or contract on the basis of necessity. A family facing a shortage of members may adopt or borrow a child from relatives (Axtell, 1981).

Inevitably, the arrival of western European settlers resulted in a clash between two incompatible modes of production and concepts of property. Contact with western Europeans undermined native Americans' system of kinship. The accumulation and concentration of wealth in one family or group led to new concepts of private property, which gradually supplanted ties of blood and reciprocity. The spread of diseases and plagues decimated large numbers of native Americans. It not only disrupted families but discredited indigenous religious and medicinal practices. The impact of contact between the two groups destroyed the symmetry of relations within native American families, eclipsing traditional ways of raising children.

Colonial America. The western European colonists who settled on the North American continent in the early 17th century initially faced a difficult period. They had to rely on the family, a predominantly patriarchal institution, as an important source of stability during the colonial period (Smith, 1982). The family resided in a household that included kin and nonkin, such as servants, who shared a common residence. It served as the foundation of society, or in the words of William Gouge, a Puritan preacher, as "a little Church, and a little common-wealth" (Morgan, 1966).

A descriptive account of Puritan life came from New England merchant and magistrate Samuel Sewall. Because newborns were regarded as embodiments of sin, parents were expected to break the will of their children. Sewall invoked his children's fear of possible eternal damnation in hell to suppress their presumed natural depravity. Another Puritan preacher, Cotton Mather, advocated shame in disciplining children (Mather, 1911/1957).

The family was the basic economic and social unit of colonial America. It formed the basis of educational and religious instruction (Demos, 1970, 1986). As a patriarchal institution, the father was seen as the head of the household, whereas other members were regarded as its limbs. His authority was not to be questioned (Mintz & Kellogg, 1988).

The birth of each child reinforced the interconnection between the family and community. Frequent childbirth among women in colonial America was a common occurrence with an average of six children (Wells, 1982). A large number of women usually attended the expectant mother's labor to provide comfort and aid. Their presence in the home often displaced the husband, as Ebenezer Parkman recorded in 1738 shortly before the birth of his fourth daughter:

> A little after 4 in the morning my Wife called Me up by her extreme pains prevailing upon her and changing into signs of Travail. I rode over to Deacon Forbush's and brought her [Mrs. Forbush] over as our midwife. Sister Hicks, old Mrs. Knowlton,

Mrs. Whipple, Mrs. Hephzibath Maynard, Mrs. Byles and Mrs. Rogers were call'd and brought and stay'd all Day and Night. (Parkman, 1961, p. 447)

Death in childbirth provoked fear among many. An estimated 1 in 30 childbirths resulted in the mother's death because of protracted labor, unusual birth, hemorrhages and convulsions, and infection (Wertz & Wertz, 1977). After birth, infants were commonly breastfed until the end of their first year of life and were kept largely in their mother's care. Children were loved but disciplined sternly. The combination of affection and harshness exemplified colonial child-rearing practices. Puritan poet Anne Bradstreet wrote affectionately of her children but commented that at times, like pieces of land, they needed "the plough of correction" (Bradstreet, 1981).

Early Republic.   In 1831, French historian Alexis de Tocqueville arrived in the United States to study the nation's new system of prisons. He used the occasion to analyze the forces that provided the bedrock of the nation. His conclusion was that the spirit of "individualism" was its distinguishing trait. It dramatically influenced, he believed, the foundation of American society. The family started to focus on the psychological needs of their children. At the same time, a married couple sought companionship and mutual affection.

In the early 19th century, a distinctive feature of the typical American family was its isolation from society. The family had come to be defined as a private place—a shelter or refuge from the public sphere of life. Whereas the colonial family had been seen as a microcosm of society and cornerstone of church and state, a radically different notion of the family emerged after the American Revolution. The family referred not to a household but to an isolated group. It consisted of a father and mother and their children. It changed from a social institution with economic functions to one with the primary responsibility of raising children and providing emotional support to its members (Coontz, 1988).

During the 19th century, humane attitudes about children increased. A number of diarists recognized infancy as a separate, distinct period in life. New England educator

HISTORICALLY SPEAKING

EARLY REPUBLIC

Abigail Adams, wife of John Adams
Abigail Adams to Mercy Otis Warren, 1773
. . . I have an important trust committed to me; and tho I feel myself very un[equal] to it, tis still incumbent upon me to discharge it in the best manner I am capable of.

Source: Adams (1961), p. 85.

Amos Bronson Alcott referred to his children with affection as "objects of great delight." He added,

> "They are indeed the charm of my domestic life. They keep alive and vivid the sentiment of humanity." (Alcott, 1938, p. 55)

Many celebrated the arrival of a new child. Henry Wadsworth Longfellow stated in 1847:

> "This morning was born in the Craigie House a girl, to the great joy of all." (Longfellow, 1886, p. 85)

Late 1800s to 1990s. In the closing decades of the 19th century, increased industrialization and urbanization transformed the United States. The majority of the population earned its livelihood in mills, mines, and factories. Many traced their heritage to a variety of religious, cultural, and ethnic backgrounds as waves of immigrants arrived from other countries. Their diverse origins shaped the nation's attitudes about the role of the American family. As in the past, the family provided stability and flexibility in adapting to a constantly changing environment. It not only eased the stresses of immigration but facilitated the family's adjustment to a modernized industrial and urbanized way of life (Dubofsky, 1996).

The family adopted different strategies to meet the economic realities of life. It provided the only reliable source of mutual assistance and support. Decisions were made on the basis of the needs of the entire family instead of individual choices. Among different ethnic groups, daughters commonly left school at an early age to work or to take care of their parents while sons finished school. Wives and mothers contributed to the family in diverse ways. Typically, they managed the family's finances and husbanded its limited income. Some supplemented the family's income with low-paying work called "outwork" because it occurred at home (Golab, 1977).

In the early 20th century, a small but influential group of experts—psychologists, educators, and legal scholars—developed a new conception of the family, one suited to a modern society. The increasing number of divorces, a pattern that started after 1870, spurred widespread public concern. It was primarily a manifestation of the painful economic and social transition to an increasingly industrialized society. Industrialization and urbanization deprived the family of its traditional economic, educational, and religious functions. The goal of marriage was no longer seen as a matter of financial security or a private place of refuge but one of emotional fulfillment and compatibility (Coontz, 1988).

From 1890 to 1930, a number of reforms were instituted to improve the welfare of children. The progressive reformers consisted of psychologists who advocated strict, rigid feeding and sleeping schedules (see Table 1–3), doctors who transferred the process of childbirth to the hospital to reduce the high mortality among mothers and infants, and lawmakers who enacted programs to provide prenatal and medical care to pregnant mothers and their infants and financial aid to a family with dependent children. New theories such as behaviorism advocated different approaches. John B. Watson wrote in 1928 that "children are made not born" (Watson, 1928, p. 7), arguing that the use of reinforcement and punishment shaped a child's behavior.

TABLE 1-3 THEN AND NOW

There has been a proliferation of child-rearing advice from experts since the turn of the 20th century. The following two contrasting sets of advice—one from the Children's Bureau and the other from a prominent pediatrician—reflect the prevailing view of infants at the time.

U.S. Children's Bureau

Infant Care, 1914

The rule that parents should not play with the baby may seem hard, but it is without doubt a safe one. A young, delicate, or nervous baby especially needs rest and quiet, and however robust the child much of the play that is indulged in is more or less harmful.

Benjamin Spock

Dr. Spock's Baby and Child Care, 1998

From what some people—including some doctors—say about babies demanding attention, you'd think they come into the world determined to get their parents under their thumbs by hook or by crook. This isn't true.

Don't be afraid to love her and enjoy her. Every baby needs to be smiled at, talked to, played with, fondled—gently and lovingly—just as much as she needs vitamins and calories.

Interestingly, both sets of advice focused on the "dos" and "don'ts" of raising an infant. However, each one provided a fundamentally different view of the needs of the infant and the role of his or her parents in providing basic care.

Sources: (1) Cohen (1974), p. 2359 and (2) Spock and Parker (1998), p. 72.

The second half of the 20th century in the United States witnessed the continued transformation of the family. The percentage of working mothers increased substantially. In two-income families, an inordinate amount of stress sometimes arises because working mothers still tend to perform their traditional roles and responsibilities at home. Divorce continues to be a public concern. About half of all marriages end in divorce, resulting in further fragmentation and isolation of families. The high rate of divorce has led to an increase in the number of single-parent households and blended families, the remarriage of parents with children from previous marriages.

In the United States, the family has shown a remarkable ability to transform itself repeatedly during the past four centuries. From the early settlements in the colonial period to the eventual industrialization and urbanization of a new nation, it has faced numerous challenges along the way. The family is not only a description but also a prescription. It is not just a means of legitimizing socially sanctioned relations and responsibilities among its members, but also a means of transmitting a prescribed set of cultural beliefs and practices from one generation to the next.

ETHNIC FAMILIES IN THE UNITED STATES

The previous section focused primarily on the western European roots of families in the United States. However, other ethnic groups have contributed to its social and economic fabric. Today, the United States is seen as a mosaic of diverse ethnic groups that came to the

CHANGES IN ATTITUDES ABOUT INFANTS IN THE 1900S

The 20th century ushered in a new era of public interest in infants that irrevocably altered child-rearing attitudes and practices in the United States. The changes resulted primarily from the following factors:

■ **Breakthroughs in medicine.** Since the turn of the 20th century, medical care and treatment have steadily improved. Once scourges of childhood, the incidence of diseases such as diphtheria and poliomyelitis have declined dramatically as a result of immunizations. Medical technology has advanced to the point of detecting and correcting possible complications before birth and increasing preterm infants' chances of survival.

■ **Contributions of psychology.** Psychological research has focused public attention on the importance of the early years. Influential theorists have made a significant contribution to child-rearing practices. Freud, in particular, warned

about the possible harmful effects of traumatic experiences on later emotional development.

■ **Legislative laws and policies.** The federal government's involvement has steadily increased since the early 1960s. Although each state determines its own priorities, the federal government establishes laws and policies affecting the entire nation. For example, in 1975, PL 94–142, a federal mandate, later extended to include infants and toddlers in 1987, was enacted to provide free, appropriate education to children with special needs.

■ **Technological progress.** There has been a significant increase in the availability of information in print, on television, and on the Internet. Topics have ranged from ensuring a healthy pregnancy to increasing an infant's IQ. Sesame Street and other programs on television have provided valuable teaching tools.

country over a period of time. They each brought or developed unique cultural beliefs and traditions that affected the way parents raised children. In particular, African American, Hispanic American, and Asian American families will be examined because of their distinct patterns of kinship and intergenerational relationships. However, regardless of differences, they all share a common attribute: the family is viewed as a central organizing force.

AFRICAN AMERICANS

A generation or two after enslavement, African Americans created their own distinctive system of family and kinship. Each succeeding generation of African Americans managed to forge strong, durable relations within the institution of slavery, even when it cruelly separated husbands from wives and parents from children. Ties to a network of

Families play a critical role in the development of infants and toddlers.
Photo courtesy of Tami Dawson, Photo Resource Hawaii.

extended kin strengthened the bond of the family as a unit. Because of their flexibility, African Americans were able to endure the devastating effects of discrimination and deprivation.

The historical roots of the African American family were planted during the mid- to late-18th century when African and American cultural practices were combined into a unique African American system of family with its own rules of courtship and marriage. It was not simply a continuation of African patterns or an imitation of the American system of family. It was instead the adoption of both African and American beliefs and practices in dealing with slavery.

The continued separation and dispersal of the family caused extreme hardship. A letter from Abream Scriven, a slave living in Georgia, to his wife expressed the anguish he felt from the forced breakup of his family in 1858:

> My Dear wife for you and my Children my pen cannot Express the griffe I feel to be parted from you all. I remain your truly husband until Death. (Gutman, 1976, p. 36)

To sustain a sense of identity and continuity, African American parents often named their children after their own parents, grandparents, recently deceased relatives, and other kin. Slaves took the names of their ancestors' owners instead of their current owners. The separation and dispersal of the family led to a reliance on a network of extended kin. When children were sold to neighboring plantations, grandparents, aunts, uncles, and cousins of the family often took on the functions of parents (McAdoo, 1998).

Although slavery imposed severe discrimination and hardship, African American parents succeeded in holding their family together and providing their children with love and wisdom. As they raised their own vegetables on their own small plots and hunted game, slaves asserted their independence. Parents were able to instill values and pass on their wealth of experience to their children. Folklore and religion further transmitted a sense of history, morality, and identity from one generation to another.

The structure of African American families has changed significantly since the mid-19th century. The last half of the 20th century witnessed a dramatic increase in divorce, the number of female-headed households, the proportion of births to unmarried mothers, and the percentage of children living in poverty (Taylor, 1994). Joblessness has been identified as one of the major contributing factors in the changing patterns of marriage and the family. Unemployment among African American men is associated with the high incidence of divorce and proportion of children born to unmarried women (Farley & Bianchi, 1991). Another major factor is the growing economic independence among African American women. Financial independence decreases the economic utility of marriage, sometimes resulting in the postponement of marriage or the resolution of unhappy marriages.

The African American family is a lasting legacy of the past. It endured deprivation and hardship but survived to perform its primary responsibility: to meet the diverse needs of its members, particularly children, and to pass on a prescribed set of cultural beliefs and traditions from one generation to the next. The African American family is a shining example of its adaptability and flexibility in facing and dealing with numerous obstacles and challenges. Even today, it continues to be the primary unit of emotional sustenance and nurturance.

HISPANIC AMERICANS

Hispanic American families consist of diverse ethnic subgroups. They share ancestral and cultural ties to Puerto Rico, Cuba, Mexico, or other Central American countries. Although each subgroup is usually combined into a generic Hispanic label, there are important differences. The largest subgroup, Mexican Americans, constitutes one of the fastest growing segments of the American population today with major concentrations in the Southwest (Zinn, 1994).

Mexican American families consist largely of descendents from immigrants who came to the United States to find work in the Southwest. Others just recently entered the country. The uniqueness of Mexican American families lies in their close proximity to their original homeland and continuous interaction with recent immigrants. Recent immigrants tend to maintain and reinforce traditional Mexican cultural values (Eitzen & Zinn, 1989). Familism, a set of beliefs with strong emotional ties to the family and extended family, is thought to be a defining feature of Mexican American families. It seems to reflect families' economic adaptation to life in the rural, isolated areas of the Southwest. Extended kinship is another characteristic trait of Mexican American families. The proximity of extended families brings new parents into contact with experienced adults (Miller-Loncar et al., 1998). However, the gradual movement of families to the urban centers of the Southwest has had a profound impact on Hispanic American families. In particular, the increasing rate of maternal employment has transformed traditional Hispanic views of wives' subordinate role in marriage and child-rearing responsibilities (Becerra, 1998).

ASIAN AMERICANS

After African Americans and Hispanic Americans, the third largest group of ethnic minorities consists of Asian Americans. Asian Americans vary widely in terms of cultural origin, language, and recency of immigration to the United States. The remainder of the chapter focuses on Chinese and Japanese American families because of their long tenure in the United States. Still other Asian Americans with a sizable presence in the United States include Korean, Vietnamese, and Filipino American families.

Chinese Americans.   Chinese Americans immigrated to the United States as laborers in the second half of the 19th century. At the time, the economy of the West needed a vast pool of laborers to build the region's infrastructure (Glenn & Yap, 1994). Because they

SOCIOCULTURAL INFLUENCES

CHANGING PERCEPTIONS OF FATHERS' INVOLVEMENT IN URBAN CHINA

Changes in urban Chinese families today generally reflect worldwide patterns. Chinese fathers have been taking an increasingly an active role in raising their children (Jankowiak, 1992). The transformation of urban Chinese families started in 1949 with the communist revolution. The elimination of property that belonged to individual families forced the populace to depend on bureaucratic agencies to secure shelter and other critical resources. The traditional patrilineal forms of familial organization were weakened. In the process, Chinese kinship was changed forever.

After the communist revolution, Chinese women gained parity with men. Women were encouraged to seek employment. Their wages contributed to their families' income. Women became partners in the household. However, the transformation of the socioeconomic status of

urban Chinese women did not completely eliminate traditional cultural expectations of Chinese men's involvement with their children. Today, total obedience and respect of the father are still expected (Lee, 1993). Fathers undertake their duties seriously and strive to morally instruct their children. Emotional indulgence with children is not the norm.

Fathers' role is limited in the first year of their children's lives. In urban China, women give birth in hospitals while the men are asked to wait in another room. Women take care of their infants' basic needs. However, after the first year, fathers' involvement increases significantly. As their children start to walk and talk, they go on short trips in the neighborhood and spend time in playful activities. Clearly, culture does play a critical role in Chinese men's involvement with their children.

were not allowed to bring their wives and children, families were separated. Even in the absence of their fathers, children were taught to respect their parents and other figures of authority (Wong, 1998).

Increasing racial and ethnic antagonism culminated in the first national exclusionary act in 1882, which barred a particular group from immigrating to the United States. However, soon a loophole was found. The relatives of Chinese American citizens born in the United States were allowed to migrate. Families were eventually allowed to join their relatives.

Traditional Chinese families maintained their close ties to China, which helped to preserve a sense of continuity. The males, particularly the father and oldest son, played dominant roles in Chinese American families. However, tremendous changes and adaptations have occurred during the last half of the 20th century. Geographic dispersion and acculturation have resulted in gradual divergence from traditional practices, particularly in marriage and child-rearing patterns.

Japanese Americans. The first Japanese laborers came to the United States in the late 19th century in the wake of the Chinese exclusion. Between 1880 and 1930, there was a sharp and steady rise in the Japanese population, first in Hawaii in the 1880s and later on the West Coast in the 1890s (Kitano & Kitano, 1998). As with the Chinese, Japanese immigrants consisted of young men who intended to return to their homeland after a period of time. The first generation, or *issei*, came with minimal knowledge of English and American culture and faced severe hardship and discrimination (Takagi, 1994). They thought of themselves as a sacrificial generation and devoted their lives to the advancement of their children, the *nisei*, or second generation.

Japanese American families have undergone dramatic changes since the arrival of the initial Japanese laborers. The *issei* continued traditional Japanese customs in their new homeland. In particular, the primary unit of social organization centered on the *ie*, or family. The needs of the family superseded the demands of its individual members (Ogawa & Grant, 1978). Respect and filial piety to parents were considered an obligation of the children, and the father had overall jurisdiction of all matters that concerned the *ie*. The shift from the traditional role of the *ie* continued with subsequent generations. The participatory rate of Japanese American women in the workforce outranks the trend of other ethnic groups in the United States (Adler, 1998).

In sum, from ancient Rome to the present, families underwent dramatic changes to meet their child-rearing responsibilities and other obligations. In particular, ethnic families in the United States demonstrated an unlimited capacity to adapt to life's challenges.

SUMMARY
....

Importance of Infancy in Human Lifespan

■ Infancy literally means "without speech." Today, it refers to the period from conception to the first few years of life.

- People have long debated the issue of infancy as a critical period in the lifespan. Current research supports the view of infancy as a sensitive period in life, or a vulnerable time in life with long-lasting but not necessarily irreversible consequences.

Sociocultural Context of Infancy

- In a sociocultural model, the primary socializing agents during infancy consist of the infants' primary caregivers, the family, and the culture. Relevant variables in the model include the temperamental qualities of both infants and their caregivers, the composition of their families, and the expectations of the cultural group.

Recurrent Themes in Infancy

- The study of infants' physical, cognitive, and psychosocial development involves recurrent themes that appear and reappear during the first few years of life. Each provides evidence of dynamic processes at work, such as the influence of heredity and environment and the reciprocal nature of development.

Historical Perspectives

- The current view of infancy as a separate, distinct period in life is not a recent phenomenon. Rather, it is a culmination of centuries of changes in Western cultural values and philosophical beliefs about infants.

- The cornerstone of society from antiquity to the present is the family. It has performed its important function as the primary socializing agent in the lives of infants and children.

Ethnic Families in the United States

- Other ethnic groups have contributed to the social and economic fabric of the United States. Each brought unique cultural beliefs and traditions that affected the way parents raised their children.

- African Americans, Hispanic Americans, and Asian Americans represent the three largest ethnic groups in the United States. Although their historical circumstances differ, they each tell a compelling story of the adaptability of families in the face of prejudice and hardship.

PROJECTS
....

1. Discuss your personal beliefs about the importance of infancy in human development.

2. Make a collage with magazine pictures of infants to illustrate today's view of infancy as a distinct stage of development.

3. Make a list of 10 things you would put in a time capsule to convey current perceptions of infants to a future generation.

THEORIES
OF DEVELOPMENT

The whole of science is nothing more than a refinement of everyday thinking.
Albert Einstein, *Out of My Later Years*

Assumptions about human behavior and development are made every day. We constantly try to interpret someone else's behavior. Sometimes we succeed, but most of the time we miss the mark. On the other hand, scientific theories are not based on personal assumptions and biases. They provide a systematic framework that describes and explains developmental changes. Chapter 2 focuses on the application of theories to understand development during the first few years.

SCIENTIFIC THEORY

Efforts to study children began in earnest at the end of the 19th century and led to the construction of theories. A **theory** is defined as *a set of interrelated statements used to describe and explain unobservable mechanisms or processes* of development. It can be translated into hypotheses or tentative assumptions about the relations between events, objects, properties, or variables. A hypothesis becomes a fact when the results of scientific research support its claims (Miller, 1993).

A theory organizes and makes sense of disparate pieces of information about the world. French mathematician Jules Henri Poincare summarized the importance of scientific theories in the following way:

> Science is built up of facts as a house is with stones. But a collection of facts is no more a science than a heap of stones is a house. (Poincare, 1913, p. 127)

Just as a collection of stones needs an architect to design a house, a series of observations about children requires a theorist to integrate facts. Theories serve as frameworks in describing changes in behavior and mapping their course of development over time.

Theories often focus on a specific area of interest. Psychoanalytic theorists are concerned with understanding the role of emotional conflicts at different stages in life. Behavioral theorists concentrate on a person's behavior. They contend that environmental stimuli shape behavior. Cognitive theorists are interested in the processes of thought. Ethological theorists examine the evolution of behavior within a particular species. Ecological theorists view the developmental process as the mutual accommodation between people and the changing social contexts of their development. Each theory has provided a rich commentary on the study of development (see Tables 2–1 and 2–2).

PSYCHOANALYTIC THEORIES

Two influential figures in psychoanalytic theory are Freud and Erikson. Freud stressed the underlying forces that motivate behavior, whereas Erikson focused on cultural factors that influence development.

Theories explain some aspect of development, such as the role of early experience or the interactive relationship between individuals and their environment.
Photo courtesy of Tami Dawson, Photo Resource Hawaii.

TABLE 2-1 MAJOR THEORIES OF DEVELOPMENT

Psychoanalytic Theories

Psychoanalytic theories stress the importance of early experiences and the role of emotions in shaping personality and behavior. Major theorists: Sigmund Freud and Erik Erikson

Behavioral Theories

Behavioral and social learning theories emphasize the influence of environment and experience in shaping behavior. Major theorists: B. F. Skinner and Albert Bandura

Cognitive Theories

Cognitive theories focus on the active involvement of children in their acquisition of knowledge at each stage of development. Major theorists: Jean Piaget and Lev Vygotsky

Ethological Theories

Ethological theories are concerned with the adaptive value of behavior and its evolutionary history. Major theorist: Konrad Lorenz

Ecological Theories

Ecological theories examine the importance of sociocultural context in shaping the course of development. Major theorist: Urie Bronfenbrenner

Eclectic Theoretical Orientation

An eclectic theoretical orientation takes into account the contributions of each of the five major theories in understanding the complex process of development.

FREUD

Sigmund Freud (1856–1939) was the founder of psychoanalysis. He believed people repressed or subdued traumatic memories of childhood into their unconscious mind (Freud, 1920). To tap into the unconsciousness, he relied on free association, which allowed the verbal expression of anything that came to his patients' mind without censorship. He felt that repressed thoughts and urges interfered with people's ability to deal with conflicts in their lives (Freud, 1900/1950).

TABLE 2-2 EVALUATION OF THEORIES

Each theory has its strengths and weaknesses. The following criteria (Green, 1989) have been used to evaluate the worthiness of five major theories in the chapter:

- **Testability.** Are the claims about developmental phenomenon in a theory objectively verified by research?

- **External validity.** Does the theory provide an accurate description of human nature?

- **Predictive validity.** Is the theory able to make predictions about human behavior?

- **Internal consistency.** Are the concepts of the theory rationally interconnected?

Freud developed a framework of the personality consisting of three components: id, ego, and superego. The **id** represents *the source of instinctual urges and needs that a person seeks to satisfy* or, in Freud's words, a cauldron of "seething excitations" and "untamed passions" (Freud, 1933/1964, pp. 73, 76). It attempts to satisfy its impulses immediately from birth, but it often interferes and conflicts with the demands and expectations of other people and society. The vigorous cries of infants because of hunger provide a compelling demonstration of the id in action.

The second component of the personality in Freud's theory—the **ego** or *the conscious, rational part of the mind*—emerges during the first year of life. Infants gradually learn to control or delay their desires. They increasingly rely on their mental processes or "reason and good sense" (Freud, 1933/1964) in dealing with difficult situations. For example, toddlers need to use words to request a snack instead of crying when hungry. The ego, therefore, serves to reconcile or find common ground between the internal pressures of the id and external realities of life.

The **superego** houses *parental and societal expectations and prohibitions*. It develops at about the age of 3 or 4 and becomes the conscience as it tries to influence a person's behavior in conforming to society's moral or ethical standards (Freud, 1923/1961). Once it is formed, the ego is faced with the complex and difficult task of reconciling the demands of the id, the external world, and the conscience. A good example is a toddler who is tempted to gratify his or her id in taking an enticing toy from another child. The superego weighs the social consequence of his or her unruly behavior. The ego then makes a choice or takes another appropriate course of action, such as asking for the toy or getting help from an adult. Table 2–3 gives an evaluation of Freud's theory.

Freud conceived of two stages of psychosexual development from birth to the age of 3. He stirred considerable controversy in arguing that infants and toddlers develop sexual urges that shift from the oral to anal regions of their bodies, called erogenous zones, the sexually sensitive areas of the body (Freud, 1905/1953).

The first stage is called the oral stage. During the first year of life, erotic pleasure comes from the oral region of the body such as sucking or biting on things (the mother's breast, the rubber nipple of a bottle, a thumb, or a rattle). Freud theorized that people sometimes develop a **fixation**, or *an obsessive or unhealthy preoccupation because of insufficient or excessive gratification in a particular stage*, manifested later in life when they bite their fingernails or chew on pencils. The quality of the relationship between children and their parents in the first few years forms the foundation of healthy psychosexual development.

TABLE 2–3 EVALUATION OF FREUD'S THEORY			
Criteria	High	Moderate	Low
Testability			X
External Validity		X	
Predictive Validity		X	
Internal Consistency			X

Source: Green (1989).

BIOGRAPHICAL SKETCH

SIGMUND FREUD (1856–1939)

Sigmund Freud moved to Vienna from Germany at the age of 4, remaining there until 1938. He died in London the next year after he and his daughter fled from the Nazi occupation of Austria during World War II. Although interest in his psychoanalytic theory has waned considerably since his death, he has made a tremendous contribution to the study of human behavior. He was a prolific writer: the standard edition of his collected works fills 24 volumes.

Freud studied neurology, earning a medical degree at the age of 25. He was appointed as a lecturer of neuropathology at the University of Vienna in 1885. In the same year, he traveled to Paris to study with a French neurologist, Jean Charcot, who treated his patients' ailments with hypnosis. Charcot believed that some physiological symptoms stemmed from a psychological origin, not an organic dysfunction.

Freud returned to Vienna and started his own private practice, using hypnosis to relieve his patients' symptoms. His private practice provided an opportunity to develop a theory of psychoanalysis, a term first he used in 1896. In a collaborative work with Josef Breuer, Freud speculated on the origin of hysteria in the case of a woman who exhibited a variety of symptoms (partial paralysis, disturbances in vision and speech, hallucinations, and even a hint of multiple personality) that resulted after the fatal illness of her father. He described the cathartic effect of recalling memories and releasing emotions during hypnosis (Breuer & Freud, 1895/1957).

Freud eventually decided to drop the use of hypnosis and simply listened to his patients. During the next few years of his private practice, he shifted from active intervention to passive attentiveness. He recognized the importance of free association, or the expression of emotions without control or censorship, as a way to access the unconscious mind. The first decade of the 20th century witnessed the gradual acceptance of his theory (Freud, 1925/1959). The publication of *The Interpretation of Dreams* in 1900 established his reputation. At the invitation of G. Stanley Hall, he traveled to the United States in 1909 to deliver a series of lectures at Clark University in Massachusetts (Freud, 1910/1957).

World War I had an influential effect on Freud. His income dropped severely as his private practice declined. As he approached his 60th birthday, he turned his attention to death. He remarked, "If you want to endure life, prepare yourself for death" (Freud, 1915/1957, p. 300).

Freud endured grief and pain with long hours of work. He was trying to come to terms with his own eventual death even before he was diagnosed with cancer of the jaw in 1923. During the two remaining decades of Freud's life, he continued to practice psychoanalysis although he endured the discomfort of numerous operations. Neither did he forsake his cigars, a lasting trademark of one of the giants in psychology (Muckenhoupt, 1999).

TABLE 2–4 EVALUATION OF ERIKSON'S THEORY			
Criteria	High	Moderate	Low
Testability			X
External Validity		X	
Predictive Validity		X	
Internal Consistency		X	

Source: Green (1989).

The anal stage begins in the second year of life when the focus shifts from the oral to anal regions of the body. Erotic pleasure, in Freud's view, is derived from using the anal muscles' ability to expel or retain feces. The onset of the anal stage coincides with parents' interest in training their children to use the toilet. He believed when parents praise their toddlers' achievement and permit reasonable freedom, a sense of increasing independence is gained.

ERIKSON

An influential psychoanalyst who trained with Freud's daughter, Anna, Erik Erikson (1902–1994) modified and expanded Sigmund Freud's theory. Although he accepted the basic framework of Freud's psychoanalytic theory, Erikson stressed the importance of the ego because of its ability to reason and solve problems.

Erikson theorized that people face a series of psychological challenges throughout life. Whereas Freud concentrated on the influence of sexuality in his theory, Erikson recognized the importance of culture and society (Mitchell & Black, 1995). Erikson contended that the healthy resolution of challenges that people face at each of his eight stages depends on their relationships with other people and social institutions. An evaluation of Erikson's theory is given in Table 2–4. The first two stages of Erikson's theory, which parallel Freud's oral and anal stages, will be further discussed in Chapter 10.

BEHAVIORAL AND SOCIAL LEARNING THEORIES

The psychoanalytic theories of Freud and Erikson dealt primarily with the influence of unconscious urges on behavior. Introspection was used as the primary investigative tool in analyzing the structure of the mind. However, as the psychoanalytic movement reached its apex in the first half of the 20th century, a radically different theoretical approach, behaviorism, emerged in the United States. As its name implies, it focuses not on internal mental processes but on external environmental factors shaping people's behavior.

PAVLOV AND WATSON

Behaviorism's roots began with the work of Russian physiologist Ivan Pavlov (1849–1936) who investigated the salivating reflex of dogs. He made an accidental discovery when he found in his laboratory that the dogs salivated not only at the sight of

BIOGRAPHICAL SKETCH

Erik Erikson (1902–1994)

Freud's theory inspired a diverse group of brilliant and creative theoreticians and therapists. The neo-Freudians accepted Freud's basic tenets, particularly the nature and composition of the unconscious mind. However, an increasing number of neo-Freudians, particularly Gill (1959) and Rapaport (1960), differed from Freud in their emphasis on the influence of sociocultural factors in the development of the individual's personality. Their contributions resulted largely from the work of German-born American psychoanalyst Erik Erikson.

At the age of 18, Erikson decided to skip college and wander in search of his purpose in life. He settled on art as a career and lived as a vagabond in different European cities for about 6 years. When he again returned to his hometown in Germany, he received a letter from a former classmate who happened to be living in Vienna. His friend had met an American mother of four children who had come to receive psychoanalysis from Freud. Hired to work with her children, his friend had started a school and needed an assistant to help. Erikson accepted the offer, and the erstwhile wanderer's life had forever changed (Friedman, 1999).

During the 6 years Erikson stayed in Vienna, psychoanalysis turned into a widespread intellectual movement. Erikson began to take theoretical courses in psychoanalysis, even as he continued to teach children. However, the Great Depression changed everything. It stemmed the flow of people who sought psychoanalysis. One after another, Freud's intimates and followers began to leave. Erikson decided move to the United States because of the political uncertainty in an increasingly violent Europe in the years before World War II.

Erikson settled in Boston and became the city's first psychoanalyst who specialized in children. He was appointed to a teaching position at Harvard University Medical School. There he enrolled in graduate courses in psychology. The ideas of scholars such as Margaret Mead, an anthropologist, and Kurt Lewin, a psychologist, had an influential impact on his professional life.

Erikson eventually left Boston in 1936 after he accepted a position at Yale University. He took an interest in the "normal" growth and development of infants. In 1939, at the age of 37, he moved to San Francisco and resumed his work with children, after he lived with the Sioux in South Dakota and later the Yurok in northern California. His experience with native Americans shaped his theoretical views on the importance of culture on development.

After 10 years in California, Erikson returned to the East Coast to take an appointment at a prominent psychiatric center. Until his publication of *Childhood and Society* in 1950, he worked on expanding Freud's psychoanalytic theory based on his observations of children and adults (Stevens, 1983). His career came full circle when he returned to Harvard as a professor of human development in 1960. Before his death in 1994, he wrote another influential book, *Identity: Youth and Crisis*, establishing his reputation as an expert on the subject.

food but later at the sound of the approaching trainer who brought the food. In other words, the dogs established *an association, after repeated trials, between two events*, the food and the trainer, a process referred to as **conditioning**. In a series of subsequent experiments later known as classical conditioning, the dogs were taught to salivate at the sound of a bell.

John B. Watson (1878–1958), an American psychologist, took Pavlov's ideas and founded behaviorism. Dissatisfied with psychoanalytic theory, he strove to change the direction of psychology from a science of the mind to a science of behavior, "a purely objective, experimental branch of natural science" (Watson, 1914, p. 27).

Watson embarked on a new theoretical approach. His interest led to a classic study of fear as a conditioned response in a 9-month-old child (Watson & Rayner, 1920). Watson used the method of pairing a loud noise with the presentation of a white rat. After a number of trials, the child developed a fear of the rat and cried in its presence. His response was generalized to other similar stimuli not previously feared, such as a rabbit and even a mask of Santa Claus. Although his study raised serious ethical issues, Watson established behaviorism as the central focus of American psychology for the next 50 years.

SKINNER

After Watson came American psychologist B. F. Skinner (1904–1990). In his long and distinguished career, Skinner stirred considerable controversy. He advocated the application of behaviorism in tackling social and educational problems. His contributions led to technological and therapeutic innovations still widely used today (Schultz & Schultz, 1999).

Skinner found in his extensive research that the recurrence of behavior depended on the consequences of actions, not on the identification of stimuli, as in the case of Pavlov and Watson. Skinner therefore discovered a new form of learning he called operant conditioning. In 1938 he published the results of his work in *The Behavior of Organisms*, which outlined the theoretical foundation of his theory. In his terminology, **reinforcement** refers to *a consequence that increases the repetition of a particular behavior*. Rats and

---

HISTORICALLY SPEAKING

BEHAVIORAL THEORY

John B. Watson
Behaviorism, 1924
I should like to go one step further now and say, "Give me a dozen healthy infants, well-formed, and my own specified world to bring them up in and I'll guarantee to take any one at random and train him to become any type of specialist I might select—doctor, lawyer, artist, . . . and yes, even . . . thief, regardless of his talents, penchants, tendencies, abilities, vocations, and race of his ancestors."

Source: Watson (1924), p. 82.

TABLE 2–5 EVALUATION OF SKINNER'S THEORY

Criteria	High	Moderate	Low
Testability	X		
External Validity	X		
Predictive Validity		X	
Internal Consistency	X		

Source: Green (1989).

pigeons performed certain tasks in his experiments because of the consequences of their actions. In particular, food was used to shape and reward a desired behavior.

Skinner's principles of behavior take place not only in a controlled laboratory but in real life. If children perform a task (drinking from a cup or putting on a shirt) and receive words of praise from parents afterwards, they would probably engage in the same behavior again at the next opportunity. Likewise, if children throw a tantrum and receive attention from a parent, the probability of the same behavior occurring again in the future increases substantially. One possible way of handling a tantrum is to ignore children's behavior as long as they are not hurting themselves or others. **Extinction**, *the elimination of a learned behavior*, results when adults do not reward or pay attention to children's tantrums. Another way of reducing an inappropriate behavior is to punish the child, such as scolding or removing privileges. **Punishment** refers to *the presentation of an unpleasant stimulus or the withdrawal of a pleasant stimulus as a consequence of a particular behavior*. Whereas reinforcement serves to increase the likelihood of a behavior, punishment discourages its occurrence. Table 2–5 provides an evaluation of Skinner's theory.

People usually equate punishment with discipline. When immediate compliance is required to protect a child in a dangerous situation, a verbal reprimand is justified. For example, an adult must take immediate action if a child tries to touch a hot stove or cross the street. Often, a stern verbal reprimand or simple reminder is all that is needed. However, harsh and punitive methods, especially spanking and belittling a child, only result in a temporary suppression of an unacceptable behavior and often lead to resistance. Once the adult removes threat of punishment, the suppressed behavior may reappear (Schneider-Rosen & Wenz-Gross, 1990).

Behaviorism is based on the notion of continuous development. In contrast to Freud and Erikson who proposed a series of distinct stages, behavioral theorists stipulate that development depends on reinforcement from the environment, not biological maturation. Sometimes, elements from different theories are sometimes combined to produce a new theory, as in social learning theory. It stresses the importance of both environmental and social and cognitive influences on a person's behavior (Grusec, 1992).

BANDURA

A prominent social learning theorist, Albert Bandura (1925–) extended Skinner's theory to include social and cognitive factors that can influence a person's behavior. He and other social learning theorists built on, rather than dismantled, Skinner's basic

B. F. SKINNER (1904–1990)

Burrhus Frederic Skinner spent the first 18 years of life in a small town in eastern Pennsylvania. During his childhood, he liked to tinker with and invent things. Inclined to experiment later as a psychologist, he viewed science as a matter of improvisation and accidental discovery rather than a premeditated process. His resulting inventions led to scientific discoveries that changed the face of psychology (Wiener, 1996).

Skinner enjoyed not only mechanical but intellectual pursuits as a boy. In high school, a caring teacher encouraged his intellectual independence, a reputation he later earned as a scientist. Although disillusioned and socially isolated in college at first, he enjoyed his English classes and longed to be a writer. In his last year of college, he received confirmation from the distinguished American poet Robert Frost, who praised his short stories.

After college, Skinner returned to his parents' house in 1926 to become a writer. During a period he referred to as his "Dark Year," he developed a growing curiosity about behaviorism, an emerging field of psychology. He was plagued with doubts about his writing career and future. In a letter to a friend, he wrote, "I had failed as a writer because I had nothing important to say" (Bjork, 1993, p. 55).

Skinner changed course and decided to pursue psychology as a career. At the age of 24, his acceptance to graduate school at Harvard forever altered his life. He devised a modified box that accurately measured of the behavior of rats. Skinner found that reinforcing consequences shaped rats' seemingly spontaneous behavior. In 1938, the results of his work were published in *The Behavior of Organisms*, a book that stamped his place in history.

Before his death in 1990, Skinner fashioned social inventions to improve living conditions. In 1944, he built a thermostatically controlled crib-sized living space after the birth of his second daughter. He wrote in a article, "Baby in a Box," that his device freed the mother from constantly watching her child. Later, he started to write about a fictional community, Walden Two, as an expression of his faith in the potential use of behaviorism in tackling social problems, an idea that culminated in 1971 with the publication of *Beyond Freedom and Dignity*, sparking considerable controversy.

Skinner built a teaching aid to promote individualized instruction after he observed his second daughter's chaotic fourth-grade class. His teaching box provided positive reinforcement whenever a child answered a question correctly. His interest in programmed instruction dominated his time in the 1950s to 1960s. Although he retired from Harvard University in 1974, he continually sought to shape a better world until his death.

conclusions but rejected his mechanistic view of behavior as a mindless response to stimuli. Bandura proposed instead the concept of **triadic reciprocity**, depicted in Figure 2–1, which states that *learning results from the mutual interaction between cognitive factors as well as environmental contexts*. It recognizes the contributions of cognitive processes in shaping behavior.

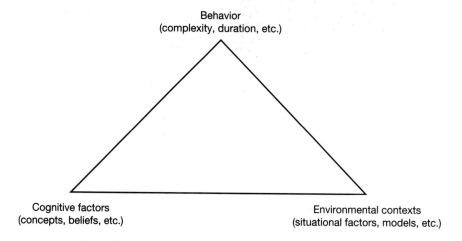

FIGURE 2–1 Diagram of Bandura's Triadic Reciprocity
Source: Bandura (1986), p. 24.

Bandura studied the determinants of observational learning, a term he used to describe the process of learning through imitation. He recognized the inherent limitations of behavioral theory in explaining that the acquisition of complex social behavior concentrated on the important role of imitation in the learning process (Bandura & Walters, 1959). However, children and adults do not simply mimic things. Instead, a specific action is imitated when a tangible reward is received, a process called **vicarious reinforcement**, or *the repetition of another person's behavior in an observed event*. Correspondingly, a model's behavior is not likely to be imitated if its action is punished (Bandura & Walters, 1963).

Bandura's social learning theory describes the process of learning new behavioral patterns on the basis of observation. There are four main parts in his model (Bandura, 1986):

- **Attention.** Learners—both children and adults—do not learn passively. Rather, they attend to relevant cues in the model's actions and ignore any irrelevant stimuli.

- **Retention.** A visual image or semantic code of the observed act is recorded. The process involves the transformation of the event into mental representations that will facilitate recall at a later time.

- **Production.** The stored mental images are then converted into appropriate actions. The learners' level of maturity affects their ability to reproduce the observed behavior.

- **Motivation.** The learners' motivation may explain any discrepancy between observation and actual performance. It is embedded in the consequences, positive or negative, of the model's actions.

Therefore, Bandura describes a model that takes into account the social context of behavior. It also involves cognition because it requires observers to judge the expected outcomes about their own behavior (Bandura, 1977).

SPOILING BABIES

Parents often worry about spoiling their infants when they respond to their frequent cries during the first few months of life. Is it better to let a child cry? A long-time authority to generations of parents since the first edition of *Baby and Child Care* in 1946, Benjamin Spock answered, "No." Below is his response to a letter from a concerned parent (Spock, 1995):

> Dear Dr. Spock: I usually pick up my three-month-old when she cries. At what point does this attentiveness lead to spoiling?

> [Dr. Spock replies:] Up to three months of age, I don't think you can spoil a child if you are responding to her needs and using common sense. During these early days and weeks, she needs to be held, fed, changed, cuddled, and talked to.
> If after three months, she still cries every time you put her down and you always respond by picking her up again (even after she's been changed or fed), then you may be inviting a situation that could lead to spoiling. With practice, however, you will discover just the right balance between being too strict and being too submissive.

Spock is adhering to an eclectic theoretical orientation. His response to the parent's question reflects both psychoanalytic and behavioral theories. Erikson theorized that infants learn to trust the world when adults respond to their cries immediately. At the same time, Spock takes a page from Skinner's theory in saying that parents can reinforce infants' cries. In other words, behavior is likely to be repeated if it is rewarded with attention. As Spock mentions, parents should respond to their infants' needs but use their common sense in determining the right balance between overprotection and insensitivity. Infants thrive in the company of attentive, supportive adults who provide an atmosphere of security and certainty (MacDonald, 1992).

COGNITIVE THEORIES

As interest waned, behavioral theories faced external challenges from other competing theories. The emergence of cognitive theories started, in the words of Hebb (1960), a "second revolution" after the rejection of introspection as an investigative tool and the establishment of psychology as a scientific field of study.

PIAGET

Jean Piaget (1896–1980), a Swiss cognitive theorist, was interested in understanding the development of human cognition. He referred to himself as a genetic epistemologist, a person who studied the origins of knowledge.

Intriguing glimpses of children's behavior and thought fired Piaget's imagination. In daily records of his own three children, he saw a remarkable process of cognitive development:

> At 0;2 (21), in the morning, Laurent spontaneously bends his head backward and surveys the end of his bassinet from this position. Then he smiles, returns to his normal position and then begins again. I observed this several times. As soon as Laurent awakens after the short naps . . ., he resumes this activity. (Piaget, 1936/1952, p. 70)

Piaget's theory was firmly rooted in biology. He was attempting to find a "biological explanation" of knowledge. His detailed observations of mollusks led to general principles that he later applied to human cognition. Mollusks adapted continually to the existing conditions of the environment, he found. Different species of mollusks evolved over time from a process called **adaptation**, or *the process of adjusting to the external world.* Just as mollusks adapt to their physical environment, so does human thought. Knowledge results from a person's interaction with the changing circumstances of the external world.

In Piaget's theory, infants construct a way of mentally representing the external world. *An organized pattern of behavior* that is used to structure a person's knowledge is referred to as a **scheme**. Two kinds of schemes are formed during infancy. The first guides a particular action, such as sucking on a bottle or grasping a rattle. The second combines sequences of actions, such as climbing on a chair to reach an object on a table. Schemes develop as infants repeat regular sequences of behavioral patterns, a process known as **circular reactions**, *the use of familiar actions to achieve the same results.* For example, at birth, infants rely on genetically programmed reflexes in dealing with the environment. They tend to suck on anything that enters the mouth, which initially is a reflexive response, but over time becomes a sucking scheme to explore the properties of new objects.

Other concepts—assimilation, accommodation, and equilibrium—play an important role in Piaget's theory. **Assimilation**, one of two related factors in adaptation, describes *the process of incorporating new information from the world into existing schemes.* Infants initially attempt to fit reality into their existing cognitive organization, such as referring to a cow

---

HISTORICALLY SPEAKING

COGNITIVE THEORY

Jean Piaget
The First Year of Life of the Child, 1927
The child's first year of life is unfortunately still an abyss of mysteries for the psychologist. If only we could know what was going on in a baby's mind while observing him in action, we could certainly understand everything there is to [in] psychology.

Source: Piaget (1927/1977), p. 199.

TABLE 2–6 EVALUATION OF PIAGET'S THEORY			
Criteria	High	Moderate	Low
Testability		X	
External Validity	X		
Predictive Validity		X	
Internal Consistency			X

Source: Green (1989).

as a dog because of similar features (both are animals with four feet and a tail). **Accommodation**, on the other hand, relates to *the process of altering existing schemes to fit reality*. Instead of relying on his or her existing cognitive structures, infants learn to adapt to new circumstances. **Equilibration** occurs when an infant reaches *a balanced state of cognitive structures*. It does not last long, however, because infants' biological maturation and accumulation of experience lead to new imbalances. Their attempt to restore equilibration is the source of their natural curiosity in the world. Table 2–6 provides an evaluation of Piaget's theory.

Piaget postulated that intelligence unfolds systematically over time. His four stages of cognitive development share the following salient characteristics:

- Each stage is seen as a structured whole in a state of equilibration. The schemes or operations of each stage are interconnected to form a whole. A state of balance is achieved at the end of a stage.

- The stages follow an invariant, universal sequence. The four stages proceed in the same sequence across the world. Each stage is derived from the preceding one.

The sensorimotor stage starts at birth and ends at the age of 2. Piaget traced the cognitive development of infants in an aptly titled book published in 1936, *The Origins of Intelligence in Children*. Knowledge is derived from infants' ability to coordinate their sensory perceptions with motoric actions. Although infants initially process sensory information at the reflexive level, they gradually begin to initiate their own actions, such as looking at, listening to, smelling, tasting, and touching objects. Over time, qualitative transformations occur in infants' cognitive structure. At the end of the second year, infants are able to understand the permanent existence of objects and anticipate the results of their actions mentally.

VYGOTSKY

Piaget's theory views cognitive development primarily as an individual activity. Although he acknowledges the contribution of adults to children's acquisition of knowledge, he generally emphasizes the interaction between the person and physical environment. However, cognitive development occurs in a social context. Infants learn not just from their interaction with objects but from other people who guide the learning process and interpret events as they unfold. The roots of the current interest in the social context of

BIOGRAPHICAL SKETCH

JEAN PIAGET (1896–1980)

Jean Piaget has been referred to as the "Einstein of psychology" and "the classroom's Freud" in recognition of his influence in both psychology and education. The only son of three children, Piaget showed a tremendous aptitude as a child. He wrote a short article about a partly albinic bird he saw in a park at the age of 9 and studied mollusks from the surrounding freshwater lakes of western Switzerland. As a young assistant to the director of the local museum, he had, in his words, "the rare privilege of getting a glimpse of science" (Piaget, 1952, p. 239).

At 16, Piaget faced a personal crisis as he tried to reconcile the opposing views of science and religion. In the aftermath, he found a new passion: philosophy (Piaget, 1952). Four years later, Piaget published a novel of a fictional person who struggled, as he did in real life, to resolve the conflict between science and religion. The book disclosed the roots of his theoretical ideas, which resurfaced later in his career (Chapman, 1988).

After he received his doctorate in biology in 1918, Piaget traveled to Paris. His first job involved the standardization of Alfred Binet's reasoning tests. After 2 years, Piaget felt that he at last found his niche in life. He wanted to pursue his interest in studying the origins of knowledge in children. In 1923, he accepted a job as director of studies at the Institut Rousseau in Geneva and wrote such influential books as *The Language and Thought of the Child* (1923/1926). His books found immediate international acclaim in psychology and education and led to numerous invitations to speak at professional conferences (Vidal, 1994).

Piaget met his wife, one of 20 collaborators working with him, at the Institut Rousseau. He conducted extensive observations of his three children's intellectual development during their first 2 years of life. His observations led to the publication of *The Origins of Intelligence in Children* (1936/1952). As he stated in his autobiography, "The main benefit which I derived from these studies was that I learned . . . how intellectual operations are prepared by sensory-motor action, even before the appearance of language" (Piaget, 1952, p. 249).

Piaget continued his work at the Institut Rousseau in the ensuing years. He was an amazingly prolific writer. A conservative estimate of his work is over 40 books and 100 articles on children's thinking skills alone. Piaget attributed his productivity in part to his assistants but provided the following glimpse into his personality:

> . . . I owe it to a particular bent of my character. Fundamentally I am a worrier whom only work can relieve. (Piaget, 1952, p. 255)

cognitive development have been largely attributed to Russian psychologist Lev Vygotsky (1896–1934). After his untimely death at the age of 38, his theory has received considerable attention (Wertsch, 1985, 1991).

Vygotsky and other supporters of his theory share certain basic assumptions about the acquisition of knowledge. They stress the reciprocal interaction between children and

Infants and toddlers learn not only from interactions with objects in their environment, but also from people who guide the learning process.
Photo courtesy of Tami Dawson, Photo Resource Hawaii.

their social context, which structures their experiences with the physical environment (Rogoff, 1998; Wertsch & Tulviste, 1992). Adults, particularly parents and teachers, guide children's engagement with objects. As a result, children acquire culturally shared values and beliefs from direct interactions with experienced learners. Cultural norms are eventually internalized over time. In Vygotsky's theory, culture constructs the human mind because it provides the psychological tools it needs to learn (Vygotsky, 1978, 1987).

RECENT APPROACHES

Another theoretical approach provides a unique perspective into cognitive development. Information-processing theory takes its inspiration from current technology: the way computers analyze and process data (Klahr, 1992). It has been called "the psychology of boxes and arrows" because of its reliance of diagrams and charts in outlining the flow of information in the model. The flow generally begins with an input, usually a stimulus, and ends with an output, a behavior or decision.

A series of mental operations occur in a typical information-processing flowchart. First, a person selectively attends to a particular stimulus in the environment. The information received from his or her senses is not merely photocopied but rather interpreted and evaluated on the basis of past experience. If it is deemed of value, it is stored in a person's memory. Then, the information is retrieved and used to make a decision or solve a particular problem at a later time. Each component is presumed to change gradually and lead to an overall improvement in cognition (Canfield et al., 1997; Richards & Casey, 1992).

Do infants use information-processing strategies? Research has shown that infants are able to remember and store information in an orderly fashion (Klahr & MacWhinney, 1998). Even at an early age, infants are able to categorize events. In a classic experiment, 3-month-old infants were taught to kick when a mobile that was made of a uniform set of stimuli—small blocks, all with the letter A on them—was secured to one of their legs. After a delay, if the form was changed (from As to 2s), the subjects no longer kicked vigorously. In an amazing demonstration of infants' mind in action, they started to kick again if they saw the same features as before (Hayne, Rovee-Collier, & Perris, 1987).

Information-processing theory acknowledges the active involvement of infants in learning about the world, as Piaget did. Although information-processing theory does not ascribe to his developmental stages, it does describe general processes of thought that presumably occur at all ages in terms of memory, planning strategies, categorization of information, and comprehension of spoken and written language. However, it does fail to explain other components of cognition, such as creativity and imagination. Further, it does not answer questions about the links between cognition and other areas of development, particularly emotional and social experience (Greeno, 1989).

ETHOLOGICAL THEORY

Ethology is concerned with the adaptive value of behavior and its evolutionary history. It is linked to the work of Darwin's painstaking observations of plants and animals. Darwin concluded in *On the Origins of Species*, published in 1859, that nature selects characteristics that may lead to a species' survival. Each member of a species carries a slightly different set of genes, which contributes to the observed individual variations in appearance and behavior. Inherited characteristics result from natural selection. If they increase the chances of survival, they pass on to the next generation; if they do not, they disappear (Lorenz, 1965).

LORENZ

A separate branch of zoology, ethology began with the work of Konrad Lorenz (1903–1989) in the 1930s. He developed, often in collaboration with other European zoologists, two basic ethological concepts (Charlesworth, 1992):

■ **Species-specific innate behavior.** Just as physical development is genetically determined, so are certain types of behavior. Each member of a species exhibits **species-specific innate behavior**, or *behavioral patterns that occur only in one particular species and that result from natural selection.* An example is the attachment between a parent and infant, a behavior that is seen in mammalian species. Although all mammals nurse their young, nursing styles differ from species to species. Mother cats nuzzle and lick their babies; mother monkeys groom and carry their infants. Humans typically look at, talk to, and touch as they nurse their babies. The concept of species-specific innate behavior was applied to human infants in John Bowlby's theory of attachment. According to Bowlby, infants and adults are predisposed to respond to each other. An attachment to one or a few specific adults usually occurs at about 8 months of age (Bowlby, 1969).

■ **Learning predispositions.** The biological control of behavior is seen not only in innate behavioral patterns, but also in learning predispositions of a species. The influence of learning predispositions is shown in a species' sensitive periods and general abilities. A widely known example of sensitive periods comes from Lorenz. He found in his research that shortly after birth, usually in the first day or two, certain birds, particularly geese, follow the mother, a phenomenon known as **imprinting**, *a biological ability to establish an attachment with an object or person during a limited period of time.* Imprinting increases the survival of the young because they learn to find food and shelter and avoid predators and other dangerous situations. In the absence of the mother, geese form an attachment with other objects, even a squatting, honking Lorenz. In addition to sensitive periods, biology controls a species' behavior in other ways (Miller, 1993). The genetic endowment of humans includes the ability to learn from experience. Human survival depends on cultural adaptation, the transmission of a set of behavioral patterns and traditions: "Conceptual thought and syntactic language . . . opened unprecedented possibilities not only for . . . sharing knowledge among contemporaries but also for transmitting it from one generation to the next" (Lorenz, 1981, p. 342).

Human intelligence, language, social attachment, and even aggression serve, or once served, a purpose. To understand the adaptive and evolutionary significance of human behavior, ethologists conduct studies of a particular behavior's eliciting conditions in a natural context, as Mary Ainsworth did in her study of attachment between infants and adults (Ainsworth & Bell, 1970; Ainsworth et al., 1978) discussed in Chapter 10.

ECOLOGICAL THEORY

Ethological theory emphasizes the biological foundations of a person's development. In contrast, ecological theory examines the totality or pattern of relations between the individual and his or her environment (Bronfenbrenner, 1995; Moen, Elder, & Luscher, 1995).

BRONFENBRENNER

Urie Bronfenbrenner (1917–), a Russian-born American psychologist, proposed a theoretical framework that examines the complex interrelationship between a person and his or her sociocultural context of development. The ecology of human development, in his words, involves the scientific study of

> the progressive, mutual accommodation between an active, growing human being and the changing properties of the immediate settings in which the developing person lives. (Bronfenbrenner, 1979, p. 21)

Infants are not viewed as a tabula rasa but instead as dynamic entities that shape their interaction with others. There is a bidirectional influence, a two-way street, between infants and their immediate environment. A good example involves the reciprocal interaction between infants and their parents or other caregivers. The sociability of infants can shape adults' interactions with infants. Adults generally like to look at and respond to infants who smile and vocalize. In turn, the social attentiveness of adults reinforces their infants' continued sociability.

The environment is perceived as a series of interconnected structures and is represented in a series of expanding concentric circles (see Figure 2–2). The interconnected structures are referred to as **systems**, or *a set of interdependent components*. Developmental change is understood only in its entirety, not just on the basis of one component. Bronfenbrenner's theoretical framework includes four interrelated components of the environment:

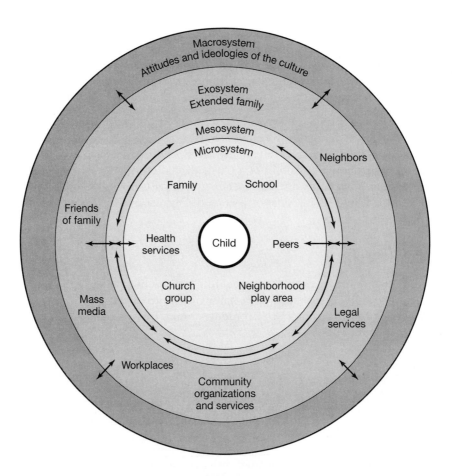

FIGURE 2–2 Bronfenbrenner's Ecological Model

▪ **Microsystem.** *The interaction between a developing infant and his or her immediate environment* occurs in the innermost circle of the **microsystem**. It includes not only the family but also the neighborhood and school. Elements of the microsystem interact with the infant. His or her reciprocal interaction with others generates a momentum of its own that motivates the participants to engage in progressively complex behavioral patterns.

▪ **Mesosystem.** The **mesosystem** refers to *the interrelationship between microsystems,* such as the family and school. As the basic unit of any society, the family reciprocally interacts with other microsystems. In recent years, for example, an increasing number of working parents are relying on out-of-home care because of economic necessity. As a result, professional caregivers play a major role in contributing to the lives of infants and their families.

▪ **Exosystem.** An extension of the mesosystem, the **exosystem** consists of *social units that indirectly influence the infant.* The exosystem includes the institutional fabric of any society such as its economic system and form of government.

SOCIOCULTURAL INFLUENCES

INFANCY AMONG !KUNG OF SOUTHWEST AFRICA

The interaction between infants and parents takes different paths in different cultures. Across the world, parents and other adults transmit their culture's traditions and values to their children. A hunting and gathering group in the northwest corner of the Kalahari Desert in Africa, the !Kung, illustrate the influence of culture on development. They refer to themselves as *Zhu/twasi* meaning "real people" and live in semipermanent villages of 15 to 40 people. Their subsistence consists primarily of hunting animals and gathering vegetables. Three days of each week are spent in finding food (Konner, 1976).

!Kung infants are kept in close physical contact with their mothers. They are either held on their mothers' laps or carried, awake or asleep, in slings at their mothers' side during the first year. The slings not only keep infants in constant skin-to-skin contact with their mothers, but also provide opportunities to observe their moth-

ers' work, interact with other children, and play with the decorative objects hanging from their mothers' necks. Infants nurse whenever they fuss and sleep face-to-face with their mothers at night (Konner, 1977).

In a culture with minimal possessions, objects have to be collectively shared. The !Kung encourages infants' interpersonal interaction with adults (Bakeman et al., 1990). A system of reciprocity is instituted soon after birth. Infants are taught about the importance of exchanging things. Adults begin to teach the concept of giving something to others between the sixth month and first year of life. First words include *na* or "give it to me" and *i* or "here, take this" (Shostak, 1976, p. 256).

The !Kung provide a good example of ecological theory. The interconnectedness between infants and other components of their surrounding environment is clearly evidenced.

■ **Macrosystem.** *The influence of culture, particularly its beliefs and traditions,* is found in the outermost circle, or **macrosystem**. A societal blueprint, it represents the totality of the other systems and regulates behavior. A culture's customs and values shape parents' child-rearing expectations and practices at home. The ability to construct and function in a culturally organized environment is a distinctive, universal human characteristic (Cole, 1999).

ECLECTIC THEORETICAL ORIENTATION

Each theory focuses on an entirely different aspect of development. Whereas one theory examines stages of emotional or cognitive development, another describes general rules governing behavior. A theory is sometimes extended or refined, as in the case of Erikson and Bandura. Each theory stands until empirical observations cast doubts on its validity. An important point to remember is that there is "only one established dogma in science" and that is not to blindly accept established dogma (Brush, 1976, p. 68).

An eclectic theoretical orientation is based not on just one theory but on several theories. The following list is intended to paint a picture of development during the first few years of life:

■ Infants are biologically predisposed to elicit and maintain contact with their caregivers (ethological theory).

■ Babies rely on genetically programmed reflexes in engaging with their physical and social world initially after birth (ethological theory).

■ Involuntary reflexes are gradually replaced with increasingly voluntary movement and intentional behavior (cognitive theory).

■ Knowledge of the world is constructed from infants' interaction with a variety of sensory experiences and direct manipulation of objects (cognitive theory).

■ Infants are not raised in a vacuum but rather are actively involved in reciprocally influencing their immediate environment (ecological theory).

■ Development is shaped not only by the family, but also by the child-rearing beliefs and practices of the culture in which the family lives (ecological theory).

■ The building blocks of a person's emotional development and eventual personality are laid during the early years (psychoanalytic theory).

■ An attachment with caring, loving caregivers provides lasting benefits, such as an increased willingness to take risks in interacting with others and exploring an ever-widening world (psychoanalytic theory).

■ Infants learn to repeat, or suppress, certain behavioral patterns when adults reward, or punish, their actions (behavioral theory).

■ However, babies do not just react mechanically to external stimulation but selectively observe and imitate others, particularly parents or even situations on television (social learning theory).

In conclusion, theories provide an orderly, integrated set of standards that describe and explain observed and unobserved processes of human behavior and development. Numerous theories with diametrically opposing assumptions about the nature and course of development have surfaced since the turn of the 20th century. A single, comprehensive theory does not currently exist. However, the diversity of theories attests to the complexity of human behavior and development (Scarr, 1985).

SUMMARY

Scientific Theory

■ A theory is defined as a set of interrelated statements used to describe and explain unobservable mechanisms and processes. It serves as a framework for examining and predicting infants' behavior and their course of development over time.

Psychoanalytic Theories

■ Psychoanalytic theories emphasize the importance of early experience and unconscious motivation in influencing behavior. Freud, the originator of psychoanalysis, and Erikson are two influential theorists.

Behavioral and Social Learning Theories

■ There are two basic types of learning in behavioral theory. One is learning to associate two events; the other is learning to repeat or suppress an action on the basis of its consequences.

■ Social learning theory rejects the mechanistic view of behavioral theory. It focuses on the mediating factors of cognition on behavior.

Cognitive Theories

■ In Piaget's cognitive theory, knowledge is acquired from successive adaptations to changing circumstances. The sensorimotor stage involves the ability of infants to coordinate their sensory perceptions with motoric actions.

■ The information-processing model examines the way people analyze and process information. It describes a series of mental operations, beginning with an input and ending with an ouput such as behavior or decision.

Ethological Theory

■ Ethology is concerned with the study of a species' adaptive behavior. Lorenz and other ethologists believe that a species' behavior evolves from natural selection and serves to ensure its chances of survival.

Ecological Theory

■ Bronfenbrenner's ecological theory examines the relationship between people and the changing properties of their immediate and extended environment. A series of interconnected components underscore the reciprocal nature of development.

Eclectic Theoretical Orientation

■ An eclectic theoretical orientation draws on the contributions of many theories. Because of the complexity of human behavior and development, each theory contributes a piece of a richly varied mosaic.

PROJECTS

1. Interview a parent or professional caregiver who works with infants and toddlers and ask about his or her views on:

    Importance of early development.

    Child-rearing practices.

    Role of the family.

    Influence of cultural expectations.

2. Select a theory and discuss its:

    Major points.

    Child-rearing implications.

3. Take the role of a major theorist (Freud, Erikson, Skinner, or Piaget) and debate his view of the:

    Nature of infants.

    Course of development during the first few years of life.

    Role of parents.

    Influence of society.

RESEARCH METHODS

That is the essence of science: ask an impertinent question, and you are on the way to a pertinent answer.

Jacob Bronowski, *The Ascent of Man*

For a long time, many people assumed that newborns could not see at birth or that they saw objects only in black and white. After all, newborns spend a lot of time squinting and blinking their eyes in reaction to light. Yet, today we now know that newborns, although extremely nearsighted, can take in and process visual stimuli. In fact, they have definite preferences, such as looking at human faces. How did our perceptions of babies change? Chapter 3 examines the methodological tools researchers rely on to investigate infants' impressive abilities.

A scientific investigation generally begins with a researcher's prediction about some aspect of infants' behavior. In other words, a **hypothesis**, or *a tentative statement about the relationship between variables* is formulated. Researchers use systematic, objective procedures in verifying the accuracy of information they gather and generalizing the results of their research to other infants. The **scientific method** refers to *the collection of information that either supports or refutes a hypothesis.*

47

Historically, the scientific study of infants began with written accounts of babies in the 19th century. At first, a few philosophers and scientists took advantage of their new-found status as fathers to describe the development of their own infants. They wanted to establish norms, the average age infants displayed certain skills. Take the example of Dietrich Tiedemann (1748–1803), a German philosopher who described a startled reaction in an infant in 1787:

> If [the infant] was held in arms and then suddenly lowered from a considerable height, he strove to hold himself with his hands, to save himself from falling; and he did not like to be lifted very high. Since he could not possibly have had any conception of falling, his fear was unquestionably a purely mechanical sensation. (Tiedemann, 1787/1927, p. 216)

British naturalist Charles Darwin (1809–1882) made similar remarks on his son's own reaction to a loud noise almost a century later. He wrote:

> During the first fortnight he often started on hearing any sudden sound, and blinked his eyes. Once when he was 66 days old, I happened to sneeze, and he startled violently, frowned, looked frightened, and cried rather badly. . . . (Darwin, 1877/1971, p. 1)

Both Tiedemann and Darwin provided a descriptive account of the Moro reflex. Infants across the world react in the same way to loud noises. They arch their backs, throw their heads backward, fling their arms and legs outward, and rapidly close their arms and legs to the center of their bodies. It typically disappears at 4 months of age.

The detailed accounts of infants in the 19th century marked the starting point of the scientific inquiry of development. Naturalistic observations of babies contributed to the emerging field of psychology in two ways. First, they accurately described babies' responses to visual and auditory stimuli. The following two accounts focused on infants' sensory abilities during the first few hours of life:

HISTORICALLY SPEAKING

SCIENTIFIC METHOD

Morris Cohen
An Introduction to Logic and Scientific Method, 1934
Scientific method is the only effective way of strengthening the love of truth. It develops the intellectual courage to face difficulties and to overcome illusions that are pleasant temporarily but destructive ultimately.

Source: Cohen and Nagel (1934), p. 402.

> As she gradually awoke and was exposed to light, she opened her eyes as if intent on adjusting these for the purpose of seeing. (Alcott, 1882)

> Medical works give six to ten hours as the earliest time at which hearing is possible, but my boy, born at 1:30, certainly heard, and nervously started at the sound of the cock crowing at 4:30. (Talbot, 1882)

Second, the detailed accounts provided longitudinal information. Developmental changes such as the disappearance of reflexes and the emergence of language were recorded.

Nevertheless, significant flaws can be found. Observers often included their own personal biases in their interpretation of data or selectively ignored evidence. Another problem involved the generalizability of results from a single baby to the entire population of infants. Piaget, another biographer who made painstaking observations of his own children, derived his entire theory of cognitive development from his descriptive accounts of his children. His small sample raised serious questions about the generalizability of his theory until other researchers replicated his studies. Because of the limitations of small samples, researchers today insist on conducting systematically controlled studies with large numbers of subjects. The intent is to increase not only the accuracy but generalizability of their results.

SCIENTIFIC METHOD

The limitations of detailed accounts of individual infants were solved with the emergence of the scientific method as the investigative tool in studying human behavior. It was designed to promote objectivity in the collection of information and consistency in the interpretation of results.

The scientific method consists of four steps:

- **Selecting a problem.** The first step in scientific research is to select a problem to study. The researcher can draw on a number of different sources in identifying a problem. A review of previous research frequently lends itself to possible ideas. Even theories provide fertile ground. A case in point is ecological theory. Bronfenbrenner's theory has spurred interest in examining the interdependent relationship between infants and the sociocultural context of the surrounding environment. Psychological research lacks, he believes, "ecological validity" because it does not emphasize the totality of development. Instead, it often focused on "the strange behavior of children in strange situations with strange adults" (Bronfenbrenner, 1977, p. 513).

- **Formulating a hypothesis.** After a problem is identified, the second step is to develop a tentative statement, or hypothesis, about the causal relationship between variables. The term comes from *hypotithenai*, a Greek word meaning "groundwork." It plays an important role in the scientific method because it affects decisions researchers make, such as the specific variables they manipulate and measure in their studies. Therefore, their selection of a problem sets the stage. For example, if researchers are interested in studying the effects of parents' emotions on infants' exploratory behavior, a tentative statement is formed. It might be hypothesized that infants rely on the emotional cues of parents in dealing with an unfamiliar situation.

■ **Testing the hypothesis.** The third step is to test the hypothesis. It involves a twofold process: a method of research, such as a naturalistic observation or an experiment, is chosen to gather information; a **sample**, or *a group of subjects who are asked to participate in a study*, is selected on a random basis. The sample is supposed to represent statistically the population from which it is taken in order to generalize the results of the study. **Generalizability** refers to *the applicability of a study's conclusions to the entire population of subjects.*

■ **Drawing conclusions.** The last step is to analyze the data that are collected in the study and draw conclusions about the hypothesis. Sometimes, the results confirm the hypothesis; sometimes, they do not. If the results refute a hypothesis, then a process of refinement begins. The investigator either revises the hypothesis and begins the entire process again or modifies components of a theoretical framework and suggests further study (Miller, 1998).

In sum, the ability of the scientific method to prove or disprove a hypothesis forms the basic foundation of scientific research today. It provides a powerful check on the validity of its conclusions. Although objectivity is a stated goal of any scientific research, in reality, as human beings, researchers do make subjective judgments in selecting the problem to study and method to employ. Therefore, although every effort should be made to eliminate subjectivity, preconceptions and beliefs do play a role, sometimes influencing even the conclusions drawn.

CRITERIA OF SCIENTIFIC RESEARCH

People often make everyday judgments about infants. One person might comment, "She is such a good baby because she never cries." Unfortunately, subjective observations can never serve as a reliable source of information, because they are usually based on limited observations of only a few children. On the other hand, scientific research provides an objective way to increase knowledge of infants' abilities. The hallmark of scientific research is its adherence to rigorously controlled procedures. Four criteria have been used to evaluate scientific research: objectivity, reliability, validity, and replicability (see Table 3–1).

OBJECTIVITY

To increase the accuracy of scientific research, **objectivity**, *the investigator's suspension of judgment about the outcome of his or her research*, is an important requirement. Therefore, the collection of data should not be based on researchers' preconceptions or biases about development. Total objectivity cannot always be achieved because of researchers' own beliefs and experiences with infants. However, it remains a significant goal in scientific research.

TABLE 3-1   CRITERIA OF SCIENTIFIC RESEARCH

Scientifically accepted guidelines are followed in conducting research. The following four criteria can be used to judge studies on infants' development:

- **Objectivity.** The description of infants' behavior should not be based on the researchers' preconceptions of development.
- **Reliability.** The measurement of infants' behavior should yield the same results on repeated occasions with agreement among independent observers.
- **Validity.** The observed behavior should reflect the underlying psychological phenomenon that the researchers claim it does.
- **Replicability.** Similar results should be obtained when the same procedures are followed in other investigations.

In addition, scientific research requires a representative sample of subjects. The subjects should be randomly chosen to represent the general population of infants in order to increase the generalizability of the results.

RELIABILITY

Another requirement of scientific knowledge involves **reliability**, *the consistency of a measurement an investigator uses in collecting information.* A reliable measure yields identical or at least highly similar results on separate occasions. Reliability can be achieved in one of two ways. First, the same measurement may be readministered to determine its consistency. The accuracy of a measurement increases whenever researchers obtain similar results at two different times. Second, independent observers may be asked to rate the same behavior on just one occasion. The degree of agreement between the two observers indicates the measurement's reliability.

For example, if an investigator is interested in examining attachment, the emotional bond between infants and their caregivers, a reliable measure is needed to record qualitatively distinct behavioral patterns. To study attachment systematically, Ainsworth and

HISTORICALLY SPEAKING

CRITERIA OF SCIENTIFIC METHOD

Ruth Strang
An Introduction to Child Study, 1938

Three kinds of information about children are especially useful to teachers and parents. The first is knowledge of methods of studying children; the second is knowledge of the kind of behavior which may be expected of children in each of the overlapping stages of development; the third is knowledge of how this behavior is acquired and modified.

Source: Strang (1938), pp. 1-2.

her associates devised a method of categorizing infants' responses in the "strange situation" (Ainsworth, 1982). It measured infants' behavior with their mothers in a room together, when their mothers leave, when a strange woman tries to offer comfort, and when their mothers return. Accumulated evidence shows that Ainsworth's descriptive measures of attachment occur routinely with a high degree of reliability (i.e., it occurs repeatedly in different situations) although some researchers criticize her research because of its focus on the caregivers' and not the infants' role in the formation of attachment (Vaughn et al., 1992).

VALIDITY

Validity involves *the accuracy of the conclusions researchers make.* A valid measure reflects the underlying psychological phenomenon researchers claim it does. There are two types of validity: internal and external validity. The first addresses causality, whereas the second deals with generalizability. Internal validity is achieved when controlled procedures are followed to eliminate or reduce the likelihood of extraneous explanations. Problems occur when other variables such as the level of noise or humidity in the room affect the subjects' performance and consequently confound the results of the study. On the other hand, external validity refers to the generalizability of the results. Even internally valid research lacks usefulness if researchers conduct their studies in an artificial environment such as a laboratory. Although researchers attempt to achieve a high degree of both internal and external validity, in practice, the steps they take to increase one type of validity tend to decrease the other. A controlled experiment conducted in the laboratory affords a high degree of internal validity but limits the generalizability of the results.

REPLICABILITY

Another important criterion in judging any research is its **replicability**, *the likelihood of obtaining the same results as the original study.* In other words, if other researchers follow the same procedures, they should obtain similar results. Although the scientific method is designed to ensure not only objectivity but also consistency, errors can be made. Studies may fail to replicate because of methodological flaws or confounding variables. If the sample of two separate studies differs, then the results possibly reflect other extenuating factors such as socioeconomic level or ethnic background of the subjects. Perhaps historical circumstances such as the use of anesthesia in childbirth today may have changed from one point in time to another. In practice, researchers often change selected parameters in order to verify the original results of another experiment as well as provide new information.

In addition to the four criteria of scientific research, a representative sample is needed. In contrast to the detailed accounts of individual infants in the 19th century, studies today rely on large groups of subjects. Statistical inferences about the population at large can be made on the basis of a limited number of subjects. Subjects are supposed to be randomly selected from a variety of socioeconomic levels and ethnic backgrounds to increase the generalizability of the results. A sample is said to be biased if not selected properly. Possible factors that may taint a sample include a limited sample (the results of a study with 10 subjects may not represent the entire population of infants because of increased variability). However, random selection is rarely attained in research. It not only takes a tremendous amount of financial resources but also depends on the availability of willing volunteers. Unfortunately, in research involving infants, a typical group of volunteers usually consist of highly educated, nonworking mothers who can bring their infants to the laboratory. Therefore, the results of any scientific study ultimately hinge on its selection of subjects and methodology.

TYPES OF RESEARCH

Scientific research typically falls into one of two broad categories. Nonexperimental and experimental methods each play a strategic role in developing a body of scientific knowledge.

NONEXPERIMENTAL METHODS

Nonexperimental methods provide descriptive information of infants' behavior in either a natural or structured context. The data gathered are not intended to establish a causal relationship between two variables.

The systematic observation of infants can be done in one of two ways. One approach is to observe infants' behavior in the field, a method referred to as **naturalistic observation**, *the description of behavior in unstructured situations.* It evolved from the detailed accounts of infants during the late 19th century. Whereas they centered on only one child, researchers today generally observe a large number of subjects.

American anthropologist Margaret Mead made extensive use of naturalistic observations of infants in different cultures in the early 1930s. In the northeast region of New Guinea, she observed the impact of cultural beliefs and child-rearing patterns of two

Researchers gather information about infants and toddlers from a variety of methods, including naturalistic observations in everyday settngs.
Photo courtesy of Tami Dawson, Photo Resource Hawaii.

PARENTING ISSUES

OBSERVATIONAL SKILLS

. . . .

Many parents develop observational skills on the job in reporting concerns to their pediatricians. Also, some professional caregivers record the developmental progress of infants in their care to share with parents. The developmental checklist in Appendix A covers typical expectations of development from age 6 months to 3 years in four major areas: physical, cognitive, language, and psychosocial development. It is meant only as a learning tool, not as a method of comparing individual infants.

geographically separate groups (Mead, 1935). In one, husbands shared caregiving responsibilities with their wives. At birth, although cultural tradition banned fathers from childbirth, they gathered the leaves their wives used to make a special sling in which to carry their infants. Water was also brought to bathe the newborns. During the first several weeks and months, infants were kept in close contact with their mothers and were comforted whenever in distress.

In contrast, adults of another culture in New Guinea placed their newborn infants, their arms strapped in place to their sides, in coarse baskets that blocked contact with their mothers' body. Adults did not feed on demand or respond to the infants' cries immediately. Without looking at the infants, without touching their bodies, mothers scratched the outside of the baskets with their fingers. If the sound did not soothe their babies, they eventually suckled their infants. Mead and others, especially American anthropologist Ruth Benedict, drew inferences from their naturalistic observations. To Benedict, culture plays a profound role in shaping development:

> From the moment of his birth the customs into which he is born shape his experience and behavior. By the time he can talk, he is the little creature of his culture, and by the time he is grown and able to take part in its activities, its habits are his habits, its beliefs his beliefs. . . . (Benedict, 1934, pp. 2–3)

The strength of naturalistic observation is its ability to describe infants' behavior in an unstructured context. On the other hand, its main weakness is its lack of control. Researchers sometimes use a different approach to observe infants' behavior but maintain control of events. *A method of observing and recording a behavior of interest in a laboratory* is called **structured observation**.

Structured observations of infants' recognition of emotional responses in others have been made in the laboratory. Considerable evidence suggests that their interpretation of events in a social context serves to regulate their behavior (Tronick, 1989). Infants and their parents, in other words, actually affect the emotional experience of one another.

The remarkable reciprocal interaction between infants and their parents is shown in the example below (Rogoff, 1991):

> An infant and his mother are playing a game of peek-a-boo. The infant abruptly ends the game and begins to suck on his thumb while he stares into space. The mother herself stops and waits. After several seconds, the infant turns back to her with an inviting expression. The mother moves in, smiles, and says in an exaggerated, high pitched voice, "Oh, you're back!" The infant smiles in response and starts to vocalize. As they both finish another round of peek-a-boo, the infant again reinserts his thumb into his mouth and stares into the distance. The mother waits again and after several seconds, joins in her infant's smiles and vocalizations. (p. 269)

Differences between unstructured and structured observations lie in location. Reciprocal exchanges such as above in which parents were instructed to engage in an everyday spontaneous manner can be recorded in a laboratory. In another example, infants were observed to overcome uncertainties when parents were sending positive instead of neutral or negative messages. When infants were confronted with a visual cliff (a table with an illusion of a vertical drop), none of the subjects were willing to cross over to mothers who were displaying fearful facial expressions on the other side of the table (Sorce et al., 1985). However, 74% did crawl over to the other side when their mothers smiled. Similarly, infants were more likely to approach and contact a toy when their mothers were asked to speak in a joyful tone of voice (Walden & Baxter, 1989).

Another type of nonexperimental method is called a **correlational study**. It refers to *a method of collecting information on existing groups without altering their experience in any way*. It is used when investigators are specifically interested in examining the relationship between two events. When changes in one are associated with changes in another, both are said to be correlated with each other (see Figure 3–1). A statistical number provides a quantitative index, symbolized as *r*, of the degree of association between the two events to distinguish between a relationship occurring because of chance or regularity. The number itself varies both in magnitude and direction from +1.00 to −1.00. The magnitude of the number indicates the strength of the relationship. The sign (+ or −) refers to the direction of the relationship. A positive sign (+) means as one variable increases, the other also increases; a negative sign (−) shows that as one variable increases, the other decreases. A zero implies the absence of any relationship between two events. However, a correlation does not in any way imply causation (i.e., when two things are correlated, it cannot be implied that A is causing B or the other way around).

A correlational study is generally used to identify potentially relevant variables. For example, Belsky (1980) observed four separate groups of infants at 9, 12, 15, and 18 months as they played with their mothers at home. During his observations, he counted the frequency of the mothers' physically pointing to and verbally naming objects in the room while at the same time observing the frequency of the infants' manipulation of objects. The results of his study indicated that measures of maternal stimulation and level of exploration correlated positively. Mothers who stimulated their babies apparently sparked their infants' natural curiosity in the world. However, the results do not explain whether maternal stimulation actually provoked the infants' exploration or whether competent infants elicited stimulation from their mothers.

(1)

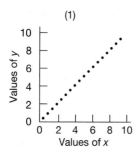

As *x* increases, *y* also increases.
A correlation of +1.00 is produced.

(2)

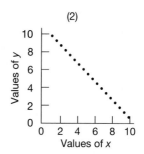

As *x* increases, *y* decreases.
A correlation of –1.00 is obtained.

(3)

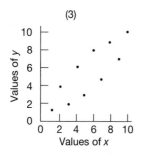

As *x* increases, *y* often increases, but there are exceptions.
A correlation between 0 and +1.00 is produced.

(4)

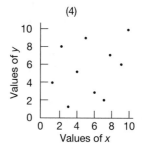

As *x* increases, *y* shows a weak relationship.
A correlation of 0 is obtained.

FIGURE 3–1 Examples of Correlation
A correlation refers to the possible relationship between two variables. Changes in one are associated with changes in the other. However, a correlation does not imply causation, a major limitation of correlational research. The four examples of correlation above indicate different relationships between two factors.
Source: Cole, M., & Cole, S. R. (2001). *The development of children* (4th ed.). New York: Worth, p. 23. Reprinted with permission.

EXPERIMENTAL METHODS

One major weakness of nonexperimental methods involves lack of causality. However, in experimental methods, researchers can establish cause-and-effect relationships and generalize the results of their studies to other infants.

An **experimental approach** consists of *controlled procedures that introduce a change in subjects' experience and then measure its effect on their behavior.* It provides a means of proving or disproving a hypothesis or prediction about the relationship between events. In a typical experiment, researchers control **independent variables**, *the variables that they manipulate*, to determine their effects on other variables (called **dependent variables** or *the changes caused by the independent variables*). Because researchers control the independent variables, they can make inferences about causal factors influencing the outcome of the experiment. For example, subjects who are asked to participate in a study are randomly assigned to one of two groups to minimize the possibility of biases and increase the generalizability of the results to other infants. One group receives the treatment. The subjects are then observed to measure the effects of the treatment on their behavior. The other group of subjects does not receive the treatment in order to compare the differences, if any, between the two groups.

A study of infants' fear of high places demonstrates the major features of the experimental method and its ability to resolve uncertainties about causal factors. Bertenthal, Campos, and Barrett (1984) hypothesized that the fear of heights develops from experience once infants begin to crawl. Previous evidence suggests that fear of heights results because of innate factors. Bertenthal and his associates initially observed a group of infants between 6 and 8 months of age, just as they started to crawl. The researchers found that all the subjects crossed a visual cliff on the first several opportunities. However, on subsequent trials, the infants did not venture onto the platform. Something apparently influenced their behavior. The investigators decided to conduct an experiment to find the answer.

Bertenthal et al. (1984) designed an experiment to test the hypothesis that fear of heights resulted from infants' accumulated experience. The researchers randomly assigned infants who participated in their study to one of two groups. In the first, the infants were placed in special walkers prior to the time they were beginning to crawl. In the second group, the subjects did not participate in the treatment. After 40 hours in the walker, the infants in the first group displayed heightened fear on their first exposure to the visual cliff. In contrast, the other group did not exhibit the same level of fear. The experiment provided evidence that the fear of heights resulted from the emergence of locomotion. In later studies, the researchers isolated the causal factors that contributed to the subjects' fear of heights (Bertenthal, 1996; Bertenthal & Boker, 1997).

LONGITUDINAL AND CROSS-SECTIONAL DESIGNS

Researchers sometimes attempt to gather information about the way subjects change over time. To answer questions about the possible causes of changes, they incorporate measures of subjects' behavior at different ages into their scientific research (see Figure 3–2).

In a **longitudinal design**, or *the repeated collection of data on the same group of subjects over a long period of time*, researchers are interested in evaluating individual stability or change over months, years, or sometimes even decades. Its strengths include the following two factors. First, because it tracks the subjects' performance over time, it identifies not only common developmental patterns but individual differences. Second, it examines the relationship between early and subsequent events in infants' development. However, longitudinal research does pose serious methodological problems. It requires a personal sacrifice and financial commitment on the part of researchers. Another drawback is attrition. In other words, the subjects (or in the case of infants, their parents) may decide to withdraw from a lengthy investigation.

Nonetheless, longitudinal studies provide extensive information about the stability of development. For example, in Yellow Springs, Ohio, a team of investigators at the Fels Research Institute examined the psychosocial development of a large group of children from birth to the midteens (Kagan & Moss, 1962). They conducted repeated

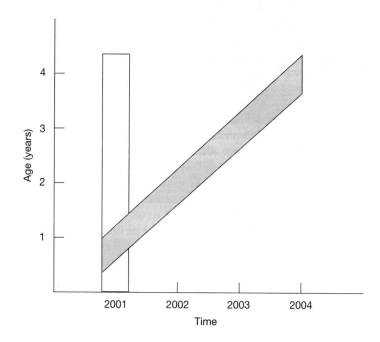

FIGURE 3–2 Longitudinal and Cross-Sectional Designs
Longitudinal research traces changes in the same persons over a specific period
of time (see shaded line). Cross-sectional research studies persons at different
ages at a single point in time.

observations and interviews, along with a battery of tests to track changes in the children's development over a period of years. Other influential studies that employed longitudinal designs included parenting styles (Baumrind, 1971), mental health (Werner &
Smith, 1982), and temperament and intelligence (Plomin & DeFries, 1985).

On the other hand, in a **cross-sectional design**, or *the collection of data from two or more
groups of subjects of different ages at the same time,* researchers are interested in comparing
similarities and differences among infants. In contrast to longitudinal studies, cross-
sectional designs provide a convenient and inexpensive way of collecting information
about development. For example, a cross-sectional study was conducted to compare
emotional distress among three groups of infants with an average age of 9, 12, and 24
months. The subjects were randomly drawn from the same socioeconomic background
and repeatedly observed during separation from their parents at a center-based program. The results showed definite differences among the three groups. The 12-month-
old subjects were more likely to cry and cling to their parents than either the 9- or
24-month-old subjects (Field et al., 1984).

Although cross-sectional research provides comparative results between groups of
subjects at different ages, it has its share of weaknesses. In particular, cross-sectional
studies do not provide information about individual changes over time. Further, studies
of young children of different ages do not necessarily yield accurate results. Perhaps

Longitudinal studies examine developmental changes of individual infants and toddlers over a long period of time.
Photo courtesy of Tami Dawson, Photo Resource Hawaii.

differences between two groups of subjects, say 1-year-olds versus 3-year-olds, may stem from other competing developmental factors.

In sum, both longitudinal and cross-sectional designs provide a wealth of information about infants (see Table 3–2). Each has its advantages and disadvantages. However, the accuracy of conclusions in any study depends on the specific type of design it employs. Therefore, the strengths and weaknesses of a longitudinal or cross-sectional study should be considered to judge its relevance to a particular group of infants (Hartmann & George, 1999).

TABLE 3–2 COMPARISON OF LONGITUDINAL AND CROSS-SECTIONAL DESIGNS

	Longitudinal	**Cross-Sectional**
Description	Studies same infants repeatedly over time	Studies infants of different ages at same point in time
Advantages	Follows development over time	Takes short period of time to complete (inexpensive)
	Examines relationship between early and later events	Compares differences between infants of different ages
Disadvantages	Takes long time (expensive)	Lacks ability to compare individual changes
	Loses subjects after long period of time (attrition)	Suffers from generational differences (cohorts)

SOCIOCULTURAL INFLUENCES

ROLE OF PRACTICE IN MOTOR DEVELOPMENT

During the first half of the 20th century, researchers were interested in examining the relative effects of heredity and environment on development. For example, American pediatrician Arnold Gesell believed that experience played an insignificant role in the development of infants' motor skills such as learning to sit or walk (Gesell, 1940). In his view, motor development followed a predictable pattern that unfolded without environmental intervention. A widely cited study to support the maturational view of motor development was Wayne and Marsena Dennis's study of native American Hopi infants in the southwestern United States (Dennis & Dennis, 1940).

In traditional Hopi families, infants were strapped to flat cradleboards during their first 3 months of life. They were unwrapped only once daily to be bathed or changed (Dennis & Dennis, 1940):

> The infant's arms are extended by his sides and the right side of the blanket is pulled tight over the right arm and is put between the left arm and the left side and tucked under the infant's body. . . . The infant, thus wrapped, is tied to the board by strips of cloth which encircle the baby and the board. . . . (p. 78)

The cradling practices did not permit any movement of the arms and legs or experience in mastering complex movements such as rolling over or sitting. Only prior to the end of the first year did the Hopi infants get the opportunity to practice beginning walking skills. The Dennises compared both traditionally and nontraditionally raised infants. The results showed that the two groups of babies began to walk without assistance at the same age, which they believed provided evidence that the Hopi infants' basic motor skills did not depend on experience.

Researchers have once again begun to explore the influence of maturation and experience on motor development. Naturalistic observations of Kipsigi infants in Kenya appear to provide evidence of environmental influences on motor development. Kipsigi parents begin to teach their babies to sit, stand, and walk shortly after birth. To teach their infants to sit, Kipsigi parents place their infants in shallow holes in an upright sitting position. The same procedure is followed until the skill is eventually acquired. Walking skills are taught at about 8 weeks of age. The infants are held under the arms with their feet on the ground and gradually propelled in a forward motion. On the average, Kipsigi infants acquire sitting and walking at 5 and 3 weeks earlier, respectively, than their European American counterparts (Super, 1976, 1981).

So, does practice accelerate motor development? Based on cross-cultural studies, the answer highlights the complex but dynamic interaction between heredity and environment. Basic motor skills such as sitting and walking do seem to be genetically determined. However, specialized motor skills require considerable practice (Thelen, 1990; Thelen & Ulrich, 1991). Highly valued skills such as playing a musical instrument or dancing are usually mastered with repeated practice in different cultures. Apparently, genetic inheritance can make a difference, but it does not diminish the benefits of actual experience in achieving high levels of proficiency.

ETHICAL CONSIDERATIONS

When research is conducted with infants, ethical questions are raised. Because of their vulnerability, infants need to be protected from any physical and psychological harm in research (Thompson, 1990). The central tenet of research is: Have sufficient steps been taken to promote infants' dignity and safeguard their welfare? The following ethical guidelines have been developed in conducting research with infants (Meltzoff, 1998; Sommer & Sommer, 1997):

- **Informed consent.** Informed consent requires the permission of parents to conduct research with infants. It includes a detailed explanation of its nature and purpose before the research can actually begin. Because parents are volunteering to participate, they are allowed to discontinue their infants' involvement at any time.

- **Protection from harm.** Researchers must take appropriate steps to minimize any possibility of physical or psychological harm or stress to infants during the study. Otherwise, investigators are required to find other ways of obtaining the desired information or abandon their research altogether.

- **Privacy.** Confidentiality is needed to protect the identity of the subjects and their families.

- **Knowledge of results.** Parents are entitled to be informed of the results of the research at its conclusion.

Ethical standards have been developed to protect infants and their families. The rights of the researcher can never at any time supersede the rights of the subjects (Bersoff, 1999).

SUMMARY

Scientific Method

- Historically, the scientific study of infants began in the late 19th century with detailed accounts of individual babies. Early biographers were interested in establishing norms of infants' development.

- The scientific method has been developed to facilitate objectivity and consistency in the collection and interpretation of data about infants. Its hallmark consists of selecting a problem, formulating a hypothesis, testing the hypothesis, and drawing conclusions.

Criteria of Scientific Research

- The foundation of scientific research lies in its adherence to rigorously controlled procedures. Four criteria can be used to evaluate scientific research: objectivity, reliability, validity, and replicability.

■ A representative sample of subjects is needed in any scientific study. It increases the generalizability of the results to the entire population of infants.

Types of Research

■ Two broad methods of scientific research have emerged since the turn of the 20th century. Each has played a significant role in expanding an ever-increasing body of knowledge about infants' development.

■ Nonexperimental methods provide detailed observations of behavior in either a natural or structured context. Although the flow of events can be described, causal relationships between two variables cannot be established.

■ In contrast, experimental studies introduce a change in one group of subjects. Then, its effect on their behavior is measured.

Longitudinal and Cross-Sectional Designs

■ Researchers are often interested in gathering information about the way infants develop over time. To answer questions about causality, they may measure subjects' behavior at different ages.

■ One method, longitudinal designs, collects information on the same group of subjects over a long period of time. On the other hand, cross-sectional designs gather data from two groups of subjects of different ages at the same point in time.

Ethical Considerations

■ When research is conducted with infants, stringent ethical guidelines must be followed. Ethical standards include informed consent and protection from physical and psychological harm.

PROJECTS
. . . .

1. Observe an infant or toddler in a naturalistic setting, with permission of his or her parents or legal guardians, and follow the guidelines below:

   Child's name

   Age

   Date

   Time

   Motor development: List his or her large and small muscle activities.

   Cognitive development: Comment on how he or she tries to solve any problems.

   Language: Did he or she vocalize words or use gestures to communicate his or her needs?

   Psychosocial development: What was the quality of his or her interactions with other adults or children?

2. Select an article from a scholarly journal such as *Infant Behavior and Development* or *Developmental Psychology* and then:

     Cite article in APA style.

     Briefly summarize its major points.

     Describe its intended audience.

     Discuss the usefulness of its information.

3. Discuss any ethical concerns regarding the following passages from a study by Watson and Rayner (1920):

     . . . the infant was confronted . . . successively with a white rat, a rabbit, a dog, a monkey, . . . masks with and without hair, cotton wool, burning newspapers, etc.

     . . . to determine whether a fear reaction could be called out . . . a loud sound was made. The sound was that made by striking a hammer upon a suspended steel bar (p. 2).

     The steps taken to condition emotional responses are shown in our laboratory notes:

     11 Months 3 Days

     1. White rat suddenly taken from the basket and presented to Albert. He began to reach for rat with left hand. Just as his hand touched the animal the bar was struck immediately behind his head. The infant jumped violently and fell forward, burying his face in the mattress. He did not cry, however.

     2. Just as the right hand touched the rat the bar was again struck. Again the infant jumped violently, fell forward and began to whimper.

     In order not to disturb the child too seriously no further tests were given for one week. (p. 4)

CONCEPTION AND PRENATAL DEVELOPMENT

*My children I would not change for all the ease, leisure, and pleasure that I could
have without them.*

Harriet Beecher Stowe, *Life and Letters of Harriet Beecher Stowe*

We tend to think development begins at birth. In reality, the foundation of development begins at the moment of conception. Each of us is the product of biology, but even before we are born, outside forces are already at work. Maternal nutrition and environmental hazards can disrupt the normal course of prenatal development. Chapter 4 examines the interaction between heredity and the environment in addition to the remarkable journey from conception to birth.

The genetic building blocks of every person are acquired at the moment of conception. The unique combination of **genes**, or *units of hereditary information*, directs the physiological sequence of events during **gestation**, or *the elapsed time between conception and* *birth.* The newly formed fertilized egg is eventually transformed into a person with billions of specialized cells, forming an intricate network of organs. The process of prenatal development illustrates the principles of qualitative and quantitative changes, two recurring themes in later chapters.

GENETIC BASIS OF LIFE

Although the scientific study of genetics did not begin until the last half of the 19th century, in the past, agricultural communities intuitively relied on basic genetic principles. When farming villages were started, different species of plants were cultivated to provide a stable source of food. Animals such as horses were bred to serve specific functions. Some were used as beasts of burden to pull plows or carry heavy loads; others were prized because of their swiftness or agility. The inherited traits of plants and animals were therefore purposefully manipulated. Hundreds of domesticated species were derived from a process of trial and error.

The science of genetics began with the observations of Austrian monk Gregor Mendel (1822–1884) who experimented with peas he cultivated in the garden of his monastery. In 1856, he started to record the physical traits of the plants (the color and shape of their seed) over successive generations. Ten years later, he reported the results of his work, although others did not realize its importance until the 20th century. On the basis of his observations, Mendel inferred the existence of genetic factors, or in his words, "characters," that controlled the physical traits of the plants that he studied (Edelson, 1999). Only later were his "characters" referred to as genes. The genetic mechanism he described operates in the same way with all forms of life, including people (Mange & Mange, 1998).

HISTORICALLY SPEAKING

GENETIC BASIS OF LIFE

Laurence Snyder
The Principles of Heredity, 1935
Parents and their offspring are usually alike in some ways, unlike in others. Some of these similarities and differences are the direct results of the relationship. Others apparently come about as a consequence of outside influences acting upon the individuals. The study of inherent similarities and differences is embodied in the science known as genetics.

Source: Snyder (1935), p. 1.

CHROMOSOMES AND GENES

Each person consists of billions of specialized cells. The center of each cell is called the **nucleus,** *a spherical body that contains the hereditary material of the cell, controlling its growth and reproduction.* The nucleus contains *threadlike structures that store and transmit genetic information* called **chromosomes.** The exact number of chromosomes vary from species to species (46 in humans but 48 in chimpanzees). Chromosomes come in matching pairs. Each member of the matching pair corresponds to the other not only in size and shape but also in genetic functions (*a pictorial arrangement of chromosomes* is known as a **karyotype**). One is inherited from the mother; the other from the father. There are 23 pairs of chromosomes in each human cell (see Figure 4–1).

Chromosomes consist of **deoxyribonucleic acid** or DNA, *long strands of molecules that contain the genetic code of the cell.* These molecules are arranged in the form of a twisted ladder known as a double helix. Pairs of chemical substances, referred to as bases, join each side of the ladder. Four molecules—A (adenine), T (thymine), C (cytosine), and G (guanine)—form the rungs of the ladder. Although the bases are always paired in the same way (A with T and C with G), the particular sequence of the pairs is varied along the sides. The four letters comprise a genetic alphabet that provides hereditary instruction. A gene refers to a segment of DNA that occupies a fixed location on a chromosome. It varies in length, perhaps a hundred to several thousand rungs long, and each one differs because of the specific arrangement of pairs.

The structure of DNA was discovered in the early 1950s. Two scientists, James Watson and Francis Crick, used x-rays to study the atomic architecture of DNA (Strathern, 1999). When x-rays strike an atom or set of atoms, they cast shadows on a photographic plate. The photographs suggested that DNA looked like a spiral staircase. Watson and

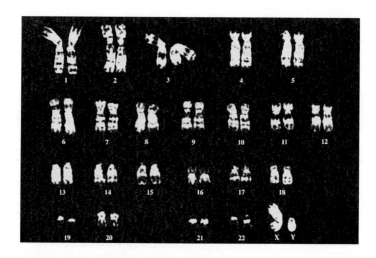

FIGURE 4–1 Human Chromosomes
Chromosomes are ordered in matching pairs, a pictorial arrangement called a karyotype.
Biophoto Associates, Photo Researchers, Inc.

Crick then undertook the task of building a three-dimensional model of DNA. Their work culminated in the publication of "Molecular Structure of Nucleic Acids" in 1953 (Watson & Crick, 1953) and a joint Nobel Prize in 1962.

MITOSIS AND MEIOSIS

A unique factor of DNA is its ability to duplicate itself. *The division of a cell into two identical cells* is called **mitosis**. Basically, the twisted ladder of DNA splits in half. During mitosis, each half builds a new ladder. In effect, the ladder straightens itself and unfastens lengthwise in the center of each rung. The members of each pair of bases are exposed to the cytoplasm of the cell, which contains the DNA's molecular building blocks and other raw materials of life. Each base pairs itself with a corresponding partner. When the splitting and pairing process is finally completed, two ladders are formed. Each of the two halves has assembled a new half. The genetic code is transmitted to each new cell.

The process of mitosis continues until death. New cells are continually created to replace old ones. Each new cell contains copies of the original 46 chromosomes that people inherit from their parents at the moment of conception. The replication of cells ensures continuity over the course of development. The passage of time does not alter the genetic information of each cell. However, increasing evidence suggests that repeated exposure to radiation and certain hazardous chemicals may result in mutations, or changes in the composition of genes.

A different process controls the production of two special cells, *the sperm and ovum.* Referred to as **gametes** or reproductive cells, they contain only 23 chromosomes, half of the total in a regular cell. **Meiosis** involves *the division of cells that reduces the number of chromosomes.* First, the reproductive cells produce copies of themselves, just as in mitosis. However, the cells then divide not once, as in mitosis, but twice. The result of meiosis is four separate cells, each with only 23 chromosomes. It occurs differently in males and females as shown in Figure 4–2.

Because the sperm and the ovum contain only 23 chromosomes each, the newly created cell receives its 46 chromosomes at conception. Each person therefore differs genetically from his or her father and mother because half of the fertilized cell comes from a different parent. Each generation differs from the one before. **Crossing over**, *the exchange of genes between a pair of chromosomes*, occurs during the first phase of meiosis and increases genetic diversity further. One section of a chromosome may switch places with the corresponding section of another chromosome. The exchange alters the genetic composition of both chromosomes and creates new hereditary combinations.

The process of meiosis produces considerable genetic variability even among children of the same parents. Although each child receives the same genetic inheritance, chance determines the specific combination of genes at the moment of conception. In terms of probability, there are 2^{23}, or about 8 million, possible genetic combinations whenever a sperm and an ovum are united. When the possibilities of crossing over are factored in, there is only 1 chance in 64 trillion that a particular genetic combination is ever duplicated (Hartl & Jones, 1998). In addition, because the production of reproductive cells varies in males and females, the childbearing lives of men and women differ. After reaching sexual maturity, men continue to produce sperm throughout their lives. In contrast, women are born with a finite set of ova. Of the 1 to 2 million ova at birth,

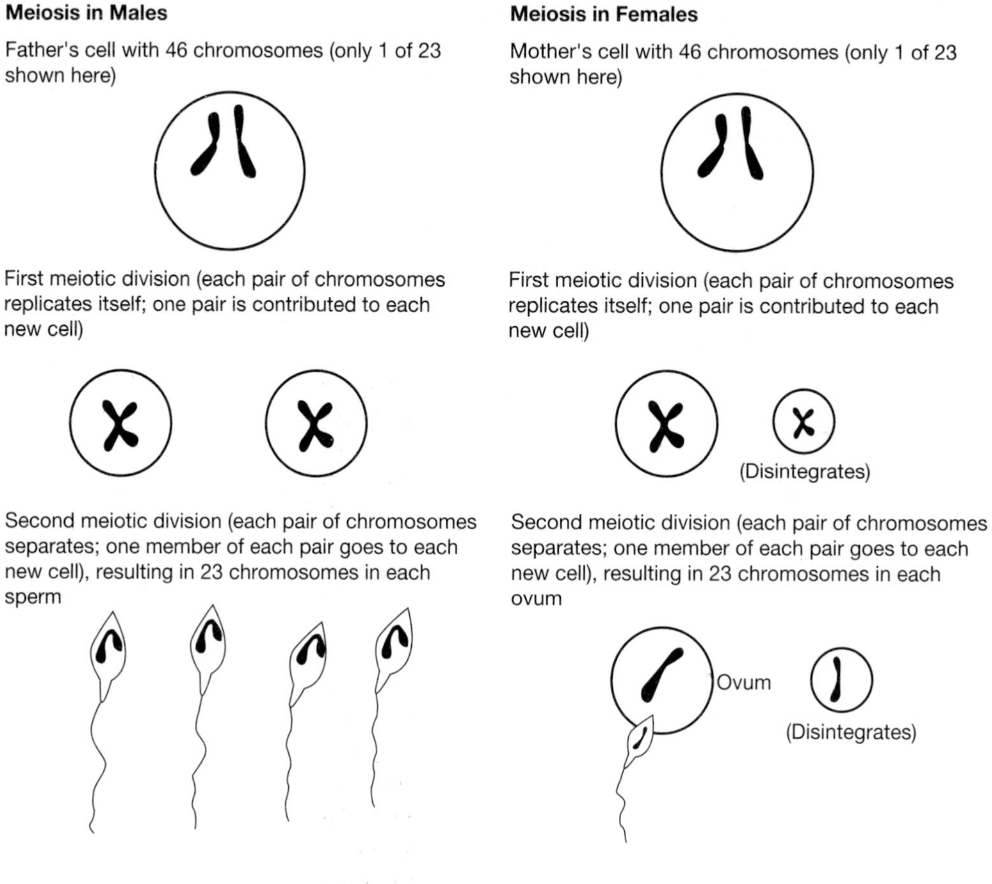

Meiosis in Males

Father's cell with 46 chromosomes (only 1 of 23 shown here)

First meiotic division (each pair of chromosomes replicates itself; one pair is contributed to each new cell)

Second meiotic division (each pair of chromosomes separates; one member of each pair goes to each new cell), resulting in 23 chromosomes in each sperm

Meiosis in Females

Mother's cell with 46 chromosomes (only 1 of 23 shown here)

First meiotic division (each pair of chromosomes replicates itself; one pair is contributed to each new cell)

 (Disintegrates)

Second meiotic division (each pair of chromosomes separates; one member of each pair goes to each new cell), resulting in 23 chromosomes in each ovum

 Ovum (Disintegrates)

FIGURE 4–2 Process of Meiosis in Males and Females

40,000 remain during adolescence and approximately 400 during women's remaining childbearing years (Sadler, 2000).

CONCEPTION

Development begins at the moment of conception when a sperm and ovum unite. The male produces an average of 300 million sperm a day in the testes, two glands located in the scrotum. Each sperm, in the final process of its development, develops a tail, which permits movement. The sperm move into a thin tube, the *vas deferens,* which leads to the penis, and mix with semen, a protective fluid, during sexual intercourse. In contrast, the female's ova, tiny spheres 1/175 of an inch in diameter (about the size of a period at the end of a sentence), are produced in two reproductive glands, the ovaries. About once every 28 days, in the middle of a woman's menstrual cycle, an ovum erupts from

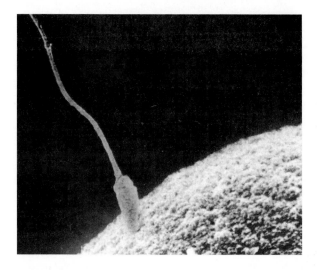

Physical traits and sex are determined at the moment of fertilization.
D. W. Fawcett, Photo Researchers, Inc.

one of her ovaries. Cilia, microscopic hairlike structures of the Fallopian tubes, propel the ovum toward the uterus. Hormones from the ovaries prepare the uterus to receive the ovum (Gould & Keeton, 1996).

A man ejects hundreds of millions of sperm, about 200 to 400 million, into the vagina at sexual climax. The pumping action of both the vaginal and uterine muscles propels the sperm into the uterus and then Fallopian tubes, a distance of about 6 inches. Only a few hundred sperm—300 to 500—actually reach the Fallopian tubes within 60 to 90 minutes after ejaculation, because of the acidic fluid of the vagina and structural defects of some sperm such as the lack of a head. The sperm eventually die if they do not encounter an ovum within a period of 24 to 48 hours, whereas the ovum can survive about 24 hours (Nilsson & Hamberger, 1990).

Only one sperm can penetrate the ovum. To strip away the protective barrier of the ovum, the sperm releases digestive enzymes. However, once fertilization occurs, the ovum immediately seals its surface from all other competitors. The chemical composition of the ovum then changes. The sperm's tail separates from the head as its genetic content spills out in an explosive but orderly manner. The genetic material is drawn into the nucleus of the ovum and is soon fused. Instantaneously, the genetic traits of the new person are determined. The fertilized ovum is now referred to as a **zygote**, or *the union of the sperm and ovum at conception.*

DETERMINATION OF SEX

Of the 23 pairs of chromosomes in a human cell, all but one resemble each other. The first 22 *matching pairs of chromosomes* are referred to as **autosomes**. They are arranged from the longest to shortest pair. However, the last pair, consisting of the sex chromosomes, differs because it determines the sex of the person. In females, both members of the twenty-third pair are the same. They are called the X chromosomes. In males, the twenty-third pair consists of one X chromosome and one Y chromosome. Since the

SOCIOCULTURAL INFLUENCES

MULTIPLE CONCEPTION

After conception, the cells of the zygote divide in half repeatedly. Sometimes, it separates and develops into **monozygotic**, or identical, **twins**—*two individuals who come from one fertilized egg.* Monozygotic twins occur in about 4 of every 1,000 births. Because they originate from the same egg, they inherit identical genetic information. The exact cause of the separation during the first few mitotic divisions of cells is not yet known. Neither the mother's age nor parity—nor the number of children that she has given birth to previously—has apparently any effect.

Another classification of twins is derived from not one but two separate fertilized eggs. **Dizygotic**, or fraternal, **twins** refer to *two individuals who come from different fertilized eggs.* They share the same genetic endowment but not the same chromosomes as with monozygotic twins. The fertilization of two eggs does not necessarily result in twins of the same sex (one may be a boy and the other a girl). Possible causes of dizygotic twins include the mother's age, the number of prior pregnancies, ethnicity, and drugs that stimulate the production of eggs. In other words, women between the ages of 35 and 40, who have given birth to four or more children, who are African American, and who have taken drugs to induce their fertility are more likely to give birth to dizygotic twins.

Researchers are interested in conducting research on twins to answer fundamental questions about nature and nurture. A comparison of similarities between identical and fraternal twins provides valuable information about the contributions of genetic and environmental factors. Robert Plomin and his colleagues, in particular, have examined temperamental traits such as level of activity and persistence and measures of personality such as introversion, extroversion, compulsivity, and anxiety of twins. They found a high degree of correlation between identical but not fraternal twins (Plomin & DeFries, 1985).

Recent studies suggest that genetic factors may play a moderate role in the development of temperament and personality. About half of the similarities between identical twins is believed to be genetically determined (Plomin, 1995). Nevertheless, heredity interacts with the environment. The unique temperamental traits of a person influences the kinds of experiences he or she receives over the course of life.

twenty-third pair in females consists of two X chromosomes, the ova always contain an X chromosome. The sperm in males carry either an X or Y chromosome. If the sperm contains an X chromosome, the resulting person at the time of conception becomes a female (XX). If it contains a Y chromosome, it then develops into a male (XY). Therefore, fathers determine the sex of their children.

The sex of a person is determined at the moment of conception. During the 13th week of gestation, a single gene on the Y chromosome triggers the sexual development of males. When it is switched on, male sex hormones are produced. In the absence of a biochemical signal from the Y chromosome, the fetus begins to develop female sex organs (Aitken, 1995).

Interestingly, the existence of either the X or Y chromosome in sperms does not result in an equal number of boys and girls at birth. In reality, boys outnumber girls at conception. At birth, the ratio between boys and girls narrows. The reason is not exactly known. Males may be at a higher risk for genetic complications and other problems both before and after birth. If a male inherits a defective X chromosome, the Y chromosome does not always contain a corresponding gene to compensate. Another factor involves culture. In some countries, selective abortion may be practiced to prevent the birth of girls. With the advent of medical procedures that can identify the sex of the fetus prior to birth, the disparate ratio between boys and girls may reflect deeply ingrained cultural traditions. For example, an unusually high ratio of boys has been reported in China because of its official policy on one child per family to reduce its birthrate, putting tremendous pressure on families to produce a son as the firstborn (Li & Ballweg, 1995; Rylko-Bauer, 1996).

SOCIOCULTURAL INFLUENCES

AIDS

The acquired immune deficiency syndrome (AIDS) refers to a viral disease that destroys the body's ability to defend itself from fatal illnesses. An estimated 3,000 infants are infected each year with the human immunodeficiency virus (HIV), the cause of AIDS. The virus is transferred from an infected mother to her infant before, during, or after birth. The mother acquires the virus when she either engages in sexual contact or shares needles with an infected person. The transfer of bodily fluids is involved in the transmission of the virus (Stine, 1998a).

The disease progresses at a rapid rate in infants infected before birth. Symptoms usually begin to appear at 6 months. They include neurological and respiratory complications in addition to fever and diarrhea. Dysmorphic features—a prominent forehead and widely spaced eyes—will be noted. Infected infants experience serious delays in their physical and mental development. Other concerns are raised because the mothers of infected infants are themselves stricken with the virus and therefore are not able to provide appropriate care.

Until a cure is found, widespread education is required to prevent the spread of AIDS. In particular, women who engage in unsafe sex or use intravenous needles should be informed of the detrimental effects of their habits not only on themselves but also on their unborn infants. Even doctors are placed at risk during a delivery of an infected infant. The cost of hospitalization of an infected infant ranges from $90,000 to $200,000 annually, a staggering amount (Stine, 1998b).

TABLE 4–1 SELECTIVE LIST OF GENETIC DISEASES AND CONDITIONS

Disease or Condition	Description	Mode of Transmission
Cystic fibrosis	Lack of enzyme causes mucous obstruction in lungs and digestive tract	Recessive gene
Hemophilia	Blood fails to clot readily	Recessive gene
Huntington's disease	Central nervous system and muscular coordination deteriorate	Dominant gene
Muscular dystrophy	Gradual deterioration of muscles occurs	Recessive gene
Sickle cell anemia	Abnormal red blood cells develop	Recessive gene
Tay-Sachs disease	Lack of enzyme causes accumulated waste in brain	Recessive gene

LAWS OF GENETIC INHERITANCE

When the sperm and ovum fuse at conception, the zygote acquires the genetic inheritance from its parents, and ultimately its ancestors. Pairs of genes determine particular traits. Each pair is found in the same place on chromosomes with the exception of the sex chromosomes. An **allele** refers to *each member of a pair of genes.*

Mendel discovered the laws governing genetic inheritance. The peas he planted came in two colors, either yellow or green. When he crossed two plants that produced yellow peas, he obtained offsprings with yellow peas. Likewise, two plants that yielded green peas produced offsprings with green peas. However, when he crossed one with yellow peas and one with green peas, all the offsprings produced yellow peas. If he then bred the hybrids, 75% of the offsprings had yellow peas; the remaining 25% had green peas.

Mendel explained his results with the law of dominant inheritance. It states that when a plant inherits competing traits, such as the color of peas, one overrides the other. A **dominant allele,** *an allele that is expressed when it is paired with an identical or recessive allele,* is written with an uppercase letter; a **recessive allele,** *an allele that is expressed only when it is paired with a matching recessive allele,* is written with a lowercase letter.

Different combinations of genes clearly produce different traits. A **genotype** is *the underlying genetic pattern of a person,* whereas a **phenotype** consists of *the observable physical and behavioral traits of a person.* The genotype does not change during the course of one's lifetime. However, their phenotype is constantly interacting with both genetic and environmental factors. Any discussion of genetic influences on development relies on inferences of genotype based on observations of phenotype. The determination of genetic influences is complicated because of polygenetic traits, the interaction between a number of genes and the environment.

GENETIC AND CHROMOSOMAL ABNORMALITIES

Genetic factors influence a wide range of human traits. Physical appearance, intellectual capacity, temperament, and even talent reflect a person's genetic inheritance. In addition,

TABLE 4–1 CONTINUED

Incidence	Treatment	Prenatal Detection
1 in 2,000 white births	Bronchial drainage, prompt treatment of infections, and dietary management	Yes
1 in 10,000 males	Blood transfusions; preventive measures to reduce risk of injury	Yes
1 in 18,000	None; death occurs about 10 to 20 years after onset of symptoms	Yes
1 in 5,000 males	None; death results from respiratory infection or weakened heart muscles in adolescence	Yes
1 in 500[1]	Blood transfusions and prompt treatment of infections	Yes
1 in 3,000[2]	None; death occurs within 3 to 4 years of age	Yes

[1]African American births.
[2]Jewish people of European descent.

a number of disorders are genetically linked (see Table 4–1). Researchers are interested in studying genetic and chromosomal anomalies in order to detect congenital defects and ameliorate their effects. Only a small number of zygotes with genetic or chromosomal abnormalities are able to survive the prenatal period. In most cases, they are spontaneously aborted (Clayman, 1989). Of the infants who do survive, 3% to 5% of newborns will exhibit genetic or chromosomal abnormalities. However, the incidence of disorders increases to 6% as doctors identify other disorders later after birth (Plomin et al., 1997).

The variety of genetic and chromosomal abnormalities broadens the range of individual variability. They pose a challenge not only to the adaptive capabilities of the afflicted child but also to the caregiving abilities of parents. Several congenital defects have been linked to a single gene or specific chromosome. Phenylketonuria and Down syndrome illustrate the effects of genetic and chromosomal abnormalities on development.

PHENYLKETONURIA

First discovered in 1934, phenylketonuria (PKU), an inherited recessive autosomal disorder that can lead to severe mental retardation, provides a dramatic example of the role of the environment in controlling the effects of a genetic defect. Although the incidence varies among different ethnic groups, PKU affects about 1 in 8,000 infants (Cunningham et al., 1993). It stems from the inability of the liver to produce an enzyme that neutralizes phenylalanine, an amino acid found in common types of food such as milk, eggs, bread, and fish. When a high concentration of phenylalanine and other abnormal metabolic products accumulates in the body, it damages the normal growth of the brain.

In addition to severe mental retardation, other symptoms of PKU include hyperactivity and behavioral problems. Infants with PKU display normal signs of development during the first 3 months after birth. Between 3 and 6 months, they increasingly exhibit either listlessness or extremely irritable behavioral patterns. Developmental milestones such as rolling over or sitting are not achieved on schedule. A highly preventable disorder, it is routinely screened before phenylalanine is allowed to accumulate. Blood is drawn from a newborn's heel within a few days after birth and is then added to a bacterial culture to determine the presence of phenylalanine (Koch, 1999).

After a diagnosis is made, infants and children are placed on a highly restrictive diet. The dietary treatment must be monitored carefully to prevent an accumulation of phenylalanine but not to stunt growth. The diet is frequently started in the first or second month of life. Infants treated prior to 6 months had IQs in the range between 70 (borderline) to 100 (average). If it was not started until after 2 years, severe to profound retardation was likely to occur. Clearly, the starting point of intervention plays a critical role.

DOWN SYNDROME

A chromosomal disorder, Down syndrome occurs in roughly 1 in 800 births. It was the first human disorder to be linked with a specific chromosomal defect (Behrman, 1999). In 95% of the cases, it results from the failure of the 21st pair of chromosomes to divide properly during meiosis. When a pair of chromosomes fails to separate, a reproductive cell sometimes receives both chromosomes instead of just one. Consequently, when it joins the reproductive cell from the other parent, the fertilized egg contains an extra chromosome. Rather than 46 chromosomes in all, there are 47. In rare cases, a broken piece of a chromosome is attached to the 21st pair.

English neurologist Langdon Down first referred to the chromosomal disorder eventually named after him as "mongolism" in 1866. He noted the similarities between the distinctive facial and physical features of children with Down syndrome and a particular ethnic group (slanted eyes with an epicantric fold on the eyelids). However, the term is never used anymore because of its obvious negative connotations. Instead, it is now called Down syndrome or Trisomy 21 because of the presence of a third chromosome on the 21st pair (Elias, 1995). Other stigmata, or physical features, of Down syndrome include a flattened face, an enlarged tongue, and a short body. Also, an unusual crease extends in a straight line across the palm of both hands instead of curving downward as it does in 90% of all people.

In addition to the external physical features of Down syndrome, there are internal complications. Because of cardiac complications, infants with Down syndrome sometimes die within the first few years. Numerous metabolic and respiratory problems further complicate the picture. With the advent of heart surgery and better metabolic treatment, children typically live to an average age of 30 years (Hassold, Sherman, & Hunt, 1995). Another prominent feature of Down syndrome involves mental retardation. An estimated 10% of institutionalized mentally retarded children and adults are afflicted with Down syndrome. IQs range from 20 to 80 with the majority in the moderate range of mental retardation. Special education and other related services are frequently required because of delayed motoric skills and limited vocabulary (Kliewer, 1998). Nevertheless, the adaptive functioning level of children with Down syndrome depends on the severity of the disorder and quality of intervention. Effective parenting and educational practices can make a significant difference in facilitating the development of children with Down syndrome.

Down syndrome dramatically increases with the mother's age. It occurs roughly in about 1 in 1,900 births at the age of 20 but rises sharply to about 1 in 30 births over the age of 45 (Halliday et al., 1995). Geneticists believe that women's ova weaken with age. Current research has not found direct evidence of increased risk on the basis of paternal age unless fathers over 40 have been exposed to possible harmful teratogens in the environment (de Michelena et al., 1993).

PRENATAL DIAGNOSIS

Prospective parents are able to seek the assistance of a specially trained medical doctor or genetic counselor to determine the probability of conceiving a child with congenital defects. Two basic steps are involved (Baker, Schuette, & Uhlmann, 1998). Information is initially gathered to assess a couple's genetic history. Prospective parents are sometimes worried about the existence of genetic problems in one or both of their families. Other concerns include a high incidence of repeated miscarriages in previous attempts or age since the overall rate of chromosomal problems rises significantly after age 35. Specific screening tests, particularly a complete analysis of a couple's chromosomes, are routinely requested (Gardner & Sutherland, 1996).

Next, a genetic counselor interprets the results of the screening tests. Statistical probabilities are used to counsel a couple about its potential risks. The chances of an occurrence or recurrence of a congenital defect are calculated. A multitude of factors is taken into account: random or inherited genetic or chromosomal abnormality, environmental factors, or multifactorial inheritance (a combination of both genetic and environmental factors). Even though a genetic counselor can provide valuable information, the couple must ultimately make its own decision of taking a chance or exploring other options such as adoption. A rate of success with adoption has improved in recent years because of social agencies' careful selection of adoptive families.

If a couple faces the possibility of conceiving a child with genetic or chromosomal abnormalities, medical procedures exist to detect potential problems before birth. They include amniocentesis, chorionic villus sampling, ultrasonography, and fetoscopy.

AMNIOCENTESIS

An **amniocentesis** involves *a medical procedure of removing fluid with a hollow needle from the amniotic sac to analyze the chromosomes of the fetus.* To perform an amniocentesis, a doctor first determines the position of the fetus with an ultrasound sonogram, or a computerized image of the fetus in the amniotic sac. A hollow needle is inserted into the mother's abdominal wall and amniotic sac. A syringe is then placed into the hollow needle to extract discarded cells of the fetus in the amniotic fluid. The cells are then analyzed to determine the presence of certain genetic and chromosomal disorders such as muscular dystrophy, Tay-Sachs disease, spina bifida, and Down syndrome. It can also be used to determine the sex and age of the fetus before birth (Curtis, 1997).

The procedure is generally performed during the 16th week after conception. The results are usually reported 2 weeks later. Since maternal age is related to the incidence of Down syndrome, women after the age of 35 are encouraged to undergo an amniocentesis. If the results detect a genetic or chromosomal abnormality, prospective parents face a difficult decision of whether to abort the fetus or raise a child with special needs. A few risks are associated with an amniocentesis such as fetal damage, spontaneous abortion, and maternal infection or hemorrhage. However, clinical studies do not reveal any significant concerns with the procedure in terms of actual prenatal injuries or problems during labor, delivery, or the newborn period although there is a small risk of miscarriage (Hsu, 1998).

CHORIONIC VILLUS SAMPLING

A recently developed procedure to detect genetic and chromosomal disorders, **chorionic villus sampling** refers to *a prenatal diagnostic test that analyzes cells taken from the hairlike villi on the membrane of the placenta.* A hollow tube is inserted into the abdominal wall or the cervix of the mother with a needle, as in an amniocentesis, to obtain a sample of chorionic villi. The procedure is typically performed from 6 to 8 weeks after conception. The results of the test are reported within a few days after the procedure is completed. There is, however, an increased risk of spontaneous abortion. In addition, the safety of the procedure and accuracy of its results have been questioned (Brambati & Tului, 1998).

ULTRASONOGRAPHY

Computerized visual images of the fetus and its internal organs in the amniotic sac can be obtained with **ultrasonography**, a technique that is used to detect fetal abnormalities. Ultrasonic waves are transmitted to and from the mother's abdomen with a transducer that is moved over the surface of the skin. The picture that is obtained is referred to as a sonogram. A painless and nonevasive procedure, an ultrasound, as it is known, is administered in conjunction with an amniocentesis or chorionic villus sampling to determine the fetus's position. A doctor can track the physical growth of the fetus and determine its age and size in addition to the presence of multiple pregnancies and structural anomalies such as spina bifida. Also, it is utilized to study fetal behavior because the fetus is capable of moving in the amniotic sac and responding to environmental stimuli.

FETOSCOPY

In a **fetoscopy**, *a procedure that photographs the fetus and samples its tissue and blood,* the doctor inserts a fetoscope, a thin tube with a diameter of a large needle, into the mother's abdomen and amniotic cavity. A high-powered light is attached to the end of the fetoscope to inspect the fetus directly. A small needle can take a sample of the fetus's blood to detect sickle cell anemia and neural defects. The procedure is performed during the third month of gestation.

Recent advances in prenatal diagnosis have led to further improvements in treating certain medical complications before birth. Fetal surgery has been used to repair malformations of the heart and neural defects (Koop, 1997). However, any intrusive measure entails the possibility of risks such as premature labor and miscarriage. To make an informed decision, parents of the unborn child should seek information from a doctor not performing the procedure (Harrison, 1996).

PRENATAL DEVELOPMENT

Harvey Jordan and James Kindred
A Textbook of Embryology, 1932

Human development includes all that lies between the event of fertilization, the union of egg and sperm, and the attainment of [adulthood]. Birth, adolescence, and maturity are only epochs in a continuous process.

Source: Jordan and Kindred (1932), p. 1.

PRENATAL DEVELOPMENT

The period before birth marks a time of extremely rapid growth. At conception, a zygote is formed with the union of a sperm and an ovum. It develops over 9 months, or about 280 days on the average, from a single cell into a competent newborn. The prenatal period can be divided into three major stages: germinal, embryonic, and fetal (see Table 4–2).

TABLE 4–2 STAGES OF PRENATAL DEVELOPMENT

Stage	Weeks	Length and Weight	Description
Germinal	0–2		The zygote multiplies and forms a blastocyst. As it enters the uterus, the blastocyst burrows into the uterine wall. Structures that nourish and protect the developing person start to emerge.
Embryonic	3–4	1/4 inch	The brain and spinal cord begin to appear. The internal organs—the heart, digestive tract, bones, and muscles—start to develop.
	5–8	1 inch	The external structures (arms, legs, fingers, and toes) form. The developing person begins to move.
Fetal	9–12	3 inches; <1 ounce	A rapid increase in size begins. External genitals are formed.
	13–24	12 inches; 2 pounds	Further enlargement occurs. Fetal movements are felt. The fetus reacts to light and sound.
	25–40	20 inches; 7 pounds	Rapid development of the brain expands sensory and behavioral capabilities. Lungs gradually mature. A layer of fat is added. Antibodies are transmitted to fetus from mother.

GERMINAL STAGE

The germinal stage covers the first 2 weeks of prenatal development. As the zygote travels to the uterus, a distance of about 4 inches, it begins to divide in half repeatedly. The first mitotic division of the zygote, or cleavage, occurs within the first 24 hours after the moment of conception. It separates into two cells, each with an identical set of chromosomes. The two cells then divide into four, four into eight, and so on. The repeated division of cells results in the formation of a **blastocyst**, *a mass of cells that forms a ball of fluid.*

After about 3 to 4 days, the blastocyst enters the uterus. Even before it is implanted into the mother's uterine wall, it is continually developing. Two distinct layers of cells are formed. The inner layer eventually becomes the developing person, whereas the outer layer flattens to form the **placenta**, *the organ that separates the mother's bloodstream from the fetus but permits the exchange of nutrients and wastes.* The outer layer of cells, or trophoblast, begins to differentiate into membranes that develop into the amniotic sac. Trophoblast comes from *trophos*, a Greek word, meaning "to nourish."

As the blastocyst enters the uterus, tiny fingerlike projections begin to emerge from the trophoblast. They eventually burrow into the spongy wall of the uterus sometime between the seventh and ninth day. Once they come into contact with the mother's blood vessels, the placenta starts to develop. The developing person is connected to the placenta with an **umbilical cord**, *a long cord that delivers nutrients and removes wastes.* It initially appears as a primitive stalk but gradually grows to a length of 1 to 3 feet. It actually contains one artery that delivers the nutrients from the mother and two veins that remove the wastes.

The implantation of the blastocyst into the uterine wall marks the end of the germinal stage. However, development continues at a breathtaking pace. Two broad principles illustrate the direction of physical growth during prenatal development (and even after birth). The first, **cephalocaudal**, literally means that *development proceeds from "head to tail"* or top to bottom. During the embryonic stage, the head develops before the trunk and the arms before the legs. The second, **proximodistal**, literally means that *development*

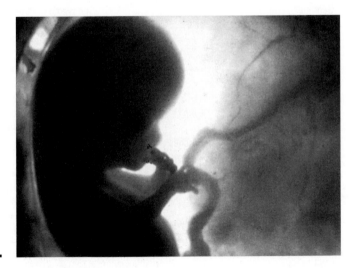

The fetus, immersed in the amniotic sac, receives oxygen and nourishment from the placenta.
Pearson Education/PH College.

proceeds from "near to far" or center of the body outward. For example, the trunk develops before the limbs and the arms and legs before fingers and toes. The physical growth of the brain and spinal cord clearly follows an organized pattern because of their significance to the further development of the embryo and fetus.

EMBRYONIC STAGE

The embryonic stage lasts from the moment the blastocyst implants itself into the uterine wall until the 8th week of gestation. It represents a period of extreme vulnerability in the development of an unborn person. Extremely rapid physical growth takes place during the next 6 weeks. Because the major organs are forming, any environmental insult can result in a serious and irreversible congenital malformation.

After implantation, the blastocyst is now referred to as the embryo. It is derived from the Greek word *embryon* meaning "to swell." *The inner mass of cells of the blastocyst,* known as the **embryoblast**, begins to differentiate into specialized tissues and organs. The inner mass of cells separates into three layers. The **ectoderm**, or *the outer layer of cells of the embryoblast,* eventually develops into the skin and central nervous system (the brain, spinal cord, and nerves); the **endoderm**, or *the inner layer of the embryoblast,* becomes the lungs and digestive system. Shortly afterward, the **mesoderm**, or *the middle layer of the embryoblast,* appears, which turns into the skeleton and muscles, the circulatory system, and inner layers of the skin.

During the 3rd week of gestation, a cylindrical body forms. The ectoderm folds to form the **neural tube**, *a primitive spinal cord,* and the brain. The production of neurons, cells that store and transmit information, starts. Gradually, the neurons travel on tiny threads to their permanent locations in the brain. As the central nervous system develops, the heart fuses into a tube and begins to pump blood into the embryo's circulatory system. Primitive blood vessels are beginning to form. During the 4th week, components of the digestive system (the esophagus, stomach, and liver) appear. So, at the end of the first month, the curved embryo, just one-fourth of an inch, consists of millions of organized groups of cells with specific functions.

During the 2nd month, rapid physical growth continues. The eyes and ears form as tiny buds become arms, legs, fingers, and toes. The trunk of the body begins to straighten. The heart develops into separate chambers as other organs—the liver and spleen—take control of the production of blood cells. The brain's internal structures take on a discernible shape. Neurons are developing at a rate of thousands per minute. Now just an inch long at the end of the 2nd month, the embryo is beginning to move, although the mother is not able to feel the flutters yet. It responds to touch in areas of the mouth and on the soles of its feet. Further, other senses are gradually coming into contact with the uterine environment. The unborn child can taste bitter, sweet, or sour flavors in the amniotic fluid (McCarthy, 1999).

FETAL STAGE

The last stage of prenatal development covers the period from the 3rd month until birth. The embryo is now referred to as a fetus because of its distinctive human appearance. The size of the fetus increases dramatically as further enlargement of its rudimentary organs occurs, particularly during the 3rd to 5th month. The fetal stage ends with the birth of the child.

During the 3rd month of gestation, coordination among the major organs, muscles, and central nervous system of the body can be seen. The fetus can now open its mouth and even suck its thumb, bend its arms, form a fist with its fingers, and kick its feet as the brain sends signals to different parts of its body. Its small lungs start to expand and contract in preparation of later breathing movements. Evidence of its sex emerges as external genitals form. Sexual differentiation begins during the 7th week when the gonadal ridges start to form testes in response to a biochemical signal from the Y chromosome. In the absence of the Y chromosome, ovaries appear several weeks later (Carlson, 1998). The testes produce male hormones, principally testosterone, which determines maleness. Femaleness depends on the absence of testosterone at the time the ovaries begin to form (Wilson, George, & Griffin, 1981).

The remainder of the fetal period can be divided into two 3-month trimesters. The second trimester marks the period from the 4th to 6th month of gestation. It covers a time of further refinement. At the end of the 2nd trimester, the fetus reaches a length of about 12 inches and weighs almost 2 pounds. Its body is evenly proportioned. The eyelids separate while eyelashes and eyebrows appear in addition to hair on the head. All the neurons have been formed in the brain. However, the glial cells, which support the neurons, increase at a rapid rate. They not only nourish the neurons but manufacture myelin, the fatty insulating sheath that improves the rapid transmission of signals between neurons. The process of myelinization continues even after birth as the brain makes further gains in overall size.

During the final 3 months of the last trimester, further gains in height and weight are being made. The fetus adds about 8 inches and almost 6 pounds. Its chances of survival outside of the womb slowly increases. Its **age of viability**, *the likelihood of sustained life*, occurs sometime between 22 and 26 weeks. Even then, a preterm infant will likely experience distress because of its inability to use its lungs or maintain its body temperature. A ventilator is needed to assist the infant until the lungs are fully developed. During the last 3 months, the brain continues to make progress. The cerebral cortex, the center of human intelligence, enlarges. A detailed picture of the fetus's sensory capabilities has emerged from recent studies. The fetus is capable of actively responding to internal and external stimulation before birth.

The ability to learn is a remarkable human achievement. Even prior to birth, the fetus can remember the recurrence of an event. Newborns have been observed to prefer the reassuring sound of a human heartbeat, although almost any rhythmic stimulation has been noted to be comforting. Confirmed in another study (DeCasper & Sigafoos, 1983), babies who heard a recorded heartbeat of 80 beats per minute found the sound to be soothing (Salk, 1973).

To illustrate the fetus's ability to remember, pregnant women in one study were asked to read a passage from Dr. Seuss's *The Cat in the Hat* aloud twice a day during the last 6 weeks of pregnancy (DeCasper & Spence, 1986). Two to 3 days after birth, the infants were tested with a specially wired pacifier. The sucking rate of the subjects was recorded to establish a baseline. Afterwards, changes in their sucking rate triggered their mother's

PARENTING ISSUES

ASSISTED REPRODUCTION

Infertility occurs in about one-sixth of all couples. Alternative methods of conception have been developed over the past 2 decades because of reproductive problems such as blocked or diseased Fallopian tubes (Begley, 1995). First performed in 1978, in vitro fertilization (IVF) has been used to fertilize an egg in an artificial environment. After an initial consultation with a team of specialists, at least one egg is surgically removed from the mother's ovary. It is then combined with the father's sperm. Once it is fertilized, it is placed into an incubator and then, after 2 days, inserted into the mother's uterus.

Although IVF has given hope to thousands of infertile couples, questions have been raised about the procedure itself. Not only do multiple pregnancies and miscarriages sometimes occur, but serious moral and legal issues arise such as the fate of unused fertilized eggs (Kiernan, 1995). Are they discarded or preserved until a later time? Further, a costly procedure, only couples with medical insurance or sufficient financial resources are able to seek IVF (a single cycle of IVF costs about $6,000 to $10,000). Currently, its rate of success is about 20%. Only one in five pregnancies comes to full term.

Other reproductive techniques have received attention in recent years. Four common methods are:

■ **Gamete intrafallopian transfer (GIFT).** A doctor, using a laparoscope, inserts sperm and eggs directly into a woman's Fallopian tube. Rate of success is 28%; cost is $6,000 to $10,000 per attempt.

■ **Zygote intrafallopian transfer (ZIFT).** The eggs are fertilized in the laboratory and transferred to a woman's Fallopian tubes. Rate of success is 24%; cost is $8,000 to $10,000 per attempt.

■ **Intracytoplasmic sperm injection (ICSI).** A doctor, using a specially designed tube to insert a single sperm into an egg, inserts the zygote into a women's uterus. Rate of success is 24%; cost starts at $10,000 per attempt.

■ **Intrauterine insemination (IUI).** Frozen sperm—either from the husband or unknown donor—is inserted directly into the uterus. Rate of success is 10%; cost is $300 with a donor's sperm.

recorded voices. Half of the babies heard the story they heard during the last 6 weeks of pregnancy; the other half listened to another story they never heard before. Because the infants learned to modify their sucking rate when they heard only the familiar story, the subjects clearly recognized a recurring event. In another study, two researchers asked pregnant women to sing "Mary had a little lamb" during the last several weeks prior to birth (Panneton & DeCasper, 1986). The newborns could perceive the difference between two songs, preferring to listen to the one they heard prior to birth.

INFLUENCES ON PRENATAL DEVELOPMENT

The prenatal period represents a time of significant change and vulnerability. A number of external factors can influence the internal environment—the womb—of the fetus. In addition to essential nutrients, potentially harmful substances can also cross the placental barrier from the maternal bloodstream. The remainder of the chapter examines environmental influences that can complicate the growth of the fetus, particularly **teratogens**, *environmental agents that result in congenital abnormalities.*

TERATOGENS

The study of congenital defects is known as teratology. It comes from the Greek word *teras* meaning "monstrosity." Until the turn of 20th century, the causes of congenital defects were not known. They were often attributed to magical or supernatural forces or interpreted as omens or signs. Two widely prescribed drugs in the 1950s demonstrated the devastating effects of teratogens on fetal development. Thalidomide was once used as a mild tranquilizer in the early months of pregnancy to control nausea and insomnia. Later, the presence of heart defects and deformed or missing limbs in infants was traced to their mothers' use of the drug. Another drug, diethylstilbestrol (DES), a synthetic hormone, was also given to pregnant women to prevent miscarriage. The effects of the drug did not appear until adolescence. It resulted in vaginal cancer in teenage girls and sterility and other genital abnormalities in teenage boys.

In general, the effects of teratogens on the fetus depend on the following four principles:

■ **The susceptibility of a developing organism to a teratogenic agent varies according its developmental stage at the time of its exposure.** Extensive structural damage to the developing organism generally occurs during the embryonic stage. The effects of the teratogenic agent peak during rapid differentiation of the major organs and limbs (O'Rahilly & Muller, 1996).

■ **Each teratogenic agent acts in a specific way on different tissues and causes a particular pattern of abnormal development.** Rubella, a viral infection, causes mental retardation and extensive damage to nerves that control the visual and hearing apparatus. Maternal use of cocaine and crack, a highly addictive form of cocaine, increases the risk of stillbirth and low birth weight and leads to possible neurological and behavioral problems later (Coles et al., 1992).

■ **The susceptibility to a teratogenic agent depends on the physiological status of the mother.** The mother's age and diet both influence the effects of teratogens on a developing organism. The risk of malformation increases with age, and maternal malnutrition intensifies the devastating consequences of teratogens.

■ **Teratogens produce delayed or indirect psychological consequences.** Congenital defects can restrict the infant's interaction with others and exploration of the environment. In turn, the lack of opportunities to actively engage with the world can hinder the development of certain skills.

Therefore, teratogenic agents can cause serious damage to the developing organism during the embryonic stage (see Table 4–3). The concept of a critical period refers to its vulnerability at a time of rapid physical growth. Although the effects of several teratogens, including lead poisoning, on the fetus have been well-documented, isolating the specific effects of other teratogens has proved difficult. Two potentially harmful drugs, alcohol and nicotine, may sometimes be abused during pregnancy. Although research has concentrated primarily on maternal factors, more recently, researchers have begun to focus on fathers' roles. For example, research shows that infants of fathers who smoke tend to be underweight at birth because of their mothers' inhalation of secondhand smoke during pregnancy (Dejin-Karlsson et al., 1998; Makin, Fried, & Watkinson, 1991).

Alcohol.   Pregnant women are advised not to drink any alcohol during the entire duration of pregnancy. Numerous studies indicate that the excessive abuse of alcohol contributes to fetal alcohol syndrome (FAS), a set of physical and mental disorders including facial abnormalities, physical deformities of the limbs, retarded physical growth, and mental retardation (Braun, 1996). It may lead to other complications later such as attentional and behavioral problems. In turn, it may affect cognitive processes and interfere with academic performance in school (Kopera-Frye, Olson, & Streissguth, 1997). In recent years, research has focused on the effects of moderate consumption of alcohol during pregnancy, a condition known as fetal alcohol effects (FAE). Infants with FAE are not likely to display physical deformities. However, they may suffer from delayed physical growth and mild to severe learning disabilities in childhood (Streissguth, 1997; Weiner & Morse, 1990).

Because it crosses the placental barrier, alcohol hinders the development of the primitive neural tube of the embryo. Long-term exposure to alcohol results in major structural abnormalities of the brain. To metabolize alcohol, large quantities of maternal

TABLE 4–3   POSSIBLE EFFECTS OF TERATOGENIC AGENTS ON PRENATAL DEVELOPMENT

Category	Agent	Possible Effects
Illegal drugs	Cocaine	Stillbirth, low birth weight, congenital defects, and neurological and behavioral problems
	Diethylstilbestrol (DES)	Cancer of cervix and testes and infertility in teenage girls and boys
	Marijuana	Premature delivery and failure to habituate
	Thalidomide	Deformed or missing limbs
Legal drugs	Alcohol	Mental retardation, retarded growth, facial and heart defects, and behavioral problems
	Nicotine	Premature birth and low birth weight
Maternal	Rubella	Mental retardation and damage to nerves that control vision and hearing
	Syphilis	Miscarriage or stillbirth
Environmental hazards	Radiation	Malformation of organs and miscarriages
	Mercury	Mental retardation and neurological problems

oxygen are required. The embryo or fetus is therefore deprived of oxygen that is critically needed as the brain and other parts of the body are developing (Abel, 1998).

In addition, the psychosocial development of alcohol-exposed infants is severely curtailed after birth. In general, infants with FAS display an increased risk of insecure attachment to their mothers. Alcohol apparently interferes with mothers' ability to provide a responsive, supportive environment. To complicate matters, the increased irritability of infants because of FAS hinders the development of a loving, caring relationship. The effects of alcohol illustrate the dynamic interaction between the biological constitution of infants and their environment. Physically and mentally compromised before birth, babies are placed in an environment that is not prepared to cope with the realities of FAS (Jenkins & Culbertson, 1996).

Nicotine. Studies of the harmful effects of nicotine, an addictive drug found in cigarettes, during pregnancy were initiated during the 1940s and 1950s. Although the results were largely ignored at the time, the evidence today is overwhelming. Smoking during pregnancy increases the risk of spontaneous abortion, stillbirth, prematurity, and low birth weight. Therefore, pregnant women are advised not to smoke. Even if women decide to stop smoking in the last trimester of pregnancy, they immediately reduce the likelihood of possible complications (Haustein, 1999).

In recent years, research has examined the harmful effects of nicotine on the developing fetus. A teratogenic agent, nicotine adversely affects the development of the placenta. The fetus is not able to gain sufficient weight if proper nourishment is not received. Nicotine depresses maternal appetite and reduces nutritional intake. Further, the level of carbon monoxide in the maternal and fetal bloodstream increases. Carbon monoxide displaces oxygen in the maternal circulatory system (Britton, 1998). Therefore, lack of oxygen can damage development of the fetus's central nervous system. Fathers who smoke may place their unborn infants at risk. Pregnant women inhaling passive smoke increase their chances of giving birth to infants with low birth weight (Sadler et al., 1999).

Even if physical anomalies do not appear at birth, behavioral problems sometimes arise later. Tobacco-exposed infants do not readily respond to their immediate environment because of attentional difficulties (Fergusson, Horwood, & Lynskey, 1993). As with alcohol, unresponsive infants may not elicit the kind of care they need from adults. Longitudinal studies show concerns in a number of different areas, particularly increased hyperactivity and poor achievement in school (Fried, Watkinson, & Siegel, 1997). Continued inhalation of smoke after birth can cause serious problems. The incidence of respiratory infections and asthma increases significantly among children of smoking parents (Infante-Rivard et al., 1999).

MATERNAL FACTORS

In addition to teratogens, maternal factors can influence the fetus's development. Nutrition can play a crucial role because of the rapid development of major organs sustaining life after birth. Maternal exercise and stress can also impinge on the developing fetus. In addition, the social context of pregnancy, particularly the role of expectant fathers in providing emotional support, has an indirect effect on the fetus.

Nutrition.   After the implantation of the fertilized egg, the developing organism receives its nourishment from its mother. Its continued development depends on its mother's adherence to a healthy, balanced diet. Research indicates that pregnant mothers need to consume at least 2,700 calories daily, gaining on the average about 25 to 30 pounds. They are now eating for two.

A host of complications can result from poor maternal nutrition. Serious damage can be sustained during **organogenesis**, *a period during the embryonic stage that marks the formation of the major organs.* Malnutrition causes severe problems as the central nervous system develops. Autopsies of malnourished infants who died at or shortly after birth reveal a significantly reduced number of brain cells, particularly if nutritional deprivation happens during the first 3 months of pregnancy. During the last trimester, severe malnutrition can result in retarded fetal growth and low birth weight (Luke & Keith, 1992).

Pregnant women should check with their doctors about nutritional guidelines. However, a healthy diet during pregnancy includes the following (Somer, 1995):

■ Protein—found in fish, poultry, lean red meat, and nuts—assists in the proper growth of fetal tissue and formation of antibodies to fight infections.

■ Calcium—concentrated in milk, cheese, yogurt, and leafy vegetables—supports the development of the fetus's bones and teeth.

■ Iron—found in lean red meat, liver, tuna, and spinach—leads to the formation of healthy red blood cells.

■ Folic acid—concentrated in green vegetables and nuts—contributes to the development of the fetus's nervous system.

■ Carbohydrates—found in grains and breads—provide needed energy.

■ Vitamin C—concentrated in fresh fruits and vegetables—builds the body's resistance to infection.

Exercise.   Physical activity is recommended during pregnancy. Although pregnant women are cautioned to avoid bouncing and jogging movements, certain activities such as walking, hiking, swimming, and light aerobics are allowed (Spencer, 1998). Special exercise classes for expecting mothers are typically offered at hospitals. Exercise strengthens the use of abdominal and pelvic muscles and other parts of the body later in labor and delivery. Pregnant women often cut back on exercise during the last trimester because of the strain resulting from having to counterbalance their heavy abdomens. Nevertheless, physically fit women usually report less discomfort later in pregnancy (Kitzinger, 1996).

Emotional State.   Pregnant women experiencing stress may place their unborn children at risk. Intense anxiety is associated with an increased incidence of miscarriage, prematurity, low birth weight, and respiratory illness (Glover, 1997). In times of stress, hormones are released into the bloodstream in a defensive response. Consequently, the fetus can be deprived of its supply of oxygen and nourishment. Because hormones can cross the placental barrier, the fetus's level of activity rises dramatically. After birth,

SOCIOCULTURAL INFLUENCES

COUVADE: PRACTICES IN PREINDUSTRIAL SOCIETIES

Men's involvement in their partners' pregnancies has gained widespread acceptance. They are increasingly taking an active role in providing physical and emotional support during a period of profound changes.

Historically, in several preindustrial societies, men marked their transition to fatherhood with special rituals. Known as *couvade,* a French word meaning "to hatch," husbands attempted to simulate childbirth at the same time as their wives' labor to deflect evil spirits (Frazer, 1910), as shown in the following example from India:

> . . . [the wife] informs her husband, who immediately takes some of her clothes, puts them on, places on his forehead the mark which the women usually place on theirs, retires into a dark room, where there is only a very dim lamp, and lies down on the bed, covering himself up with a long cloth. When the child is born, it is washed and placed on the cot beside the father. (Dawson, 1929, pp. 20–21)

In other cultures, expectant fathers limited their physical activities and followed dietary restrictions. The following ritualized custom was observed in the Solomon Islands:

> . . . it is not only the expectant mother who is careful what she eats, the father also both before and after a child's birth refrains from some kinds of food which would hurt the child. . . . and he abstains from the movements which are believed to do harm, upon the principle that the father's movements affect those of the child. A man will not do hard work, lift heavy weights, or go out to sea. . . . (Dawson, 1929, p. 40)

Today, in industrialized countries, expectant fathers do not practice ritualized customs like *couvade.* However, an estimated one in five men may experience similar physical symptoms of fatigue and nausea (Klein, 1991). Psychological problems—irritability and depression—sometimes accompany expectant men's perceived physical symptoms. Their symptoms invariably disappear after their partners give birth. When expectant fathers are able to share their wives' experiences, they are more likely to offer emotional comfort. In the process, they may develop a bond with the fetus even before birth (Elwood & Mason, 1994).

increased irritability is observed among infants of highly stressed mothers (Van den Bergh, 1990).

In addition, emotional stress can lead to other unintended consequences. Pregnant women under stress usually engage in unhealthy habits. They might consume alcohol or smoke cigarettes to reduce their overall level of stress. Likewise, they may neglect to eat properly at a time when their unborn child undergoes rapid physiological changes.

However, social support can minimize the risks of maternal stress. Just as proper medical care is needed, a supportive network of relatives and friends is required during pregnancy (Blechman & Brownell, 1998; Litt, 1997).

Social Context.   Pregnant women undergo profound physical and psychological changes. In view of the possible harmful effects of maternal stress on prenatal development, the emotional state of a woman's pregnancy deserves special attention (Pierce et al., 1996).

An increasing number of men today are taking an active role in their partners' pregnancy. Many choose to be involved at each step of the way (Heinowitz, 1995). Just as women do, men themselves may experience apprehension and anxiety about impending parenthood. Men should acknowledge and accept their fears and uncertainties in order to support their partners and meet the new challenges of parenthood:

> As men become more involved in the process of fatherhood, we must expand our understanding of their needs and fears. The father-to-be cannot be fully a part of the pregnancy and birth unless his fears are fully recognized by himself, by his spouse, by his family and by society in general. (Shapiro, 1987, p. 42)

When men are involved, they are participating in an extremely rewarding experience. The provision of an emotionally supportive environment indirectly benefits their unborn children when they create a healthy emotional climate: encouraging proper nutrition and exercise and abstinence from harmful substances, particularly alcohol and nicotine; choosing an obstetrician who recognizes the importance of men's involvement; scheduling regular prenatal visits with the obstetrician; and participating in childbirth (Biller & Trotter, 1994).

The stage is now set. The next major transition is the birth of the new baby.

SUMMARY

Genetic Basis of Life

■ The interaction between biological and environmental factors results in considerable variability. The developing organism's unique combination of genes determines its physical and temperamental traits.

■ There are billions of specialized cells in the human body. The nucleus contains exactly 46 chromosomes that store and transmit genetic information.

Conception

■ Development begins when one sperm penetrates the protective surface of the ovum. The genetic traits of the new person are determined instantaneously as the genetic content of the sperm and ovum is combined.

■ At the moment of conception, there are 8 million possible genetic combinations. Clearly, different combinations of genes produce different traits.

Genetic and Chromosomal Abnormalities

■ Congenital anomalies are linked to a single gene or specific chromosome. PKU provides a good example of an inherited genetic disorder.

■ Down syndrome, a chromosomal abnormality, results from the failure of chromosomes to divide properly during meiosis. Internal complications include cardiac, metabolic, and respiratory problems and mental retardation.

Prenatal Diagnosis

■ Today, couples can seek the assistance of a doctor or genetic counselor to determine the probability of giving birth to a child with congenital defects. Information is gathered to assess possible risks.

■ Prenatal diagnostic methods can detect potential problems prior to birth. They include amniocentesis, chorionic villus sampling, ultrasonography, and fetoscopy.

Prenatal Development

■ The 9-month period before birth marks a time of rapid changes. It is divided into three stages: germinal, embryonic, and fetal.

■ The germinal stage covers the first 2 weeks of prenatal development. As the fertilized egg travels from the Fallopian tube to the uterus, it begins to divide in half repeatedly.

■ The embryonic stage (2 to 8 weeks) is a period of extreme vulnerability because the major organs are developing. Any environmental insult is likely to result in a serious and irreversible congenital defect.

■ The fetal stage covers the remaining period from 8 weeks until birth. The sex of the child is determined in the 13th week of gestation.

Influences on Prenatal Development

■ Teratogens can cause serious damage to the developing organism. Maternal factors such as proper nutrition and physical activity play an important role.

■ Increasingly, expectant fathers are taking an active role in providing a supportive emotional atmosphere during pregnancy. Suggestions include encouragement of proper nutrition and exercise and abstinence from harmful substances and lifestyles.

PROJECTS

1. National organizations with local chapters can provide information on a variety of genetic disorders. Complete the following project on your own or with a small group of students:

Select a genetic disorder.

Call the local chapter in your community to obtain a brochure about services it provides.

Write a short summary of the organization.

Share your experience with the class.

2. State-of-the-art medical technology provides a wide range of options to infertile couples. Discuss the pros and cons of assisted reproduction in addition to ethical questions such as "Are we tampering with nature?" and "Are you in favor of utilizing current technology to select the sex of the child?"

3. Parenting magazines can provide information about the detrimental effects of teratogens, particularly alcohol and nicotine, on prenatal development. Select and read one article about a particular teratogenic agent.

BIRTH

> *. . . babies show their individualism from the beginning by arriving on their own schedule and nobody else's. . . .*
>
> Rose Kennedy, *Times to Remember*

Birth *marks an important transition in development. Once residing in a thermostatically controlled environment, the fetus is thrust into a whole new world. Its umbilical cord is clamped and cut, ending its supply of nourishment from its mother. Its lungs inflate, taking in oxygen. It now cries to signal hunger and distress, eliciting the attention of and starting a symbiotic relationship with adults. Chapter 5 covers the remarkable process of childbirth.*

Physiologically speaking, birth occurs roughly in the same way across the world. A transforming experience, it shifts the focus of development from the inside to the outside of the womb. In the process, birth touches and forever changes the lives of the key players. The very survival of the new child depends on the active involvement of parents and other adults. Culture plays a major role as it influences the expectations and child-rearing patterns of parents. Before discussing the stages of childbirth, past historical practices of childbirth will be examined.

HISTORICAL PRACTICES

The history of obstetric practices in the United States during the last three centuries resembles a pendulum. **Obstetrics** refers to *a branch of medicine that deals with the care of women before and after childbirth.* Until the turn of the 20th century, childbirth was viewed as a natural process. It was then placed in the hospital to protect the lives of mothers and their newborns. However, once the move was made, it was no longer seen as a natural event but as a diseased condition. Only during the last half of the 20th century have obstetric practices once again shifted. Today, childbirth is again viewed as a natural event. It occurs primarily in hospitals although some expecting mothers choose to give birth at home or alternative birthing centers.

During the colonial period of American history, women were expected to fulfill their role as childbearers. The high birthrates at the time reflected not only the availability of land and scarcity of labor but religious expectations and social attitudes that viewed women's childbearing status as a divinely ordained mission in life (Scholten, 1985). The average woman gave birth to eight children before her 40th year of life. Therefore, women generally devoted a large portion of their lives to bearing and raising children.

American women followed traditional western European customs during the colonial period. Childbirth took place in the company of other women, primarily members of the family and neighbors who aided each other. After childbirth, women were expected to "lie in" or stay in bed for a few days, sometimes weeks. Others performed the chores and managed the household. Midwives were employed on the basis of their level of education and experience in attending to laboring women and delivering babies. They did not receive any formal medical training but nevertheless performed an essential function. During the early stages of labor, a woman's friends dropped in to offer encouragement. The midwife took full control during the final stage of labor. As it progressed, she caught the child and tied the umbilical cord. Alcohol constituted the only painkiller. If labor proceeded slowly, the midwife sometimes prescribed remedies of doubtful efficacy such as the use of a magnet or horseshoe to expedite delivery. Her main duty was to provide comfort to a woman in labor (Rooks, 1999).

At the end of the colonial period, the customs of childbirth started to change. Toward the end of the 18th century, fertility declined in urban areas and settled regions of the United States. Men began to study and practice midwifery in increasing numbers. They argued that childbirth required the expertise of trained physicians but at the same time denied women admittance to medical schools. Many women initially resisted men's involvement because of the long-standing association of childbirth as a feminine event. However, over time, women were persuaded of the value of men's medical education (Shyrock, 1960).

The acceptance of men in childbirth signaled a significant historical shift. Childbirth was increasingly regarded as a medical enterprise (Borst, 1996). During the mid-19th century, the increasing professionalism of medicine, at least in the minds of men who formed medical associations and set the standards in the field, excluded women's participation. Physicians even began to refer to themselves as obstetricians, which did not convey the feminine connotations of midwives.

The level of interference in childbirth increased yet another notch during the late 19th and early 20th century. A leading obstetric textbook in the mid-1830s viewed childbirth as a natural process and frowned on the use of **forceps**, *an instrument that resembles a pair of pincers and that assists the expulsion of a child at birth* (Blundell, 1834). Later, in the late 1880s, the use of forceps was advocated only in difficult deliveries. An **episiotomy**, *a surgical incision in the perineum that widens the vaginal cavity in order to expedite the delivery of a baby,* was occasionally performed (Martin, 1881).

During the early 20th century, childbirth moved from the home to the hospital. In 1900, only about 5% of expecting mothers, especially poor women, delivered in hospitals. However, in just a short time, the rate jumped significantly. Half of all births took place in hospitals during the 1920s, and before the end of the 1930s, three-quarters of all women delivered in hospitals. The marked transformation of childbirth can be traced to concurrent medical advances. Physicians believed that hospitals prevented the spread of infectious diseases and reduced the likelihood of complications during labor. Other reasons included using hospitals to train medical students and upgrading the obstetric profession. Even society's expectations changed as contraception reduced fertility and social progress freed women from the confinement of home.

Once the move from the home to the hospital took place, the medical establishment viewed childbirth as a diseased state. Pregnant women were treated as patients. The philosophy of medical intrusion reached its apex in the 1950s. Fathers were excluded from the birthing process and were required to wait in an adjoining room. Because mothers were heavily sedated, forceps were routinely used to expel the infant. Aseptic conditions prevailed. Delivery was performed on metal tables, and the feet of laboring women were placed in stirrups. After delivery, the baby was then kept in a secluded nursery and seen only on a rigid schedule.

During the same period, obstetricians were gradually forced to reevaluate their own practices. Advocates of **natural** or **prepared childbirth**, *a method of childbirth that tries to reduce medical intervention,* warned about the possible harmful effects of anesthesia on both mother and child. In particular, English obstetrician Grantly Dick-Read attained enormous popularity. In his book, *Childbirth Without Fear*, birth was again viewed as a natural process (Dick-Read, 1944/1953). He glorified motherhood as women's true fulfillment in life. After his own experience in delivering a baby without chloroform, he sought to educate women about their bodies and taught exercises that strengthened their muscles and reduced their fear of pain during labor and delivery.

The next advance in natural childbirth came from an unexpected source. During the 1930s and 1940s in Russia, Pavlov's theory of conditioned reflexes was being applied to childbirth. Fernand Lamaze, a French doctor, traveled to Russia to study the new method. He simplified the Russian techniques and added a rapid breathing procedure, which became the hallmark of his own method he called *accouchement sans douleur* or childbirth without pain (Lamaze, 1956/1970). In the late 1950s, an American mother who lived in

HISTORICAL PRACTICES

Grantly Dick-Read
Childbirth Without Fear, 1944
Superstition, civilization and culture have brought influences to bear on the minds of women which have introduced justifiable fears and anxieties concerning labor. The more cultured the races of the earth have become, so much the more positive have they been in pronouncing childbirth to be a painful and dangerous ordeal.

Source: Dick-Read (1944/1953), p. 12.

Paris wrote of her experience with the new method. It immediately found a foothold in the United States and eventually led to obstetric changes in the late 1960s and early 1970s.

Today, childbirth is seen as a natural process. Many women take classes in natural childbirth. They learn breathing techniques to relax and lessen pain during labor. Hospitals have tried to create a homelike atmosphere in order to alleviate fear. Labor and delivery usually occur in the same comfortable room. Fathers are encouraged to participate in the birthing process itself. Although a large percentage of childbirths take place in hospitals, an increasing number of women and their families choose to deliver in the privacy and comfort of their homes or alternative birthing centers. Their decisions reflect either personal preferences or religious beliefs.

METHODS OF CHILDBIRTH

Birthing practices reflect the cultural traditions of people. In the United States, childbirth occurred at home in the presence of the family and in the company of women before shifting to the hospital in the first few decades of the 20th century. Since then, alternative methods to giving birth have developed. Known as natural or prepared childbirth, two approaches—Lamaze and Leboyer—attempt to limit medical intervention and involve the family. Each has its distinct advantages and disadvantages. Parents-to-be need to weigh the pros and cons of each before actual labor begins, because both methods of childbirth require special preparations (Al-Azzawi, 1998; Bean, 1990).

LAMAZE

French obstetrician Fernand Lamaze introduced a radically different method of childbirth. In the 1950s, he attended a conference in Russia and learned about painless childbirth without medication. Russian doctors at the time were applying Pavlov's theory of conditioned reflexes in childbirth. Women, they reasoned, associated pain with labor. Fear of pain led to tension, which interfered with contractions during childbirth; in turn, tension further intensified the sensation of pain. Laboring women were therefore taught to block their experience of pain without the use of anesthesia.

Lamaze made a number of changes to traditional obstetric practices when he returned to Paris. First, expecting women were required to attend a series of classes during the last few months of pregnancy. They learned about labor and practiced breathing techniques to control pain. Second, obstetricians used anesthesia sparingly, if at all, in order not to interfere with laboring women's ability to view childbirth as a rewarding experience. Until then, French women traditionally played a passive, medically managed role in childbirth. In the late 1950s, Marjorie Karmel's book, *Thank You, Dr. Lamaze*, popularized Lamaze's method of childbirth in the United States (Karmel, 1959).

Other steps have been taken in the United States since Lamaze's initial efforts. Today, labor, delivery, and recovery usually occur in one room instead of two or three separate rooms to maximize the mother's comfort. The father and other members of the family are encouraged to participate in the process. After birth, the baby is allowed to stay in the same room with the parents, instead of being placed in the hospital nursery, to facilitate bonding.

Because of Lamaze and other advocates of natural childbirth, the birthing experience has forever changed. Women generally report a more positive impression of their birthing experience (Hetherington, 1990). Further, doctors do not use anesthesia indiscriminately since many women want to take control. Fathers' involvement in the birthing process creates a positive experience. Studies suggest that emotional support during labor provides important benefits. When a doula, or female companion, is assigned to a woman during labor, the length of labor and the likelihood of complications are significantly reduced (Kennell et al., 1991; Sosa et al., 1980).

LEBOYER

Another French obstetrician, Frederick Leboyer, focused attention on the experience of the baby during childbirth. In 1975, he outlined a method of childbirth called "birth without violence." Advocates of his method take steps to ensure a "gentle" birth. It includes:

■ Dimming the lights in the birthing room.

■ Placing the baby on the mother's abdomen after delivery.

HISTORICALLY SPEAKING

METHODS OF CHILDBIRTH

Irwin Chabon
Awake and Aware, 1966
Today's young women, in ever-increasing numbers, look upon childbirth as one of the most precious of life's experiences. They want to be awake and aware; they want to participate actively in the birth of their children.

Source: Chabon (1966), p. 23.

■ Gently massaging the baby before the umbilical cord is cut.

■ Submerging the baby in warm water afterwards.

Leboyer suggests his method minimizes the trauma of birth in contrast to traditional obstetric practices. Although couples usually report a positive experience, studies do not offer substantial proof of long-term benefits to infants. Furthermore, not all obstetricians accept Leboyer's ideas. Critics argue that his method actually postpones the examination of newborns' vital signs until later because of the dimly lit environment at the time of birth.

STAGES OF CHILDBIRTH

Not surprisingly, the process of birth itself is referred to as labor because of the physical exertion the body undergoes. It begins with a series of hormonal changes in the mother's body, resulting in contractions. Before labor actually begins, the muscles of the uterus contract and expand at irregular intervals (the contractions are often called false labor or prelabor). The cervix begins to dilate, or widen, about a centimeter, or three-fourths of an inch. The fetus then moves into position with its head in the mother's pelvic cavity in preparation for its eventual delivery. A definite sign of impending labor involves the discharge of reddish mucous, or bloody show, that sealed the cervix during pregnancy.

Regular uterine contractions signal the onset of labor. The remainder of labor and childbirth has been divided into three distinct stages: dilation and effacement of cervix, delivery, and placental expulsion (see Figure 5–1).

DILATION AND EFFACEMENT OF CERVIX

The first stage of childbirth lasts from the first intense contractions of the uterus, at intervals of 10 to 15 minutes apart, until the cervix dilates to a diameter of 10 centimeters, or 4 inches. As labor progresses, the contractions increase in frequency and duration. At their peak, they occur every 2 to 3 minutes and last 45 to 60 seconds on the average. The uterine contractions cause the cervix not only to **dilate**, or *to widen*, but to **efface**, or *to thin*, prior to the delivery of the child.

When the cervix opens completely, the fetus moves into the mother's pelvic cavity. *The end of the first stage of labor* is called the **transition**. The frequency and duration of the uterine contractions reach their climax during the transition. It generally lasts an hour or two. A natural urge to push the fetus is often felt. However, the mother is encouraged to counteract the urge to push until complete dilation. Others, particularly the mother's partner, can play an important role in providing emotional support during an uncomfortable period just before birth.

The duration of the first stage of labor varies from person to person. Its average length is about 14 hours. Labor does take a toll on the body. Some women experience nausea and other discomforts such as sweating and shivering during the transition.

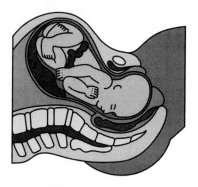

Stage 1: Dilation and effacement of cervix.
Contractions of the uterus cause the cervis to
dilate, or widen.

Transition. The cervix opens completely as the
frequency and strength of the contractions reach
their peak during labor.

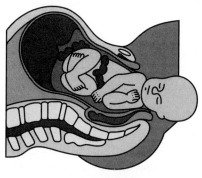

Stage 2: Delivery. The mother pushes with her
uterine muscles until the baby's head appears
and the rest of the body emerges.

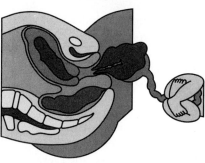

Stage 3: Placental expulsion. The placenta or
afterbirth is separated from the uterine wall with
other fetal membranes and expelled.

FIGURE 5-1   Three Stages of Childbirth

DELIVERY

Childbirth enters its second stage when the cervix fully widens to 10 centimeters, or 4
inches. The baby then moves into the mother's vaginal cavity. Typically, the head crowns
or appears in a downward position. The vulva, or external female genitalia, encircle the
circumference of the baby's head. The strong uterine contractions continue while the
mother pushes with her uterine muscles. The baby emerges within 45 minutes to an
hour on the average.

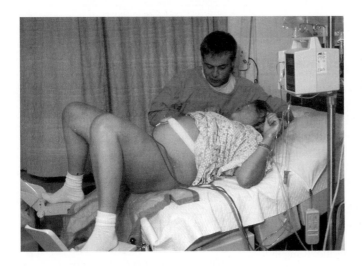

After about 9 months in healthy pregnancies—an eternity to many parents-to-be—development continues on the outside of the womb.
Dennis MacDonald, PhotoEdit.

When the baby's head crowns, the shoulders rotate, and the head turns to the side. Sometimes, an episiotomy may be performed to protect the woman's perineum, the area between the genital region and anus, expediting delivery (Scott et al., 1999). Currently, the widespread use of the surgical procedure has been criticized. Critics argue that it unnecessarily causes pain and discomfort during the postpartum period and sometimes results in infection or loss of blood (Thorp & Bowes, 1989). In the event of fetal distress, such as an irregular fetal heart, forceps or other obstetrical devices such as a vacuum pump might be used to extract the baby. In using mechanical forceps, the possibility of bruises or injuries to the baby's head or face must be weighed.

Once the baby's head emerges, the doctor or nurse removes mucous from the mouth to clear the breathing passageway from obstruction. The procedure is again repeated when the baby is fully delivered. When the baby is breathing independently, the umbilical cord is clamped and severed with a pair of surgical scissors. The remaining cord eventually dries and falls off within the first 2 weeks after birth.

PLACENTAL EXPULSION

The third and final stage of childbirth involves the expulsion of the placenta from the mother's body and typically lasts from a few minutes to an hour after delivery. After hours of labor, the uterus continues to contract. The contractions now cause the placenta and other fetal membranes to separate from the uterine wall. The contents are expelled and delivered as the afterbirth, which is inspected to ensure none is left in the uterus.

MEDICAL INTERVENTION

In the United States and the rest of the industrialized world, childbirth is a medically monitored and controlled event. A number of procedures are followed not only to protect the mother and child but also to ease the discomfort of labor. Historically, people

CULTURAL VARIATIONS IN CHILDBEARING PRACTICES

Birth is not only a biological but also a human event. Labor occurs in the same way everywhere, but the cultural context of birth varies greatly. Cultural traditions provide parents with a prescribed set of procedures to follow during the birthing process. Even after birth, parents will behave in accordance with cultural expectations that will invariably affect the developmental outcomes of infants.

In many preindustrial societies, childbirth is viewed as a natural process and is experienced without special preparations. Among the hunting and gathering !Kung in southwest Africa, childbirth is unassisted:

> The first labor pains came at night and stayed with her until dawn. That morning, everyone went gathering. Mother and I stayed behind. We sat together for a while, then I went and played with the other children. Later, I came back and ate the nuts she had cracked for me. She got up and started to get ready. I said, 'Mommy, let's go to the water well, I'm thirsty.' She said, 'Uhn, uhn, I'm going to gather some mongongo nuts.'
> We walked a short way, then she sat down by the base of a large nehn tree, leaned back against it, and little Kumsa was born. (Shostak, 1981, pp. 53–54)

In other cultures, childbirth is seen as the exclusive province of women. Men are totally excluded from the birthing process as among the Ngoni of central Africa. Expecting women even attempt to conceal their pregnancy from their husbands until the last moment. They assert their authority, claiming that:

> Men are little children. They are not able to hear those things that belong to pregnancy. (Read, 1959, pp. 49–50)

During labor, the mother-in-law and other female relatives banish the husband from the hut and take charge. They remove everything belonging to the husband. Only old mats and pots are kept. The laboring woman sits on a mat and leans against another woman:

> Though she might be in great pain, she was not expected to cry out or even to groan. The older women talked to her encouragingly, and wiped her face, or gave her a little water to drink. (Read, 1959, p. 51)

Later, from the door of the hut, the mother-in-law announces the birth of the child. "A new stranger has come," she proclaims.

In the peninsula of Yucatan, Mexico, midwives are employed to assist in childbirths of indigenous Mayan Indians. Midwives learn their trade from other experienced midwives. Birth usually takes place at home but may shift to the hospital if complications arise. Midwives are treated with the utmost respect in their communities because of their expertise (Jordan, 1993).

Midwives still play a critical role across the world. In the United States, many Mexican American women living in communities bordering Mexico rely on culturally sensitive midwives (Burk, Wieser, & Keegan, 1995). Likewise, in western Europe, large numbers of expecting parents employ certified midwives. The comprehensive services of midwives in Britain and Sweden continue into the postpartum period and often the first year with periodic visits to the home to ease the transition to parenthood (Mothander, 1992; Oakley et al., 1996).

have always found ways to assist childbirth. Preindustrialized societies discovered naturally occurring drugs that midwives used to stimulate labor. In native American cultures, selected leaves or roots have been prescribed to hasten delivery or facilitate the mother's recovery after birth. Today, the following medical procedures are utilized: fetal monitors, medication, induced labor, and cesarean delivery.

FETAL MONITORS

During the first stage of childbirth, a **fetal monitor** is sometimes used. It refers to *an electronic device that tracks the fetal heart rate and measures the frequency and duration of the mother's contractions.* Two broad types of fetal monitors are used in American hospitals. One is externally strapped to the mother's abdomen during labor. If complications are detected, such as an abnormal fetal heart rate, then another type of fetal monitor is employed. Electrodes are attached to the baby's scalp to obtain vital information about the progress of labor.

Safe and reliable, fetal monitors have undoubtedly saved countless lives. Their routine use has nevertheless been criticized (Chez, 1997). Fetal monitors have been linked with an increased number of cesarean deliveries, an alarming trend. Women often complain about the uncomfortableness of fetal monitors, preventing normal movement and possibly interfering with the course of labor. However, the use of fetal monitors is likely to be continued in American hospitals. Obstetricians may worry about accusations of malpractice, or negligent treatment, if serious complications arise during labor (Malnory, 1993).

MEDICATION

Childbirth has always been associated with the pain of labor. Since the late 19th century in the United States, medical advances have led to the development of medication, initially chloroform, to alleviate the discomfort of childbirth. Today, medication is used in about 80 to 95% of births in the United States. **Analgesics** refer to *drugs that relieve pain,* whereas **anesthesia**, a Greek word meaning "the loss of sensation," involves *an artificially induced painkiller that blocks sensation to the affected area of the body.* General anesthesia affects the entire body, and because it puts the mother to sleep, it actually slows or stops labor. It is rarely used today because of its potential harmful effects on the fetus during labor. Regional anesthesia, on the other hand, is administered to block pain in a specific area of the body. Different types of regional anesthesia are listed in Table 5–1.

TABLE 5–1   DIFFERENT TYPES OF REGIONAL ANESTHESIA

Type	Description and Effects
Pudendal	Local injection of novocain into the vulval and perineal region. It has minimal effect on the infant.
Paracervical	Local injection of novocain into the cervix and uterus. It lowers the mother's blood pressure and fetal heartbeat.
Spinal	Regional injection into the spinal column to anesthetize the entire area from the waist to the toes. It requires the use of forceps to deliver the baby.
Epidural	Regional injection that is administered continuously with a catheter and needle in the back. It numbs the entire area from the waist to the toes but sometimes causes a drop in the mother's blood pressure.

In complicated deliveries, medication permits medical intervention to protect the mother or infant. However, concerns have been raised about the routine use of general anesthesia in the past. When it is used, the mother is prevented from participating in the birthing process. If she is not able to push, then forceps are required to deliver the baby. In addition, general anesthesia crosses the placental barrier and enters the bloodstream of the fetus. In large doses, it results not only in diminished alertness and increased irritability but also in poor reflexes and feeding difficulties (Brackbill, McManus, & Woodward, 1985). Because of the infant's immature liver and kidney, the effects of medication persist even after birth. A mother is likely to encounter difficulties in trying to establish an emotional bond with her infant immediately after birth (Murray et al., 1981).

Does the use of anesthesia result in lasting effects on infants' physical and mental development? Some claim it does (Monk, 1996). Concerns about the possible harmful effects of anesthesia have led to a reevaluation of obstetric practices in the late 1960s and early 1970s. The impact of anesthesia on the emotional bond between infants and their parents raises a legitimate concern about its continued use. Today, as the level of medical technology improves, regional anesthesia minimizes the negative effects of medication on infants. Expectant parents are encouraged to check with their obstetricians about their views of anesthesia (Mander, 1998).

INDUCED LABOR

Labor may be induced if the pregnancy is not progressing smoothly. An **induced labor** refers to *an obstetric procedure of rupturing the amnion*, the amniotic membranes that protect the fetus (an event that typically takes place on its own in the first stage of childbirth) *or administering oxytocin, a hormone that hastens contractions* (Bowes, 1994). Once labor is induced, childbirth follows a different course. The mother's contractions tend to increase in both frequency and duration. The supply of oxygen to the baby is therefore reduced. Consequently, drugs and forceps are used in the delivery of the baby (Friedman, 1987).

The decision to induce labor is usually based on justifiable reasons, such as prolonged labor or fetal distress. However, occasionally, it is determined on the basis of convenience, not health. For example, the birth of the baby might coincide with an obstetrician's planned vacation, or the parents may wish to arrange the date of their baby's birth to fit with their own plans. Doctors must weigh both the pros and cons of an artificially induced labor before making a final decision.

CESAREAN DELIVERY

In the past, a **cesarean delivery**, or C-section, was performed primarily to save the life of the mother, baby, or both. It refers to *the removal of the baby from the uterus through a surgical incision on the mother's abdomen.* Today, doctors generally use a C-section because of unexpected complications during labor. A woman's previous history of a cesarean delivery is often used as a justification because of the possibility of rupturing the uterine scar during a vaginal delivery. In rare cases, the position of the fetus during childbirth justifies the procedure. If its buttocks or feet are positioned first instead of its head in a breech delivery, its supply of oxygen might be cut off, causing irreparable damage to the brain.

Once a rare procedure, the incidence of a cesarean delivery has risen sharply in the United States. It has climbed from 3% in 1970 to 22% of all births in 1996 (National Center for Health Statistics, 1999). Because it requires a surgical incision on the mother's abdomen, a cesarean delivery can prolong her recovery from childbirth and interfere with her ability to take care of her newborn immediately after birth. Because anesthesia, like any drug, crosses the placental barrier, it may affect infants' behavior after birth. They may not be able to respond to others because of grogginess. Although the percentage of cesarean deliveries appears to have peaked, critics still question the procedure's use and intrusion in healthy pregnancies (Young, 1997).

COMPLICATIONS

Most pregnancies end with the birth of a healthy newborn. However, in 5 to 6% of all deliveries, the newborn is considered to be at risk (Klein & Ganon, 1998). The newborn may be suffering from difficulties in breathing and digesting food because of immature respiratory and digestive systems and poor sucking and swallowing reflexes. Other complications result from prematurity, low birth weight, or both (Manginello & DiGeronimo, 1998).

PREMATURITY AND LOW BIRTH WEIGHT

After 40 weeks of gestation, the average newborn weighs about 3,400 grams, or 7.5 pounds, at birth. The normal gestational period is 38 to 42 weeks. A healthy newborn's weight can range from 2,500 to 4,500 grams, or 5.5 to 10 pounds. A newborn infant is referred to as **premature** or preterm if he or she is born *before the 37th week of gestation.*

A reliable measure of infants' continued survival and subsequent development involves birth weight. **Low birth weight**, *a birth weight of 2,500 grams, or 5.5 pounds, or less*, affects 7% of newborns in the United States. Maternal malnutrition may be tied to low birth weight, particularly during the last few months of pregnancy. Premature infants may be born with low birth weight. However, not all low-birth-weight babies are born prematurely. Other causes of low birth weight may include:

- **Poor maternal health and prenatal care.** Unhealthy maternal habits, such as smoking and consuming alcohol, impair fetal nourishment and may possibly precipitate premature labor. If the mother fails to visit the doctor or take care of herself, the fetus may be affected.

- **Maternal age.** The incidence of low birth weight increases sharply among women 18 and under and 35 and over. The poor or inadequate diet of teenage mothers on the one hand and the aging process itself on the other probably affect the healthy development of the fetus.

- **Simultaneous pregnancy.** Twins gain weight normally at the same rate until the 7th week of gestation. Because of the nutritional and placental difficulties in sharing a common uterine environment, they tend to be born early, about 3 weeks on the average, and weigh about 5 pounds.

Of particular concern is the impact of poverty on infants. Poverty and maternal nutrition are closely linked. Economically deprived women may be malnourished. Also, they may not be receiving adequate prenatal care during pregnancy. Sociocultural factors consequently contribute to conditions causing low birth weight. There is a wide economic disparity between countries across the world. Most low-birth-weight infants are found in developing countries. However, even in developed countries such as the United States, the incidence of low birth weight rises sharply in heavily populated urban areas because of increased poverty.

Consequences. Research has been conducted on the consequences of prematurity and low birth weight. Premature infants may experience developmental delays later. In particular, many encounter difficulties in cognitive development and verbal ability. Learning problems, especially distractibility, are noted when other complications, such as **anoxia**, *the temporary absence of fetal oxygen during labor,* and respiratory distress at birth, are involved. Physical and social competence of infants may also be affected. Premature infants exhibit not only perceptual impairments but increased problems in interacting with others because of their irritability and unresponsiveness (Landry et al., 1990). When low birth weight is associated with poverty, its effects on development are intensified. Therefore, the severity of low birth weight depends on medical and sociocultural factors.

Although premature infants may be at risk because of low birth weight and other possible complications, they are capable of making considerable developmental gains. Parents especially play a critical role in meeting their premature infants' unique needs (Meyer et al., 1998). Special programs provide parents with the needed tools. Premature infants generally score in the average range on measures of developmental progress after intervention (Achenbach et al., 1993). In one program, premature infants who participated in early intervention made remarkable strides. The results clearly indicate that early intervention benefits premature infants and their parents (Sparling et al., 1991).

Intervention. At birth, premature infants require immediate intensive care in hospitals. Medical advances have increased their chances of survival. Even preemies with extremely low birth weight, fitting in the palm of a hand, have been able to survive life on the outside of their mothers' womb. Preemies are placed in an **isolette**, *a modified crib that is designed to provide a regulated environment.* The temperature is controlled and the air is filtered to prevent infection. Although the needs of premature infants are artificially met, every attempt is made to provide physical contact and stimulation.

Unfortunately, the physical appearance and displacement of premature infants can affect the response they receive from others. Their relatively small size and restrictive living condition in an isolette often discourage contact from parents. However, steps have been taken in recent years to improve premature infants' living conditions in the hospital and at home. Premature infants can be suspended in hammocks or lie on waterbeds to simulate the gentle rocking motion of their mothers' womb. Familiar sounds, particularly the mothers' heartbeat and voice, can be recorded and played back. A mobile can provide additional visual and auditory stimulation. Further, touch has been found to play a critical role in premature infants' development (Field, 1995; Heller, 1997). It triggers a chemical reaction. To examine the therapeutic effects of touch, premature

PREEMIES

As medicine made remarkable advances during the last half of the 20th century, the rate of survival among premature infants improved dramatically. In fact, the likelihood of survival of preemies with extremely low birth weight (<1,000 grams or 2 and a quarter pounds) has reached a rate of 50% in comparison to nearly zero in 1970. Some go on to live normal lives after they leave the hospital. Unfortunately, severe disabilities may occur in about one-third of the cases; another one-third encounter learning difficulties in school later (Vohr & Garcia-Coll, 1988).

Today, medical intervention is able to save the fragile lives of countless preemies. However, risks remain:

■ Blindness may occur from highly concentrated oxygen to aid respiration.

■ Cognitive deficits may result from respiratory failure.

Parents are faced with making agonizing decisions between life and later possible visual and cognitive impairment. Still, miracles do occur:

A room away, unknown to us, Daniel [at 1 pound, 3 ounces] was facing the most important screening committee of his life. The medical team gave him a little oxygen, then watched and waited. He was so small, a nurse told me later, that they decided that if his heart rate dropped below 100 beats a minute, or if he stopped trying to breathe, they would let him slip away. But he kept struggling for air, and his heartbeat never wavered. (Kantrowitz, Wingert, & Hager, 1988, p. 69)

The key to minimizing the likelihood of prematurity is prevention. Proper prenatal care and nutrition both play an essential role. Healthy development begins before birth. Although modern medicine works miracles, expecting women should obtain not only factual information on the effects of certain unhealthy habits but also emotional support from others in order to start a new life on the right track.

infants were massaged several times each day in the hospital. At the end of the first year, they made demonstrable physical and cognitive gains in contrast to premature infants not receiving any massage (Field et al., 1986; Scafidi, Field, & Schanberg, 1993).

In sum, early intervention, coupled with parental involvement, appears to make a world of difference. The bulk of research shows that stimulation leads to increased gains in weight and alertness during the first few weeks after birth. Although premature infants may face seemingly insurmountable obstacles, a highly trained nursing staff and involved parents can even the odds. Premature infants thrive in an environment of responsive and developmentally appropriate care.

POSTMATURITY

The normal length of a pregnancy is 38 to 42 weeks. A **postmature** or postterm infant is born *after the 42nd week of pregnancy.* An estimated 10% of pregnancies end in postmature deliveries. A postmature birth, in and of itself, does not pose any significant difficulties to the mother.

The cause of postmaturity is not known. Perhaps the exact date of the mother's last menstrual period may have been miscalculated. However, after the 42nd week of gestation, there may be reasons to be alarmed. The fetus usually begins to lose weight because the placenta no longer functions properly and the amount of amniotic fluid declines. Because the fetus continues to grow during the few extra weeks, the possibility of injuries during the birthing process increases. Lastly, fetal movement may put pressure on the umbilical cord, possibly depriving oxygen to the developing child.

Therefore, because of possible complications, doctors may induce labor. Oxytocin can be administered intravenously to stimulate uterine contractions, and a fetal monitor may be used to detect any abnormalities in the fetal heartbeat. After birth, postmature infants may exhibit a distinctive appearance of abundant hair, long nails, and cracking skin. Although early cognitive skills may lag slightly during infancy and early childhood, postmature infants usually do not encounter any serious developmental difficulties otherwise.

Table 5–2 summarizes the classification of newborns.

INFANT MORTALITY

Infant mortality rates are used to assess the overall health of a country's children. It refers to the incidence of deaths during the first year of life per 1,000 births. Although the United States has one of the best health care systems in the world, the infant mortality rate has actually risen over the past half century (see Table 5–3 for international comparisons). A number of factors are involved, with poverty as a leading contender. When expectant women lack adequate prenatal care and nutrition, their unborn children suffer. Further, other developmental concerns may appear later in life, such as behavioral and learning difficulties in school (Hale, 1990).

In countries where the infant mortality rate is low, the following elements are noted. Prenatal care is usually subsidized, and national standards monitor its quality. In western

TABLE 5–2 CLASSIFICATION OF NEWBORNS AT BIRTH		
Description	**Gestational Age**	**Average Weight**
Preterm	<37 weeks	<2,500 grams[1]
Full term	37 to 42 weeks	At least 2,500 grams
Postterm	>42 weeks	

[1]5.5 pounds

TABLE 5–3 INFANT MORTALITY RATES AMONG DIFFERENT COUNTRIES	
Country	Rate[1]
Japan	4.4
Singapore	5.5
Sweden	6.2
Hong Kong	6.2
Norway	6.2
Canada	6.4
Netherlands	6.5
Switzerland	6.8
Germany	6.9
Australia	7.1
France	7.2
United Kingdom	7.4
Austria	7.5
Spain	7.7
Ireland	8.2
Greece	8.2
New Zealand	8.3
Italy	8.3
Belgium	8.4
United States	8.9

[1]Rate per 1,000 live births.

European countries, a paid leave of absence is typically granted to provide new parents, including fathers, with the opportunity to spend time with their newborns during the first few weeks and months of life. Additional paid leave is permitted in the event of a serious illness or emergency in the family. Countries with low infant mortality rates place a premium on the benefits of preventive care and parental involvement in improving the welfare of their citizens. Some experts believe there is a definite link between the commitment of national resources and the incidence of infant mortality (Kotelchuck, 1995).

POSTPARTUM PERIOD

After birth comes a period of adjustment. *The newborn,* or **neonate**, starts to cry and breathe independently. The circulatory system fully functions on its own. The color of the skin soon changes as oxygen circulates. Any remaining mucous is removed, and the umbilical cord is clamped and cut. The neonate is wiped and swaddled with a blanket to maintain warmth.

In industrialized countries, neonatal health and behavior are generally measured with a number of tests typically referred to as scales. To assess the neonate's physical condition at birth, the **Apgar scale**, *a rating system of five vital signs*, is administered. Also, the neonate's behavior may be examined to determine neurological condition and continued adjustment in the first month of life. In particular, the Brazelton Neonatal Behavioral Assessment Scale (BNBAS) has been used to monitor the progress of premature infants in addition to providing comparative information of newborns living in different countries. Further, the emotional and psychological adjustment of new parents after birth has been extensively studied. **Postpartum depression**, *a prolonged state of depression during the period after birth* may affect some women.

MEASURES OF NEONATAL HEALTH AND BEHAVIOR

The Apgar scale is named after a pediatrician. In 1953, Virginia Apgar devised a scale to assess a neonate's condition at 1 and 5 minutes after birth (Apgar, 1953). Five vital signs are checked to determine whether further medical intervention is needed to sustain life. A score of 0, 1, or 2 is assigned to each of five categories: neonate's appearance, pulse, grimace, activity, and respiration (see Table 5–4). A score of 7 or better signifies a healthy neonate. Any combined score falling in the range of 4 to 6 warns of a possible problem, whereas a score of 0 to 3 requires immediate medical attention.

In addition to the Apgar scale, a complete physical examination of the neonate is performed in the first few hours of life. The examiner, typically a nurse or pediatrician, measures the neonate's height, weight, and size of the head and checks his or her eyes, ears, nose, mouth, and throat, sucking and swallowing reflexes, breathing pattern, genitals, and appearance. The neonate's ability to urinate and move bowels is noted. Antibiotics—such as erythromycin, tetracycline, or silver nitrate—are administered to the eyes within the first hour of birth to prevent infection.

If the examiner is interested in assessing the neonate's responsiveness to physical and social stimuli, reflexes, motor abilities, and other reactions, the BNBAS, named after

TABLE 5–4 APGAR SCALE

	Score		
Sign	0	1	2
Appearance	Blue body, arms, and legs	Pink body with blue arms and legs	Body, arms, and legs entirely pink
Pulse	None	Slow (<100 beats per minute)	Rapid (100 to 140 beats per minute)
Grimace[1]	None	Weak reflexive response	Strong reflexive response
Activity	Completely limp	Weak movements of arms and legs	Strong movements of arms and legs
Respiratory	None	Irregular breathing	Strong breathing and crying

[1]Sneezing and coughing.
Source: Wegman (1996).

well-known pediatrician T. Berry Brazelton, can be employed. Consisting of 26 items, it requires only a rattle, ball, flashlight, and pin. To record changes in a neonate's organization of behavior, the BNBAS is administered repeatedly during the first week of life. Typical items include (Brazelton & Nugent, 1995):

■ **Visual and auditory orientation to stimuli.** The examiner calls the baby's name in a high-pitched voice. Does the baby focus on and follow the examiner visually?

■ **Traction.** The examiner puts a forefinger in each of the baby's palms and gently pulls into a sitting position. Does the baby try to right his or her head?

■ **Cuddliness.** The examiner holds the baby in an upright position. Does the baby react passively or cuddle against the examiner's body?

■ **Defensive movement.** The examiner places a cloth on the baby's face. Does the baby attempt to remove the cloth?

Since its introduction in 1973, the BNBAS has been used to compare babies in different parts of the world. Cultural differences reveal the effects of child-rearing practices on neonatal behavior. For example, disparities between Asian and European American mothers in handling their babies' irritability have been found. Asian mothers typically provide close physical contact, nursing their babies at the first sign of discomfort, whereas European American mothers often try distract their infants' attention (Muret-Wagstaff & Moore, 1989). Furthermore, in Zambia, Africa, undernourished neonates were found to benefit from sensory stimulation while straddling their mothers' hips during the day. After 1 week of extra stimulation, unresponsive newborns were transformed into alert babies (Brazelton, Koslowki, & Tronick, 1976).

Nevertheless, the predictive value of the BNBAS and other neonatal scales has been called into question. A single score cannot predict later development (Francis, Self, & Horowitz, 1987). Although the BNBAS does highlight neonatal capabilities and cultural influences on parents' child-rearing practices, critics believe a reliable estimate of future performance can only come from repeated observations. Only then can the combination of newborn behavior and parenting style be revealed (Sameroff, 1978).

EMOTIONAL AND PSYCHOLOGICAL ADJUSTMENT

Many parents experience a period of psychological adjustment after their children's birth. Some may feel an emotional letdown after several months of anticipation. Temporary emotional fluctuations affect a large number of women from all walks of life. An estimated 50 to 80% of new mothers undergo a reaction psychologists refer to as postpartum blues. Possible causes involve hormonal changes and situational circumstances, particularly fatigue or uneasiness in caring for an infant demanding considerable attention. As new mothers make the transition, reassurance from a supportive social network, particularly their partners, relatives, friends, and coworkers, can help. Even some men may experience postpartum blues. Perhaps a heightened sense of their parenting role may trigger a similar reaction.

In some cases, a prolonged duration of sadness and apathy after birth, coupled with a sense of worthlessness and withdrawal, continues over several weeks or months. About

10% of women are afflicted with a condition known as postpartum depression (Emerson, 1999). Their depressive state will affect their relationship with their infants. Depressed mothers rarely talk to or respond to their infants' signals (Cohn et al., 1990). Because infants receive important cues from their parents, depressed women's inability to relate to their infants entails serious consequences. After a protracted period of maternal depression, infants may begin to exhibit emotional and cognitive problems (O'Hara, 1997; Whiffen & Gotlib, 1989).

Maternal factors are involved in postpartum depression. However, often forgotten is the effect of infants' temperamental qualities. Prolonged and vigorous crying episodes, in addition to irregular sleeping and eating patterns, can produce considerable stress in any parent. Fatigue may lead to a sense of helplessness. Signs of postpartum depression usually occur before birth in half of all cases. Therefore, successful treatment may depend on early identification of at-risk parents to counteract the debilitating effects of postpartum depression on infants' development.

FATHERS' INVOLVEMENT

When childbirth shifted to the hospital, fathers were often excluded from the birthing process. In large hospitals, they had to wait in a separate room. Only afterwards, many were allowed to see their babies in the nursery from the sterile corridor. Some believe that the exclusion of fathers interfered with their opportunity to experience birth as an important milestone in life.

Since then, obstetric practices have changed dramatically. The forgotten link in the family is now seen as an important contributor. Fathers today are encouraged to be actively involved. Many not only attend prenatal classes and sit in on doctors' visits, but also coach their partners and even cut the umbilical cord of their newborns. Many fathers are beginning to recognize the benefits of their involvement. As Brazelton and Cramer (1990) explain:

> The father learns his role on the job, as does the mother. He adjusts his behavior, his own rhythms . . . and learns about his capacity to respond and to nurture. (p. 106)

Fathers' involvement in childbirth can ease the transition to parenthood. The rewards of parenthood are linked to fathers' level of involvement in sharing child-rearing responsibilities (Brott & Ash, 1998). Even everyday activities such as feeding and diapering provide endless opportunities for fathers to bond with and stimulate their infants. Fathers can play an important role in facilitating their infants' sense of trust in and exploration of the world through give-and-take interactions.

In the United States, the Family and Medical Leave Act, enacted in 1993, has enabled many new parents, including fathers, to take unpaid leave of up to 3 months per year from their jobs to care for their infants and children. It affects only businesses with 50 or more employees. The law guarantees job security and continued medical benefits. Its enactment seems to reflect society's increasing recognition of the difficulties facing many fathers and mothers alike today in trying to balance work and family.

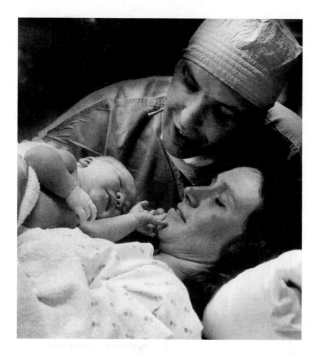

Many fathers take an active interest in their children's development before and after birth.
Ulrike Welsch, Photo Researchers, Inc.

SUMMARY

Historical Practices

■ Childbirth was seen as a natural process in the United States until the turn of the 20th century. It occurred at home in the company of other women who provided comfort and performed the household chores as the mother recuperated from childbirth.

■ Because of advances in medical science, the birthing process was moved from the home to the hospital. Unfortunately, childbirth was no longer viewed as a natural process but a diseased state.

■ Medical intervention reached its apex in the mid-20th century. The laboring mother was heavily sedated to eliminate pain while the father was excluded from childbirth.

■ The foundations of natural or prepared childbirth were laid in the 1950s. The pendulum has swung back to the view of childbirth as a natural process.

Methods of Childbirth

■ Other methods of childbirth have been developed to create a positive experience. Lamaze and Leboyer focus on breathing techniques to minimize fear of pain and easing the transition from the womb to the outside world.

■ Natural or prepared childbirth has had some positive outcomes in terms of women's attitudes toward labor and delivery. Also, reduced pain is reported.

Stages of Childbirth

■ The process of childbirth begins after roughly 40 weeks of gestation. It begins when the fetus sends a biochemical signal to its mother's body.

■ Contractions signal the onset of labor. Childbirth is divided into three stages: dilation and effacement of cervix, delivery, and placental expulsion.

Medical Intervention

■ Childbirth is medically monitored and controlled. Certain procedures are followed to protect the lives of the mother and child and ease the discomfort of labor.

■ Labor may be induced if the pregnancy is not progressing smoothly. Reasons include prolonged labor or fetal distress.

Complications

■ Most pregnancies end with the birth of a healthy newborn. However, in some cases, the newborn is considered to be at risk because of prematurity, low birth weight, or both.

■ The newborn is referred to as premature if born before the 37th week of gestation. Premature infants may experience developmental delays later.

■ Steps have been taken to improve the living conditions of premature infants in hospitals. In addition to visual and auditory stimulation, touch plays a critical role and leads to demonstrable physical and cognitive gains.

Postpartum Period

■ Neonatal health and behavior can be measured. To assess the neonate's physical status, the Apgar scale, a rating system of five vital signs, is administered at 1 and 5 minutes after birth.

■ The emotional and psychological adjustment of new parents after birth has been studied. Some parents, particularly mothers, may experience postpartum blues, a period of emotional and psychological fluctuation after birth.

Fathers' Involvement

■ Obstetric practices have changed since the mid-20th century in the United States. A once forgotten link in the birthing process, the father is now viewed as an important contributor.

PROJECTS

1. Discuss the historical context of natural childbirth in the United States and compare the pros and cons of different methods.

2. Interview a parent of an infant or young child and ask about his or her experience during childbirth.

3. Borrow an up-to-date book on childbirth and summarize the major points regarding any possible harmful effects of medication or other intrusive procedures during labor or delivery.

NEWBORN

And when our baby stirs and struggles to be born
It compels humility: what we began
Is now its own.
Anne Ridler, *For a Child Expected*

To many, newborns appear to be completely helpless. Their only means of communicating with their caregivers is crying. However, they are not as helpless as people once believed. In fact, newborns are very adept at eliciting attention to themselves and interacting with their physical and social environment. They demonstrate definite sensory preferences as they seek out certain kinds of stimuli. Chapter 6 examines the first month of development after birth.

Scientific interest in the newborn period, defined as the first month of life, started toward the end of the 19th century. At first, the newborn was seen as a squirming mass of flesh. Early American psychologists believed that the newborn spent the first weeks of life without the ability to see or hear. In his classic work, William James described the newborn's perception of the world as "one great blooming, buzzing confusion" (James, 1890/1950). He felt that the newborn remained in a state of complete helplessness until further physiological maturation occurred. Another American psychologist, G. Stanley Hall, unflatteringly depicted the newborn in the following way:

. . . with its red, shriveled, parboiled skin . . . , squinting, cross eyed, pot bellied, and bow legged. (Hall, 1891, p. 128)

Even today, many parents are startled to see their newborn immediately after birth. The newborn's elongated head and swollen features do not always conform to their parents' perception of healthy babies. In the last few decades, a completely different picture of newborns has begun to emerge. In contrast to previous views of "immaturity" (Gesell, 1928b), newborns have been found to be quite capable of processing sensory information from the very start:

> Newborns are not just as helpless as they look. First of all, the activities needed to sustain life function at birth. A newborn can breathe, suck, swallow, and get rid of wastes. He can look, hear, taste, smell, feel, turn his head, and signal for help from the first minute. (Caplan, 1993, p. 32)

The physical appearance, reflexive capabilities, physiological states, sensory and perceptual development, and social world of newborns will be examined. During the first month, sometimes called the neonatal period, infants make the transition from dependence to increasing independence.

PHYSICAL APPEARANCE

Newborns are the product of their genetic inheritance. They are designed to survive childbirth and adapt to the external world. The average height and weight of newborns in the United States is roughly 20 inches and 7.5 pounds at birth. Because of individual variations, 95% of newborns fall between 18 and 22 inches and 5.5 and 10 pounds. Newborns typically lose about 5 to 10% of their total birth weight during the first few days because of the loss of fluid. However, they regain their original weight at birth before the end of the second week as they take in their mothers' milk (initially **colostrum** or *the milk secreted during the first few days after birth*) or commercial formula.

The size of the newborn at birth depends on a number of factors, such as genes, the mother's length of pregnancy, parity (the number of children she has borne), health and nutrition, and ethnicity.

Newborns across the world share similar physical characteristics. Their heads tend to be misshapen from childbirth. Their nose and ears are similarly flattened. Because physical growth takes place in a cephalocaudal direction, or top to bottom, at birth, the muscles of their neck are not able to support their disproportionately large heads, accounting for about one-quarter of their total length. The separate plates of the skull do not completely fuse until after birth in order to overlap during childbirth and permit further development of the brain. *The space between the cranial bones of the newborn* is referred to as **fontanels** or soft spots (see Figure 6–1). The plates return to their normal location sometime before the third day after birth. They do not, however, fully close until about 18 months of age. The closure of the plates is not related to the ethnicity or sex of the newborn. Further, delayed closure is not an indication of abnormal development (Kataria et al., 1988).

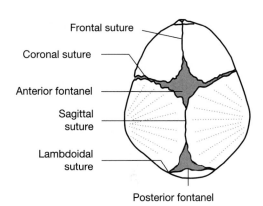

Frontal suture

Coronal suture

Anterior fontanel

Sagittal suture

Lambdoidal suture

Posterior fontanel

FIGURE 6–1 Skull at Birth
Fontanels are gaps between the bony plates of the new-born's skull.

Newborns display other distinctive physical characteristics. **Vernix caseosa,** *an oily sub-stance that covers the newborn's skin,* prevents infection during childbirth. It dries in a few days' time. A yellow complexion of the skin indicates jaundice because of an excessive accumulation of bilirubin that causes yellowish-red pigmentation. It is normally trans-formed into bile. If, however, the liver does not function properly, it collects in the new-born's body. Jaundice usually begins on the second or third day after birth. A relatively common condition affecting about 60% of all infants, it is often treated with special fluo-rescent lights. It gradually disappears in about 5 to 10 days. In addition, the newborn may be covered with soft, fine hair. **Lanugo** refers to *the newborn's prenatal hair that disap-pears within a few days of birth.* Parents may need to be reassured about their newborn's appearance. Their preconception of a healthy baby may not always fit reality (Ritter, Casey, & Langlois, 1991).

REFLEXIVE CAPABILITIES

Newborns come into the world with a wide range of capabilities. They are equipped to engage with their immediate environment from the outset. Initially, newborns rely on reflexes to survive the first days and weeks. **Reflexes** refer to newborns' *inborn, involun-tary responses to specific stimuli.* Newborns possess dozens of reflexes at birth, although a number of reflexes disappear within months. A description of the major reflexes can be found in Table 6–1.

Reflexes serve different purposes. Some, such as rooting and sucking reflexes, facili-tate the newborn's survival. Because they occur automatically, the newborn does not have to learn the complex task of finding the mother's nipple or bottle and coordinat-ing the complex muscles of the lip and tongue in order to swallow. The vast array of re-flexes reflects the development of the brain. Because the subcortex controls reflexes, their disappearance denotes the increasing dominance of the cerebral cortex with matu-ration and the eventual replacement of voluntary behavior. Since reflexes follow a predictable timetable, their presence or absence offers a way to evaluate the newborn's neurological development.

TABLE 6–1   NEWBORN REFLEXES

Reflex	Stimulus	Response	Age of Disappearance	Function
Babinski	Stroke sole of foot from toe to heel	Toes spread and curl as foot twists in	8 to 12 months	Provides index of normal neurological condition
Blinking	Shine light in eyes	Eyelids blink	Permanent	Protects infant from aversive stimuli such as bright lights and foreign objects
Grasping	Place finger in infant's hand	Infant grasps finger	3 to 4 months	Prepares infant to grasp objects voluntarily later
Moro	Hold infant and drop head slightly or produce sudden loud noise	Infant extends arms and legs outward and makes embracing motion	6 to 7 months	Ensures survival because infant clings to adult in emergency
Rooting	Stroke cheek with finger or nipple	Head turns in direction of stroke as mouth opens and infant sucks	3 to 6 months	Helps infant to find source of nourishment
Stepping	Hold infant vertically and permit bare feet to touch flat surface	Infant lifts one foot and then another in rhythmic manner	2 months	Prepares infant to support weight and later take first steps
Sucking	Put finger into mouth	Infant sucks on finger rhythmically	Permanent	Permits infant to obtain nourishment
Tonic	Turn infant's head to one side on back	Infant lies in fencing position with one arm in flexed position	4 months	Allows infant to reach objects

SIDS: UNEXPECTED DEATH

The death of any infant is a tragic event. Parents are stricken with grief at the unexpected loss of life. Most deaths in infancy occur in the first month as a result of congenital defects. However, another cause of death is sudden infant death syndrome (SIDS). It affects 3,000 infants each year in the United States, peaking between 2 to 4 months of age during the winter months. There is a greater incidence among native Americans and African Americans. Still a great mystery, it strikes seemingly healthy infants during sleep regardless of socioeconomic level (Horchler & Morris, 1997).

After decades of research, the actual cause of SIDS is not known. However, several theories have been proposed:

■ **Suffocation.** Suffocation is presumed to be one possible cause of SIDS. It results in about 900 deaths each year. The American Academy of Pediatrics and National Institutes of Health recommend that parents dress their babies in pajamas instead of using blankets, which can mold to infants' faces. The resulting accumulation of carbon dioxide is thought to deprive infants from oxygen (Consumer Product Safety Commission, 1999).

■ **Bacterial or viral infection.** A small percentage of infants suffered from a cold within days of their unexpected deaths. A case of the sniffles may increase susceptibility to SIDS. However, not all infants who died had symptoms of a cold or another minor illness. In one study, an examination of autopsies revealed that the presence of a cold did not cause sudden death (Cotton, 1990).

■ **Apnea.** Infants' voluntary responses gradually replace defensive reflexes from 2 to 4 months of age. When infants experience apneic episodes, or the temporary suspension of respiration, they may shift the position of their bodies or cry to get help. However, some infants may fail to take another breath. Respiratory problems may therefore be a factor in SIDS (Guntheroth & Spiers, 1997).

■ **Environmental factors.** Current research is focusing on a variety of environmental factors such as smoking and sleeping position. Infants of smoking mothers are found to be two to three times more likely to die from SIDS (Dwyer, Ponsonby, & Couper, 1999; Schoendorf & Kiely, 1992). Some think that maternal smoke puts added strain on infants' respiratory system. In addition, babies who sleep on their stomach instead of their backs suffer from a high risk of SIDS (Poets & Southall, 1993; Ponsonby et al., 1993).

Until a definitive cause or a combination of causes is found, parents are advised to take steps to minimize the risk of SIDS. Recommendations include removing soft bedding materials (blankets, quilts, sheepskins, and pillows) and stuffed toys from the cribs, dressing infants in warm pajamas, putting them to sleep on their backs instead of their stomachs, and refraining from smoking.

Newborns demonstrate an amazing ability to adapt. Initially relying on reflexes to engage with the world, they attempt to respond purposefully to stimuli in a short span of time. Piaget traces the origin of human intelligence to the reflexive capabilities of the newborn. In his theory, reflexes provide the basic building blocks of cognitive development (Piaget, 1936/1952). Reflexes are gradually transformed into the first acquired adaptive behavior during the first several weeks of life. For example, the sucking reflex provides not only nourishment but information about the properties of objects (Flavell, 1963).

Moreover, reflexes promote social interaction with others. While feeding their newborns, many parents usually touch or talk to them. Newborns' sucking behavior is highly organized. It fosters the establishment of reciprocal social exchanges. Newborns suck in short bursts. In turn, mothers tend to jiggle their babies during pauses between sucking bursts. Some believe jiggling represents the emergence of dialogue. Newborns may be learning to wait and take turns after a few short bursts, an occurrence that may foreshadow later human conversation (Kaye, 1982; Kaye & Wells, 1980).

REGULATION OF PHYSIOLOGICAL STATES

During the first month of life, distinct periods of rest and activity are beginning to emerge. *Newborns' different levels of sleep and wakefulness* are referred to as **states**. Sleep initially dominates wakefulness. Newborns typically sleep about two-thirds of the day. Both sleep and wakefulness alternate in cycles of 4 hours: 3 hours hours asleep and 1 hour awake.

Peter Wolff and other researchers have made extensive observations of newborns' patterns of sleep and wakefulness. The results of their research indicate newborns' states play a critical role in their responsiveness to stimuli (Wolff, 1959, 1966). The frequency of newborns' responses increases, in particular, during quiet alertness, one of six states that Wolff identifies. Other states include regular and irregular sleep, drowsiness, active alertness, and crying. An electroencephalograph, or EEG, is used to record the electrical activity of the brain. Distinctive patterns are associated with different states (DiPietro & Porges, 1991; Thoman & Whitney, 1990).

Sleep consists of two distinct states. During irregular sleep, rapid eye movement (REM) is observed. The electrical activity of the brain resembles the state of wakefulness. Not only do the eyes dart, but fluctuations in heart rate occur along with increased movements of the body. REM appears to serve an important function. It apparently stimulates the brain. In contrast, nonrapid eye movement (NREM) is noted during regular sleep.

Irregular and regular sleep occurs in both newborns and adults. REM occupies about half of newborns' sleep. However, it rapidly declines to about one-quarter of their sleep at 2 years of age. At 5 years of age, the proportion drops to 20% of their sleep, the same percentage it consumes in adulthood (Roffwarg, Muzio, & Dement, 1966). Researchers think newborns probably do not dream in the same way adults do. Because newborns spend only about 10% of the total waking hours in a state of quiet alertness, a time when they focus on external stimuli, REM seems to fulfill a different need. A newborn's brain may be stimulating itself during irregular sleep. The stimulation it provides may support the development of the brain (Fletcher, Page, & Jeffrey, 1998).

The unique behavioral patterns of newborns signal their individuality and influence their social relationship with their parents. The state of quiet alertness seems to invite their parents' interaction because newborns appear to be interested in the environment. Newborns track objects that move and attend to their parents' social overtures such as vocalizations and gestures. Although sleep occupies a large portion of the day during the initial weeks of life, experts believe that parents should pay close attention to their newborns' different states of wakefulness. Many parents like regularity. However, a predictable schedule of sleep and wakefulness generally does not happen until 3 months of age.

Infants cry to elicit their parents' attention. Their cries communicate physiological and emotional needs. Hunger, in general, triggers an intense cry, but as infants develop,

---

PARENTING ISSUES

CRYING INFANTS: SOOTHING TECHNIQUES

Many parents worry about the best course of action to follow in responding to crying infants. They may wonder if a prompt response may spoil babies. In many preindustrialized societies, parents usually sooth and nurse their crying infants immediately. Many may even share their mothers' bed at night. However, in the United States and other industrialized countries, infants typically sleep in a separate room from their parents. Differences in childrearing strategies reflect not only socioeconomic factors but also ethnic differences. For example, in response to crying infants, many African American mothers prefer to use pacifiers or engage in physical stimulation. In contrast, European American mothers rely on nursing their infants or using physical touch (Burchinal, Follmer, & Bryant, 1996; Garcia-Coll, 1990).

Different crying patterns have been identified. Hungry infants will engage in a rhythmic, repetitive cry. A loud, shrill crying obviously denotes pain, whereas a whiny, nasal crying signifies an illness. Nevertheless, experts generally recommend a prompt response to infants' cries during the first few months of life. The duration of crying episodes usually declines whenever parents respond immediately because consistency seems to facilitate infants' sense of trust and security. Other soothing techniques include

■ **Using a pacifier.** Infants like to suck on their thumbs and fingers as well as other objects. During the first year, 60 to 70% of all infants engage in nonnutritive sucking. It often continues until about 4 to 7 years of age. In rare instances, some may continue to suck their thumbs until adolescence.

Should parents be concerned about pacifiers? Sucking on pacifiers immediately induces a state of calm although many parents wonder about possible dependency. The soothing effect probably results from infants' conditioned association between the intake of nourishment and the sucking response itself.

(continued)

In one study, pacifiers produced the desired calming effect during routine medical exams (Campos, 1994). Some doctors worry about the indiscriminate use of pacifiers and its unintended effect on breast-feeding. The increased use of pacifiers has been found to interfere with breast-feeding duration (Barros, Victora, & Weiderpass, 1995; Righard, 1998).

■ **Swaddling.** Swaddled infants are tightly wrapped in blankets with their arms at their sides. It usually produces an immediate calming effect because the blanket minimizes startled movements. In one study, 2-week-old infants were swaddled before their heels were pricked to draw blood. Crying was significantly reduced (Campos, 1989). However, some experts question the indiscriminate use of swaddling infants. They worry that it may restrict free movement of the arms and legs or delay physical development.

■ **Rocking.** The effects of rhythmic movement have been examined. Infants in one study were rocked either vertically or horizontally (Byrne & Horowitz, 1981). The results indicated that rhythmic movement of any form produced a soothing effect. Also, distressed infants can be effectively calmed when they are rocked intermittently instead of continuously. In many cultures, infants are carried in slings or on the hips of parents. Such arrangements encourage skin-to-skin contact and mutual engagement (Korner, 1974).

■ **Listening to auditory stimuli.** Repetitive auditory stimulation can produce a calming effect as parents who sing lullabies to their infants already know. However, not just any kind of sound will work (Brackbill, 1970). Continuous sounds decrease infants' state of arousal. Brackbill (1975) varied the intensity of the sound and found that loud noise at 80 dB soothed crying infants. In addition, developmental changes are noted in the effectiveness of various sounds. White noise works effectively with newborns (Kopp, 1982), but at 3 months, infants prefer their mothers' voices (Kopp, 1989).

In sum, newborns' cries signal hunger or distress. Parents and other adults play a critical role in fostering their newborns' sense of trust and security. However, if parents notice that their efforts just do not seem to work or that their infants cry in an unusual way, they should call their pediatrician. Prolonged crying can possibly indicate a disorder, such as colic (severe abdominal pain), requiring medical intervention (Adams & Davidson, 1987; Lester & Zeskind, 1982).

their cries vary in intensity from a whimper to a forceful expression of discomfort. Infants cry in response to both internal states, such as pain, and external stimuli, such as loud noises. Interestingly, the cry of another infant precipitates a similar reaction. The response possibly reflects infants' innate ability to react to the distress of others (Martin & Clark, 1982; Sagi & Hoffman, 1976).

Infants' crying is presumed to be genetically determined to ensure their survival. The unpleasant sounds of their cries evoke a similar reaction in most adults—parents and nonparents and men and women alike (Boero et al., 1998; Boukydis, 1985). Although parents may not understand the intent of their cries, experience gradually improves the accuracy of their judgment. Zeskind and others have found that even inexperienced adults are able to distinguish different crying patterns in newborns (Zeskind & Lester, 1978; Zeskind & Marshall, 1988). Adults' rate of response to newborns' crying can influence its duration. When adults respond immediately, crying typically will decrease.

Research has examined the effects of infants' cries on abusive parents. Abusive parents may react differently to infants' communicative signals. In particular, premature and sick infants are likely to elicit aversive responses from abusive parents. Abusive parents often mention their infants' grating cries as the factor leading to abuse (Cuisinier et al., 1998; Zeskind & Shingler, 1991). Further study is needed to establish a relationship between abusive parents' behavioral patterns and their infants' physiological responses. Nevertheless, abusive parents may benefit from learning to engage in soothing ways of alleviating infants' cries such as rocking or swaddling crying infants when everything else fails.

In sum, different physiological states play an important role in infants' development. Their bodies require periods of rest to consolidate their resources and further sustain their physical growth. Further, their attention to the external stimuli fosters their cognitive and social development during the state of quiet alertness. Parents' awareness of physiological states may increase sensitivity to their infants' needs.

SENSORY AND PERCEPTUAL DEVELOPMENT

Newborns are able to see, hear, smell, taste, and touch at birth. A distinction between sensation and perception has been made. **Sensation** refers to *the body's ability to detect a particular stimulus.* **Perception**, on the other hand, involves *the brain's capacity to make sense of information that it receives from the body's sensory modalities.*

Newborns' sensory and perceptual capabilities have been extensively documented because of technological advances over the last few decades. Researchers basically introduce a change in the environment and observe its effect on the physiological or behavioral processes of newborns (Morse, 1995). For example, if newborns see a flashing light or hear a tone, they may suck on a modified pacifier at a different rate. If the stimulus is no longer maintaining their attention, they are said to be habituated. **Habituation** refers to *the gradual decline in attention that results from prolonged exposure to a particular stimulus.* In contrast, **dishabituation** involves *increased attention to a different set of stimuli.*

SEEING

Newborns' visual apparatus is not fully developed at birth. Because of physiological immaturities, their vision is blurred. The muscles controlling the lenses of the eyes lack coordination in adjusting to varying distances. The retinas (membranes that line the walls of the eyeballs) receive and transmit improperly focused visual images to the optic nerves. Both the optic nerves and area of the brain that processes visual information

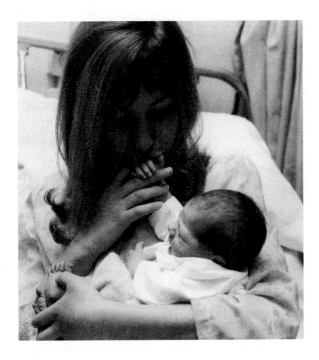

From the moment of birth, newborns utilize all five senses in processing information about the world.
Hulton Getty, Archive Photos.

continue to mature during the next several weeks and months. Newborns take a long time to respond to visual stimulation and become visually fatigued after prolonged exposure (Caulfield, 1994).

Newborns are extremely nearsighted. Their **visual acuity**, or *sharpness of vision*, is quite limited. It is estimated to be 20/500 (Cornell & McDonnell, 1986). In other words, newborns can perceive objects at a distance of 20 feet that adults with perfect vision can see clearly at 500 feet. Nevertheless, newborns are able to focus on objects at a distance of

---

SENSORY AND PERCEPTUAL DEVELOPMENT

Wilhelm Preyer
Mental Development in the Child, 1893
The newborn child enters a world of light and sound, but he cannot yet see or hear. He does not feel, in the degree that he will feel at a later time; single pricks of a needle often produce not the least expression of pain in him, and in the first moment of existence he cannot properly smell or taste.

Source: Preyer (1893/1897), p. 2.

8 to 10 inches from their faces. Therefore, they are likely to see their caregivers' faces while being held.

As further neurological maturation occurs, newborns benefit from increased coordination of the optic muscles and efficient transmission of neural signals to the brain. Their visual system begins to approximate adults' capabilities at 6 months of age, although **visual accommodation**, *the ability of the eyes to bring objects into focus,* gradually improves during the first 2 months (Hainline & Abramov, 1992).

The visual acuity of preterm infants with extremely low birth weight has been assessed. Results show that their visual acuity falls within the normal limits (Courage & Adams, 1997). However, at the end of 1 year, in comparison to full-term infants, delays in visual development have been found. Significant developmental lags have been found in the visual acuity of infants with Down syndrome, especially after 6 months (Courage et al., 1994).

Newborns can visually attend to both stationary and moving objects. They generally focus on a single feature or contour of an object (Freeseman, Colombo, & Coldren, 1993; Haith, Bergman, & Moore, 1977). However, at 2 months of age, they scan the external edges and internal features of objects. Similarly, infants at 1 and 2 months of age examine different features of the human face. One-month-old infants look primarily at the contours of the face and ignore the internal features. In contrast, 2-month-old babies are drawn to both the eyes and mouth of the face. Newborns track a moving object in a somewhat haphazard fashion (Slater & Johnson, 1998). A smooth, sustained visual

---

PARENTING ISSUES

NEWBORNS' ABILITY TO IMITATE

Are newborns' able to imitate facial gestures? Meltzoff and Moore (1977, 1979) reported that newborns only a few days old can mimic certain actions of adults. In their study, newborns were first exposed to the expressionless face of an adult. The adult then performed, in random order, four distinct gestures: pursing the lips, opening the mouth, protruding the tongue, and opening and closing a hand. Afterwards, trained observers viewed each infant on videotape. The results indicated that newborns consistently tried to match the adult's gestures.

Meltzoff and Moore's research seems to provide evidence that newborns demonstrate an innate ability to imitate the gestures of others. Their imitative actions may play an active role in influencing their parents' behavior (Meltzoff & Moore, 1989, 1997). However, not all agree with Meltzoff and Moore's conclusions. Ullstadius (1998) found that in a nonrestrictive environment, newborns did not copy their mothers' oral gestures. Newborns usually protrude their tongues in response to almost any object within their visual range. According to Jones (1996), newborns are manifesting exploration, not imitation.

pursuit of an object occurs only about 15% of the time. Newborns are capable of following an object to an arc of about 90 degrees (Bronson, 1994).

Newborns can perceive color. In fact, they react differently to visual stimuli on the basis of color just as adults do (Adams, Courage, & Mercer, 1994). The different wavelengths of light determine the range of color. The colors of the spectrum (red, orange, yellow, green, blue, and violet) are arranged in order from the longest to shortest wavelength. Newborns can discriminate different colors. However, researchers encounter difficulties in studying newborns' perception of color (Adams & Courage, 1998). Two components, hue and brightness, are involved in the newborns' ability to perceive color. If newborns are able to distinguish between two stimuli, are they responding to differences in hue or brightness? Although the extent of their ability is not fully known, newborns are quite capable of discriminating color at 1 month of age. The neural pathways processing visual information continue to mature during the first several weeks of life (Banks & Shannon, 1993; Brown, 1990).

Visual Preferences.   Newborns do not just randomly attend to objects in their environment. They selectively look at certain things (Fantz, Fagan, & Miranda, 1975). In particular, human faces are appealing to newborns. They appear to be genetically programmed to focus their attention on human faces. Early research of infants' visual preferences relied on schematic outlines of human faces. Robert Fantz and his associates found that infants from 10 hours to 5 days after birth preferred to look at a black and white face instead of a patch of newsprint (Fantz, 1963). Since then, research has shown that infants are able to differentiate between photographs of two different faces at 3 months of age. Babies prefer photographed faces of their parents rather than strangers (Barrera & Maurer, 1981). At 5 months, faces are apparently perceived as integrated configurations of internal and external contours, not just collections of separate features. Infants prefer real to schematic faces, familiar to unfamiliar ones, correctly drawn to scrambled ones, and moving to immobile ones (Valenza et al., 1996).

In addition, infants seek visual stimulation with complexity. They prefer to attend to novel rather than familiar stimuli and complex rather than plain patterns such as bull's-eyes and checkerboards instead of simple circles and squares (Simion, Valenza, & Umilta, 1998). The results of research in recent years have led to an appreciation of infants as "little scientists" who strive to make sense of their world. As Haith (1993) comments, "babies actively try to organize their world" (p. 262). Infants attend to and process selective stimuli while ignoring others. They also demonstrate selectivity in response to auditory stimuli.

HEARING

In contrast to vision, newborns' hearing apparatus is fully functioning at birth. They can hear even prior to birth (Bernard, 1946). Early researchers relied on fetal movement to determine the fetus's ability to respond to a variety of auditory stimuli. With the advent of ultrasonography, however, fetal reaction to sudden noises is noticed at 24 and 28 weeks in 50 and 100% of fetuses, respectively (Birnholz & Benacerraf, 1983). The repeated presentation of auditory stimuli gradually results in a decline of interest after

28 weeks, an example of habituation. Fetal ability to hear is closely tied to the maturation of the auditory nerve and anatomy of the ears.

A person's sensitivity to auditory stimuli depends on the loudness and pitch of sounds. Loudness is measured in terms of decibels (dB). A normal conversation is 60 dB, whereas a whisper is 40 dB. On the other hand, pitch is measured in terms of hertz (Hz). Researchers rely on physiological changes in newborns' behavior to determine their sensitivity to sounds. Their absolute threshold of sound falls in the range of 40 to 60 dB although their sensitivity gradually improves during the first year of life (Cone-Wesson & Ramirez, 1997). Their ability to detect a sound hinges not only on its frequency but also on its duration. Infants have difficulties in hearing sounds of short duration (Clarkson et al., 1989).

Auditory Preferences. Just as with vision, newborns selectively attend to different sounds. Not surprisingly, they prefer to hear human voices. They often turn their heads to locate the source of adults' voices. Research indicates that newborns prefer to hear their mothers' voices (DeCasper & Fifer, 1980) but cannot differentiate their fathers' voices (DeCasper & Prescott, 1984). The subjects had only minimal contact with their mothers during the time between their birth and the testing session a day later. Newborns' ability to discriminate their mothers' voices probably stem from their prenatal experience.

Newborns are able to detect closely related sounds. At 1 month of age, they perceive the difference between /b/ or "buh" and /p/ or "puh" (Eimas et al., 1971). The subjects in the now classic study activated a tape that played /b/ whenever they sucked on a modified pacifier. Their sucking response slowly decreased as they habituated to the repeated presentation of the same sound. Then, the sound was changed from /b/ to /p/ on the tape. The infants' increased sucking activity indicated that they perceived the difference between the two sounds. In addition, infants are capable of discriminating between sounds not found in their own language. Therefore, there seems to be a genetically predisposition to tune in to human speech at birth (Cooper et al., 1997; Kaplan et al., 1995).

In reality, newborns are simply not exposed to pure tones but complex sounds. They prefer to listen to high-pitched sounds, although their preference peaks at about 2 months of age (Cooper & Aslin, 1990). Adults typically use a distinctive pattern of speech consisting of high-pitched sounds and exaggerated intonations in talking to infants. Known as parentese or infant-directed speech, adults make a deliberate effort to address infants in a particular way. It reflects sensitivity to infants' increased attention to certain frequencies of sounds. About 80% of the total vocalizations between parents, particularly mothers, and infants resemble parentese during the first 6 months of life (Fernald, 1989; Fernald & Kuhl, 1987).

Nonhuman sounds can elicit specific responses from newborns and affect their emotional states. Very high (4,000 Hz) and very low frequencies (70 Hz) can cause considerable distress in newborns (Hutt et al., 1968). However, low frequencies can produce a calming effect. Newborns are clearly able to detect extremely high- and low-pitched sounds. Several studies have focused on the effects of repetitive auditory stimuli in soothing fretful or crying infants. In one study, researchers compared newborns' response to heartbeats to other sounds such as a metronome or a lullaby, finding that all three resulted in a calming effect (Tulloch et al., 1964).

MOZART EFFECT: SOUND BEGINNINGS?

Music is supposed to soothe the savage beast. Does it also stimulate the mind? Researchers have studied the effects of music on college students' ability to solve complex spatial tasks (Rauscher, Shaw, & Ky, 1993). They found that Mozart's Sonata for Two Pianos, K. 448 (hence, the term *Mozart Effect*) apparently had an enhancing effect but lasted only for 10 minutes. According to the researchers, listening to Mozart and executing complex spatial tasks share similar neural pathways in the brain. Therefore, listening to music may improve the efficiency of the brain in solving certain kinds of problems (Rauscher, Shaw, & Ky, 1995).

Can infants, like college students, benefit from the Mozart Effect? The answer is not clear-cut. There are anecdotal accounts of music's enhancing effect on infants. Campbell (1997) presented a case of an extremely premature baby, weighing just over 1.5 pounds at birth. At the mother's request, Mozart was piped into the Neonatal Intensive Care Unit (NICU) at the hospital. Not only did her daughter survive but, at 3 years of age, scored "far ahead of her years" on developmental measures. In one study, the soothing effect of music on premature infants had been verified. According to Caine (1991), exposure to normal noise in NICUs can cause potential stress, but recorded music of children's lullabies and songs can improve nutritional intake, cut initial weight loss, and shorten the length of the hospital stay.

Therefore, the long-term effects of classical music, particularly Mozart's, have yet to be proven. The initial euphoria has diminished somewhat when other researchers tried to replicate Rauscher and colleagues' (1993) initial findings. Newman and colleagues (1995) found no evidence of the Mozart Effect with a larger sample of college students. Likewise, Stough, Kerkin, Bates, and Mangan's study (1994) also failed to support the beneficial effects of music. Nevertheless, some experts advocate that parents should provide a stimulating auditory environment both before and after birth. Recent research has shown that prenatal music can have some positive effects on infants' later gross and fine motor coordination and cognitive and linguistic development (Abrams et al., 1998; LaFuente et al., 1997).

SMELLING

Research on newborns' olfaction or the sense of smell has not received extensive attention. However, the ability to smell does play an important role in development. At about 7 months of gestation, the nostrils open. Although an accurate determination of fetal olfaction is somewhat restricted because of obvious methodological limitations, premature infants at a gestational age of 28 weeks are able to respond to strong odors (Sarnat, 1978).

Newborns can react to and differentiate odors in the same way adults do. They avoid unpleasant odors such as asafetida or ammonia, which produce a nauseating smell. They are able to utilize their sense of smell in discriminating different smells. Their olfactory capabilities continue to improve during the first month of life (Self, Horowitz, & Paden, 1972).

Studies have demonstrated the sensitivity of newborns' sense of smell. Their ability to recognize their own mothers' odors has been documented (Makin & Porter, 1989; Porter et al., 1992). Newborns at 2 days of age typically turn their heads to a pad from their mothers' armpits instead of a stranger's. Breast-fed babies recognize pads containing their mothers' underarm odors, probably because of extended physical contact. Bottle-feds infants, on the other hand, do not show similar signs of recognition. Neither breast- nor bottle-fed babies exhibit any recognition of their fathers' underarm pads perhaps because lactating mothers' bodies produce chemical substances that appeal to nursing infants.

The sense of smell influences early contact between parents and their infants. Mothers have been found to recognize their own infants' odors after only 1 or 2 days of exposure in the hospital (Porter, Balogh, & Makin, 1988; Russell, Mendelson, & Peeke, 1983). Their extended physical contact in the first few days of life may have heightened their sensitivity to their babies' distinct odors. The mutual olfactory abilities of both mothers and their infants may contribute to the formation of an emotional bond.

TASTING

Gustation or the sense of taste is fully developed before birth. It starts to function during the 4th month of gestation. The fetus is able to open its mouth and swallow amniotic fluid. Because the chemical composition of amniotic fluid continually changes, it can actually stimulate the fetus's sense of taste.

Taste is detected on the tongue. Tiny receptors are located in raised areas on its surface. As saliva dissolves food, it seeps into pores connected to receptors. The chemical composition of the food is then transformed into neural impulses transmitted to the brain. The sense of taste is clearly used in infants' exploration of the world. Their mouth becomes an important source of information in learning about the physical properties of objects.

Newborns are quite capable of differentiating a variety of tastes at birth. They exhibit distinctive facial expressions when researchers place different substances on their tongue (Crook, 1978; Steiner, 1979). In general, a sweet solution elicits a relaxed response. It usually results in a smile. In contrast, sour and bitter solutions produce quite different reactions. The lips purse and the mouth gapes in response to a sour and bitter taste, respectively. Both evoke an expression of disgust.

Sweet solutions can reduce the sensation of pain. Newborns 1 to 3 days old undergoing circumcision or having their heel pricked will cry less when given sucrose (Blass & Hoffmeyer, 1991). Decreased heart rate and activity level have been noted. The soothing effect was found in preterm and full-term infants (Smith & Blass, 1996).

TOUCHING

Tactile capabilities or the sense of touch develop before birth. Tactile responsiveness first appears at about 8 weeks of gestation, particularly in the region of the mouth (Spears & Hohle, 1967). At birth, the sensitivity of the tactile system is manifested in newborns' reflexive responses. If the cheek is touched gently, a rooting reflex is triggered. Physical contact between newborns and their parents can provide a reassuring sense of security. Newborns are able to detect changes in temperature and respond to textures such as the fabric of their clothes and blankets or the surface of the bed or floor. Research indicates that parents generally rely on physical contact to establish an emotional bond with their newborns. In one study, mothers of newborns successfully identified their babies just on the basis of tactile cues (Kaitz et al., 1992).

Tactile stimulation can soothe and arouse infants. In different cultures, mothers maintain continuous physical contact with their babies (Small, 1999). For example, the Gusii of Kenya never leave their infants on their own, day or night. When infants are carried in slings or pouches, they are exposed to a variety of visual, auditory, and olfactory stimuli in their parents' day-to-day activities (LeVine & LeVine, 1988).

INTEGRATING SENSORY AND PERCEPTUAL CAPABILITIES

With the exception of vision, all the senses are functioning at birth. Newborns' ability to process sensory information steadily improves because of further physiological maturation of the brain. However, environmental stimulation further facilitates sensory development. The senses mature independently but function simultaneously. They operate in an interconnected manner in making sense of the world. For example, nursing babies use visual, olfactory, and tactile cues to find and suck on the nipple or bottle. As they coordinate sucking and swallowing movements, they concentrate on a variety of stimuli, including the physical features of their parents' face, the sound of their voices, the smell of their body, and the taste of the milk. Sensory impressions stimulate their interest not only in the physical but also in the social world.

Recent research has found that infants can code faces and speech at an early age. Referred to as intermodal perception, infants are able to link visual and auditory stimuli (Meltzoff & Kuhl, 1994). The conventional view is that visual and auditory signals are

---

HISTORICALLY SPEAKING

SENSORY AND PERCEPTUAL DEVELOPMENT

Winifred Rand
Growth and Development of the Young Child, 1930
Infants are more than cunning and amusing objects; they are rapidly developing bodies, minds, and personalities. . . . Once the child has learned to use his eyes, his ears, his tongue, his nose, and his fingers, he is placed in possession of the means of exploring everything that comes within his immediate environment.

Source: Rand, Sweeney, and Vincent (1930), p. 195.

recognized through unimodal mechanisms. In other words, infants are thought to process faces and voices separately at first. However, they can make connections between the face and the sound of the voice. In one study, 4-month-old infants matched unfamiliar faces and voices, suggesting that they detected relations between the two senses (Bahrick, Netto, & Hernandez-Reif, 1998). Infants apparently learn to organize intermodal information from coordinating observations of others and movements of their bodies. Other studies confirm that stimulation from the external world coupled with continued neural development contribute to intermodal organization (Lewkowicz, 1994; Schmuckler, 1996).

SOCIAL WORLD OF NEWBORNS

From the moment of birth, newborns come into extended contact with others. Although it does not happen in the same way to all parents, many remark on bonding with their newborns within the first few hours after birth, as in the following account:

> I just touched him for a really long time and then they took him over but something had already happened. But it was much more than I ever felt or thought I would feel. Just instant love. And I can remember when they would bring him into the room afterwards—it didn't diminish at all. (Davis-Floyd, 1992, p. 143)

Do all parents feel an instantaneous bonding at birth? Studies of hoofed animals and other species may lead some to believe it does. Immediate physical contact apparently ensures the survival of certain species. For example, if a goat is separated from its mother after birth and returned a few hours later, it is ignored or rejected, but if it is nuzzled and suckled during the first 5 minutes after birth and later returned, it is welcomed back (Klopfer, 1971).

Early studies on bonding suggested that the same phenomenon occurs with humans. In the pioneering work of two pediatricians, Marshall Klaus and John Kennell, mothers were asked to spend an extra hour with their newborns after birth, touching their newborns' fingers and toes and massaging their arms and legs (Klaus et al., 1970). Klaus and Kennell reported that mothers receiving extended physical contact with their newborns benefited from the experience. A year later, the mothers maintained physical closeness and soothed their babies when they cried (Klaus & Kennell, 1976).

Klaus and Kennell's research stirred considerable debate. Obstetric changes were made in hospitals because of their efforts. Today, parents are encouraged to hold and "bond" with their newborns after birth. Newborns are no longer whisked to the nursery and are permitted to "room in" with their parents. Even parents of premature infants are not barred from extended physical contact as in the past. However, Klaus and Kennell's research has been criticized because of serious concerns. Did the results actually reflect the benefits of extended physical contact or the mothers' knowledge of the treatment they received? In addition, subsequent studies have failed to confirm the benefits of early physical contact (Goldberg, 1983).

SOCIOCULTURAL INFLUENCES

CULTURAL BELIEFS OF NEWBORNS' CAPABILITIES

In the past, expectations of newborns' capabilities were passed on from generation to generation. Today, experts in medicine and psychology play an increasingly important role in providing advice to parents. For example, in the early part of the 20th century, American psychologist John B. Watson advocated principles of behavioral theory in child-rearing practices. Parents were told to ignore their infants' cries and follow an inflexible 4-hour feeding schedule (Watson, 1928). Three-quarters of a century later, flexibility is advocated. Parents are encouraged to respond promptly to their babies' cries and feed on demand (Spock & Parker, 1998). Parents generally hold a high opinion of their newborns' capabilities. Their beliefs are reflected in their actions, talking to and stimulating their newborns' interest in the world.

Other cultures may hold a different set of beliefs about infants. The Kaluli, a nonliterate, egalitarian community living in the tropical rainforest of New Guinea, view infants as helpless creatures (Ochs & Schieffelin, 1984). Because of their perceived helplessness, mothers rarely leave their infants in the care of others. They carry their infants in bags suspended from their heads as they perform their daily chores. Although they greet their infants, they do not talk to them directly. Nor do they gaze into their eyes. Instead, infants face other members of the social group on their mothers' laps. Their mothers speak to others on their infants' behalf. Not until their infants actually utter two critical words, *mother* and *breast*, do the Kaluli acknowledge their infants' ability to learn. Thereafter, their mothers use direct instruction to teach the social uses of language.

The above two contrasting examples of differing child-rearing styles demonstrate the role of culture on parents' child-rearing patterns. The kinds of experiences infants encounter depends on the beliefs of the parents. Infants' interactions with trusted adults can affect the outcome of development. In the words of American anthropologist Margaret Mead, "each human infant is transformed into the finished adult" (Mead, 1930, p. 1).

Most experts acknowledge the importance of extended physical contact between parents and newborns. However, according to Eyer (1993), over time a bonding myth, or an expectation of instantaneous affection, has gained a foothold. In fact, some parents may experience a sense of guilt if they do not feel immediate infatuation with their newborns. Too often other unforeseen circumstances such as premature birth can exacerbate parents' emotional anguish. The bonding myth may have resulted from the increasing depersonalization of traditional obstetric practices in hospitals during the mid-20th century. Advocates may have seized on Klaus and Kennell's research as scientific validation of early physical contact to make changes. Nevertheless, current evidence seems to indicate that early postpartum experiences play an important but not critical

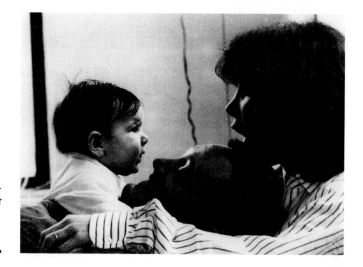

Newborns have definite preferences, particularly looking at their
parents' faces.
Shirley Zeiberg, Pearson Education/
PH College.

role in parents' relationships with their infants, as millions of affectionate and dedicated
parents with adopted children demonstrate. With humans, what matters is the quality of
care, not the actual moment when parents fall in love with their children.

As time passes, infants exert considerable influence on the social environment. As
Harriet Rheingold observes:

> . . . the infant arouses and reinforces nurturant behavior in his parents; of men and
> women he makes fathers and mothers. (Rheingold, 1968, p. 283)

Because of their presumed helplessness, newborns are assumed to be passive participants in their own development. Research indicates otherwise. Newborns initially rely on
genetically programmed reflexes not only to survive but also to interact with their parents. They cry to signal distress and draw attention to their immediate needs. As their reflexes gradually disappear, they engage in increasingly purposeful behavior. Infants
attempt to maintain close physical contact with their parents as a reciprocal emotional
bond develops (Lewis, 1977). The mutual interaction between infants and their parents
resembles a kind of a symbiotic dance. A smile from one will likely trigger a similar response in the other.

The emotional or temperamental qualities of newborns can elicit different responses
from parents. A "difficult" baby who constantly cries may evoke a negative reaction. The
stress may wear parents' patience and sometimes exceed their coping capabilities. Un-
soothable babies unfortunately are overrepresented among abused children. On the
other hand, an "easy" baby may respond predictably to parents' overtures. In either case,
parents must learn to accept each child's individuality.

SEEING AND HEARING

Newborns are able to respond to a wide variety of stimuli from the moment of birth. Parents can play an important role in providing numerous opportunities to foster their newborns' interest in the world and sensory and perceptual development.

Seeing

■ Provide lots of face-to-face contact.

■ Purchase, or make, simple mobiles with contrasting patterns and faces.

■ Imitate infants' facial expressions.

■ Play peek-a-boo.

■ Hold infants securely in an upright position at the shoulder, taking a walking tour of the home.

Hearing

■ Constantly talk to infants during everyday activities and diapering and feeding routines.

■ Vary the tone of voice.

■ Gently shake a variety of different safe objects such as a rattle or set of large plastic keys.

■ Use words to describe the properties and actions of objects.

■ Read simple stories in children's books.

SUMMARY

Physical Appearance

■ The average newborn is 20 inches in length and 7.5 pounds at birth. Ninety-five percent of all newborns fall between 18 and 22 inches and 5.5 and 10 pounds.

■ All newborns share certain physical characteristics. Fontanels refer to the soft spots of the skull that do not completely fuse until about 18 months of age.

■ Vernix caseosa, an oily substance covering the newborn's body, provides protection from infection at birth. Lanugo, or prenatal hair, is soon lost.

Reflexive Capabilities

■ Newborns are equipped with a variety of reflexive capabilities. Reflexes serve specific adaptive functions.

Regulation of Physiological States

■ Distinct periods of rest and activity emerge during the first month of life. Newborns' different levels of sleep and wakefulness are referred to as states.

■ Newborns' states influence their social relationship with their parents. The state of quiet alertness can encourage mutual interaction because of newborns' interest in the world.

Sensory and Perceptual Development

■ The ability to detect a particular stimulus is known as sensation. Perception involves the brain's capacity to interpret information that it receives from the senses.

■ Although vision is not fully developed at birth, newborns are able to see objects clearly from a distance of 8 to 10 inches. Their visual acuity begins to approximate adults' capabilities at about 6 months of age.

■ All the other sensory systems are fully functioning at birth. Newborns are capable of hearing, smelling, and tasting in addition to responding to tactile stimulation.

■ Newborns selectively attend to stimuli in their environment. They prefer to look at human faces and listen to high-pitched voices and recognize their mothers' odors.

Social World of Newborns

■ Newborns are programmed to engage with other people. The mutual interaction between newborns and their parents provides the building blocks of later social development.

■ Researchers have studied the benefits of early physical contact during the first few hours. The results of Klaus and Kennell's work have led to a bonding myth, or expectation of immediate infatuation, but have not been substantiated in later studies.

PROJECTS
....

1. Lie down on your stomach at home. Write a short summary of your experience (things you see, hear, smell, and feel in addition to possible hazards in the environment).

2. Using homemade materials, make a mobile reflecting current knowledge of newborns' visual and auditory preferences. Discuss the mobile's benefits to newborns.

3. Visit a store that sells toys for infants and toddlers. Use the following format to evaluate a newborn toy:

    Brand

    Cost

    Sketch of toy

    Manufacturer's description of toy on package

    Developmental value

PHYSICAL GROWTH AND DEVELOPMENT

Wise is the way of Nature, first to make
This tiny model of what is to be . . .
Hartley Coleridge, *To an Infant*

I nfants grow at a phenomenal rate. In just a few years, they gain increasing independence as they develop control over their bodies. Reflexes dominate the first weeks and months. Gradually, they are replaced with voluntary movement and intentional behavior. Infants will begin to sit, crawl, stand, and walk. They will seek and manipulate objects in their immediate vicinity. Chapter 7 explores infants' rapid progression of physical growth and mastery of motor skills.

Physical growth plays an important role during the first few years. The pituitary gland, in conjunction with the hypothalamus, secretes hormones that regulate the body's physical growth. In general, physical growth unfolds in an orderly manner. Although individual infants may differ in the actual rate of physical maturation, they will typically follow the same sequence of developmental change.

PHYSICAL GROWTH

Physical growth takes two directions simultaneously: cephalocaudal, or top to bottom, and proximodistal, or center of the body outward.

PATTERNS OF PHYSICAL GROWTH

The cephalocaudal principle is evidenced in infants' physical growth. During prenatal development, the head is the first to develop. It represents one-half of the entire body during the second month after conception. From birth to adulthood, the head doubles in size, but because the trunk and limbs continue to develop, it later comprises only one-eighth of the entire body in adults. Motor ability also follows the cephalocaudal pattern. Infants first learn to control the muscles of the head and neck. Then, they gain control of their arms, trunk, and legs. Therefore, infants learn to hold their heads upright before they can sit, sit before they can stand, and stand before they can walk.

Proximodistal development adheres to a different but complementary process. Again, it is illustrated in prenatal development. The head and trunk grow first. The arms and legs and the hands and feet follow later. Control of the large muscles precedes control of the small muscles of the body. Therefore, toddlers' ability to jump and run, activities involving large muscles, develop before they can draw and put a simple puzzle together, activities involving small muscles. Over time, toddlers perform increasingly precise and sophisticated tasks such as using a spoon to eat or fastening a button on a shirt. As a result, they develop a sense of competence as they succeed in accomplishing desired actions.

In addition to cephalocaudal and proximodistal development, physical growth reflects increasing differentiation and integration during the first few years of life. *The progression from global to specific movements of the body* is referred to as the **orthogenetic principle** (Werner, 1957). In other words, at first, newborns exhibit generalized, undirected movements of the body. When one part moves, other parts of the body will follow such as the simultaneous movement of both arms and legs. Infants gradually begin to engage in refined, coordinated movements as further maturation of the brain occurs. As infants integrate different movements of the body, they will start to perform complex tasks successfully such as grasping and manipulating objects with their thumb and forefinger instead of using the whole hand.

Physical growth is genetically determined. Genes control the timetable that directs the sequence of physical growth. However, in extreme circumstances, environmental conditions can have an impact on physical growth. Noted British biologist Conrad Waddington used the term **canalization** to refer to *the tendency of physical growth to return to its normal pattern after prolonged illness or dietary deficiency* (Waddington, 1957). Not all

HISTORICALLY SPEAKING

PHYSICAL GROWTH

Arnold Gesell

The Psychology of Early Growth, 1938

There has been considerable controversy about the use of the word *growth.* Some have maintained that its meaning should be restricted to changes in size, while others have employed it to denote all of the changes which an organism manifests in its progress with age.

Source: Gesell and Thompson (1938), p. 194.

aspects of physical growth are canalized. Environmental factors such as extreme malnutrition will inevitably affect children's physical growth. Therefore, although genetic factors determine the specific sequence of physical growth, the environment plays an important role.

CHANGES IN HEIGHT AND WEIGHT

During the first few years, extremely rapid physical growth occurs in both height and weight. At birth, newborns are 20 inches long and weigh 7.5 pounds on the average. On the first birthday, their height increases 50% (10 inches) to 30 inches. Before the end of the second year, it increases another 25% to 35 inches. Infants do grow in spurts, sometimes a half an inch in 24 hours, after a period of minimal change. Before each growth spurt, infants may exhibit increased irritability (Lampl, Veldhuis, & Johnson, 1992).

With inches come pounds. Weight doubles before the end of 5 months after birth and triples before the first birthday. However, it slows considerably during the next 2 years. Only 4 to 6 pounds, or about a half a pound per month, is gained thereafter (Lowrey, 1986). Figure 7–1 shows the height and weight gains from birth to age 2.

SKELETAL GROWTH

Changes in infants' height and weight result from the growth of bones. *The formation of bones,* or **ossification**, actually begins during the embryonic period of prenatal development. The embryonic skeleton consists of fibrous tissues. During the 6th week, the tissues start to harden as calcium and other minerals accumulate. Skeletal growth actually occurs at both ends of every bone. Just before birth, **epiphyses**, *areas of the bone that manufacture new cells,* appear. Columns of newly formed cells are stacked in the spaces between the epiphyses and the main shaft of the bone. The cells extend the length of the bone, a prolonged process that continues until the end of adolescence (Tanner, 1990). Eventually, the production of new cells ceases. The main shaft of the bone then fuses with the epiphyses.

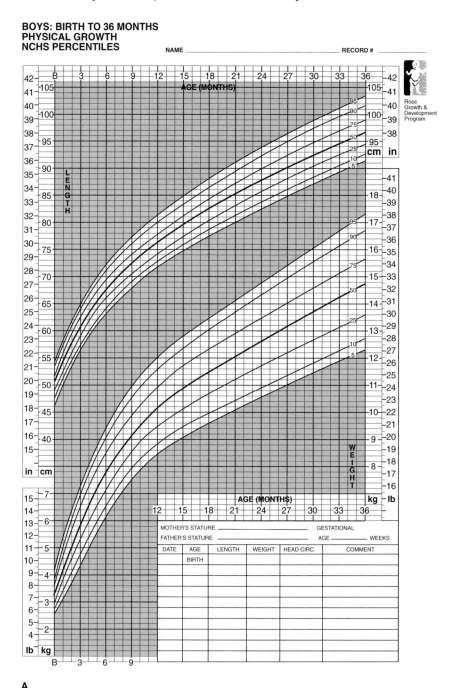

A

FIGURE 7–1 Gains in Height and Weight from Birth to 2 Boys (A) and Girls (B)
Source: Snow, C. W. (1998). *Infant Development* (2nd ed.). Upper Saddle River, NJ: Prentice Hall, pp. 322–323.
Reprinted with permission.

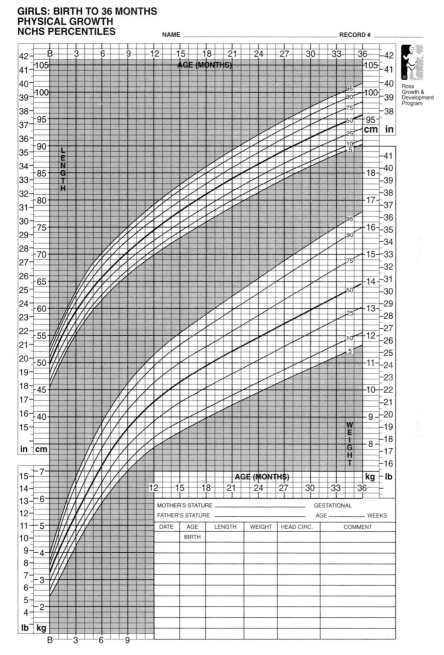

FIGURE 7–1 Continued

If there are medical concerns about infants' physical growth, x-rays are taken to obtain a measure of maturity. The wrists and hands of infants provide an accurate index of skeletal maturation. A series of x-rays record changes over time. The number of manufactured cells is counted and compared to the norms of children of the same age. Differences between the sexes have been found in studies. Girls tend to mature at an accelerated rate and reach their eventual height before boys. The trend begins before birth. Girls' skeletal age during the fetal stage is 3 weeks ahead of boys, but at birth, the gap widens to about 4 to 6 weeks, a trend that continues until puberty (Loesch et al., 1995).

APPEARANCE OF TEETH

Two sets of teeth appear in the normal course of physical growth. *The first set of teeth* is known as **deciduous**, or primary, **teeth** (the Latin root of the word literally means "to fall"). The primary teeth, embedded in the jaws of the fetus, begin to calcify from the 4th to 6th months of gestation. The first tooth usually erupts at 6 months of age. The central incisors appear first on the lower jaw and later on the upper jaw. Next, the lateral incisors, first molars, cuspids, and second molars follow in sequence. Although there are individual variations, the average infant has about six to eight teeth at 12 months and 14 to 16 teeth at 2 years of age. A complete set of 20 primary teeth is in place before the third birthday (see Figure 7–2).

Not all infants teethe or react with discomfort to sore or swollen gums as their primary teeth emerge. Some exhibit severe symptoms such as biting or fretting, but others do not appear to be affected at all. To alleviate any discomfort, a number of steps can be followed. Medication can be prescribed to numb painful gums. However, a teething ring is generally used to relieve discomfort. Parents can massage the inflamed gums with a clean fingertip. Some teething infants may chew or gnaw on objects. Consequently, nursing mothers may decide to wean their infants or switch to a bottle.

Proper dental care starts with the primary teeth. Permanent teeth do not appear until about 6 years of age on the average. The primary teeth perform a number of important functions. The premature loss of primary teeth leads to serious problems such as improper occlusion, or alignment of permanent teeth, and poor speech later. Cavities result from plaque and food containing sugar. The bacteria in plaque produce acids dissolving the protective enamel of teeth. Parents are advised to take appropriate actions to prevent premature decay. The following steps have been suggested:

■ **Ask a pediatrician or dentist about fluoride.** Fluoride increases the resistance of teeth.

■ **Clean the infant's teeth initially with a clean washcloth and later a toothbrush.** After 18 months of age, a small, soft toothbrush should be used at least once a day, preferably before bedtime.

■ **Use a bottle only during mealtimes.** The infant should be held at an incline to prevent possible ear infections.

■ **Never give a bottle with milk, juice, or any other sweetened beverage at nap or bedtime.** The sugar in the liquid is extremely damaging to teeth if left to puddle in the mouth.

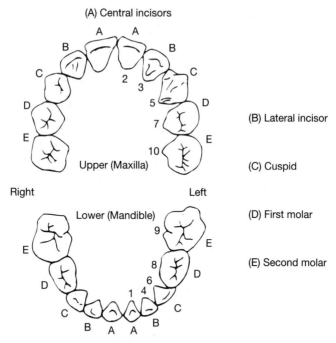

Tooth	Upper jaw (months)	Lower jaw (months)
Central incisor	8–10	6–10
Lateral incisor	9–13	10–16
Cuspid	16–22	17–23
First molar	13–19	14–18
Second molar	25–33	23–31

FIGURE 7–2 Appearance of Primary Teeth

■ **Do not put a sweetening agent on a pacifier.** As with a bottle, sugar increases the chances of decay.

■ **Visit a dentist on the first birthday and at regular intervals thereafter.** Parents should remember that good dental hygiene starts before, not after, the appearance of permanent teeth.

MATURATION OF BRAIN

The brain begins to develop during the first few weeks after conception. As the fertilized egg enters its 2nd month of prenatal development, rapid division and differentiation of cells continue. At the end of 8 weeks, the brain and spinal column appear. At birth, the brain contains about 100 billion **neurons**, or *cells that receive and transmit information in the brain* (see Figure 7–3). It weighs about 1 pound and represents about 15% of the total

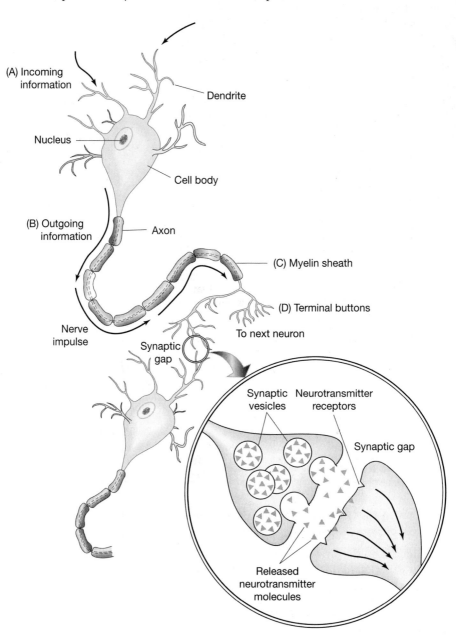

FIGURE 7–3 Structure of Neuron

body weight. In comparison, the brain of adults weighs 3 pounds, or about 2% of their total weight. The brain continues its rapid growth during infancy, particularly the first 6 months after birth. It gains about 50 and 75% of its eventual weight at 6 months and 2 years of age, respectively.

DEVELOPMENT OF NEURONS

The brain consists of two distinct types of cells. Neurons refer to the nerve cells of the brain. Each neuron contains a nucleus and cytoplasm, the substance surrounding the nucleus. Connected to each neuron are **dendrites** and **axons**, *branchlike structures that either receive information from or transmit information to other neurons.* Neurons differ in size because of the length of their axons. Axons vary from a fraction of an inch in the brain to several feet long in the spinal cord. Information sent from one neuron to another is received in the dendrites. *The chemical substances that are involved in the transmission of neural information* are called **neurotransmitters**. Neurons themselves are not tightly packed. *The spaces between neurons* are known as **synapses**.

Glial cells occupy half of the cellular volume in the brain. They do not transmit information as neurons do but support **myelinization**, *a process that coats the axons of neurons with an insulating sheath of **myelin**, a white, fatty substance that improves the efficiency of neural transmission.* Myelinization parallels the development of the brain after birth. It proceeds at a rapid rate during the first few years, dramatically increasing the brain's volume, but it continues until the late teens. Newborns are equipped to process basic sensory information. The neural pathways between the brain and sensory organs have already been coated with myelin during the prenatal period. However, the acquisition of highly complex skills depends on further myelinization. The sequential progression of developmental milestones, such as crawling and walking, tying shoelaces and kicking a ball, is tied to the process of myelinization.

Further maturation of the brain results from repeated engagement with the real world, sometimes alone but often in the presence of supportive adults.
Photo courtesy of Tami Dawson, Photo Resource Hawaii.

During the first few weeks and months, a series of extraordinary changes transforms the brain. Trillions of connections between neurons are formed "in a display of biological exuberance" (Nash, 1997, p. 50). The brain requires appropriate stimulation to thrive. Deprived of stimulation, the brain suffers. Whenever infants look at visual patterns, hear their parents' voices, smell and taste new kinds of food, and feel a soothing stroke, the brain exhibits a burst of neural activity. Although brain development involves physiological transformation, changes occur in a distinctly human context (Greenspan, 1997). In the first few months, the brain explodes with the formation of new connections resulting from parents' interaction with their infants and, conversely, infants' interactions with their physical and social world (see Figure 7–4). The profusion of connections provides exceptional flexibility and resiliency in infants and young children as they learn new skills or overcome setbacks from injuries to the nervous system (Bell & Fox, 1994). As part of its normal develoment, the brain begins to prune excessive connections between neurons. Repeated practice and experience can ensure the survival of neural connections controlling the first steps to the first words (Huttenlocher, 1994).

DEVELOPMENT OF CEREBRAL CORTEX

The brain is composed of three major parts. The hindbrain and midbrain attain maturity before the forebrain, which contains the cerebral cortex, the seat of highly developed human intelligence. Basic functions of the body are controlled in the hindbrain. An area of the hindbrain involved in the regulation of respiration and circulation is known as the *medulla oblongata*. It is directly connected to the spinal cord. Another area, the cerebellum, meaning "little brain," regulates complex voluntary muscular movement. It develops rapidly during the first year and reaches its full size on about the fifth birthday. The midbrain controls reflexes and emotions and relays visual and auditory information to the cerebral cortex (Haines, 1999).

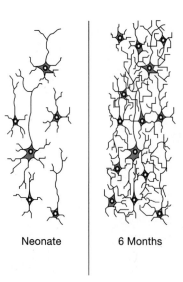

Neonate 6 Months 2 Years

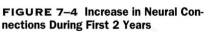

FIGURE 7–4 Increase in Neural Connections During First 2 Years
An intricate network of neurons develops rapidly during the first few years of life. The brain's functional maturity depends on the increased connectivity between neurons.

The diligent work of Jesse Conel contributed to modern knowledge of the cerebral cortex. In a series of eight volumes spanning a period of 28 years, he published his studies of the cerebral cortex from birth to 6 years of age (Conel, 1939–1967). The cerebral cortex controls not only perception and voluntary movement but also distinctly human functions such as reasoning ability and language. The largest structure of the brain, it represents 85% of the brain's total weight. It is divided into two separate hemispheres connected by a band of fibers referred to as the *corpus callosum,* meaning "callous body." Each hemisphere regulates the opposite side of the body (i.e., the left hemisphere controls the right side, and the right hemisphere controls the left side). The two cerebral hemispheres are the last part of the brain to develop. Therefore, environmental conditions exert a profound influence during the first few years of development.

The cerebral cortex is divided into four different lobes, or areas, of the brain. Each lobe performs highly specific functions. Located at the back of each hemisphere are the occipital lobes. They interpret visual information. At the top of each hemisphere lie the parietal lobes. They control the sense of touch and spatial information. Situated on

AMAZING BRAIN

Scientific research has started to unravel the mysteries of the human brain. The rapid changes occurring during the first few years result from the brain's physiological maturation. At birth, it contains about about 100 billion neurons. Over time, the neurons establish contacts with each other, eventually forming an intricate network of 100 trillion connections. Essential functions such as breathing, controlling the heartbeat, and regulating the body's temperature have been programmed before birth. However, trillions of other neural connections are made afterwards. Connections are formed continuously as stimulation from the environment is received. When infants scan a human face or touch a textured surface, neurons in the visual cortex of the brain form connections (Begley, 1996).

Sensory input is required to connect neurons in the different areas of the brain. Neural connections are maximized when sensory input is received during critical periods in the brain's development. Language is a good example. When infants repeatedly hear certain phonemes such as /b/ and /p/ in their parents' speech, the sounds their ears receive stimulate the establishment of neural connections in the auditory cortex. The brain actually begins to map the phonemes of the parents' language. The basic neural circuitry is completed before the first birthday. The window of opportunity to learn a second language may be closed before age 10 (teens and adults can learn a second language but only with difficulty). Once connections are established, the ability to form new connections may be lost. Therefore, ample sensory stimulation is needed in the early years to encourage optimal brain development. Parents and other adults assume the responsibility of providing a varied environment at home or in other contexts (Greenough, 1991).

the side of each hemisphere are the temporal lobes. They regulate auditory information and store verbal memory. Finally, positioned in the front of each hemisphere are the frontal lobes. They are involved in reasoning and solving problems. Different areas of the cerebral cortex mature at different rates. The frontal lobes take years to develop. Any accidental injury to the frontal lobes results in an inability to reason and plan. However, the brain demonstrates remarkable **plasticity**, or *the ability of other areas of the brain to assume the functions of the damaged regions.* If the injury occurs in infancy, the brain can reorganize itself and find compensatory neural pathways. Other parts of the brain can take over tasks handled in the damaged region.

Although the two hemispheres resemble each other, they specialize in different functions. *The specialization of functions in the two hemispheres of the cerebral cortex* is referred to as **lateralization**. The left hemisphere, in particular, handles verbal functions, both spoken and written language. Two areas of the left hemisphere are specifically related to language—Broca's and Wernick's areas are involved in using and understanding language (Pinker, 1999). The right hemisphere, in contrast, specializes in nonverbal functions, including artistic and musical abilities and the expression of emotions. The division of labor increases the brain's efficiency. Different regions of the two hemispheres develop at different rates. New abilities begin to emerge as the brain matures. For example, coordination between the eyes and hands gradually increases infants' exploration of the immediate environment. However, areas of the brain controlling reasoning ability, the frontal lobes, continue to develop even into the second and third decades of life. Both heredity and the environment play a mutual role. Although genes provide the initial building blocks, further development of the brain results from direct involvement with the physical and social environment.

As the two hemispheres continue to lateralize, or specialize in specific functions, infants begin to exhibit handedness. The preference of one hand over the other reflects the dominance of one hemisphere (Kolb & Winshaw, 1995). Because each hemisphere controls the opposite side of the body, the left hemisphere dominates among right-handed people. Others rely on their left hand or use both with equal facility. Handedness begins to appear in infancy but continues to develop in early childhood. At 6 months of age, the majority of infants grasp objects primarily with their right hand (Hopkins & Ronnqvist, 1998). Research on infants' electrical patterns in their brains show distinct differences between the left and right hemispheres. However, handedness does not stabilize until 2 years of age as lateralization accelerates (Chiron et al., 1997; Simon, 1997). Further, handedness does not always follow a consistent pattern in the first few years. Although intellectual precocity has been linked to left-handedness (Benbow, 1986), children should never be forced to choose a particular hand or switch hands.

INFLUENCES ON PHYSICAL GROWTH

Physical growth involves the mutual interaction between heredity and the environment. Although physical growth follows a genetically determined course, environmental factors such as diet and malnutrition can affect infants' optimal development.

TOILET TRAINING

Toddlers' control of the bladder and bowel is directly linked to their bodies' maturation. During the first year, infants eliminate body wastes reflexively. They must learn to regulate the muscles governing the retention and elimination. Only toward the end of the second year do toddlers gain increasing control of their body. Research indicates that parents waiting patiently until about 2 years of age tend to reduce the average length of time it takes to train their toddlers. In general, parents trying to "push" their toddlers may actually prolong the process and even aggravate the situation (Eden, 1992; Spitz, 1993).

Toddlers gain a sense of competence when they learn to use the toilet on their own. Their success depends on the following factors:

■ **Readiness.** The age toddlers begin toilet training varies. Some start during the last half of the second year; others wait until the following year. Each toddler's readiness underscores individual rates of development. However, it typically starts when two milestones converge: increasing control of muscles, namely, the bladder and rectum, and communication of need ("I have to go!").

Toddlers generally follow a predictable sequence in learning to use the toilet. First comes control of their bowels. Next, daytime control of the bladder is attained. Last comes nighttime control of the bladder. Toddlers usually indicate need with consistent words and gestures to communicate. Parents, of course, may need to assist in removing and putting on clothes.

■ **Equipment.** Because toilets are basically designed to accommodate adults, modified equipment is often required to meet the special needs of toddlers. A modified seat is often used to adjust the rim of the toilet to toddlers' size. A non-slippery stool can be used to provide easy access to the toilet. It further serves as a footrest while toddlers sit on the toilet.

Parents can purchase a commercial potty instead of using a standard toilet. A potty is specifically designed to meet toddlers' needs. A container on the bottom is used to dispose of the contents. A plastic, not wooden, frame is recommended to prevent the spread of infectious diseases.

The ability to control the bladder and bowel will foster toddlers' sense of independence. Parents' loving, caring attitude can go a long way in ensuring success. The best advice is to take their cues from the child. Other helpful hints include never force a child to sit on a toilet or potty and always give positive feedback and encouragement.

DIET

Because the brain and body develop rapidly during infancy, a balanced diet plays a critical role. It sustains physical growth and provides energy to support infants' physical activity (Pipes & Trahms, 1993). During the first year of life, human milk or commercial formula is well-suited to infants' nutritional needs. Semisolid food is generally introduced during the last half of the first year. Many parents face a difficult question in deciding whether to breast- or bottle-feed infants. Until the turn of the century, all infants were fed with human milk. However, during the 1930s to 1940s, a period corresponding to the increasing medicalization of childbirth, "experts" advised parents to bottle-feed. In the early 1970s, about 75% of all infants in the United States were bottle-fed. Since then, based on research emphasizing the importance of bonding, obstetric practices started to change again, highlighting the nutritional benefits of breast-feeding. Today, about 60% of all mothers breast-feed their infants.

Human milk offers numerous physiological benefits. Its nutritional superiority has never been contested. Commercial formula contains the same basic nutritional content of human milk but differs qualitatively. Specifically, the right balance of protein in human milk increases its digestibility compared to commercial formula (Springen, 1998). Further, human milk provides immunological protection during the first few days of life. Mothers' breasts produce colostrum, a yellowish fluid containing antibodies, before the actual production of milk begins. Colostrum reduces respiratory illnesses and allergic reactions because it increases resistance to infections. Therefore, human milk contains built-in protections.

Commercial formulas also offer numerous benefits to mothers who choose not to breast-feed and fathers and others wanting to bottle-feed. The decision to breast- or bottle-feed depends on situational factors such as cost and convenience (the advantages and disadvantages of each are further discussed in Chapter 11).

MALNUTRITION

Worldwide, large proportions of children suffer from malnutrition. An estimated 40 to 60% of children are undernourished, and another 4 to 7% are severely malnourished (UNICEF, 1998). Infants represent a particularly vulnerable group. Prolonged malnutrition during pregnancy and the first few years can lead to irreversible damage. Optimal development of both the brain and body can be adversely affected. Long-term malnutrition is associated with stunted physical growth and mental retardation. In particular, it actually hampers the process of myelinization and interferes with the structural organization of the brain. Malnourished infants will exhibit decreased responsiveness and heightened irritability, affecting their ability to engage in social interaction with others (Brazelton et al., 1977).

Although infants show remarkable resiliency, demonstrating the ability to recover from setbacks, malnutrition invariably leads to permanent intellectual deficits if it occurs in the first year of life. In a longitudinal study conducted in Barbados, the effects of severe malnutrition on infants were examined (Galler, 1984; Galler & Ramsey, 1989). The researchers found that at age 11, children experiencing severe malnutrition during the first year of life later exhibited significant cognitive and behavioral deficits such as poor performance in school and impaired attention. The problems continued until age 18. Even mild to moderate malnutrition had adverse consequences on the physical and cognitive development of infants. In other long-term studies conducted in Egypt, Kenya, and Zimbabwe, mildly to moderately malnourished infants demonstrated delayed forms of play and cognitive abilities (Cosminsky, Mhloyi, & Ewbank, 1993; Wachs et al., 1992).

Two dietary diseases can result from severe malnutrition. **Marasmus**, *an extreme form of malnutrition that leads to a wasted condition of the body*, occurs in the first year. Physical and behavioral consequences can be seen (swollen stomach and listlessness). The scarcity of food can become a deadly cycle. If mothers themselves are severely malnourished, they may not be able to produce a sufficient supply of breast milk. **Kwashiorkor**, *a form of severe malnutrition that results from a deficiency of protein in children's diets*, affects children from 1 to 3 years of age. Symptoms include enlarged abdomens, swollen feet, loss of hair, and lethargy. Death is likely to follow if not treated immediately (Franco et al., 1999; Manary, Broadhead, & Yarasheski, 1998).

Even mild to moderate malnutrition entails serious repercussions. In the United States, poverty is the leading cause of malnutrition, affecting an estimated one in five children. The lack of resources limits the overall quality of their diet. In addition, poverty increases the level of stress in families, which can interfere with children's optimal physical growth and cognitive and psychosocial development. Preventive steps are needed to ameliorate the devastating effects of malnutrition. Children need a well-balanced diet, and parents need to increase their awareness of children's nutritional needs.

MOTOR DEVELOPMENT

Coordinated movements of the body are known as motor skills. There are two broad types. **Gross motor skills** refer to *movements that involve the entire body*. When infants crawl and walk, they use large muscles to control their arms and legs. **Fine motor skills** involve *movements that require complex coordination between the eyes and hands*. When toddlers stack blocks and eat with a spoon, they use small muscles to control manual dexterity. The sequential progression of gross and fine motor skills is connected to further maturation of the brain.

Motor development fosters interaction with the immediate environment. **Locomotion**, or *movement from one place to another*, greatly expands infants' exploration. As they learn to crawl and walk, for example, infants encounter a multitude of experiences. Gradually, they begin to exercise individual choice in seeking or avoiding objects or people. Similarly, the emergence of fine motor skills fosters cognitive processes. Infants will acquire specific information about the physical properties of objects, such as texture, as **prehension**, or *the ability to grasp objects*, develops. Deliberate exploration of the world facilitates the development of the brain. In turn, as the brain's structural organization improves, highly complex skills foster new ways of exploring the world.

GROSS MOTOR DEVELOPMENT

Scientific observations of infants did not start until the late 19th and early 20th centuries. In the United States, the pioneering work of Arnold Gesell and others, notably Mary Shirley (1931–1933) and Nancy Bayley (1935), spurred interest in infants' development. Attention centered primarily on the establishment of norms, providing information about infants' current development in comparison to a standardized sample. Gesell accepted the long-held view that heredity plays a dominant role in motor development. He filmed infants to record developmental changes over time. His collection of over 3,000 photographs filled two volumes in *An Atlas of Infant Behavior*, published in 1934.

HISTORICALLY SPEAKING

MOTOR DEVELOPMENT

Myrtle McGraw
Growth, 1935
    Whenever there is development or growth there is also a period of inception, incubation, consummation, and decline. Nothing springs forth full-grown. Development is extremely gradual. There are spurts and rhythms in development, but it can safely be said that nothing is created without preparation.

Source: McGraw (1935), pp. 304–305.

Gesell devised a normative scale on the basis of his detailed work. It consisted of four broad areas: motor, language, adaptive behavior, and personal and social behavior (Gesell, 1925). Motor development was further divided into two sections. Postural control and locomotion involved the use of large muscles, whereas prehension focused on the control of small muscles. The inclusion of postural control in Gesell's scale reflected his view of maturation as a genetically determined mechanism. In his own words, he remarked:

> Posture is behavior. Postural patterns . . . are determined by the maturity and organization of the infants' central neural equipment. (Gesell, 1934, p. 44)

Gesell amassed an enormous amount of descriptive and normative data during his career. However, his work depicted motor development as a collection of unrelated skills (Thelen, 1987, 1989). Currently, researchers view motor development as a system, or a series of interdependent components forming a whole. In other words, new milestones build on previously acquired skills in producing increasingly complex behavior (Hofsten, 1989; Thelen & Spencer, 1998). Evidence is seen in postural control and locomotion. Infants are able to sit, crawl, stand, and walk once control of the head and trunk is achieved.

Postural Control and Locomotion.   Postural control involves the position of the head and trunk. Cephalocaudal development progresses from the top to the bottom of the body (see Figure 7–5). When infants are held upright, control of the head is typically achieved at about 6 weeks of age. At 2 months, infants begin to elevate the head with their arms while in a prone position. They later learn to sit independently at 7 months. Then, at 11 months, before they actually start to walk, they learn to stand independently. Proximodistal development is clearly demonstrated in the acquisition of postural control. Infants' control of the head, trunk, arms, and legs appears before coordination of their hands and feet.

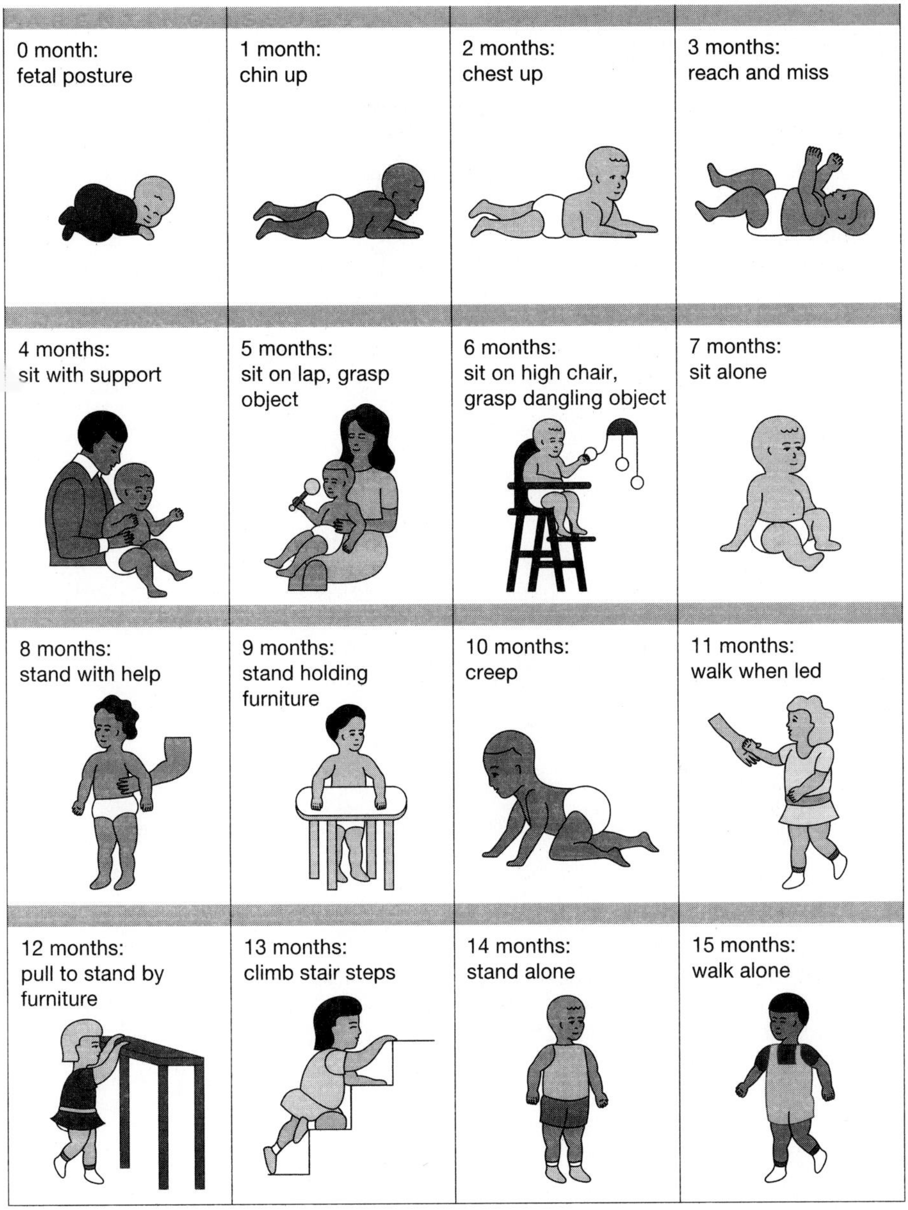

0 month: fetal posture	1 month: chin up	2 months: chest up	3 months: reach and miss
4 months: sit with support	5 months: sit on lap, grasp object	6 months: sit on high chair, grasp dangling object	7 months: sit alone
8 months: stand with help	9 months: stand holding furniture	10 months: creep	11 months: walk when led
12 months: pull to stand by furniture	13 months: climb stair steps	14 months: stand alone	15 months: walk alone

FIGURE 7–5 Sequence of Gross and Fine Motor Development

(A) Newborns push with their knees and toes to creep.

(B) Infants lift their heads, but pushing movements diminish in the lower extremities.

(C) Control of head and shoulders improves.

(D) Ability to support the upper body increases.

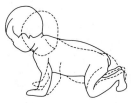

(E) The midsection is raised, but rocking movements of the arms and legs are made.

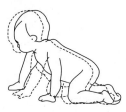

(F) Coordinated activities of the arms and legs allow crawling movements.

FIGURE 7–6 Postural Phases in Development of Creeping and Crawling

Changes in postural control correspond with infants' increasing ability to move from one place to another. Infants enter a new chapter as they master locomotion. As they learn to walk, they gain an increased sense of independence and competence. Not surprisingly, an interest in doing things on their own is expressed. Frequently heard is "no," an affirmation of their growing autonomy. They too begin to hear "no" from adults. Parents and professional caregivers must take preventive steps to protect infants' safety. Specific recommendations are further discussed in Chapter 11.

Locomotion follows an orderly sequence. As with postural control, it proceeds according to the principles of cephalocaudal and proximodistal development. Infants first learn to roll from side to back at 2 months and back to side at 4 months of age. Their ability to coordinate movement begins to improve dramatically during the remainder of the first year. Once infants roll onto their stomach, they usually engage in crawling movements, their first effective mode of locomotion. A series of increasingly complex steps are taken in mastering the ability to crawl (see Figure 7–6). Control of the head and shoulders is attained at 2 months of age. However, the coordinated movement of the midsection of the body takes time. Even when they do get onto their hands and knees, infants lack the ability to coordinate movements of both their arms and legs. Only after repeated practice are different units of the entire body integrated into alternating movements of the arms and legs at about 7 months of age (Adolph, 1997; Adolph, Vereijken, & Denny, 1998).

During the next 4 to 5 months, infants' mode of locomotion gradually shifts from crawling to walking. The ability to walk caps an exciting year of rapid physical growth and development. Maturation of the brain is linked to concomitant progress in locomotion. As myelinization of the cerebral cortex accelerates and neuromuscular control of the body improves, infants typically take their first independent steps at the age of 12 months. Balance steadily increases as time passes. Infants' characteristic gait in walking has earned a new moniker of toddlers, as they take short, unsteady steps with a wide base. Toddlers soon start to run after they learn to walk. Although coordinated running movements are not acquired until 18 months, a few rapid steps are taken to reach the next base of support, such as a piece of furniture or set of loving hands. Their first attempts to jump also are observed at about 18 months. Toddlers like to jump from a low surface such as the last step of the stairs but do not obtain the ability to jump in place until 6 months later.

Although postural control and locomotion follow a predetermined course, demonstrating the influence of heredity, the environment plays a limited but important role. At first, research supported Gesell's view of maturation on infants' motor development (Gesell, 1940). A widely cited study was often used to bolster his claim. Dennis and Dennis (1940) examined traditional Hopi's cradling practices in southwestern United States. Infants were tightly swaddled on a flat board during the initial months of life. Only when they were required to be washed or changed were they unwrapped. The subjects were compared with nontraditionally raised infants to determine the cultural effects of cradling practices on motor development. The results showed that the two groups of infants did not differ significantly in their acquisition of basic motor skills. However, since then, researchers realize that infants do need opportunities to practice emerging motor skills. Repeated practice does not necessarily accelerate the rate of motor development, but it does foster infants' sense of competence, as any adult who observes a child's mastery of a previously difficult task knows.

FINE MOTOR DEVELOPMENT

As infants gain increasing control of their body, their ability to explore their world correspondingly improves. They begin to manipulate objects in highly effective ways during the first 6 months. Their active exploration and direct involvement expand both their physical and cognitive development. The voluntary coordination of the eyes, arms, hands, and fingers is required in learning about the physical properties of objects. It occurs in two stages. The first stage, prereaching movements, begins shortly after birth (Van der Fits & Hadders-Algra, 1998). Newborns frequently attempt to reach for an object as they simultaneously make grasping movements with their hands. They often fail to grasp an object, even after repeated attempts, because they close their hands too early or too late. Prereaching movements demonstrate the proximodistal direction of physical development. Initially, poorly coordinated swiping actions precede eventual refined movements of the hand and fingers (Bertenthal & Hofsten, 1998).

Infants enter the second stage of voluntary coordination at 3 months. Global attempts to grasp objects are gradually replaced with visually guided reaching movements. Considerable concentration is needed to grasp objects successfully. Infants at first glance back and forth at the objects that they want to grasp and at their hands. The ability to grasp objects improves steadily with practice. Infants soon start to guide their reaching movements with a single glance (Out et al., 1998). The eventual shift from prereaching to visually guided reaching actions corresponds with simultaneous changes of the cerebral cortex. Infants' increased neuromuscular control of the body accompanies continued maturation of the cortical structures of the brain. However, behavioral complexity does not depend only on biological maturation. The opportunity to manipulate a variety of objects will induce changes in the brain that in turn result in complex behavioral patterns (Rochat & Goubet, 1995).

Prehension. In addition to infants' voluntary coordination improving, their ability to grasp objects also makes remarkable strides during the first year. Infants initially rely on an **ulnar grasp**, *a clumsy motion that involves the closure of the fingers on the palm,* at about 4 months of age. They typically hold on to objects indefinitely until something diverts their attention and the hand opens. Because objects are likely to be placed in the mouth, constant vigilance is required to prevent any accidental choking. Toys that contain small pieces pose a serious danger. Before the end of the first year, a **pincer grasp**, *a highly refined grasp that involves the thumb's opposition to the forefinger,* appears such as being able to pick up a raisin. Infants' manipulation of a wide range of objects improves significantly once it develops. Thereafter, exploration of the world is now taken to new heights.

During the next 2 years of life, toddlers continue to spend a lot of time in exploring and manipulating objects. They are successfully able to build a tower with cubes, remove a pellet from a bottle, put pegs in a pegboard, and do simple puzzles. They begin to scribble on pieces of paper with a crayon. A straight line can be imitated if modeled. Improved coordination of their eyes and hands increases toddlers' ability to drink from a

LOCOMOTION AND PREHENSION

LOCOMOTION

Infants typically take their first steps at the end of the first year. With practice, other complex activities such as running and jumping begin to emerge during the second and third years.

Birth to 1 Year

- Place the infant on his or her side and, with a toy, encourage a rolling movement to his or her stomach or back.

- Put a toy in front of the infant while on his or her stomach to initiate a forward movement on his or her hands and knees.

- Create a path with obstacles such as chairs and boxes and play "follow the leader."

- Support the infant's efforts to hold on to low tables and chairs as he or she "cruises" from one place to another in the room.

- Stand the infant a few small steps from a desired object and gradually withdraw support.

1 to 3 Years

- Provide a variety of pushing and pulling activities such as pushing a box or pulling a toy with wheels.

- Make a simple line on the floor with masking tape to walk on and later connect lines that go in different directions.

- Encourage the toddler to jump from the last step of the stairs or a flat platform.

- Sing "Pop goes the weasel" to facilitate the toddler's ability to jump in place.

- Play a variety of music with fast and slow tempos to encourage physical movement in a creative way.

PREHENSION

Infants' ability to grasp and manipulate objects proceeds in an sequential and orderly manner. Although they initially make global movements in trying to reach objects, with practice, they increasingly engage in purposeful actions.

Birth to 1 Year

- Dangle an enticing object in front of the infant to encourage his or her visually guided grasping movements.

- Place an object into the infant's hand and describe its features, such as shape and texture.

- Provide a plastic hammer or wooden spoon to pound on different pots and pans.

- Put a piece of cereal in an unbreakable bottle with a narrow neck and praise the infant's efforts to retrieve the object.

- Look at pictures in durable books while turning the thick pages together.

1 to 3 Years

- Provide a pegboard with large plastic pegs to insert.

- Place small blocks on the table and build a tower together.

- Put uncooked oatmeal or puffed rice into a box and ask the toddler to find hidden toys.

- Tape a large sheet of paper to draw on the table or floor with a variety of crayons and markers.

- Give the toddler a large unused paintbrush and a pail of water to "paint" an outside wall or fence.

cup, use a spoon at mealtimes, and remove clothes, such as their shirt, socks, and shoes. Their increasing sense of autonomy frequently taxes adults' patience, but toddlers learn from trial and error. Criticisms of their efforts sometimes lead to an emotional test of wills. On the other hand, a healthy dose of encouragement works wonders in fostering toddlers' sense of pride in their accomplishments.

CULTURAL INFLUENCES

Observations of infants in different cultures provide direct evidence that repeated practice affects the onset of universal motor milestones. The Ache, a hunting and gathering group living in the rainforest of eastern Paraguay, illustrate the point (Kaplan & Dove, 1987; Morelli & Tronick, 1992). Because of the dangers of living in a rainforest, Ache mothers discourage their infants' independent exploration and locomotion during the first few years. The infants spend 80 to 100% of their time in direct physical contact with their mothers.

Although Ache infants follow the same sequence of developmental stages, they acquire certain motor skills at a later time. Ache traditional child-rearing practices seem to inhibit rather than stimulate the acquisition of sitting and walking. Ache children are gradually allowed to move on their own and engage in increasingly complex activities. In just a few years, their mastery in scaling tall trees attests to their exceptional motor skills.

In contrast, African infants usually achieve motor milestones at an early age, particularly in locomotion. The Efe, short-statured hunters and gatherers in the forested areas

Opportunities to practice emerging gross and fine motor skills enhance children's sense of competence.
Photo courtesy of Tami Dawson, Photo Resource Hawaii.

WEST INDIAN INFANTS' MOTOR DEVELOPMENT

Do particular child-rearing practices accelerate infants' motor development? Although heredity influences the universal sequence of postural control and locomotion, environmental factors affect the rate that infants acquire certain motor skills. West Indian infants in Jamaica demonstrate early maturity of neuromuscular control of gross motor behavior. They tend to be advanced in the attainment of sitting and walking skills in comparison to their counterparts in west European countries (Grantham-McGregor & Back, 1971). West Indian parents do not try to train their infants. They engage in culturally determined child-rearing practices that appear to facilitate their infants' early motor development (Hopkins & Westra, 1988).

West Indian parents follow a prescribed set of handling practices, primarily involving stretching exercises and vigorous massages during the first months after birth. The exercises and massages are incorporated into daily caregiving routines, particularly after a bath (Hopkins & Westra, 1990). The arms and legs are stretched first. Infants are then suspended from one arm at a time or upside down from both of their ankles. Next, their parents may hold their head on both sides. Their head is gently lifted and lowered. As infants lie in downward position, their parents will stroke their backs at least four times on both sides of the paravertebral line. Lastly, the infants may be gently tossed into the air and caught.

At 3 months of age, West Indian infants are encouraged to sit and walk. They are propped into an upright position with cushions to strengthen their sitting ability. Once stepping movements are noticed, infants are given the opportunity to walk. They get practice first on the lap and stomach of their parents and later on the floor. The daily exercises continue into the last half of the first year until infants learn to walk independently on their own. They receive constant reassurance and encouragement from others as their ability to walk steadily increases over time.

Therefore, West Indian parents' cultural traditions and beliefs exert a profound influence on their child-rearing practices. They believe exercises and massages minimize accidental injury and promote physical attractiveness (Hopkins, 1991).

of Zaire, share child-rearing responsibilities among all members, males and females. Efe mothers provide one-half of the total care during the first few years, but the physical and social arrangement of the group encourages the involvement of other adults (Morelli & Tronick, 1991; Tronick & Winn, 1992). Efe infants are given numerous opportunities to practice emerging motor skills during social play. Children of different ages also participate, a practice that further encourages infants' mastery of motor skills.

In sum, early motor skills, as with other aspects of development, reflect the complex interaction between nature and nurture. Heredity ensures that all infants across the world follow a similar sequence of motor development, but experience influences their individual rate of acquisition.

SPECIAL NEEDS

Infants with special needs share many similarities and differences with other children. Similarities include physiological and psychological needs such as being fed, clothed, talked to, and loved. Differences in infants' movement, thought, speech, and personality contribute to their uniqueness. However, sometimes, infants may require specialized early care and intervention to achieve optimal development. Recent advances in medical science and technology have made significant strides in improving the quality of life among infants with special needs. After an examination of the historical roots of early intervention, the remainder of the chapter focuses on the identification of infants with physical and developmental disabilities.

HISTORICAL ROOTS

In ancient times, children with special needs were often treated as outcasts. Physical deformities were sometimes attributed to divine retribution or even witchcraft (Winzer, 1993). Sporadic efforts had been made to improve the conditions of children with physical disabilities, but reformers did not succeed in instituting changes until the 19th century. Philippe Pinel, a French physician, and his student, Jean-Marc-Gaspard Itard, fought valiantly to provide humane treatment. Their pioneering work inspired other influential reformers later in western Europe and the United States. Edouard Sequin, an educator of children with mental retardation, developed methods that served as the foundation of Maria Montessori's work in Italy at the turn of the 20th century.

In the United States, federal legislation provided the impetus that educators and parents advocated on behalf of children with special needs. The Education of All Handicapped Children Act, or Public Law 94-142, enacted in 1975, was an important landmark in the history of special education. It mandated free and appropriate educational and related services to all children with disabilities, 3 to 21 years of age. Special education must be provided in the least restrictive environment along with statements of yearly goals and measurable objectives in an Individualized Education Program, or IEP. Public Law 94-142 was later amended in 1986. Special educational and related services now extend to include children from birth to 3 years (Anastasiow & Nucci, 1994).

IDENTIFICATION OF INFANTS WITH SPECIAL NEEDS

Early identification of infants with disabilities generally begins with a screening test. It is often done after but sometimes before birth. During pregnancy, a routine examination can check on the growth of the developing fetus. Ultrasonography and amniocentesis can be used to detect any physical disorders and chromosomal abnormalities during the 4th month. After birth, screening tests can be used to determine possible developmental delays. Pediatricians are able to compare the developmental status of suspected infants with a standardized sample. Screening tests do not conclusively pinpoint a particular disability. If one is suspected, a comprehensive assessment is conducted to either confirm or reject the existence of a disability (McLean, Bailey, & Wolery, 1996).

After a comprehensive assessment is completed, a diagnosis is made. In medical science, a diagnosis involves the determination of the possible etiology, or cause, of the child's disorder or delay. However, in special education, a diagnosis provides information on the specific types of services a child may require. To begin with, a multidisciplinary team of specialists administers a battery of tests. Once a disability is identified, a plan of action is then prescribed. If special educational and related services, such as physical and occupational therapy, are needed, an IEP is formulated. Two broad groups of infants are served in special education. Infants at risk exhibit vulnerabilities, whereas infants with developmental disabilities show functional limitations (Bailey & Wolery, 1992).

INFANTS AT RISK

Several factors may interfere with the ability of infants at risk to develop normally. First, there may have been prenatal complications. Maternal malnutrition may have severely hindered the formation of vital organs and therefore adversely affected the postnatal adjustment of infants. Indifference and unresponsiveness to stimulation are often observed in prenatally malnourished infants. Other factors include low birth weight, which increases the likelihood of developmental risks. Nicotine in cigarettes can result in the abnormal development of the placenta and severely restrict the transfer of nourishment. Even postmaturity poses risks. Not only does the placenta start to deteriorate after 40 weeks of gestation, but the level of amniotic fluid drops sharply thereafter.

After birth, some infants "fail" to thrive. Failure to thrive can seriously impair physical and psychological adjustment and development during the first few years (Kelsey, 1993). In the past, it consisted of two types. Organic failure to thrive resulted from a physical origin, whereas inorganic failure to thrive involved an emotional component. However, conceptualization of the disorder has changed in recent years to include both components. It is associated with delayed physical and skeletal growth and behavioral and psychological problems later (Kessler & Dawson, 1999). Deficiencies in the quality of interaction between parents and their infants pose serious risks. Infants who fail to thrive do not receive the kind of loving, caring attention they need from their parents (Coolbear & Benoit, 1999). During routine feeding and diapering activities, they are often treated with indifference and sometimes hostility. Immediate intervention is needed to rectify the situation before lasting cognitive and psychological deficits are sustained (Mackner, Starr, & Black, 1997).

DEVELOPMENTAL DISABILITIES

Developmental disabilities encompass a wide range of handicaps. They include physical disabilities in addition to visual and hearing impairments and mental retardation (Pueschel, Scola, & Weiderman, 1995). However, labels can be a problem. Although they can identify educational and related services a particular disability requires, they can result in stigmatization. Labels do not adequately describe individual strengths and weaknesses. Rather, they may accentuate the differences instead of similarities between people.

Any disability interferes with the ability of infants to interact with their environment. In particular, infants with multiple disabilities require special concern and consideration. A case in point is cerebral palsy. A muscular impairment, cerebral palsy results from damage to the brain before or during childbirth. Causes include anoxia, the lack of oxygen to the brain. Cerebral palsy impairs the coordination of muscles and involves secondary disabilities such as learning problems and difficulties with speech.

Classification of cerebral palsy is based on the affected limbs. Prefixes are used with plegia, or paralysis, to describe the paralyzed parts of the body. Paraplegia refers to the paralysis of the legs only. Quadriplegia, on the other hand, involves the paralysis of both the arms and legs. Movement of the unaffected limbs varies considerably. Terms such as *spasticity* refer to the muscles' resistance to voluntary movement. Physical therapy is used to increase the voluntary control of infants with cerebral palsy. On the other hand, involuntary movement is suppressed (Miller & Bachrach, 1998).

Visual impairments interfere with the normal course of development. However, infants with visual impairments can learn to overcome their sensory loss and lead productive lives later as adults. Instead, developmental lags result from the lack of visual stimulation (Nielson, 1991). During the first few months of life, infants with visual impairments achieve postural control, such as controlling the head, rolling from side to back and back to side, and sitting, at the same time as other infants do. In the later months of the first year, developmental lags begin to appear in the locomotion. Blind infants do not usually learn to crawl until their second year. The ability to walk is acquired soon thereafter (Holbrook, 1996; Warren, 1991).

The ability of infants with visual impairments to process sensory information is not adversely affected. It depends on the quality of stimulation they receive from their interactions with the environment. They tend to follow the same developmental sequence of cognitive and social milestones as other children. However, environmental factors such as overprotectiveness may impede optimal development. Auditory and other sensory cues should be used to stimulate interest in objects. Developmental deficits probably result from experiential poverty, or the lack of opportunity to explore the world.

Lastly, the role of parents in early intervention should not be overlooked. Parents typically react with shock and disbelief to the unexpected diagnosis of their children's disability. Long-term adjustment depends on opportunities to share intense emotions—anger and guilt—in a supportive atmosphere. A supportive network and collaborative partnership between parents and the professional staff are key ingredients to any program's success (Greenspan & Wieder, 1998).

SUMMARY

Physical Growth

- Physical development proceeds at a phenomenal rate during the first year of life. Height increases 50% and weight triples before the first birthday.

- Changes in height and weight result from skeletal growth. New cells are manufactured at each end of the bone, eventually fusing with the main shaft.

Maturation of Brain

■ The brain consists of about 100 billion neurons. Connected to each neuron are branchlike structures used to transmit and receive information.

■ The rapid increase in the brain's volume results from myelinization, a process that coats the axons of neurons with an insulating sheath of myelin. Because myelinization improves the efficiency of neural transmission, infants begin to acquire increasingly complex skills.

■ The brain is divided into three major parts. Basic functions of the body are controlled in the hindbrain.

■ The midbrain controls reflexes and emotions and relays visual and auditory information to the forebrain, the largest structure of the brain. The seat of highly developed human intelligence, the forebrain contains the cerebral cortex.

■ The cerebral cortex is divided into two separate but interdependent hemispheres. Each hemisphere controls the opposite side of the body.

■ The cerebral cortex is divided into four different lobes, or areas. Each lobe performs different functions, increasing the brain's efficiency.

Influences on Physical Growth

■ Physical growth follows a genetically predetermined path. Nevertheless, the environment plays an equally influential role.

■ Diet provides an excellent case in point. A nutritionally balanced diet is needed to sustain infants' rapid physical growth and support their physical activity.

■ Human milk contains numerous physiological benefits, reducing possible allergic reactions and increasing resistance to infections. Nevertheless, commercial formulas provide the same basic nutritional benefits.

■ Malnutrition exacts a heavy toll on many children across the world. Infants, in particular, represent an extremely vulnerable group.

Motor Development

■ Motor skills refer to coordinated movements of the body. A distinction is made between gross and fine motor skills.

■ Gross motor skills involve the entire body. When infants crawl and walk, they use large muscles to control their arms and legs.

■ On the other hand, fine motor skills require eye–hand coordination. When infants grasp and manipulate objects, they use small muscles to control manual dexterity.

Special Needs

■ Not all infants follow a predictable pattern of development. For some, early intervention is needed to facilitate their potential.

■ When a developmental disability is suspected, a screening test is given. Once a disability is identified, a plan of action, or IEP, is formulated.

■ Two broad groups of infants are served in special education. Infants with developmental disabilities demonstrate functional limitations, whereas infants at risk exhibit vulnerabilities.

PROJECTS

1. Conduct an observation of an infant or toddler between 6 months and 3 years of age using the developmental checklist in Appendix A and summarize his or her strengths and weaknesses.

2. Invite a pediatrician or pediatric nurse as a speaker to discuss normal physical growth and address issues such as nutrition.

3. Visit a community-based program serving infants with special needs and their families.

COGNITIVE DEVELOPMENT

. . . [the] baby works indefatigably at his discoveries. He is intoxicated with his newfound world. . . .

Selma Fraiberg, *The Magic Years*

Do infants come into the world with preconceived knowledge? Or is knowledge acquired from experience? Such questions have perplexed philosophers and researchers studying infants since the turn of the 20th century. Chapter 8 explores possible answers with two different approaches to understanding infants' cognitive development. In addition, it examines the social context of cognition and the role of play.

In just a few short years, infants develop from dependent newborns to independent toddlers. Before the end of their third year, toddlers are able to explore their environ-

SOCIOCULTURAL INFLUENCES

PHILOSOPHICAL VIEWS OF COGNITIVE DEVELOPMENT

The roots of scientific interest in infants' cognitive development are embedded in philosophy. Since the ancient Greeks, philosophers have tried to seek answers to two related questions:

■ Do infants inherently possess knowledge at birth?

■ Does experience influence the acquisition of knowledge?

Two opposing viewpoints, nativism and empiricism, have arisen since Plato. Each side has relied primarily on abstract arguments, although in recent years scientific verification has been provided. Nativists argue that heredity provides the initial building blocks in making sense of the world at birth. Advocates such as Immanuel Kant, a German philosopher in the late 18th century, believe that the mind imposes order on sensory input. For example, depth perception, or judgment of the distances between objects and oneself, is thought to be an inborn ability. Infants have been observed to perceive a sudden change in elevation (Gibson & Walk, 1960). However, depth perception is apparently related to experience. In a different study, precrawling infants do not express the obvious signs of distress at 4 months that they later show at 6 months after learning to crawl (Bertenthal & Campos, 1990).

On the other hand, empiricists assert that preconceived knowledge does not exist at birth. Proponents such as John Locke, an English philosopher in the 17th century, believe that infants begin life as a blank slate. Knowledge accumulates as they associate sensory perceptions with actual experiences. Sensory input, in other words, eventually aggregates, or comes together, into meaningful perceptions. In the mid-20th century, behaviorism has taken the empiricist viewpoint. Behavioral outcomes occur as a function of environmental consequences. However, difficulties soon arise whenever people take extreme positions in any debate. Some behaviorists ignored compelling evidence contradicting their argument. For example, children's cognitive skills can regulate their behavior. Their ability to extract general rules from complex sets of observed behavior influences their imitation of important adults (Haith & Benson, 1998).

In reality, both nativism and empiricism have contributed to the study of cognition. Infants' genetic inheritance provides inborn mechanisms such as reflexes to engage with the world. At the same time, they learn about their immediate environment from sensory input. Therefore, infants possess the means to adapt to different kinds of experiences (Spelke & Newport, 1998).

ment and interact with others in increasingly complex ways. The accelerated rate of development is not matched at any other period in the human lifespan. The difference between the capabilities of newborns and toddlers is quite staggering. While newborns rely primarily on reflexes to engage with the world, toddlers actively construct knowledge of the world. *The mental process involved in making sense of the world* is known as **cognition**. It encompasses a wide range of phenomena such as sensation, perception, retention, and creativity. It consists of not just a random collection of unrelated components but also an organized system of interconnected elements.

Historically, philosophy predates the modern study of infancy. Since the ancient Greeks, philosophers have sought to understand the origins of knowledge. Current interest in cognition is rooted in two philosophical traditions. Whereas nativism postulates that knowledge preexists, empiricism presumes that knowledge depends on experience. However, as the scientific study of intelligence was established in the first half of the 20th century, the validity of each was challenged. Swiss psychologist Jean Piaget offered a compelling argument that both heredity and the environment play a role. The debate continues even today. *A branch of philosophy that is concerned with the nature of knowledge* is referred to as **epistemology**. In fact, Piaget referred to himself as an epistemologist. After his theory of cognitive development is discussed, current research is examined in the context of memory and categorization.

PIAGET'S THEORY OF COGNITIVE DEVELOPMENT

Piaget was not satisfied with either the nativist and empiricist traditions. He wanted to reconcile the two. However, instead of argumentation, he adopted the scientific method. On the basis of his detailed observations of children, he developed a complex, yet comprehensive, theory of cognitive development, a theory that tried to answer questions about the origins of knowledge. According to Piaget, cognitive development involves the qualitative transformation of children's global psychological structure. Children progress through a series of four sequential stages from birth until early adolescence. The sensorimotor stage corresponds to infancy. Infants' ability to construct knowledge is tied to their sensory perceptions and direct actions on objects.

PIAGETIAN CONCEPTS

Piaget's theory was rooted in his personal and educational experience, both as a child and later as an adult. He developed an early interest in biology. In fact, he devoted his professional life in pursuit of a "biological explanation" of knowledge. Between 1925 and 1931, he kept detailed records of observations of his own three children. His explanations of cognitive changes reflected his biological background in formulating a theory integrating the philosophical views of nativism and empiricism.

The starting point in Piaget's theory involves his concept of cognitive organization. A scheme represents an organized pattern of behavior. Reflexes provide a good example. At birth, newborns respond involuntarily to a wide array of external stimuli such as turning their head and opening their mouth in response to a tactile stroke on the cheek. New schemes evolve as reflexes disappear. Infants' schemes are constantly transformed and even combined as new experiences are encountered, a process referred to as adaptation, or adjustment to the external world. For example, the sucking scheme is extended to other objects placed in the mouth such as a thumb or a rattle. Physical contact with objects not only induces pleasure but also provides important information about the physical properties of objects (Flavell, Miller, & Miller, 1993).

Two related processes exemplify adaptation. The incorporation of new information into existing schemes is known as assimilation. However, over time, new experiences do not always conform to infants' current cognitive structures. The alteration of existing schemes to fit reality, or accommodation, occurs when infants make adjustments in the way they perceive the world. The two processes are in a constant tug of war. When new information is integrated into infants' existing schemes, a state of balance, or equilibration, is said to be achieved. On the other hand, in the case of cognitive incongruity, existing schemes are modified to return to a balanced state. Cognitive development proceeds rapidly during the sensorimotor stage, because biological maturation and the accumulation of experience lead to new imbalances (Rosser, 1994).

Examples of Piaget's concepts abound. One is infants' grasping reflex. At first, infants will grasp any object touching the palm of their hands, including their parents' finger. As the grasping reflex disappears, infants will intentionally extend their hands to grasp other things. The grasping scheme can be combined with other actions such as sucking on objects put into their mouth. Assimilation and accommodation can be seen in infants' everyday actions. For example, infants will eventually learn that round objects bounce. They will have to modify their existing cognitive structures and create another classification of objects when they encounter a nonbouncing round object such as a marble.

SENSORIMOTOR STAGE

In Piaget's theory, infants are actively involved in learning about their world. They rely on their senses, which function at the moment of birth, and manipulate objects and interact with people to satiate their curiosity. The sensorimotor stage provides a

TABLE 8–1 SIX SUBSTAGES OF PIAGET'S SENSORIMOTOR STAGE

Substage	Description
1 Reflexes (Birth–1 month)	Newborns' responses are limited to basic schemes such as sucking and looking, swiping, and kicking. Information is processed at the reflexive level.
2 Primary circular reactions (1–4 months)	Infants begin to adapt their reflexes to the environment. They engage in simple actions centering on their own body.
3 Secondary circular reactions (4–8 months)	The focus of infants' exploration shifts to external events. Infants develop an awareness that objects continue to exist even when not in sight at about 8 months of age.
4 Coordination of secondary circular reactions (8–12 months)	Infants are beginning to demonstrate intentional behavior and anticipate events. They coordinate separate actions to achieve desired goals.
5 Tertiary circular reactions (12–18 months)	Although they still engage in repetitive activities, infants reach an advanced level of proficiency. They not only produce variations of the same events, but also begin to expand their exploration.
6 Symbolic representation (18–24 months)	Infants' previous cognitive advances culminate in the development of symbolic representation. They are now able to represent actions mentally instead of solving problems through trial and error.

HISTORICALLY SPEAKING

PIAGET'S THEORY OF COGNITIVE DEVELOPMENT

Jean Piaget
The Origins of Intelligence in Children, 1936
Intelligence is an adaptation. In order to grasp its relation to life in general it is therefore necessary to state precisely the relations that exist between the organism and the environment.

Source: Piaget (1936/1952), p. 3.

comprehensive framework of cognitive development. Because of its complexity, the sensorimotor stage has been divided into six substages (see Table 8–1). Although each substage is discussed separately, a cumulative effect is noted over time. Each builds on the accomplishments of the previous substage (Piaget, 1970; Piaget & Inhelder, 1969).

Substage 1. The first substage of the sensorimotor stage covers the first 4 weeks. At birth, newborns are equipped with involuntary reflexes. Reflexes provide the initial contact with the environment. A cry, for example, is triggered in response to hunger or pain. When a breast or bottle is offered, a sucking response is then activated. However, presumably newborns cannot make connections between the different sensations they receive from their sensory modalities.

The major achievement of the first substage involves the increasing efficiency of reflexive responses. With accumulated experience, newborns will begin to adapt their reflexes to new situations. For example, they will use the sucking scheme on any object that enters their mouth. Their sucking actions can now fulfill both nutritive and nonnutritive purposes. Likewise, grasping schemes are modified to manipulate objects as reflexes are replaced with voluntary control. Grasping reflexes provide the means to explore objects in subsequent substages.

The inability to distinguish oneself from others dominates the first month of life. Infants' awareness of themselves as unique entities is not acquired until the 3rd month, as evidenced in babies with access to mirrors (Bahrick, Moss, & Fadil, 1996; Rochat, 1997).

Substage 2. The next substage, a period from 1 to 4 months, provides the first hints of adaptive behavior. Infants begin to gain voluntary control of their actions. The ability to make simple connections between cause and effect will occur at about 2 months. Infants will usually repeat movements producing interesting results. For example, when an inadvertent kick shakes a mobile, infants will likely engage in the same activity over and over again. The repetition of the same behavior is called circular reactions. During the remainder of the sensorimotor stage, circular reactions change over time. Initially, circular reactions involve the body. Next, repetitive actions shift to external events. Later, in the 2nd year of life, different ways of solving problems are sought.

At the outset of the second substage, infants still rely on existing reflexive schemes. They may start to repeat simple actions discovered accidentally. For example, when a finger or fist is placed in the mouth, a sucking response is triggered. Because it produces pleasure, infants may engage in the same activity again and again. When saliva accumulates on their lips and bubbles appear, infants may continue to prolong the effect. Piaget refers to *repetitive actions that center on the body* as **primary circular reactions**. Infants soon learn to combine and coordinate different schemes at the same time. They may grasp their parents' clothing while feeding.

Substage 3.   Attention slowly shifts from internal to external events from 4 to 8 months. Instead of repeating activities centered on the body, infants now engage in **secondary circular reactions**, *repetitive actions that produce interesting results on the environment*. When infants squeeze a toy, producing an unexpected noise, they will repeat the same action until they lose interest. Adults' verbal acknowledgment or social praise can encourage infants' duplication of the same activity. Repeated actions are usually accompanied with intense concentration. Then, their repetitions will start to increase in speed, resulting in frequent smiles and gleeful squeals at the outcomes of their actions.

Toward the end of the third substage, infants begin to develop an awareness of object permanence. The ability to understand that hidden objects maintain their existence marks a major cognitive achievement. Prior to 8 months of age, infants do not actively try to find an object that drops or follow a parent who leaves the room. Although infants may often track the movement of objects, they generally abandon their search when something disappears. Only after repeated experiences do infants come to realize that objects exist as separate entities from themselves. Although the concept takes time to develop, infants start to demonstrate their awareness when they uncover a partially hidden object or smile when a parent returns from another room.

Substage 4.   Infants are beginning to organize previously learned mental structures from 8 to 12 months. They start to combine secondary circular reactions to achieve their desired goals. To illustrate, Piaget described his son's behavior with a tin can. At 10 months of age, Laurent dropped the container into a basin, a demonstration of secondary circular reaction. Piaget knew from previous observations that his son liked to bang the object on the basin. He noticed that his son later combined two actions as he remarked in the following sequence of events:

> Now, at once, Laurent takes possession of the tin, holds out his arm and drops it over the basin. . . . this is a fine example of the coordination of two [schemes] of which the first serves as "means" whereas the second assigns an end to the action. (Piaget, 1936/1952, p. 225)

Intentionality is increasingly seen in infants' actions during the fourth substage. They deliberately combine separate schemes, as Piaget's son did, to achieve a goal. The coordination of secondary schemes further advances infants' cognitive development. When they apply a different combination of schemes in a variety of circumstances, they will observe the effects of their actions. Infants' awareness of object permanence is related to the coordination of secondary circular reactions. Now, they will actively search for hidden objects. However, their awareness is not quite fully developed yet. When an object is placed under one cover and moved to another in full view, only the first cover is searched.

Substage 5.   An advanced level of cognitive proficiency is reached from 12 to 18 months. It is known as **tertiary circular reactions**, *actions that are deliberately repeated to discover new variations of established schemes.* During the first year, infants repeated actions producing the same results. Now, they will experiment with different variations of the same activities. Instead of just hitting a plastic container with a stick over and over, infants may strike other objects. In Piaget's words, they are experimenting "in order to see" the results of their discoveries (Piaget, 1936/1952, p. 272).

Two milestones converge during the fifth substage. Infants are beginning to make significant physical and cognitive strides. Locomotion provides increased opportunities to explore and interact with a variety of objects and people. At the same time, infants literally become "little scientists" who devise and test their hypotheses such as dropping different things from the high chair or stroller. In the process, they discover the relationship between cause and effect although experimentation takes the form of trial and error. They will try to find new or alternative ways of solving a problem or accomplishing a goal.

Substage 6.   Mental representation reaches its climax in the sixth and final substage of Piaget's sensorimotor stage, a period from 18 to 24 months. At last, infants can think before they act. The ability to represent the external world internally is developing. *The internalization of reality* is referred to as **symbolic representation**. In other words, infants are now able to solve problems mentally instead of having to act on things physically. Piaget provides an example of infants' increasing cognitive advances in the following account of his daughter trying to retrieve a chain from a matchbox:

> She looks at the slit with great attention; then several times in succession, she opens and shuts her mouth . . . wider and wider! Apparently Lucienne understands the existence of a cavity . . . and wishes to enlarge [it]. (Piaget, 1936/1952, p. 338)

Further advancement in imitation occurs during the sixth substage. *The ability to retain and copy a representation of an observed behavior* is known as **deferred imitation**. Infants have always been able to mimic the actions of others. Previously, imitation requires the presence of a model. For example, when parents wave "bye-bye" to a departing person, infants may copy the gesture. The behavior is reinforced when social praise is received. Later, the observed action can be imitated in the absence of a model. Infants may wave "bye-bye" while playing with a doll because of their ability to represent the external world symbolically.

EVALUATION OF PIAGET'S SENSORIMOTOR STAGE

Although methodological concerns have been raised, Piaget's basic premises, particularly the invariant sequence of his stages, continue to provide insights into cognitive development. To summarize, infants construct mental structures from direct engagement with the world. Cognitive advances are made when existing schemes are modified to

PARENTING ISSUES

CAREGIVING IMPLICATIONS OF PIAGET'S THEORY
• •

Piaget's contribution is not restricted to the laboratory. His theory has had an impact on early education. Although he never considered himself as an educator, Piaget identified environmental conditions fostering children's cognitive development. The practical application of his theory stresses two broad principles:

■ **Active involvement.** Infants take an active, not passive, role in engaging with the environment. Because they learn directly from their hands-on involvement, adults should provide a richly varied environment facilitating infants' exploratory behavior.

■ **Sensory development.** Infants rely on all of their senses in constructing knowledge about the world. Adults should provide a variety of things to look at, listen to, smell, taste, and feel, including opportunities to interact with their most favorite playthings of all— their caregivers.

conform to reality. Infants' remarkable progression has been divided into six substages, four in the first year of life and two in the second, each building on the previous substage. Basically, infants progress from reliance on involuntary reflexes to increasingly purposeful actions. As their reflexes diminish, infants begin to perpetuate interesting activities centered on their own body initially but focused on external events later. Infants eventually experiment with different ways of doing the same things. They continue to make advances in the second year from discovering solutions through trial and error to solving problems through anticipation and foresight (Siegler, 1997).

Since the publication of Piaget's original work, new discoveries have led to modifications of his theory. Alternative theories of cognitive development have been proposed in recent years. Neo-Piagetians accept the basic principles of the mechanisms that govern developmental changes in Piaget's theory. However, they reject several assumptions (Caulfield, 1996a). Contemporary research indicates that infants possess innate abilities Piaget failed to recognize. From birth, infants are apparently equipped with the ability to process information such as the numerical relation between objects (Wynn, 1992, 1995). Given the inherent limitations of Piaget's methodology, a new framework of cognitive development has been proposed. It focuses on the acquisition of increasingly complex skills instead of the construction of increasingly complex schemes as in Piaget's theory (Fischer & Bidell, 1998). The existence of four, not six, substages marks another difference between Piaget and the neo-Piagetians. The major shifts in sensorimotor development correspond to changes in the structure of the brain at 3, 8, 12, and 18 months of age (Fischer & Rose, 1996).

Nevertheless, Piaget's sensorimotor stage has been replicated in comparative studies of primates. Striking similarities have been found between the great apes (gorillas and chimpanzees) and human infants (Vauclair, 1996). The results indicate that primates progress through the same invariant sequences. Chimpanzees and gorillas, like human infants, do not skip a substage or exhibit the same features of two or more substages (Dore & Dumas, 1987). Of course, distinct species-specific differences exist, reflecting the unique adaptation of each species. In general, the great apes attain certain cognitive milestones before human infants do. The early appearance of locomotion in primates provides a temporary advantage. Yet, prehension, or the ability to manipulate objects, among the great apes is limited. Chimpanzees do not explore objects in the same way that human infants do (Poti & Spinozzi, 1994). Socialization plays an influential role in the cognitive development of both primates and human infants. Important information about socially acceptable behavioral patterns is gained from the observation of adults within the species (Boysen & Himes, 1999).

CURRENT RESEARCH ON COGNITIVE DEVELOPMENT

The studies of primates and human infants confirm the behavioral sequence of Piaget's sensorimotor stage. The universality of sensorimotor development has been further substantiated in cross-cultural research, as shown in the following box. However, Piaget's own biases have been called into question. In particular, he apparently miscalculated the approximate age children acquire specific skills because of methodological limitations. Further, he assumed that cognitive growth depends on infants' direct contact in exploring the world. Research in recent years has shown that certain mental structures may be genetically determined.

Permanence of Objects. A good example of Piaget's underestimation of infants' cognitive abilities is object permanence. In Piaget's theory, infants do not, before 8 months of age, attempt to search for objects that disappear. The ability to understand the permanent existence of objects is tied to their repeated contact with their immediate environment. Piaget concludes that only after 8 months do infants locate completely hidden objects (see Table 8–2).

In recent years, Piaget's estimation has been questioned. In particular, Renee Baillargeon's research shows that infants seem to possess rudimentary knowledge of object permanence prior to 4 months of age (Baillargeon, 1993, 1998). In one study, infants were first habituated to a screen that rotated on a 180-degree arc (see Figure 8–1). Then, two different events were shown. First, in the "possible event," a yellow box was placed in the path of the screen. When the screen rotated, it rested on the yellow box. Second, in the "impossible event," the yellow box was removed as the screen continued its movement. The screen completed a full arc, but as it reversed to it original position, the box reappeared. Infants significantly increased the length of time spent in looking at the impossible event. Their behavior suggested that they recognized the incongruity of the event and developed the concept of object permanence (Baillargeon, 1987; Baillargeon et al., 1990).

Although infants appear to realize that hidden objects exist prior to 4 months, they still face difficulties with complex tasks involving the movement of objects from one place to another. Before 10 months, infants will make mistakes that researchers call the AB error (pronounced "A, not B"). In a typical experiment, a researcher places two

UNIVERSALITY OF CULTURAL INFLUENCES ON COGNITIVE DEVELOPMENT

Cognition is closely tied to culture. Infants inherit a genetic as well as cultural endowment from their parents (Gardiner, Mutter, & Kosmitzki, 1998). Infants are predisposed to maintain their proximity to and involvement with adults. Their cries in response to external and internal stimuli typically trigger similar reactions in almost all cultures across the world. Generally speaking, cultural practices compliment genetically programmed mechanisms. Adults usually behave in ways that foster their interactions with infants. They encourage gradual participation in skilled and valued activities of their society. In addition, they modify difficult tasks and model expected performance during joint activities (Gardner, 1995).

Guided participation in culturally valued activities will contribute to infants' cognitive development. They eventually become skilled participants in the social fabric of their society (Rogoff, 1993). For example, even at age 2, Mayan infants observe and imitate their mothers each day in preparing the family's meal. Infants are given a small piece of dough to roll into a ball and flatten in making tortillas. It is then cooked and eaten with the rest of the meal. As the mothers witness continued progress, they start to add additional information (Rogoff, 1990). Mutual engagement between infants and their parents provides the building blocks of subsequent development. Together, they make use of the tools they inherit from previous generations to solve culturally defined problems. Children come into contact with a complex system involving their parents and other members of the community already participating with societal institutions and technologies. As a result of their collaboration with others, children begin to engage in culturally specific activities.

Although reciprocal interaction between infants and their parents has been consistently observed throughout the world, distinct cultural variations have been found. Differences usually center on the goals of development. The child-rearing practices of parents in Kenya and the United States provide a good example. The Gusii inhabit the southwestern corner of Kenya, an area with rich soil and abundant rainfall. They choose to live in scattered homesteads instead of isolated villages as other people in the same area do. In contrast to neighboring communities, they rely on agriculture, not cattle, to subsist. Gusii and European American mothers have been found to differ in their style of interaction with their 1-year-old infants in response to structured tasks such as building a tower with blocks or inserting pegs into a board. Gusii mothers generally offer unambiguous instructions and model the tasks in their entirety. They appear to expect the tasks to be completed in exactly the same way (LeVine et al., 1994).

In contrast, European American mothers interpret their roles differently. They tend to encourage their infants' exploration of the toys before directing attention to the completion of the structured tasks. A distinctive feature of European American mothers' strategy involves the frequent use of questions to instruct their infants. Also, they tend to reflect on their

(continued)

SOCIOCULTURAL INFLUENCES

infants' mood or behavior. Periods of inattention are countered with renewed efforts to refocus their infants' attention. The tasks are broken into manageable steps if their infants are experiencing frustration.

Gusii mothers, on the other hand, attempt to maintain their infants' attention with physical, not verbal, measures. They restrain their infants to get their attention (LeVine, 1988).

pieces of cloth on a table or floor in full view of an infant (see Figure 8–2). An enticing toy is then hidden under one. The infant will usually remember the location of the hidden object and unhesitatingly retrieve the toy. However, if the researcher hides the same toy under the other piece of cloth, the infant will look under the first cloth but will not persist in trying to locate the object (Munakata, 1997). Infants make AB errors when a specific span of time elapses. Errors are increased when infants are restrained for at least 3 seconds after the object is hidden at B, the second location. Infants are not able, before 12 months, to translate the concept of object permanence into a successful searching strategy. It appears to be tied to the rapid maturation of the cerebral cortex at the end of the first year (Diamond, 1988).

Imitation.   Researchers disagree about the exact age infants start to imitate the behavior of others. Newborns appear to copy distinctive facial expressions of adults such as opening the mouth and protruding the tongue. At 1 year, infants will imitate only in response to immediate stimulation from the environment (Barr, Dowden, & Hayne, 1996). When parents shake their heads from side to side to indicate "no," infants often respond in a similar manner. However, in the middle of their second year, infants do not just mimic others' behavior (Barnat, Klein, & Meltzoff, 1996). They begin to remember and repeat past events or actions at a different time and place, an ability that Piaget refers to as deferred imitation. Its appearance provides evidence of infants' increasing ability to represent the world internally. Infants develop a new mode of thought, symbolic representation, as the sensorimotor stage comes to an end.

TABLE 8–2 AWARENESS OF OBJECT PERMANENCE

Substage	Adaptive Behavior
1	Infants do not try to find hidden object.
2	Infants do not try to find hidden object.
3	Infants try to find partially hidden object but stop if it disappears.
4	Infants try to find completely hidden object but stop if it moves to another location.
5	Infants search new location of hidden object only if they observe its placement.
6	Infants seek to find hidden object in all possible locations.

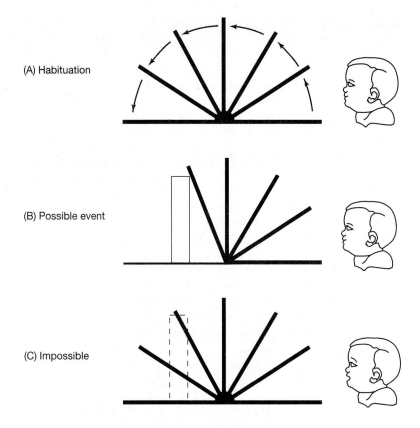

(A) Habituation

(B) Possible event

(C) Impossible

FIGURE 8–1 Current Research on Object Permanence Studies have challenged Piaget's conclusions on infants' ability to recognize object permanence only after 8 months of age. Infants at 3½ months of age in one study demonstrated their awareness of objects' permanence. (A) First, the subjects habituated to a screen that rotated 180 degrees on a table. Next, two different events were presented in full view of the subjects. (B) In the possible event, the screen slowly moved until it stopped on a yellow box and returned to its original position. (C) In the impossible event, the screen slowly rotated 180 degrees. However, as it returned to its original position, the yellow box reappeared. The results showed that infants dishabituated, or recognized the incongruence of the impossible event, at 3½ months of age.
Source: Baillargeon (1987).

In recent years, researchers have found that deferred imitation may not be confined to the last half of the second year. In one study, deferred imitation has been induced at 9 months of age in the laboratory (Meltzoff, 1988a). The subjects in the experimental group were exposed to three objects. An adult manipulated the objects in full view of the subjects such as pushing a button on a box or shaking a plastic egg. Other groups just saw the objects without the adult or the adult who only touched the toys. When they returned to the laboratory a day later, the subjects who observed the adult's modeled actions played with the ob-

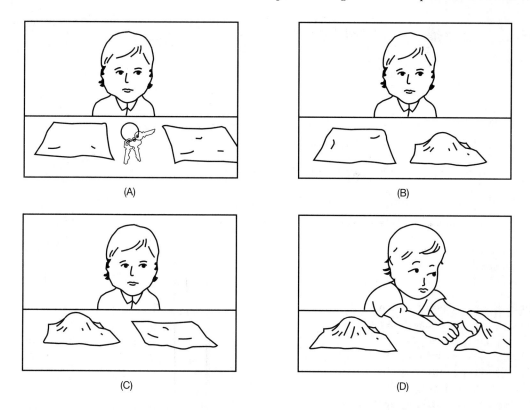

FIGURE 8–2 Demonstration of Object Permanence Infants' increasing awareness of object permanence represents a significant cognitive advancement. At 8 months of age, infants actively search for hidden objects but do not yet understand their disappearance from one location to another. (A) The infant examines a set of plastic keys. (B) The keys are hidden under one of two pieces of cloth. (C) The location of the hidden keys is changed to the other cloth. (D) The infant mistakenly looks under the wrong cloth.

jects in the same way. The results show that deferred imitation may appear almost a year before Piaget's original estimation. At 9 months of age, infants are able to keep not one but at least three separate actions in mind at least a day later. In another study, infants demonstrated the ability to imitate multiple actions after a delay of 1 week. At 14 months of age, the subjects remembered the actions they observed and guided their own subsequent behavior on the basis of internal representations of the world (Meltzoff, 1988b).

NEW PERSPECTIVES ON COGNITION

Piaget's theory does not sufficiently describe the basic mechanisms infants use to process sensory stimuli. Two components of the cognitive apparatus, memory and categorization, have been found to improve significantly during the first few years.

MEMORY

When sensory information is received, it is deposited in a storehouse. *The capacity to retain and retrieve past experience* is known as **memory**. In particular, it describes a process of recalling previous events in the absence of the original elements of the experience. It involves a series of actions:

■ Encoding, or acquiring and organizing, elements of the experience.

■ Retaining, or storing, the acquired elements.

■ Recalling, or extracting, the retained elements.

Memory is categorized in two ways. *Sensory information that is stored temporarily* is referred to as **short-term memory**. For example, when infants manipulate an object and make a startling discovery such as a unexpected noise, they may store the information in their short-term memory. *The permanent storage of sensory input* is called **long-term memory**. Infants' ability to maintain information they receive depends on their processing strategies. **Rehearsal**, or the *repetition of information*, can improve long-term retention.

In recent years, research on infants' ability to remember past events has received increased attention. Infants make marked improvement in the retention of information during the first year, but the use of memory actually begins before birth. Newborns prefer to hear a familiar story that their mothers read repeatedly during the final weeks of pregnancy. They have been found to be able to recognize information stored in their memory prior to birth (DeCasper & Spence, 1986). Even the sense of smell is used to recall a past event. Newborns demonstrate the remarkable ability to remember the odors of their own mothers only after limited exposure at birth (Cernoch & Porter, 1985).

Infants' successful retention of past experiences can be seen in the following experiments. Carolyn Rovee-Collier and her associates had been involved in training infants to kick their legs in order to shake a mobile on their crib (Rovee-Collier, 1984, 1987). The mobile consisted of blocks with either the letter A or number 2. A string was used to attach the mobile to the infants' foot. After the infants were allowed to kick spontaneously, their ability to remember the experience was examined. The results showed that at 3 months, infants resumed their learned activity after 2 weeks. Similar experiments have been conducted with infants of different ages. Again, infants have been able to recall past events (Carver & Bauer, 1999; Hartshorn et al., 1998; Rovee-Collier & Bhatt, 1993; Rovee-Collier & Shyi, 1992).

In sum, infants' ability to retain and retrieve previously learned information develops rapidly during the first year. Newborns (and perhaps even fetuses) can store and remember past events. The retention of information will initially depend on repeated exposure to environmental stimuli. However, during the next several months, major cognitive strides are made. The duration of infants' memory increases from only a few minutes to days, weeks, and months. Although their advances reflect maturation of the brain, infants develop increasingly successful strategies in remembering things (Bauer, 1996). Reminders of past experiences will facilitate retention. When a task involves environmental familiarity and personal relevance, recall improves (Lipsitt, 1990).

CATEGORIZATION

During the first year, infants are able to differentiate similarities and differences between objects. **Categorization**, an essential cognitive skill, refers to *the ability to organize information into meaningful groups mentally.* Even at birth, newborns can make discriminations. They can perceive the distinctive features of stimuli (Walton, Armstrong, & Bower, 1997). They cannot only differentiate straight and curved lines, vertical and horizontal lines, and patterns with high and low density, but also detect color. Infants focus on different elements of objects as a whole. At 2 months, they prefer to look at schematic faces, not scrambled arrangements. The results of research on infants' perception of human faces suggest that infants learn to recognize particular configurations corresponding to actual objects (Bushnell, 1998).

Infants' capacity to categorize objects represents an important cognitive achievement. Categorization facilitates the storage of sensory input and improves the efficiency of the brain in processing information. Although unanswered questions remain, research provides a glimpse into infants' ability to organize and make sense of their experiences. The

SOCIOCULTURAL INFLUENCES

BEYOND PIAGET

Other alternative models of cognitive development have been offered in recent years. They include:

■ **Nativist models.** An alternative model to Piaget's theory is referred to as modularity. Cognitive structures have been described in terms of innate modules (Gopnik, 1996). Therefore, infants' mental representations of the world are not constructed from experience. Instead, infants are innately endowed with a fixed neural architecture (Karmiloff-Smith, 1992). Examples of modularity include perception and syntax. Infants are predisposed at birth to attend to certain aspects of their immediate environment such as phonological sounds and syntactic rules adults use.

■ **Empiricist models.** Some have argued that knowledge is organized into scripts or narratives. Scripts and narratives involve cognitive structures organizing knowledge in terms of accumulated experience (Mandler, 1998). Children gradually combine initial mental representations of the world into increasingly ordered structures. Another empiricist explanation is called connectionism. The connectionist model views knowledge as a collection of concrete pieces of information. Inputs from the environment are connected into a single network. Knowledge is changed as a consequence of new experience (McLeod, Plunkett, & Rolls, 1998).

Therefore, new ideas have developed from Piaget's theory. However, instead of rejecting his theory outright, some researchers have preferred to add or revise aspects of it.

following conclusions can be drawn about sequence of categorization. First, at 3 months, infants are only able to categorize selected stimuli. In one study, when infants habituated to dotted patterns of simple geometric shapes—triangles, squares, or diamonds—they successfully detected differences in new patterns (Bomba & Siqueland, 1983). Different dotted shapes in a particular category such as triangles of different sizes were shown repeatedly. When infants saw two new objects, one from a previous category and another from a totally different category—a square—noticeable changes occurred in the length of time spent in looking at the novel shape (Younger & Gotlieb, 1988).

Next, infants can categorize a variety of stimuli from about 9 to 12 months. In another study, two imaginary classes of deer (deer with ears and feathered tails and deer with antlers and furry tails) were shown (Younger, 1990). A set of 12 pictures were presented in random order until habituation. Then, the infants' reactions to three new stimuli were examined: a deer that represented one of two already habituated categories, a deer that violated the rules of habituation (a deer with antlers and feathers), and a novel animal (a monkey). The subjects demonstrated the ability to categorize when they ignored the deer they saw previously but dishabituated to the other two animals. Similar results have been found in other studies (Sherman, 1985). Taken as a whole, the evidence suggests that infants do not just perceive differences between objects. They appear to be applying underlying cognitive principles that determine the inclusion or exclusion of objects on the basis of relevant features. Although infants' categorization may reflect biologically based mechanisms, environmental factors play a role. Opportunities to explore a wide variety of objects can provide the necessary building blocks of categorization (Eimas, 1994; Quinn & Eimas, 1996).

SOCIAL CONTEXT OF COGNITION

In Piaget's theory, the acquisition of knowledge is seen primarily as an individual activity. However, other researchers have challenged his view of infants as solitary explorers and instead focused attention on the social context of cognitive development.

VYGOTSKY'S FRAMEWORK

Born in the same year as Piaget, Vygotsky's influence is still felt today. Although only a few short articles were published in English after his untimely death in 1934, his work was introduced to the academic community with the published translation of *Thought and Language* in 1962. The past decade has seen renewed interest in his work. Six volumes of his work have been published in *The Collected Works of L. S. Vygotsky* (Rieber, 1987–1999).

The theoretical roots of Vygotsky's ideas stemmed from his own personal life with his family as a child and later as an admirer of German philosopher Karl Marx. In school, he was often referred to as "the little professor" because of his reputation as a skilled debater. Later, he studied linguistics before receiving a doctorate in psychology. He taught psychology at a small teacher's college in western Russia. There, he met children with congenital defects such as mental retardation. His interest in the social context of cognitive development started because he wanted to help children with disabilities. Shortly afterwards, Vygotsky obtained a teaching position at the Institute of Psychology in Moscow in 1924. His lectures inspired students who sat in overflowing auditoriums (Wertsch, 1985).

Vygotsky became a victim of Stalin's rule. Because of his contact with Piaget and other Western psychologists, he was viewed with suspicion. During the Stalinist purges of the early 1930s, he was blacklisted. He died of tuberculosis after only a brief professional career. Even after his death, his work was banned for 20 years. Still, his ideas survived. Vygotsky believed basic psychological tools such as language are acquired through education and transmitted from one generation to the next. Therefore, cognitive development is tied to social factors.

The importance of the social context in Vygotsky's theory can be seen in his concept of zone of proximal development. It refers to the difference between children's current cognitive level in a particular area and their potential level when they receive guidance from skilled adults. A variety of means can be used to facilitate the learning process such as modeling the behavior to be learned and engaging in joint participation as in playing with a jack-in-a-box toy. At first, parents may demonstrate the sequence to an infant, turning the handle to trigger the sudden appearance of a clown and closing the cover to start again. However, with a toddler, they may only use verbal instructions and gestures as the child tries to operate the toy. As Vygotsky (1978) wrote,

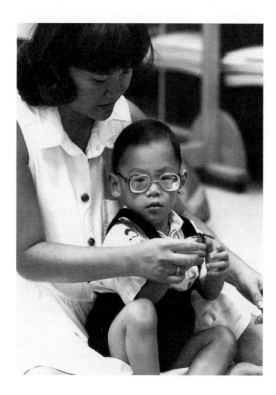

Infants and toddlers often receive guidance from skilled adults as they learn to master difficult tasks.
Photo courtesy of Tami Dawson, Photo Resource Hawaii.

learning awakens a variety of internal developmental processes that are able to operate only when the child is interacting with people in his environment. . . . (p. 90)

Vygotsky's concept is seen whenever a new task is introduced. Adults typically guide
and support their children's efforts. They may break difficult tasks into small, manageable units and direct their children's attention to the salient features. Further, adults
may use words to describe their actions or identify objects. In the process, children learn
about the different kinds of cognitive strategies adults use to solve problems. Children
gradually learn to assume increased responsibility in tackling problems on their own.
The cognitive tools they acquire reflect their unique cultural heritage. Each culture
determines the necessary skills children need to become productive members of society.

ROLE OF PLAY

Play is inextricably tied to infants' cognitive development. Spontaneous activities that are
intrinsically motivated, or, in Piaget's words, "an end in itself," are called play (Piaget,
1951/1962, p. 147). Play expands not only knowledge of the physical and social world
but also awareness of themselves. The complexity of play has lead to several theories that
explain its function (Garvey, 1990).

At the turn of the 20th century, Herbert Spencer and Karl Groos proposed two theories of play. To Spencer, animals, including children, are supplied with a limited supply
of energy to survive (Spencer, 1897). Any surplus of energy not used is expended or dis-
charged in play. In contrast, Groos speculated that children rehearse specific skills they
need later as adults (Groos, 1901). Just as kittens play with balls of string in order to
sharpen their skills in catching mice, children learn about adulthood through dramatic
play. However, early explanations of play were either discarded or incorporated into
other theories. Soon afterwards, psychoanalytic and cognitive theories emerged, shifting
attention to the psychological, not biological, contributions of play (Hughes, 1995).

PSYCHOANALYTIC AND COGNITIVE THEORIES OF PLAY

Both psychoanalytic and cognitive theories examined the importance of play on children's development. However, each had its own particular slant. The psychoanalytic
view of play is rooted in the work of Sigmund Freud, the founder of psychoanalysis. Play
is seen as an activity to reduce anxiety (Freud, 1933/1964). According to Freud, two
types of anxiety are experienced in childhood. Objective anxiety reflects children's basic
fear of the external world. It occurs when children begin to realize their helplessness.
Play lessens objective anxiety because children gain a temporary illusion of power.
Therefore, emotional conflicts can be resolved in a nonthreatening atmosphere. The
reenactment of an unpleasant situation during play may reduce children's level of
anxiety.

Another source of anxiety involves children's fears of their uncontrolled urges. Instinctual anxiety refers to socially inappropriate impulses such as destructive emotions.
Adults' excessive punishment or ridicule of children's natural impulses may result in
guilt. Play allows the healthy expression of children's instincts. Children will be able to

release antisocial emotions in socially acceptable ways. For example, they are often told not to hit someone or break a toy in anger. However, when they take their anger out on a doll or topple a tall tower of blocks, they learn to deal with their pent-up emotions. Not everyone agreed with Freud's emphasis on the reduction of fear. Erik Erikson stressed the role of play in building children's ego, or their sense of self, and developing important social skills to become contributing members of society.

Cognitive theory regards play as a tool fostering children's thinking skills. Play provides opportunities to solve problems in a relaxed but stimulating way. Piaget's theory offers insights into the importance of play. He argues that play represents the dominance of assimilation, or the incorporation of reality into children's existing cognitive schemes (Piaget, 1937/1954, 1951/1962). He cited an example of his son who, at 3 months, tilted his head to look at the world from an unusual position. His son laughed loudly as he repeatedly engaged in the same behavior because of the pleasure it brought. Play is thought to be a form of consolidation. An activity is initially learned and is repeated again as a means of incorporating new information into previously learned behavioral patterns.

PIAGET'S CONCEPTUALIZATION

Piaget describes two types of play. Sensorimotor play characterizes the first 18 months. It involves the frequent repetition of simple motor skills. Infants at first learn to master control of their bodies and focus their attention on the manipulation of objects. Then, sensorimotor play is merged with symbolic play. Interest in exploring objects such as rattles and blocks shifts to internal representation of reality.

Sensorimotor Play.   Infants are constantly learning. *The intrinsically satisfying repetition of simple motor skills* is known as **sensorimotor play**. Initially, it centers on their body through reflexes such as sucking. Their reflexive actions are gradually transferred to other objects such as a fist or rattle. At 4 months, infants begin to focus effects of their actions on the environment. For example, when they accidentally hit at a mobile with

Play, often described as a child's work, is the primary means of learning new things.
Photo courtesy of Tami Dawson, Photo Resource Hawaii.

HISTORICALLY SPEAKING

ROLE OF PLAY

Maria Montessori
The Absorbent Mind, 1949
. . . the first lesson we must learn is that the tiny child's *absorbent mind* finds all its nutriment in its surroundings. Here it has to locate itself, and build itself up from what it takes in.

Source: Montessori (1949/1967), p. 97.

their hand, its movement attracts their attention. They then try to repeat the same action. Their success depends on their ability to coordinate the complex movements of their arms and hands. The intentional actions of infants during the last half of the first year correlate with continued maturation of the brain. They are interested now in engaging in repetitive actions not just to prolong interesting activities but to produce novel consequences.

Symbolic Play.   Although sensorimotor play dominates the first year of life, a new element in infants' spontaneous activities appears before the end of the second year. *Imaginative activities that are intended to represent reality* are referred to as **symbolic play.** Just as they eventually use words to signify ideas, infants pretend inanimate objects represent real things. A wooden block can become an airplane and a doll a parent. Symbolic play does not emerge all at once. At 12 months, infants' symbolic play focuses on their everyday lives. They pretend to eat, drink, go to sleep, or take a bath. Thereafter, they will begin to incorporate inanimate objects into their play. Instead of feeding themselves, infants may pretend to feed their stuffed animals with a spoon. Frequent substitutions of objects are noticed after 18 months. Symbolic play clearly parallels Piaget's last substage of sensorimotor development with internal representation of reality.

PARENTS' CONTRIBUTIONS

Parents exert a profound influence on children's lives. Their impact is felt even in play. Some parents, particularly fathers, sometimes hesitate to play with their infants. However, play provides many developmental benefits. For example, when parents describe the properties of objects or their actions, they stimulate their infants' natural curiosity. Infants will learn to value play if their parents take the time and effort. Later, parents can encourage toddlers' burgeoning imagination during symbolic play. Imaginative play brings both parents and children together in mutually enjoyable activities (Haight & Miller, 1992). Parents can provide not only props to enrich the experience but also guidance in solving problems. Play can be an effective learning tool.

SUPERBABIES

During the last half of the 20th century, a transformation of enormous magnitude has occurred in the United States. Increasing numbers of parents seem to be preoccupied in creating superbabies or infants achieving at an advanced level in relation to their peers. Although opinions have varied on the subject, parenting experts have begun to voice their concerns. David Elkind, in his book, *The Hurried Child*, remarks:

> The concept of childhood . . . is threatened with extinction in the society we have created. Today's child has become the unwilling, unintended victim of overwhelming stress—the stress borne of rapid, bewildering social change and constantly rising expectations. (Elkind, 1988, p. 3)

The emphasis on early instruction has led to the proliferation of books and programs intended to raise the intellectual ability of infants. The "miseducation" of infants is not limited to unwarranted efforts to teach traditional academic skills such as reading and math; it has extended to all facets of children's development. The notion of early instruction has spread to sports and gymnastics, music and ballet. Contributing factors include:

■ **Postponement of parenthood.** Today, many adults of childbearing age may delay parenthood until their 30s or 40s. In the process, they may develop a competitive bent at work and view their children as extensions of themselves.

■ **Decreasing size of families.** With the postponement of parenthood comes the reality of the biological clock. Parents deciding to raise just one child may believe they need to "invest" in their child's future.

■ **Knowledge of infants' abilities.** The availability of parenting books has increased parents' knowledge of infants' abilities. Some parents may mistakenly want to "teach" their infants before the opportunity passes.

■ **Popular belief of mediocre public education.** Parents with high expectations may worry about the quality of public education because of perceived shortcomings. They may put their children in academically demanding programs to increase their chances of getting into private schools.

In conclusion, detrimental consequences can result from unrealistic efforts to accelerate development. High expectations may backfire. Instead of pushing, parents should develop an appreciation of their infants' unique needs, particularly gaining experiences with the real world. Infants are not simply waiting to be taught but instead are expending enormous time and energy in learning about things firsthand (Elkind, 1998).

SPECIAL NEEDS

About 1 to 3% of children are diagnosed with mental retardation. Some 20 to 25% of them are identified at birth because of the severity of their impairment; others are not diagnosed until the preschool years or primary grades (Burack, Zigler, & Hodapp, 1998). The term *mental retardation* refers to a variety of physical and mental conditions. Children with mental retardation vary in intellectual ability ranging from mild to profound. Some display physical disabilities; others do not. Some need constant protective care; others learn to live a productive life as adults.

MENTAL RETARDATION

Mental retardation refers to an intellectual deficiency significantly impairing a person's ability to function independently. A person with mental retardation demonstrates subaverage general intelligence with concomitant impairments in adaptive behavior (Kozma & Stock, 1993). In the context of mental retardation, adaptive behavior refers to developmentally appropriate expectations of personal independence and social responsibility. Therefore, the assessment of mental retardation depends not only on intellectual ability, but also on the cultural context (Jacobson & Mulick, 1996). Societal expectations play an influential role in establishing norms of appropriate behavior. People are expected to function in socially acceptable ways in a variety of different situations. An example of cultural influences can be seen in eating. In some cultures, people are allowed to use their fingers, but in other cultures, the same behavior is not encouraged.

Mental retardation has been classified in two main ways. One is based on severity. IQs have been used to classify children with mental retardation. Children with IQs ranging from 50 or 55 to 70 fall into the mildly retarded range, representing 80 to 85% of all individuals with mental retardation. Children with IQs ranging 35 or 40 to 50 and 20 or 25 to 35 or 40 are diagnosed as moderately and severely mentally retarded, respectively. Profound mental retardation, affecting 1 to 2% of all individuals with mental retardation, occurs with IQs below 20. IQs are used primarily to determine the placement of children with mental retardation into specially designed educational programs. They do not reflect the strengths and weaknesses of individual children with mental retardation.

In 1992, the American Association on Mental Retardation devised a new system of classification. It describes the way that people with the same IQ function. In the old system, children with similar classifications, such as mild or moderate mental retardation, are assumed to perform at the same level. However, in reality, functional capabilities vary considerably among children scoring in the same range. The new system provides a comprehensive picture of mental retardation, taking into account improvements over time. The four levels of the new system are (American Association of Mental Retardation, 1992):

■ **Intermittent.** Occasional support is required.

■ **Limited.** Certain kinds of support are needed on a consistent basis.

■ **Extensive.** Daily support is required in some aspects of life.

■ **Pervasive.** Constant support is needed in all aspects of life.

The causes of mental retardation vary. Two areas will be discussed: genetic and prenatal factors and complications during birth and infancy.

Genetic and Prenatal Causes.   A frequent cause of mental retardation is Down syndrome. Occurring in approximately 1 in 800 births, it results from the presence of an extra chromosome in the 21st pair. Instead of 46 chromosomes in a fertilized egg at conception, there is a faulty distribution of 47. The risk of Down syndrome increases substantially with the age of mothers, particularly after the late thirties, apparently because the gametes (the human sperm and ova) weaken with age and do not properly separate during meiosis.

Several teratogens have been linked to mental retardation during prenatal development. Examples include alcohol, prescribed medication, illicit drugs, and toxins such as lead and mercury. The specific effect of a particular teratogen depends on the stage of prenatal development in which it occurs. Exposure in the embryonic stage from 2 to 8 weeks of gestation severely impacts the normal growth of vital organs. Excessive maternal consumption of alcohol can result in a condition referred to as fetal alcohol syndrome (FAS). It afflicts an estimated 1 in 500 to 700 births, resulting in facial abnormalities and severe impairments of the brain.

Complications During Birth and Infancy.   Certain perinatal and postnatal factors can cause mental retardation. The deprivation of oxygen, or anoxia, during labor severely affects the healthy development of the brain. Perhaps the umbilical cord unexpectedly prolapses, or drops, during childbirth. Therefore, the head of the fetus inadvertently blocks the flow of oxygen from the umbilical cord to the brain as it enters the mother's birth canal. After birth, mental retardation may result from injuries to the head. Although automobile accidents tops the list, other common causes include physical abuse, particularly when parents shake their babies violently (called shaken baby syndrome).

EARLY INTERVENTION

In the past, children with mental retardation were severely shortchanged. Because their learning abilities were frequently underestimated, they were not even allowed to enter school. However, times have changed. Today, federal laws mandate that children with mental retardation receive appropriate educational programs and services to develop their functional daily living and vocational skills. Increasingly, many are mainstreamed, or integrated, with normally developing students. Therefore, children with mental retardation should be able to meet their educational and personal potential.

Once a diagnosis of mental retardation is made, a course of action is charted to facilitate development. Early intervention is intended to optimize children's unique learning and functional skills such as eating and dressing. Therapeutic factors are also taken into consideration. Related services, including physical and occupational therapy, are provided if motoric difficulties are noted. Parents' involvement has been identified as a critical component of early intervention. As their children's first teachers, parents play an influential role in identifying and implementing long- and short-term goals with a team of trained practitioners (Marsh, 1992).

COGNITIVE DEVELOPMENT

During the first year, infants learn from sensory exploration of objects. The following activities are designed to provide a variety of sensory experiences.

Birth to 1 Year

■ Play "peek-a-boo" with a towel held in front of your face.

■ Use a cardboard or cloth as a barrier or screen to hide an enticing object.

■ Provide toys that make noises when moved to learn about cause and effect.

■ Wear a smock—an old shirt or apron—with different textures sewn on or stuffed in pockets.

■ Put pudding or jello on a clean tray to encourage sensory play.

During the next 2 years, infants make continued progress. The following activities are intended to stimulate their natural curiosity about the world.

1 to 3 Years

■ Smear different kinds of food on a clean tray to fingerpaint.

■ Introduce simple puzzles with two separate large, knobbed pieces.

■ Make a nesting activity with plastic containers or cardboard boxes.

■ Collect different things such as leaves and rocks from the yard or park and display them on a shelf later.

■ Provide large homemade or commercial blocks to stack and create an endless variety of structures.

SUMMARY

Piaget's Theory of Cognitive Development

■ According to Piaget, cognitive development involves the qualitative transformation of children's global psychological structure. The first of four sequential stages in his theory is called the sensorimotor stage.

■ The sensorimotor stage is divided into six substages. Although infants initially rely on basic reflexes, they increasingly engage in purposeful activities over time.

■ Infants develop an increasing awareness of object permanence at roughly 8 months. Their ability to understand the existence of hidden objects marks a major cognitive achievement.

■ Piaget's theory has had a profound impact on research of infants' cognitive development. However, because of methodological limitations, some of his conclusions have been challenged in recent years.

New Perspectives on Cognition

■ Piaget's theory describes qualitative changes over time, but it does not adequately explain the basic mechanisms infants use to process sensory information. Recent studies have provided insights on memory and categorization, two important components of the cognitive apparatus.

■ When sensory information is received, it is deposited in a storehouse. The capacity to retain and recall past events is known as memory.

■ During the first year, infants make major strides in retaining information. Even newborns demonstrate the ability to remember short-term events after limited exposure.

■ Retention of information depends on infants' repeated exposure to environmental stimuli at first. Over time, duration increases from only a few minutes to days and weeks.

■ Further, infants can distinguish similarities and differences between objects. Their ability to organize information into meaningful groups is known as categorization.

■ The ability to sort objects into categories represents an important cognitive milestone. It facilitates the storage of sensory input, thereby improving the brain's efficiency in processing information.

Role of Play

■ Infants take an active role in exploring their environment. Spontaneous activities that are intrinsically motivated are referred to as play.

■ Several theories have been proposed to explain the function of play since the turn of the 20th century. Psychoanalytic and cognitive theories examine the impact of children's play on emotional and cognitive development.

■ Psychoanalytic theories are rooted in the work of Freud. In his view, children engage in play to reduce anxiety or resolve emotional conflicts.

■ Piaget's cognitive theory emphasizes the connection between sensorimotor development and play. Infants' playful activities provide opportunities to learn about the physical properties of objects and represent the world symbolically.

Special Needs

■ About 1 to 3% of all children are diagnosed as mentally retarded. One-quarter are identified at birth because of the severity of their impairment.

■ Mental retardation refers to an intellectual deficiency significantly impairing someone's ability to function independently. A person with mental retardation demonstrates subaverage general intelligence with concomitant impairments in adaptive behavior.

PROJECTS

1. Put together a homemade "feely box" to foster infants' sensory exploration of their world, using a cardboard box with a variety of securely fastened textures.

2. Conduct a Piagetian experiment by hiding a toy under a cloth to see whether an infant will actively search for it.

3. Go to a toy store and evaluate the developmental value of two toys, using the following format:

    Choose a commercial brand of toys oriented to the needs of infants and explain your decision.

    Select two toys of the same brand to evaluate.

Name of toy	Recommended Age	Cost

    Toy 1

    Toy 2

    Write manufacturer's information on each toy's developmental value.

    Toy 1

    Toy 2

    Draw sketch of each toy below.

    Toy 1

    Toy 2

    Discuss your opinion of each toy.

    Toy 1

    Toy 2

LANGUAGE ACQUISITION

If language is intimately related to being human, then when we study language we are, to a remarkable degree, studying human nature.

Charlton Laird, *The Miracle of Language*

The acquisition of language represents a remarkable human achievement. In just a short time, infants acquire the major components of their native language. On the average, infants utter their first meaningful word at about 12 months of age. Chapter 9 will show that even before children enter school, they can already demonstrate the ability to adapt their speech to suit the social and communicative nature of a situation, to pronounce and define hundreds of words in their vocabulary, and to use the correct grammatical forms—subjects, objects, verbs, plurals, and tenses.

A distinction between language and speech must be made. **Language** is defined as *a complex system of arbitrary symbols that are used to express and understand ideas and emotions.* Hereditary and environmental factors both play an equally important role in language acquisition. Infants are predisposed to acquire language. At birth, they possess the necessary cognitive tools they need learn their native tongue. Still, without environmental stimulation, they lose their capacity to gain mastery of the grammatical rules of language. Their ability to communicate transcends geographic and economic boundaries. All infants with the exception of babies with severe disabilities share a distinctly human heritage (Lenneberg, 1964, 1969). However, language involves not only a set of rules but also in most cases a vocal component. **Speech** therefore refers to *the production of spoken words and other meaningful sounds.*

THEORETICAL FRAMEWORKS

Although the scientific investigation of children's language did not begin until the mid-20th century, ancient societies certainly had pondered on its mysteries. The first recorded account of infants' development of language is found in the work of Greek historian Herodotus living in the fifth century B.C. He relates the story of Psammetichus, an ancient Egyptian king who wanted to prove that the human race originated in Egypt. To authenticate his claim, he ordered a shepherd to raise two newborns. The shepherd was not allowed to speak to them. The first spoken word of the children, the king believed, would reveal the original race of humankind. After 2 years of solitude, the children one day uttered a word of unknown origin. When the king found that the word meant bread in the Phrygian language, he decided to yield to the antiquity of the Phrygians.

Only much later in the late 19th century were studies of children's language published. Initial interest centered on the establishment of norms. Darwin himself kept a detailed diary of his son's acquisition of language. His observations provided valuable insights to other pioneers in the emerging field of psychology. American psychologist G. Stanley Hall himself was interested in "the content of children's mind." He inspired an entire school of students interested in studying children's language during the first half of the 20th century. Then, a revolution in the study of language acquisition occurred during the mid-20th century. Work in descriptive **linguistics** (Gleason, 1955), or *the science of language,* in addition to the transformational theory of Noam Chomsky (1957), provided the impetus. Linguists and psychologists eventually combined investigative techniques in their respective fields to study children's acquisition of language. **Psycholinguistics**, a branch of linguistics, emerged, involving *the study of the psychological processes that underlie language.*

At the same time, theories have been formulated to explain language acquisition. Two dominant theories have staked opposing positions. Behavioral theory stressed the influence of environmental factors. In contrast, structural theory emphasized the importance of heredity in controlling the sequential acquisition of children's language. In recent years, a new theory has emerged. Interactionist theory focuses on the interconnection between innate abilities and environment influences.

THEORETICAL FRAMEWORKS

Wilhelm von Humboldt
Wilhelm von Humboldt Werke, 1907
   The spiritual traits and the structure of the language of people are so intimately blended that, given either of the two, one should be able to derive the other from it to the fullest extent . . . Language is the outward manifestation of the spirit of people: Their language is their spirit, and their spirit is their language; it is difficult to imagine any two things more identical.

Source: Salzman (1993), p. 151.

BEHAVIORAL THEORY

Behavioral theorists take the view that language develops in response to environmental stimulation. They believe children learn to talk when adults reinforce their efforts to produce meaningful sounds. Other than the human vocal apparatus, innate features are not acknowledged in behavioral theory. Unobservable mechanisms are entirely rejected. To behavioral theorists, language acquisition follows the same laws of learning as with other types of behavior. It can be explained on the basis of both classical and operant conditioning (see Chapter 2).

   Classical conditioning involves the association between two events. In the context of language acquisition, children learn words when they make associations between external stimuli and internal responses. For example, initially, milk is a neutral word. However, the word itself refers to something that satisfies hunger. Repeatedly paired together, the word is associated with pleasure. Over time, just the word itself elicits the same reaction. The process only covers the development of receptive language. It does not explain children's ability to express themselves. Operant conditioning focuses on the consequences of behavior. Simply put, when a particular behavior is rewarded, it is repeated (Skinner, 1969). Children emit a wide range of sounds during the first year. Parents initially reward sound combinations approximating actual words. When children babble "mama" or "dada," they receive attention and social praise from parents ("Joey just said, 'Daddy'!"). Over time, children learn the correct pronunciations of words.

   Word combinations are acquired in the same way. The first word occurs in a specific context, serving as a stimulus that elicits the second word in the sentence and so on. Children do not necessarily have to hear every conceivable chain of words to engage in conversation with others. They only have to form associations between pairs of words or between single words and the environmental context (Mowrer, 1960).

   Therefore, the basic processes of learning are assumed to direct and control the increasing complexity of children's verbal behavior. However, classical and operant conditioning does not adequately explain the rapid pace of language acquisition. Behavioral theorists point to imitation as an important ingredient in language acquisition because it provides a shortcut to mature verbal behavior without laboriously reinforcing every response. Imitation involves the reproduction of behavior children observe in others. Still, the behavioral view of language acquisition has lost support over time because of its limited focus. Nevertheless, it has stimulated scientific interest in studying children's language acquisition.

STRUCTURAL THEORY

In contrast to behavioral theory, structural theorists concentrate on the biological aspects of language. Although they do not completely dismiss the influence of environmental factors, they believe language acquisition depends on innate features of the brain. Structural theorists argue that children utter novel sentences never heard before. In their view, language is not acquired on the basis of the association between stimuli or reinforcement of behavior. Instead, children's ability to generate and comprehend language follows a predetermined course across the world. The existence of universal milestones provides evidence supporting the position of structural theorists. Even deaf children spontaneously vocalize during the early months in the absence of auditory input. The brain is apparently predisposed, or genetically wired, to acquire a uniquely human characteristic: the use of language.

The work of one person has dominated the field of linguistics. American linguist Noam Chomsky has devised a comprehensive theoretical framework of language (Chomsky, 1965, 1968). He argues that each language assumes a structure or grammar. A grammar consists of a finite set of rules that all speakers of a particular language share. The rules governing any language allow the generation of an infinite number of possible sentences. A grammar resembles mathematics wherein a finite set of theorems permits the solution of an infinite number of problems.

Structural theorists presume that a physiological mechanism exists in the brain that bestows on children the ability to extract the rules that govern their spoken language. Referred to as LAD, or language acquisition device, it operates on the raw linguistic data of a particular language. Just as wings allow birds to fly, children possess enough innate knowledge of language to speak. Children are genetically endowed with innate linguistic knowledge. In fact, children are regarded as "little cryptographers," employing innate knowledge to decipher the language they hear.

Because of innate mechanisms, infants follow a predictable sequence of milestones. Although languages differ in significant ways, infants still rely on their linguistic endowment in acquiring language (Chomsky, 1999). Newborns immediately begin to detect linguistically significant sounds in their environment. As their ability to control the articulatory mechanisms matures, they produce only sounds they hear. Infants start to acquire unlabeled concepts of words that adults use. When adults say, "Do you want milk?" infants conclude that milk refers to an actual object. Children attend to milk instead of other words in the sentence because they possess the capacity to categorize words into grammatical classes. In other words, children automatically differentiate nouns from verbs because of their differing patterns in adults' speech (O'Grady, 1999).

BIOLOGICAL BASIS OF LANGUAGE

Specialized neural mechanisms in the brain are involved in the development of language. Infants are therefore predisposed to acquire language because of the neurological composition of the brain (Bates, Thal, & Janowsky, 1992; Cappa, 1999). Information regarding specialized areas of the brain controlling language comes from studies of injuries to the head. When a specific area of the brain is damaged, a person is said to suffer from **aphasia**, *a generalized communicative disorder.* Injuries to the brain generally result from either a traumatic event, a stroke, an aneurysm, or another cardiovascular condition. The effects of aphasia depend on the site of the lesion (Baum & Boyczuk, 1999; Hanlon, Lux, & Dromerick, 1999). Studies of aphasia have been limited primarily to adults. Children demonstrate remarkable plasticity wherein nondamaged areas of the brain can take over former functions.

At least three areas of the left hemisphere of the brain are associated with language. **Broca's area** involves *the front left region of the brain that controls expressive language* (the lips, tongue, and larynx). Damage to Broca's area results in Broca's aphasia, a typical aphasic syndrome. The patient demonstrates good comprehension but experiences difficulty with pronunciation. Only the important words are contained in speech. **Wernicke's area** refers to *the posterior left temporal lobe of the brain that governs receptive language.* Damage to Wernicke's area produces an aphasia that interferes with comprehension but not with speech. Neologisms, the use of nonsense words or phrases, characterize a patient's speech. The two areas of the brain are linked. A lesion in the **arcuate fasciculus**, *a bundle of subcortical fibers that connects the Wernicke's and Broca's areas,* hinders a patient's ability to repeat information.

A controversial aspect of Chomsky's work involves the limited role of the environment. He believes experience makes a difference only in the particular language children learn to speak (for example, children do not learn to speak Chinese if they do not hear it). However, criticisms have been raised about structural theory's emphasis on innate factors to the exclusion of other major influences affecting language acquisition. Just as behavioral theory ignores the contribution of heredity, structural theory dismisses the importance of the environment in shaping language acquisition. More recently, new ideas have emerged that stress not only the interaction between heredity and the environment but also the sociocultural context of language.

INTERACTIONIST THEORY

A third theory favors neither biological nor environmental explanations of language. The acquisition of language is instead viewed as an interaction between nature and nurture. Interactionalist theory recognizes and accepts the arguments of both the behavioral and the structural theoretical frameworks. Two major interactionist approaches have been developed: the cognitive theory of Piaget and the social interactionist approach.

Piaget's Cognitive Theory. Piaget's theory of cognitive development shares common elements with structural theory. Both emphasize internal structures. Yet, the two approaches do have significant differences. Basically, Piaget assumes that children's acquisition of language results largely from cognitive maturation (see Chapter 8).

The relationship between cognitive development and language acquisition is rooted in the sensorimotor stage. It centers on the concept of object permanence. According to Piaget, at first, infants do not realize that objects exist as separate entities. Once they understand the concept of object permanence, a major shift occurs at about 8 months of age. Infants gradually begin to use words to represent objects and later express ideas. In Piaget's view, linguistic ability coincides with cognitive maturation. Other cognitive accomplishments are assumed to occur before they are reflected in children's linguistic skills. Word combinations depend on children's perception of semantic relations between objects and people in their environment (Bohannon & Bonvillian, 1997; Bowerman, 1982).

Social Interactionist Approach. As with Piaget's cognitive theory, the social interactionist approach combines both traditional behavioral and linguistic frameworks. Social interactionists agree with linguists who stress that language follows biologically determined

---

PARENTING ISSUES

PARENTESE

Infants are captivated by the human voice. Questions have been raised about their preferences in listening to human speech, just as in looking at faces. Is the human voice simply an interesting thing to listen to, or do infants' preferences reflect a biological predisposition? Researchers are still seeking answers to explain infants' preferences at birth and during the subsequent months of development.

Adults themselves seem to respond to infants' selectivity in attending to the human voice. Parents engage in a special kind of speech that features a high pitch and exaggerated intonation. It has been referred to as babytalk or motherese in the past. In recent years, because fathers, like mothers, adjust or modify their verbal exchanges with their infants, researchers prefer the neutral term *parentese* or infant-directed speech (Cooper, 1993; Cooper & Aslin, 1994).

Parentese can be found in every culture. During the first year, 80% of parents' vocalizations with their infants can be classified as parentese (Stern, Spieker, & MacKain, 1982). Psycholinguists believe that parentese fulfills a variety of functions. First, it captures and maintains infants' attention because of its unique qualities (Pegg, Werker, & McLeod, 1992). Infants typically turn their heads in the direction

(continued)

of adults who use parentese. Second, parentese encourages social interaction (Ratner, 1996). Parents have been observed to respond sensitively to their infants' needs and exhibit a playful demeanor. Lastly, parentese increases the linguistic competence of infants because it encourages their ability to notice and discriminate the stream of adults' words and sentences (Grieser & Kuhl, 1988).

Adults modify their speech with infants in a number of distinctive ways. They not only use a high-pitched voice and exaggerate their intonation, but also make other modifications:

Sound

■ Loud volume

■ Slow rate of speech

■ Clear enunciation

■ Special pronunciation ("You are getting to be such as b-i-i-i-g boy!")

■ Adoption of infant's incorrect pronunciation of words ("bozer" instead of bulldozer)

Semantics

■ Substitutions ("choo-choo" instead of train)

■ Diminutives ("kitty" instead of cat)

■ Inappropriate use of words (reference to orangutan as "monkey")

■ Adoption of infant's invented words ("wa-wa" in place of water)

■ Nonstandard words ("pigeon-bird" instead of pigeon)

Grammar

■ Grammatically simple utterances

■ Short utterances

■ Use of nouns in place of pronouns ("Daddy wants Melody to take a bath.")

■ Use of pronouns in place of singular ("Shall we take a bath now?")

■ Intentional ungrammatical usage ("No eat!" instead of "Don't eat that!")

Conversation

■ Restricted topics (speech is limited to present or immediate past)

■ Provision of both questions and answers ("Shall we change your diaper now? Yes? Okay.")

■ Repetitive utterances ("Would you like some juice? Would you like some juice?")

■ Use of sentences in labeling objects ("That's a cow. A cow.")

■ Expansion of infant's utterances (adult replies, "Yes, your milk is all gone. Would you like some more?" in response to "All gone.")

mechanisms but at the same time share behaviorists' emphasis on environmental factors. Specifically, proponents of the social interactionist approach believe that children acquire language to not only communicate but engage with people. Therefore, the development of linguistic structures is tied to children's increasing ability to relate to others in social contexts. Both sides of the nature–nurture debate are accepted.

Children learn new words when adults describe the properties of objects, such as shape and texture, in spontaneous or structured activities. Photo courtesy of Tami Dawson, Photo Resource Hawaii.

Although humans are genetically predisposed to acquire language, a certain amount of cognitive maturation is needed before it is attained.

Social interactionists point to the special nature of speech that parents direct to their children during the first few years. Parents engage in *a pattern of speech that consists of a high-pitched voice and exaggerated intonation,* known as **parentese**. Children tend to improve their control of the vocal apparatus when they attend to their parents' production of sounds. Further, social play between children and their parents serves as an important basis of conversational speech later. Even when children babble, parents attempt to interpret their vocalizations. In the words of Golinkoff (1983), "conversational bouts" occur in interactions between children and their parents. If a child babbles "mama" because of hunger, the mother often tries to make an interpretation. On the basis of the mother's knowledge of the child, she offers milk, or some other food, to fulfill the child's request (Harding, 1984).

STRUCTURAL COMPONENTS OF LANGUAGE

When the grammatical rules of a language are acquired, children are said to have developed communicative competence. It refers to the internalization of the grammatical rules that speakers use to communicate with others. Researchers rely on children's actual utterances to gain insights about their underlying competence. Children of different ages produce errors as they learn about the grammatical rules of their language. To understand the development of language, researchers must study its structure. All languages consist of five basic structural components: phonology (the distinctive sounds of language), morphology (the way that sounds are combined to form words), syntax (the

SOCIOCULTURAL INFLUENCES

CULTURAL VARIATIONS IN PARENTESE

Parents often alter their speech to accommodate the perceptual and cognitive immaturity of their infants. Cultural beliefs and practices can play a critical role in determining the specific nature of parents' speech (Shatz, 1991). For example, the similarities and differences in the use of parentese between Japanese and European American mothers have been studied. Both modify their speech to accommodate their infants in similar ways, but culture influences the quality of their interactions with their babies (Tomasello, 1996).

Early research has concentrated on the structural features of parentese. However, a simple comparison of structural characteristics is fraught with difficulties because of distinctive differences between languages (Fernald, 1993). In recent years, researchers have begun to focus on the interaction between parents and their infants. The question is asked: Do differences in the form and content between Japanese and European American parents' speech result from linguistic restraints or distinctive communicative styles of cultures? The results of different studies have confirmed the universal features of Japanese and European American parents' speech with their infants. Both modify their speech (Toda, Fogel, & Kawai, 1990).

At the same time, differences in communicative style have been found. European American mothers tend to focus on and label objects that their infants attend

to and play with (Fernald & Morikawa, 1993). On the other hand, Japanese mothers do not label objects with words to the degree that European American mothers do. On the average, Japanese mothers name objects only about one-third of the time in their interaction with infants in comparison to one-half with European American mothers. Further, Japanese mothers often use onomatopoetic words in reference to objects. Because "buubuu" represents both the sound that pigs and vehicles make in Japanese, mothers refer to pigs, cars, and trucks with the same word (Fernald & Mazzie, 1991).

Therefore, culturally transmitted views influence maternal speech in both Japan and the United States. Japanese mothers encourage *amae*, translated as mutual dependence (Doi, 1973), in their interaction with children, whereas European American mothers generally value independence in children. In addition, Japanese mothers stress the importance of fitting into the social group. In an example of the pragmatic component of language, Japanese mothers often rehearse social routines with their children such as responding politely to adults and considering the needs of others (Morikawa, Shand, & Kosawa, 1988). Clearly, adults' speech reflects the complex interaction between both linguistic and cultural factors. Adults universally modify their speech to children but differ in the way they encourage culturally acceptable uses of language.

way that words are stringed to form sentences), semantics (the meaning of words), and pragmatics (the way that a language is used to communicate with others).

PHONOLOGY

Each language consists of a set of distinctive sounds that its speakers combine together to form words. **Phonology** involves *the rules that control the combination of sounds in a language.* Phonological rules determine intonation and stress, features that give a language its melody. **Phonemes**, derived from a Greek word meaning "sound" or "voice," refer to *the basic sounds of a language.* The exact number of phonemes depends on the language itself. It generally ranges from 20 to 60. In English, there are 44 phonemes. Phonemes outnumber the letters of the English alphabet because combinations of letters represent different phonemes such as ch and th.

The phonological tasks that children face vary. For example, complicated rules govern the combination of consonants in English and other Germanic languages, in contrast to Japanese with only a few clusters. Some sounds in English are not found in any other language. Combinations such as th pose a challenge to anyone who wants to learn English. Still, infants are prepared to acquire any language they are exposed to. Even at birth, they selectively attend to only certain sounds in their environment. They prefer to listen to high-pitched human voices. Within a few weeks, they are able to discriminate their mothers' voices from others (Jusczyk, 1995; Vihman, 1996).

The production of sounds involves the complex coordination of the respiratory system and vocal tract, which includes the throat, mouth, tongue, and nasal cavity. Air is pushed from the lungs into the vocal tract. The type of sound that is made is based on several factors. In particular, the articulation of sounds depends on the position of the lips and tongue. /p/ is produced in the front; /g/ is made in the back. The lips close to make /b/. The tongue flicks the area in back of the front teeth to articulate /t/. The structure of the vocal tract gradually changes with physiological maturation. Control of specific sounds increases with age.

MORPHOLOGY

Infants are quite capable of making distinctive sounds. At first, crying signals distress. Later, infants begin to string sounds into combinations of consonants and vowels. Only at the end of the first year, however, do children begin to combine sounds into meaningful words. In every language, rules determine the specific combination of sounds in words. **Morphology** refers to *the rules that govern the construction of words in a language.* Words can be broken into individual units. *The smallest units of meaning in a language* are known as **morphemes**.

In all languages, morphemes represent whole words or subsets of a whole. Single morphemes are found in words such as *open*. The addition of multiple morphemes changes the content of the word. The word *opened* is composed of two morphemes (open + ed). Children internalize the rules controlling the possible combinations of sounds in their native language on their own. They demonstrate their awareness of morphology when they engage in **overregularization**, *the application of regular grammatical rules in exceptional cases.* Children often add the plural -*s* to exceptional nouns as in *mans* or *foots* for men and feet. Further, they use, to the amusement of their parents, regular past tense -*ed* on irregular verbs such as *falled* or *goed* for fell and went. Expressions such as "I falled down" or "I goed outside" begin to appear in children's utterances between ages 2 and 3, demonstrating the creative use of grammatical rules since adults do not use overregularized words. Overregularization is used only in about 5 to 8% of the time in which irregular forms are used (Marcus, 1995; Marcus et al., 1992).

SYNTAX

An important linguistic watershed is reached at the end of the second year. Children start to combine two or more words together. Their initial sentences clearly follow certain grammatical rules. Children's utterances show evidence of **syntax**, *the combination of words into meaningful sentences.* To describe the rules that specify the relationship between words in sentences, linguists make a distinction between two different syntactic forms. While the **surface structure** of a sentence refers to *the linear arrangements of words,* **deep structure** involves *the basic grammatical relationship between the subject and object in a sentence* (Chomsky, 1957, 1965).

The systematic investigation of syntactic development has historically centered on naturalistic observations of children's spontaneous speech. Longitudinal studies of children have yielded vast quantities of raw data in the form of transcripts (Lieven, Pine, & Baldwin, 1997). Although they provide valuable insights into the acquisition of language, they do not disclose information on children's comprehension of syntactic rules. Because of methodological constraints, naturalistic observations had to be complemented with controlled studies. For example, Golinkoff and her colleagues have pioneered a new method of assessing children's comprehension of language. Subjects listen to a recorded sentence, such as "Cookie Monster is tickling Big Bird," and look at one of two monitors (Golinkoff et al., 1987). If they look at the correct monitor, the children show they understand the message. The length of time spent in looking at one monitor or the other provides an objective measure of children's syntactic development.

Children's length of sentences increases over time. The length of a sentence, not age, is a good predictor of children's syntactic development (Wexler, 1999). Each new unit, or morpheme, represents the acquisition of new linguistic knowledge. Roger Brown introduced the first major index of syntactic development in 1973: the **mean length of utterance** (MLU), *the average length of children's sentences.* Infants apparently rely on prosodic cues in speech to "bootstrap" their way into syntax. Some researchers believe infants' perceptual analyses of speech must precede their application of syntactic rules in language acquisition (Fernald & McRoberts, 1996).

SEMANTICS

As children utter their first words, their vocalizations reflect the words adults use to label objects. When children say a word, parents typically engage in naming games, pointing to and talking about specific objects in the immediate environment. The words children utter do not always mean the same things adults associate in actual usage. Children often classify similar objects in the same category. For example, they sometimes say "doggie" to refer to all animals or, to the embarrassment of their fathers, "daddy" in reference to all men. In linguistics, *the study of the meaning of words* is referred to as **semantics**.

Children's vocabulary includes words from different grammatical classes. Their first 50 words represent all the major classes that adults use in language. Studies have noted the preponderance of nouns in comparison to other types of words. In one study, nouns (general nominals such as "doggie" and specific nominals such as "mommy") represent about two-thirds of words in children's vocabulary (Nelson, 1973). First words generally refer to objects children come into frequent contact with such as food or toys and things that move such as ball or pet. Receptive vocabulary (words that are understood) always precedes expressive vocabulary (words that children are able to say). Labels of new and familiar objects are learned from parents during spontaneous play, assisting in the infants' understanding of word meanings (Masur, 1997).

PRAGMATICS

Children gain not only linguistic but also communicative competence in just a few short years. Linguistic competence involves the construction of grammatically correct sentences, whereas communicative competence relates to the use of language in different situations. In particular, children develop the ability to adapt or modify their speech when listeners signal communicative difficulty. **Pragmatics** refers to *the rules that govern the practical use of language to communicate with others in a variety of conversational and social situations.*

Communicative competence begins even before infants utter their first words. Parents respond to infants' vocalizations, facial expressions, and gestures and engage in intentional communication with their infants, even during the initial weeks and months of life. For example, parents have been observed to "jiggle" or shift their infants while breast- or bottle-feeding. Both parents and infants are believed to be engaging in a rudimentary form of dialogue (Kaye, 1982; Kaye & Wells, 1980). When one person shuts down, the other makes an effort to continue the conversation. Other forms of mutual conversation ensue later. Infants typically mirror their parents' social overtures, reciprocating with coos and babbles of their own.

Further progress is made in the mastery of communicative skills over the next few years. Toddlers' vocalizations, facial expressions, and gestures all show communicative intent. When their efforts fail, toddlers try to make "repairs." Although they sometimes experience frustration, toddlers try to repeat or alter their request both verbally and nonverbally (Golinkoff, 1986) or clarify their communicative intent when adults request additional information (Ninio & Snow, 1999). At the same time, children learn the social conventions of language reflecting their culture's values. In different cultures, children are taught specific communicative routines such as greeting or leaving someone (hi, bye-bye), making a specific request or acknowledging someone's assistance (please, thank you), and addressing someone politely (ma'am, sir).

SEQUENCE OF MILESTONES

Across the world, children follow the same sequence and timetable in acquiring language. Children's ability to acquire language can be traced in two periods: the prelinguistic and linguistic periods.

PRELINGUISTIC PERIOD

Even newborn infants are able to communicate at birth. During the first few months, infants cry to signal physiological distress such as hunger or pain. Analyses of infants' cries

READING ALOUD TO INFANTS

The development of children's language is further stimulated when books are read. Books contain repetitive and descriptive words that foster interest in the usage of language (Butler, 1998). Infants learn to become active participants in the reading process. During the last half of the first year, they can now begin to pay increased attention to words and illustrations (Trelease, 1995). Adults sometimes hesitate to read aloud, but children enjoy opportunities to listen to stories because of the skin-to-skin contact they receive. The following strategies have been suggested to enrich children's reading experiences in the first year (Eisenberg, Murkoff, & Hathaway, 1996a):

■ **Read aloud with enthusiasm.** Children like to listen to stories when adults read with exaggerated tone and inflection. Adults can stimulate children's inherent curiosity and interest when they talk about the salient features in the illustrations or ask questions about the stories' outcomes.

■ **Start a collection of books.** Hundreds of children's books are published each year. Appropriate books include sturdy construction with laminated pages and rounded edges, bold and realistic illustrations, simple text with repetitive words, and textured surfaces that encourage sensorimotor exploration.

■ **Create a reading habit.** Adults should incorporate reading into daily activities, perhaps a few minutes at first. Good reading times include before naps and bedtime and after lunch and baths.

■ **Read yourself.** Children take an interest in reading when adults themselves read. They learn to understand that adults value books and other sources of information.

The next 2 years bring ample opportunities to enjoy books. Among the different ways to nurture children's interest in reading are to (Eisenberg, Murkoff, & Hathaway, 1996b):

■ **Be selective.** Choose books with simple texts and realistic pictures. Introduce simple stories with rhyming words.

■ **Be creative.** Take literary license to increase children's listening pleasure. Abridge long passages, substitute simple words, add your own commentary, and use descriptive words to label things in the illustrations.

■ **Be interactive.** Involve children in the reading process. Point to the illustrations and ask questions about the plot.

■ **Be repetitive.** Read the same stories again and again. Exaggerate your tone of voice.

reveal distinctive crying patterns. Differences among infants' cries involving hunger and pain provide possible information about the causes of their distress (Gustafson & Harris, 1990; Zeskind & Marshall, 1988). However, parents are not always able to pinpoint the exact cause of their infants' cries. Prolonged crying usually slips into rhythmic crying patterns accompanying hunger. Newborns cry primarily because of hunger. Early studies of crying both before and after feedings confirm that it generally decreases in frequency

TABLE 9-1 MAJOR MILESTONES IN LANGUAGE ACQUISITION

Age	Phonology	Morphology and Semantics
Birth	Crying	
2 months	Cooing	
6 months	Babbling	
10 months		Understands selected words
12 months		Utters first word
18 months		Comprehends simple commands; amasses vocabulary of 50 words
24 months		Knows about 200 words
36 months		Amasses vocabulary of about 1,000 words

Sources: Bayley (1969); Leach (1997).

afterwards (Dunn, 1977; Wolff, 1969). Further, infants of different ethnic groups exhibit very distinctive crying strategies. European American infants typically prefer crying as the primary mode of communicating whereas Korean American infants do not cry as frequently (Green & Gustafson, 1997; Lee, 1994).

Cooing. Sometime between 2 and 4 months, infants begin to coo. In contrast to crying, **cooing**, *vowel-like utterances that infants make*, seems to signify contentment. Its appearance coincides with changes in the configuration of the vocal tract. Over time, the larynx, the seat of the vocal cords, gradually descends from its original position (Baron, 1992). Further, infants develop increased control of the tongue and lips. The emergence of cooing, as with other aspects of language, depends on both physiological and neurological maturation. The cooing sounds that infants make come from the back of their throat. Two consonants, /k/ and /g/, are individually paired with a vowel, /u/, to produce the characteristic sounds of cooing. Infants' cooing represents a physiological, not a linguistic, event since the ability to coo soon disappears with normal maturation of the vocal tract. However, occurring in a social context, it elicits parents' attention and promotes social interaction (de Villiers & de Villiers, 1992).

Babbling. Between 4 and 8 months, infants begin to experiment with different patterns of sounds. **Babbling** consists of *the repetition of consonants and vowels in alternating sequences that increasingly resemble adults' speech*. Initially, babbling sounds include single vowels, consonants that stop the flow of air in the mouth (/p/, /b/, /t/, and /d/), nasals (/m/ and /n/), and combinations of consonants and vowels. In the last half of the first year, children start to babble long sequences of sounds, such as pa-pa-pa-pa or ba-ba-ba-ba. Again, the transition from cooing to babbling results from further physiological and neurological control of the vocal tract. Children tend to shift back and forth between cooing and babbling in their everyday vocalizations. Babbling seems to serve two purposes. Just as children exercise their emerging physical and cognitive skills, here they seem to be exploring the parameters of sounds. A second function of babbling involves social contact. Children become rudimentary conversationalists at 10 months of age and begin to alter the intonation of their vocalizations, just as adults do. In different cultural groups, infants apparently babble in distinctive ways. Even untrained listeners

TABLE 9–1 CONTINUED	
Syntax	**Pragmatics**
	Points and gestures
	Understands gestures; responds to bye-bye
	Waves bye-bye
Uses two-word utterances; engages in telegraphic speech	Uses words to communicate needs
Makes use of pronouns and prepositions	Engages in rudimentary conversation
Uses adjectives	Follows simple directions

can detect differences between the native languages of English, French, Swedish, and Japanese learning babies (Boysson-Bardies & Vihman, 1991; Levitt, 1993).

Children make the transition from babbling to true speech between 10 and 12 months. Until now, children have been barraged with language from their parents and other sources, including television. A few dozen labels are repeatedly heard in the average household. In particular, words such as mommy, daddy, milk, and no are frequently used in children's presence. The repetitive quality of the babbling period sometimes becomes the source of children's first words. Children who are on the verge of uttering their first words are generally active babblers. Many heavily rely on the same string of sounds, particularly duh (or da). According to behavioral theory, rewards encourage the likelihood of the same behavior. In reality, parents do reinforce their children's vocalizations with frequent smiles and social praise. Children who say, "duhduh," probably receive a demonstrable reward (a hug or kiss) from their fathers. As a result of parental reinforcement and attention, babbling takes on increased importance, although in some cases, children clearly select their own early words. Children who are fascinated with boats may say buh as their first identifiable word.

Table 9–1 summarizes the major milestones children reach in acquiring language.

LINGUISTIC PERIOD

The appearance of the first word between 10 and 18 months marks a significant shift from prelinguistic to linguistic speech. Just as parents eagerly await their children's first steps, first words typically represent a momentous occasion.

First Words.   Children's first words generally consist of people ("mommy," "daddy"), parts of the body ("eyes," "nose"), domestic animals ("dog," "cat"), and objects that move ("car," "ball"). In addition, their first words include familiar actions ("bye-bye," "more") and outcomes ("wet," "hot"). Their first 50 words reflect people and objects they interact with on a daily basis. Children's first words rarely refer to stationary objects such as a table or chair (Bloom, 1993; Erneling, 1993). Early words are inextricably tied to children's cognitive advances during the same time. Their use of phrases such as "all gone" reflect their increasing awareness of object permanence. As their ability to

SEQUENCE OF MILESTONES

Helen Keller

Helen and Teacher: The Story of Helen Keller and Anne Sullivan Macy, 1980

I stood still, my whole attention fixed upon the motions of [Anne's] fingers. Suddenly I felt a misty consciousness as of something forgotten—a thrill of returning thought; and somehow the mystery of language was revealed to me. I knew then that W-A-T-E-R meant the wonderful cool something that was flowing over my hand . . . Everything had a name, and each name gave birth to a new thought.

Source: Lash (1980), p. 55.

solve problems increases, children's spontaneous expressions highlight some of their successes and failures. They like to say "there" or "uh-oh" in response to their everyday encounters with the real world.

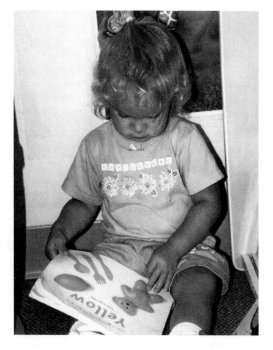

Books read aloud to children foster interest in language and facilitate the acquisition of new words.
Photo courtesy of Tami Dawson, Photo Resource Hawaii.

Not until the last half of the second year are children able to combine words into simple sentences. At first glance, single words seem to restrict the production of language, but some psycholinguists believe that children actually engage in **holophrastic speech** or *the use of single words to convey complex ideas in full sentences* (McNeil, 1970). Many examples of children's holophrastic speech abound. Depending on the context, "mama" may indicate "I want mommy" or "Mommy, put on my shoes." Sometimes, a word is used in a restrictive manner. *The use of words to refer to a narrow category* is called **underextension**. Children generally do not use the same label to refer to other objects in the same class. A "doggie" perhaps refers to a pet in the family but not to other dogs in the neighborhood. The opposite phenomenon is observed in children's overuse of words. **Overextension** involves *the application of a word to a variety of objects that share a common characteristic*. For example, a "ball" may refer to all round objects such as seasonal ornaments. An estimated 20 to 30% of all words are overextended (Nelson et al., 1978).

Two-Word Utterances. Children start to combine two words together at about 18 months. The appearance of two words coincides with the rapid acquisition of vocabulary (Goldfield & Reznick, 1990; Reznick & Goldfield, 1992). At first, children add about 1 to 3 new words per month. During the last half of the second year, they acquire about 10 to 20 words per week, resulting in a vocabulary of about 200 words on their second birthday. Before children use sentences, they enter a transitional phase and express two ideas separately, one after the other. Their utterances do not represent true sentences because a pause separates both words as in "Daddy, car" (perhaps meaning "Daddy is going. He is in the car.") Children form actual sentences soon afterwards. Two separate ideas are now combined into a simple utterance (therefore, "Daddy, car" becomes "Daddy car" meaning "Daddy is going in the car.")

When children string two words together, unimportant elements of their message are usually discarded as in an old-fashioned telegram. **Telegraphic speech** refers to *children's two-word utterances that convey an idea with a minimal number of words* (Brown & Fraser, 1963). Children's sentences consist mostly of nouns, verbs, and adjectives. Few articles, conjunctions, or prepositions appear in their utterances (such as *at, in, to,* or *with*) although adults make considerable use of them. Nor do children inflict words with suffixes or prefixes. They do not add *-s* to nouns to indicate plurality or *-ed* to verbs to signify past tense. Further, children largely ignore auxiliary verbs such as *can* or *may*. The length and complexity of their sentences gradually increase with age. At 30 months, children use between 3 and 5 words in their sentences as their vocabulary increases to about 1,000 words (McLaughlin, 1998).

Telegraphic speech can be seen across the world. Table 9–2 demonstrates the universality of telegraphic speech.

BILINGUALISM

An increasing number of children in the United States are capable of understanding and using two, or more, languages. Current estimates indicate that over 6 million children

TABLE 9–2 UNIVERSALITY OF TELEGRAPHIC SPEECH

Function	English	German	Russian	Finnish	Samoan
Location	"There book"	"Buch da" ("Book there")	"Tasya tam" ("Tasya there")	"Toussa Rina" ("There Rina")	"Punafu lea" ("Punafu there")
Recurrence	"More milk"	"Mehr milch" ("More milk")	"Yesche moloko" ("More milk")	"Anna Rina" ("Give Rina")	"Mai pepe" ("Give doll")
Possession	"My shoe"	"Mein ball" ("My ball")	"Mami chashka" ("Mama cup")	"Tati auto" ("Aunt car")	"Lole a'u" ("My candy")
Question	"Where ball?"	"Wo ball" ("Where ball?")	"Gdu papa" ("Where papa?")	"Missa pallo" ("Where ball?")	"Fea Punafu" ("Where Punafu?")

learn English as a second language (Tabors, 1997). During the linguistic period, bilingual children acquire new words from both languages. Their first words are rarely used to describe the same object or concept in both languages, particularly when one parent speaks one language and the other a different language (Yavas, 1995). A child might say "ball" to one adult and "pelota" (or ball in Spanish) to another. Later, at about 18 months, bilingual children begin to put two words together in their utterances. Because of the distinctive syntactic differences between unrelated languages, special challenges are sometimes encountered (Bhatia & Ritchie, 1999). For example, in Spanish, adjectives typically follow nouns, as in "la casa blanca" (or the white house). Bilingual children eventually use words appropriately in their respective contexts after repeated exposure and practice in their richly varied linguistic environment. Although the acquisition of two languages seems to pose insurmountable barriers, bilingual children typically progress at the same rate as their monolingual counterparts (Romaine, 1995). Also, recent research shows that bilingualism has some beneficial effects on cognitive development. Bilingual children do better than their monolingual classmates in school on measures of analytical reasoning and cognitive flexibility as well as metalinguistic awareness or the ability to think about spoken and written language (Bialystok, 1997; Bialystok & Majumder, 1998).

SPECIAL NEEDS

Perception of the world is derived from the senses. If any one of the five senses is impaired, development can be severely affected. Audition or the sense of hearing plays a critical role in infancy. A hearing impairment can restrict language acquisition and hinder children's social interactions with others. When a medical diagnosis of a hearing

EXPLOSIVE GROWTH OF VOCABULARY

Researchers once believed that infants' productive or expressive vocabulary did not differ from their comprehensive or receptive vocabulary. However, comprehension of language develops before actual production of words. *The ability to understand the speech of others* is referred to as **comprehension**. Children typically understand simple words before they can say their first word. At the end of the second year, children are beginning to understand two to three related requests combined into a single utterance. Children's comprehension of words explodes after the second year as their receptive vocabulary increases dramatically. On the other hand, **production**, *the spoken communication of children*, begins at the moment of birth with the first plaintive cries. Although crying is the first form of communication, production involves the utterance of meaningful words that adults understand.

The rate of children's production of words increases exponentially after the second year. Children generally amass a vocabulary of about 200 words at the age of 2. However, before the age of 6, it increases to an average of 10,000 words. Children are learning on average about 5 new words each day, a remarkable achievement in view of the fact that the first intelligible word takes an entire year (Anglin, 1993):

> . . . the speed and complexity of children's learning of a first language are truly impressive. Perhaps especially well-documented is the rapid pace at which children acquire the grammatical rules that enable the production and comprehension of sentences during the preschool years. . . . (p. 1)

Considerable research has tried to determine the underlying cause of children's rapid acquisition of new words. The answer seems to lie in the realization that the development of vocabulary does not result from an additive process. Apparently, the brain discovers interconnections between categories of words. Children develop a kind of mental map that charts the similarities among actual objects, a process called fast mapping (Golinkoff et al., 1992). When a new word is heard, it is placed into an existing category on the basis of its use in a particular context. Even when preschool children heard a nonsense word in an experimental study just once such as *koob* (an oddly shaped plastic ring), they quickly made a connection after a very brief encounter (Dollaghan, 1985). Parents often assist their children's ability to learn new words when they label things. A new geometric shape, a triangle, is easily acquired when another shape, a circle, is already understood. In addition, children make assumptions about new words that seem to accelerate the process. They assume that words refer to whole objects, not parts, and that each object contains only one label (Carroll, 1999).

LANGUAGE DEVELOPMENT

The first year brings dramatic changes in the acquisition of language. When adults are actively engaged in mutual interactions with infants, direct benefits include accelerated onset of first words and increased vocabulary (Dunham & Dunham, 1992; Dunham, Dunham, & Curwin, 1993).

Birth to 1 Year

■ Respond immediately to infants' cries in a soothing, reassuring tone of voice.

■ Pay attention to and talk about things that they look at and touch.

■ Imitate infants' sounds as they begin to babble.

■ Label different parts of the body when you change diapers or play in front of a mirror.

■ Play "pat-a-cake" and sing simple songs involving a variety of motions.

Children begin to combine words into telegraphic sentences and follow simple directions. Daily routines provide numerous opportunities to label objects in the immediate environment and practice beginning conversational skills.

1 to 3 Years

■ Point to and label objects and people.

■ Listen and respond to children when they vocalize and combine words together.

■ Look at pictures in a book and ask simple questions about the events in the story.

■ Describe your actions as you perform daily routines.

■ Take a short walk in the neighborhood or shopping mall and talk about the different sights and sounds.

impairment is made, immediate intervention is needed to promote children's ability to communicate effectively and function independently in a variety of contexts. Because language is acquired rapidly in the first few years, steps must be taken not only to increase amplification with corrective hearing aids but also to encourage communicative competence with aural-oral or manual approaches.

Hearing impairment has always been associated with human existence. However, efforts to educate the hearing impaired did not begin until the 16th century. Spanish monk Pablo Ponce de Leon taught a nobleman's first-born son with hearing impairment to talk in order to inherit his father's property. Over time, the education of the hearing impaired gained widespread acceptance in western Europe. In time, two opposing views of education arose. While the Abbe de l'Epee used manual communication to instruct the deaf, Samuel Heinicke in Germany and Thomas Braidwood in England relied on speech. In the United States, Thomas Gallaudet studied the manual method in France.

He returned and established the first school, still in existence, to teach the deaf in Hartford, Connecticut, in 1817 (Lowenbraun & Thompson, 1990).

CAUSES OF HEARING IMPAIRMENTS

In a normally functioning ear, sound enters the external auditory canal. It then travels into the middle and inner ear, containing the cochlea, the hearing organ, and the semi-circular canals, the center of balance. As a result, sound is transformed into neural impulses. The brain interprets the neural signals it receives and acts accordingly. Interference at any point in the auditory system results in a hearing loss. Impairment in the mechanical transmission of sound in the outer or middle ear is known as a conductive hearing loss. Children frequently experience excessive accumulation of wax in the external ear or fluid in the middle ear, hindering the transmission of sound. Conductive hearing losses are usually corrected either with medication or surgery. Impairment in the inner ear interferes with the conversion of sound into neural impulses. Sensorineural hearing losses not only reduce the intensity of the signal but also distort the perception of the sound.

Other factors may cause a hearing loss. Genetic causes account for about 50% of all cases of deafness in children. The high incidence of marriages between individuals with hearing impairments has increased the likelihood of genetic causes. Nongenetic factors, such as diseases or injury, can also cause hearing losses. Rubella, commonly called German measles, precipitates a hearing loss as it attacks the rapidly developing central nervous system during the first 3 months of pregnancy. In addition, complications during pregnancy or childbirth such as premature birth or apnea, the loss of oxygen, increase the possibility of hearing impairments. After birth, viral infections, particularly mumps, measles, and meningitis, sometimes lead to hearing losses. In a small percentage of cases, trauma, high fever, and excessive exposure to loud noises can take a toll and result in permanent hearing impairments.

INTERVENTIONAL STRATEGIES

The severity of hearing losses depends on the degree of impairment and the involvement of one or both ears. In general, persons with unilateral hearing losses tend to function normally with difficulties only in locating the direction of sounds. Persons with mild to moderate bilateral hearing losses usually benefit from amplification with hearing aids. Severe bilateral hearing losses require not only the amplification of any residual hearing but also the additional support from aural-oral or manual communication. Children with severe hearing losses do not on their own develop spontaneous speech because their hearing impairments limit their linguistic exposure. However, with therapeutic and educational intervention, they are able to communicate effectively and function independently.

Two different approaches are used to teach children with hearing losses. In the aural-oral approach, children are taught to speak and read lips. They are learning to "fit in" with the normal hearing population. Proponents of the aural-oral method believe manual communication hinders the process of normalization. On the other hand, manual communication bypasses the auditory–vocal channel in favor of the visual-motor system. Proponents of manual communication believe it facilitates children's communicative competence. Finger spelling, a system that uses manually formed symbols representing each letter of the alphabet and ordinal numbers, eliminates the ambiguities of speech reading. Another system of manual communication is known as sign language. In particular, American Sign Language (ASL) relies on the use of fingers, hands, arms, and facial expressions to communicate with others. It consists of thousands of signs and a unique syntax that does not include certain features of spoken language such as articles and prepositions. Whatever approach is used, parents of children with hearing impairments must be actively involved. They form an important link in the collaborative partnership between home and special educational programs (Roush & McWilliam, 1994).

SUMMARY

Theoretical Frameworks

- Different theories have been proposed to explain children's acquisition of language. Since the mid-20th century, two theories have dominated the debate.

- Behavioral theory emphasizes the influence of environmental factors. In other words, children acquire language because adults shape emerging sounds into meaningful words through reinforcement.

- In contrast, the structural framework of Chomsky emphasizes the role of innate factors. In his view, the brain is wired with the capacity to extract the grammatical rules of language.

- The interactionist theory, on the other hand, favors neither viewpoint. It instead focuses on the interaction between nature and nurture.

Structural Components of Language

- To understand children's acquisition of language, researchers study its structure. Every language consists of five basic components.

- Phonology refers to the distinctive sounds of a language. In contrast, morphology is defined as the way that particular sounds are combined to form words.

- Syntax involves the way people combine words into sentences. The study of the meaning of words is known as semantics.

- The way that language is used to communicate is called pragmatics. Although children can communicate intent with vocalizations and gestures during the first year, the emergence of conversational skills does not start until the last half of the second year.

Sequence of Milestones

- Children across the world follow the same basic sequence and timetable in acquiring language. Psycholinguists have distinguished two distinct periods: prelinguistic (first year) and linguistic (next 2 years).

■ During the prelinguistic period, newborns are able to communicate basic needs such as hunger or pain. Between 2 and 4 months, infants begin to coo, uttering vowel-like sounds signaling contentment.

■ Next, infants start to babble, stringing together consonants and vowels in alternating sequences. Babbling resembles the intonation of adults' speech.

■ The prelinguistic period comes to an end at when children typically say their first words between 10 and 18 months. First words generally consist of familiar people and objects.

■ Some psycholinguists believe children rely on holophrastic speech, the use of single words to convey complex ideas. Evidence of holophrastic speech can be found in children's expressive vocalizations.

■ Between 18 and 24 months, children are beginning to combine two words together. The appearance of two-word utterances coincides with the explosive growth of vocabulary.

Bilingualism

■ More and more children in the United States understand and use two languages at home. Although two languages pose special challenges, bilingual children generally progress at the same rate as their monolingual peers.

Special Needs

■ Perception of the world comes from all five senses. When audition is affected, normal language development may be severely restricted.

■ Early intervention is recommended to facilitate children's acquisition of language. Because language is acquired rapidly, corrective steps should be taken to increase amplification with hearing aids and encourage communicative competence.

PROJECTS
• • • • • • • • • • • • •

1. Videotape a mutual interaction between a 6- to 18-month-old child and adult and answer the following questions:

   Did the adult use parentese?

   Describe aspects of the adult's speech such as high-pitched voice, exaggerated intonation, and simplified vocabulary.

   Was the child a passive listener or active participant?

2. Brainstorm on strategies facilitating children's language acquisition during the prelinguistic and linguistic periods.

3. Discuss the unique features of developmentally appropriate children's books ranging from plastic-covered pages with pictures only to simple stories in storybooks.

PSYCHOSOCIAL DEVELOPMENT

*Babies control and bring up their families as much as they are controlled by them;
in fact, we may say that the family brings up a baby by being brought up by him.*

Erik Erikson, *Childhood and Society*

I nfants are unique beings from the very start. They are endowed with the capacity to respond to and engage with other people. The first few years bring dramatic changes. Infants seek to maintain close proximity to trusted adults and cry to signal distress in unfamiliar
situations. Increasing mobility provides further opportunities to expand infants' social horizons.
Chapter 10 focuses on psychosocial development, including attachment, temperament, self, and
socialization.

Historically, the scientific study of psychosocial development is rooted in Freud's psychoanalytic theory. Although he built his theory entirely on adults' recollections of their

childhood, his ideas did spur considerable interest in the influential role of the early years of life. Later, Erikson agreed with Freud's basic concepts but instead focused his attention on social and cultural factors that influence children's development. Both believed in the importance of the special relationship between parents and children, known as attachment (Crain, 1999). However, Freud and Erikson never used the term in their theoretical discussions. The first reference to children's affectional relationships with their parents was made well over a half century ago (Sears, 1943) but serves as a useful starting point.

EMOTIONAL DEVELOPMENT

Between 7 and 9 months, infants start to form enduring emotional ties with certain adults. The term **attachment** refers to *the affectional bonds that infants establish with special people in their lives and that persist over time.* In addition, the role of temperament, or infants' basic dispositions, on emotional development has been widely studied. Both attachment and temperament provide compelling evidence of the way infants affect their social environment.

ATTACHMENT

British psychiatrist John Bowlby was the first to study attachment. In 1939, he outlined his views on the effects of negative early experiences on later psychological disorders (Bowlby, 1940). He identified two factors that he believed resulted in long-lasting consequences. The first involved the death of the mother or prolonged separation from her. To buttress his point, he cited examples of children who experienced lengthy separations from their mothers and who subsequently suffered from severe emotional problems. The second concerned the emotional attitude of the mother toward her children, permeating everyday child-rearing practices such as feeding and diapering.

Bowlby sought to synthesize two theories. He tried to incorporate ethological concepts (see Chapter 2) into psychoanalytic theory (Bowlby, 1958). Ethologists such as Lorenz made important discoveries on the instinctual behavior of different species such as geese shortly after hatching. Bowlby saw similarities between human infants and other species. Behavioral patterns in infants' instinctual repertoire, such as crying and clinging, he believed, encouraged the formation of attachment with their mothers. Separation from their mothers produced disastrous consequences because it interfered with the development of attachment. Bowlby's position received support from Harry Harlow's studies of maternal deprivation with rhesus monkeys in the 1950s. Harlow separated babies from their mothers 6 to 12 hours after birth to prevent the spread of diseases in his laboratory. However, their health only deteriorated. To rectify the problem, he placed the babies with surrogate mothers made of cloth and wire, leading to marked improvements in health although still isolated from other monkeys (Harlow, 1958).

The results piqued Harlow's curiosity. He was reminded of a study with institutionalized children a decade before (Spitz, 1946). Harlow decided to replicate Spitz's study, using monkeys instead. He was interested in investigating the biological roots of

ETHOLOGICAL EVIDENCE OF ATTACHMENT

Ethical concerns preclude the possibility of conducting research with infants to examine the effects of prolonged separation from parents. Half a century ago, Harlow conducted an extensive series of experiments with rhesus monkeys (Harlow & Harlow, 1965, 1966). The monkeys were separated from their mothers soon after their birth and placed in isolated cages. Placed into two groups, they had a surrogate mother made of either wire or wire and cloth. Although the two surrogate mothers were equipped with wooden heads and large eyes, only the wire mothers were fitted with a bottle. The results of his studies showed that all the monkeys preferred to be with the cloth mothers, concluding that the monkeys' preferences demonstrated "the importance . . . of bodily contact and the immediate comfort it supplies in forming the infant's attachment for its mother" (Harlow, 1959, p. 70).

Although the isolated monkeys received adequate nourishment, they developed abnormal behavioral patterns when they returned to a large cage with other monkeys later. As adults, they displayed indifferent, abusive behavior in their contact with other monkeys. Deprived of social interaction early in life, they were not able to form normal social relationships. Harlow remarked,

> the nourishment and contact . . . provided by the nursing cloth-covered mother in infancy does not produce a normal adolescent or adult. The surrogate cannot cradle the baby or communicate monkey sounds and gestures. (Harlow & Harlow, 1962, p. 142)

Likewise, human infants require reciprocal contact to develop healthy attachments with trusted adults. Secure attachments have been correlated with improved cognitive, emotional, and social competence during later years (Cassidy & Shaver, 1999; Elicker, Englund, & Sroufe, 1992).

attachment (Karen, 1998). The surrogates Harlow placed in the cages consisted either of a block of wood covered with cloth and a circular face or a wire mesh with the same face. For some monkeys, a feeding nipple was fitted to the cloth surrogate; for others, it was simply attached to the wire surrogate. In the end, it did not matter which surrogate fed the monkeys: all the monkeys spent practically all of their time, 16 to 20 hours a day, with the cloth mother (Harlow & Zimmerman, 1959).

Theories of Attachment. Harlow's studies struck a severe blow to a long-standing belief at the time. Freud argued that babies gradually associated their mothers with the presence of food (Freud, 1933/1964) in the same way that behavioral theorists later did (Sears, Maccoby, & Levin, 1957). However, attachment does not depend on the satisfaction of basic physiological needs. Human infants can develop attachments with relatives and friends of the parents and form strong emotional ties to inanimate objects such as blankets and stuffed animals, often known as transitional objects (Triebenbacher, 1997).

Bowlby's theory of attachment has gained widespread acceptance. He describes four distinct stages in the formation of attachment (Bowlby, 1969):

- **Indiscriminating social responsiveness (birth to 6 weeks).** Newborns rely on biologically determined mechanisms to elicit adults' attention. Crying brings infants into close contact with adults. Another potent signal in infants' repertoire involves smiling, beginning in the second month. As with crying, smiling profoundly affects the behavior of others because it maintains adults' physical proximity to infants. Therefore, even in the first weeks and months, infants are influencing their social environment. As adults respond to infants' signals, they usually provide security in addition to extra stimulation such as stroking, carrying, rocking, and vocalizing. However, infants are not yet able to develop an attachment to any one particular adult. They appear to be satisfied with anyone who responds to their cries, smiles, and other similar signals.

  Initially, infants display poor motoric control and unpredictability in sleeping and waking patterns. However, as the brain continues to develop, coordination of voluntary movements and states of alertness gradually increases. During periods of alertness, adults usually hold infants in different positions, encouraging exploration of the immediate surroundings. Alert infants focus on inanimate objects and fixate not only on the prominent features of adults, primarily their faces and voices, but even their body odors. In time, infants begin to associate the presence of certain adults with the relief of distress. Crying infants rapidly learn to expect comfort and quit when they see or hear their approaching parents (Colin, 1996; Lamb & Malkin, 1986).

- **Discriminating social responsiveness (6 weeks to 6–8 months).** Infants are starting to prefer familiar adults, not just anyone, during the second and third months. They now associate pleasurable experiences resulting from regular social contacts with certain people. Infants' preferences are manifested in subtle ways. Only some adults are able to soothe crying infants and elicit smiles.

  The gradual changes can be linked to infants' increased motor control. They are now able to coordinate voluntary movement and stay alert for longer periods (Emde & Robinson, 1979). Opportunities to engage in spontaneous play with adults increase dramatically during the same period. Between 3 and 6 months, adults often reciprocate their infants' cues such as smiling or cooing in return. However, infants themselves are actively engaged in maintaining social interactions with others. They express concern when familiar adults adopt unresponsive faces and fail to respond to their own social overtures (Lamb, Morrison, & Malkin, 1987).

- **Establishment of attachment (6–8 months to 18 months to 2 years).** At about 6 to 8 months, a dramatic shift occurs in Bowlby's next stage of attachment. Whereas in the previous stage, infants do not protest when their parents leave the immediate vicinity, they now seek to remain in close contact, especially in the presence of strangers. Infants signal their distress and seek to maintain their proximity to familiar adults. **Wariness of strangers** refers to *the distressed reactions that infants display to the presence of new adults.* Infants actively follow only certain people in order to maintain their closeness and inten-

HISTORICALLY SPEAKING

ATTACHMENT

John Bowlby
Infancy in Uganda: Infant Care and the Growth of Love, 1967

When a baby is born he cannot tell one person from another and indeed can hardly tell person from thing. Yet, by his first birthday he is likely to have become a connoisseur of people. Not only does he come quickly to distinguish familiars from strangers but amongst his familiars he chooses one or more favorites. They are greeted with delight; they are followed when they depart; and they are sought when absent.

Source: Bowlby (1967), p. v.

tionally signal distress in order to reestablish contact with missing adults. The reassuring presence of trusted adults provides numerous benefits, including the use of their presence as a secure base to explore an ever-widening physical and social world.

Cultural beliefs can influence stranger wariness. Some ethnic groups do not believe in allowing anyone outside of the immediate family to take care of their children. For example, Korean Americans express concerns about leaving their children in the care of baby-sitters or other private providers. They prefer to rely on the mother's own mother or her mother-in-law to provide care in their absence (Yu & Kim, 1983). In con-

PARENTING ISSUES

EFFECTS OF OUT-OF-HOME CARE ON ATTACHMENT

Today, working parents often worry about the quality of out-of-home care their infants receive. Questions generally center on the detrimental effects, if any, of prolonged out-of-home care on attachment. In other words, can infants form multiple attachments with professional caregivers in addition to their parents? Does the length of time infants spend in out-of-home care adversely affect children's psychosocial development later in life? Parents' concerns are usually inflamed when scientific studies are published in newspapers on the effects of out-of-home care. For example, American psychologist Jay Belsky concluded that infants who spent at least 20 hours a week in out-of-home care developed an insecure attachment with their parents (Belsky, 1986). Prolonged separation in out-of-home care, he said, resulted in infants who avoided and ignored their parents. Belsky believed that out-of-home care during the first year interfered with the formation of secure attachment (Belsky, 1987).

Belsky's position sparked considerable controversy. His conclusions that pro-

(continued)

longed separation results in aggressiveness and noncompliance later on in preschool raised public fears. Although some researchers agreed with him, others criticized his analysis on two grounds. First, most infants in out-of-home care do establish secure attachment with their parents (Thompson, 1991b). A small increase of just 10% in the number of infants with insecure attachment does not warrant condemnation of out-of-home care. Second, maybe infants in out-of-home care behave in ways that actually represent a healthy sense of autonomy instead of insecurity. Their increased assertiveness may simply be a manifestation of their adjustment to their daily separation and reunion with their parents. The issue, others argue, centers not on the length of time that infants spend in out-of-home care but on the overall quality of care (Clarke-Stewart, 1989; Phillips et al., 1987). Poor-quality care can obviously contribute to infants' insecurity. In programs with a high ratio of children to adults and poorly trained staff, infants cannot receive sufficient attention or proper care. The debate clearly illustrates the importance of affordability of and accessibility to out-of-home programs of high quality. As Belsky (1990) himself stated:

> Developmental research has convincingly established that high-quality care in the preschool years not only does not carry any risks, but actually serves to enhance child development. . . . there is good reason to believe that when care in this developmental period is of high quality there should be little reason to anticipate negative developmental outcomes. (pp. 11–12)

Later research confirms the benefits of out-of-home care when trained caregivers meet the psychological needs of infants. Insecurely attached infants may actually benefit from the opportunity to form a secure attachment with responsive, supportive caregivers (Goossens & van Ijzendoorn, 1990). Further, the establishment of a secure attachment with professional caregivers may ease the transition of infants to the eventual formation of social relationships with peers. Securely attached infants usually exhibit more socially skilled patterns of behavior with their peers later during the preschool years (Howes, Hamilton, & Matheson, 1994). Because of economic necessity, out-of-home care has become a fact of life for millions of working parents and families. At the same time, many experts advise that parents should exercise good judgment in finding licensed, high-quality out-of-home care.

trast, many African American parents believe in sharing child-rearing responsibilities with multiple caregivers. In one study, more than half of African American families reportedly have access to caregivers (Jackson, 1993). Two to five adults, relatives and nonrelatives, are generally designated as supplemental caregivers to accommodate many working parents' schedules. Therefore, contacts with other adults outside of the immediate family can lead to the formation of multiple attachments.

■ **Formation of reciprocal relationship (18 months to 2 years and onward).** The last stage in Bowlby's theory of attachment reflects the continuing developmental advances infants make at the end of the second year. Rapid growth in cognitive development and language influences infants' social interactions with adults. Infants are beginning to understand the rule of reciprocity. In social interactions, partners take turns in acting and reacting to each other's behavior. Protests of separation from particular adults usually start to decline over time. Infants can now vocalize their needs and negotiate with adults instead of crying and clinging.

Bowlby's theory has generated considerable interest in the importance of attachment and its formation during the first few years. Mary Ainsworth, a noted American psychologist who worked with Bowlby, shared his views and conducted her own extensive research. She and her coworkers closely observed the social interactions between infants and their parents. On the basis of observations in Africa and the United States, she has classified different patterns of attachment.

Patterns of Attachment. Ainsworth disagreed with studies that simply measured the frequency of attachment at different ages because they provided information on the quantity but not quality of attachment. She devised a way of measuring infants' attachment with a now classic procedure, replicated in hundreds of studies, called the "strange situation" (Ainsworth, 1973; Ainsworth & Wittig, 1969). It consists of a series of episodes, lasting about 3 minutes each. Basically, parents leave their infant in an unfamiliar room with a stranger but later return to offer comfort.

Infants demonstrate distinctive patterns of attachment in reaction to the presence of the stranger and reunion with their mothers. They display one of the following four patterns:

■ **Secure attachment.** Securely attached infants play comfortably with toys in the room and react positively to the presence of a stranger. They visibly show signs of distress when their parents leave the room but quickly seek contact when their parents return. Once their distress is consoled, infants' exploration of toys is resumed. About 70% of infants fall into the category of **secure attachment**, *a warm, positive relationship between infants and their parents based on infants' trust in their parents' physical and emotional availability.*

■ **Avoidant attachment.** Avoidant infants demonstrate indifference to their parents' presence in the room. Some cry when their parents leave; others do not. When their parents return, avoidant infants tend to ignore their parents instead of seeking contact; some even increase their distance. **Avoidant attachment,** *a relationship between infants and their parents based on the active avoidance of parents after a brief separation,* represents about 20% of all infants.

■ **Resistant attachment.** Resistant infants seek closeness with parents before separation in the strange situation and fail to play with the assorted toys in the room. When their parents leave, they display considerable distress and rebuff the stranger's efforts to comfort them. When their parents return, resistant infants attempt to seek renewed contact while at the same time resisting their parents' reassurance. About 10% of the infants show **resistant attachment**, *a relationship between infants and their parents based on reluctance at separation but ambivalence at reunion.*

■ **Disorganized attachment.** Since her initial work, a fourth category of attachment has been added to Ainsworth's classification. Disorganized infants appear dazed or disoriented in a strange situation (Main & Heese, 1990; Mayseless, 1998). At reunion with their parents, they tend to cry unexpectedly or look depressed. **Disorganized attachment**, *a relationship between infants and their parents based on inconsistent patterns of behavior after a brief separation,* are thought to indicate possible parental maltreatment of infants at home.

Factors Affecting Attachment.   Ainsworth's strange situation has been replicated in numerous studies. The results consistently show that the quality of care, with both parents and other adults, in early infancy affects attachment (Thompson, 1991a). The emotional contact that adults establish with infants correlates highly with secure attachment. In particular, the following factors can influence the formation of secure attachment: sensitivity to infants' needs and responsiveness to their specific signals (Isabella, 1993). Adults' sensitive and responsive caregiving practices in the early months generally lead to secure attachment in the later months. Fathers, too, are capable of meeting their infants' basic needs if their efforts are encouraged (Bailey, 1995; Steele, Steele, & Fonagy, 1996).

Personal traits of infants can certainly affect the quality of attachment because infants vary considerably in their temperament and the intensity of their emotional reactions to different situations. Irritability has been shown to be associated with insecure attachment (Seifer et al., 1996). Further, prematurity and other complications during or after birth can tax the already burdened responsibilities and skills of highly sensitive, responsive parents. Nevertheless, infants with special needs have been found to establish secure attachment in an atmosphere of patience and acceptance (Wille, 1991).

Other factors influencing attachment center on the familial context. The extent of fathers' involvement in the care of their infants and the quality of their marital relationships can affect attachment (Goldberg & Easterbrooks, 1984; Owen & Cox, 1997). Studies have traditionally examined only the interaction between infants and their mothers without consideration of the role of fathers. Because the quality of marriage can affect parenting outcomes, infants usually exhibit secure attachment with parents who report high marital satisfaction. Significant shifts in the socioeconomic status of families can disrupt familiar patterns of interaction between parents and their children. The loss of a job adds both emotional and financial stress, reducing parental attentiveness and patience. Further, child maltreatment usually increases in families experiencing severe economic and social stress. Parents who abuse their children often lack the social support that they need to resolve potential problems (Korbin, 1994; Thompson, 1993).

Cross-cultural studies have found stable consistencies with Ainsworth's research (see Figure 10–1). About 70% of infants in other countries are securely attached (Fox, Kimmerly, & Schafer, 1991; Sagi, van Ijzendoorn, & Koren-Karie, 1991). Longitudinal comparisons between infants of European American parents and Central American im-

CROSS-CULTURAL RESEARCH ON ATTACHMENT

The concept of cultural adaptationism has been borrowed from anthropology and incorporated into the cross-cultural study of attachment. It refers to the interdependence among people (particularly the physical environment), modes of production, social organization, and cultural expectations of adults (Keesing, 1981). Adults who live in a certain ecosystem select attitudes and traditions that enhance continual harmony with their physical environment. Culture itself consists of socially transmitted behavioral patterns that ensure a group's successful adaptation to a particular environment (Segall et al., 1992).

Differences in attachment between infants and their parents reflect cultural adaptations to the immediate physical environment. The particular caregiving styles of parents and cultural expectations evolve from adaptive consequences over a period of time (Super & Harkness, 1986). Parents acquire a culturally shared set of expectations that direct their actions and their social relations with infants. The cultural transmission of values and beliefs is manifested in parents' relationship with their infants.

In one study, the effects of different cultural perceptions on the child-rearing practices of Puerto Rican and European American mothers were examined. Each group was further subdivided to represent families of low and middle incomes (Harwood et al., 1999). The mothers were asked to respond to a set of open-ended questions in order to examine their indigenous conceptions of desirable and undesir-

able behavioral outcomes in their children. The results indicated that Puerto Rican and European American mothers attended to different culturally relevant dimensions of behavior. Puerto Rican mothers adhered to qualities maintaining dignity and proper demeanor in a public context. In contrast, European American mothers expressed concerns centering on their children's independence in an unfamiliar situation.

Cross-cultural studies of attachment demonstrate the influential role culture plays in psychosocial development. Although the range of expressive behavior is biologically determined (Harkness & Super, 1985), the expression of attachment is culturally shaped (Harwood, Miller, & Irizarry, 1994). From the moment of birth, parents' affectional ties with their infants reflect cultural norms and behavioral patterns involving interpretations of appropriate emotional display in specific situations. The cultural context of infants' lives influences the way they interact with their physical and social environment.

In sum, two implications can be derived from cross-cultural studies on attachment. First, the quality of the relationship between infants and their parents provides the foundation of interpersonal norms that organize social interactions later in life. Second, specific interactional norms and rules reflect cultural standards and expectations that infants learn from their reciprocal interaction with their parents and other people. Therefore, attachment, like other forms of human behavior, is embedded in culture.

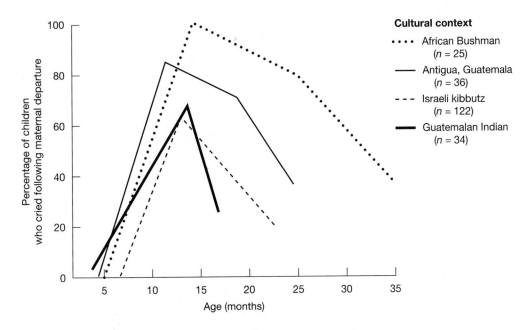

FIGURE 10–1 Cross-Cultural Comparisons of Distress in Maternal Separation. In Ainsworth's "strange situation," infants across the world exhibit distress after a short separation from their mothers. Their distress increased during the last half of the first year and declined after about 15 months of age.
Source: Kagan, Kearsley, and Zelazo (1978), p. 107. Reprinted with permission.

migrants have yielded similar results. The only difference between the two groups involve instability in the everyday living experiences of the Central American infants (Lamb et al., 1998; Scholmerich et al., 1997). However, some critics question the validity of the strange situation as a universal indicator of attachment. Infants who rarely experienced separation from their mothers or who did not come into contact with other adults had vastly different outcomes (Sagi, 1990; Takahashi, 1990). In studies of Japanese infants, over 40% showed ambivalent patterns of attachment. Japanese mothers had difficulties in consoling their infants during reunion (Nakagawa, Lamb, & Miyake, 1992; Takahashi, 1986).

Importance of Attachment.   Research shows that the quality of children's attachment to trusted adults affects cognitive and social development. Secure attachment has been found to be associated with higher cognitive competence in early (Matas, Arend, & Sroufe, 1978) and middle childhood and adolescence (Jacobsen, Edelstein, & Hofmann, 1994). Securely attached children are better able to solve challenging problems and persevere in stressful situations. Further, at age 3, securely attached children are often selected to be friends by their peers and are more likely to interact with teachers and seek assistance in resolving conflicts with their peers (Frankel & Bates, 1990; Park & Waters, 1989).

A secure attachment, based on an adult's prompt and consistent responses to a child's signals, fosters trust in oneself and the world.
Photo courtesy of Tami Dawson, Photo Resource Hawaii.

In contrast, insecurely attached children may experience difficulties in the acquisition of cognitively and socially appropriate behavior. In comparison to securely attached children, they do not display the same kind of confidence in their exploration of objects or pursuit of activities involving other children. Instead, excessive dependency on teachers is seen. They usually cling to their teachers and make inappropriate demands. Even later, significant differences between securely and insecurely attached children can be found. At age 6, observations of children's reunion with their mothers show remarkable stability from infancy to childhood (Solomon, George, & Ivins, 1987). However, the correlation between two separate events in time does not indicate a cause-and-effect relationship. Perhaps mothers of securely attached children continue to behave in ways that facilitate their children's sense of security (Jacobson et al., 1997).

DIFFERENCES IN TEMPERAMENT

Infants are actively involved in shaping their interactions with others. They exhibit distinct differences in their reactions to new situations and events in their lives. Parents often remark on the unique qualities of their children. Some sit quietly in their parents' lap and others constantly squirm. Do differences between infants result from biological or environmental factors? In other words, do genes or parenting styles shape the unique personalities of infants? Psychologists make a distinction between personality and temperament. **Personality** refers to *enduring personal qualities and behavioral patterns that define a person's own individuality,* which encompass the global physical, cognitive, emotional, and social characteristics of the person. On the other hand, **temperament** pertains to *stable, inherited dispositions that determine the quality and intensity of a person's emotional reactions to different situations.* Therefore, temperament reflects inherited biological mechanisms, but environmental factors influence its expression.

Stella Chess and her husband, Alexander Thomas, pioneered studies on temperament a half century ago. They were interested in the long-term contribution of temperament on subsequent development (Chess, Thomas, & Birch, 1959). Now referred to as the New York Longitudinal Study, the sample, consisting of 140 infants from middle- to upper-income families and 75 Puerto Rican children, was tracked over time. Questionnaires with parents were later supplemented with standardized tests and interviews with teachers (Thomas et al., 1963).

Classification of Temperament.   Analysis of the results revealed nine different behavioral traits. The children were grouped into one of the three broad temperamental categories (Thomas, Chess, & Birch, 1970):

■ **"Easy"** (about 40% of the sample). Easy infants demonstrate adaptability and regularity. They react with low to moderate levels of intensity and approach unfamiliar situations positively.

■ **"Slow to warm up"** (about 15% of the sample). Here, infants show inactivity and slowness in adaptability. They react mildly to environmental stimuli and adjust slowly to unfamiliar situations.

■ **"Difficult"** (about 10% of the sample). Difficult infants adapt to new experiences slowly. They tend to react with high intensity and negativity and withdraw from unfamiliar situations.

The three broad temperamental categories constitute only 65% of the sample in Chess and Thomas's study. The remaining infants receive a classification of "average" because they do not fit into any one of the three other profiles. Instead, they exhibit a combination of temperamental traits. The three broad temperamental categories of Chess and Thomas provide a useful inventory of emotional dispositions (Strelau, 1998).

When parents try to adapt their child-rearing expectations to meet their children's needs, their actions may produce favorable outcomes. The concept of **goodness of fit** describes *the quality of the match between temperament and the demands of the environment.* A dramatic example of the concept comes from a study of infants in the Masai, a group of nomadic warriors living in east Africa. After the researchers categorized the infants' temperamental qualities, the Masai suffered a severe drought. The subsequent famine had detrimental consequences. The researchers found that a large number of the "easy" infants died, whereas almost all of the "difficult" infants survived (deVries, 1984). Perhaps cultural expectations affected the outcome, because the Masai value boldness and assertiveness in their children. Apparently, the "difficult" infants were breast-fed on demand because of increased fussiness resulting from hunger, ensuring their survival.

Children with a "difficult" temperament have received the lion's share of attention in the literature. Some researchers have tried to use measures of difficultness to predict the likelihood of subsequent behavioral problems. Chess and Thomas's longitudinal study has confirmed the predictive value of temperament in childhood. In their study, 70% of "difficult" children eventually developed behavioral problems in contrast to 18% of "easy" infants (Thomas & Chess, 1980). Difficultness involves frequent and intense expression of negative emotions. The loud, high-pitched cries of "difficult" infants is usually associated with aversiveness (Papousek & Papousek, 1996). However, "difficult" infants do not necessarily encounter behavioral problems later if parents learn to accept their temperamental uniqueness. In one study, "difficult" children living in middle- to upper-income families usually outscore their "easy" counterparts on tests that measure intelligence at age 4 (Maziade et al., 1988). Perhaps parents are able to adapt to their

PARENTING ISSUES

SHYNESS: STABILITY OF TEMPERAMENT

Shyness is an enduring trait of the personality. Explanations focus on either inherited qualities or environmental factors. In reality, shyness reflects the contributions of both. In other words, the distinctive genetic profile of each infant interacts with the social environment.

Even in the first few months, evidence of shyness can be seen in infants' behavior. It is manifested in their reactions to unfamiliar situations. In a long-term study to examine the long-term effects of shyness, subjects were videotaped at age 4 months in reaction to varied sets of visual stimuli and sounds. Each infant's behavior was scored in two areas. A high or low score was assigned to motor activity (the frequency of waving the arms or kicking the feet) and amount of crying. Twenty-three percent displayed high levels in both areas; 37% exhibited low levels in both areas; 40% received a high score in one but a low score in the other (Kagan & Snidman, 1991).

Later, at ages 9, 14, and 21 months, the infants were again observed. The observers rated the infants' reactions to the following activities: the placement of electrodes, a facial disapproval from an examiner, a noisy rotating wheel, and a request to taste liquid from a dropper. All the infants exhibited wariness, but each reacted differently. The study yielded remarkably consistent results. Infants with high motor activity and crying at age 4 months demonstrated more fear later on. Likewise, low motor activity and crying were associated with less fear. The results found marked differences in infants' thresholds of excitability in unfamiliar situations. Most of the shy infants in the study later became shy children at 7 years of age; similarly, sociable infants became sociable children (Kagan, 1989).

Therefore, shyness has strong ties to biology. Studies of identical twins point to the same conclusion (Robinson et al., 1992). However, shyness is not an immutable characteristic. Parents can encourage sociability in shy children, perhaps resulting in a more favorable outcome. Although research can provide interesting insights into the stability of temperament, it does not suggest that biology determines people's destiny. In reality, the constellation of people's biological propensities partially interacts with the environment (Kagan, Reznick, & Snidman, 1999).

children's difficultness and stimulate their cognitive development. As Maziade and colleagues (1988) state:

> Such parents would stimulate the difficult infant more than the extremely easy infant, who is more readily left to himself. Such special stimulation would favor more rapid development. (p. 342)

Stability of Temperament.   Early studies on temperament relied on parents' reports. In Chess and Thomas's study, the stability of temperament was confirmed (Thomas & Chess, 1977). However, their study was criticized because of two serious methodological flaws. First, it did not start immediately after birth. Did hereditary or environmental factors influence the results? Second, parents' reports can be biased (Bates, 1989). Their reports did not always match the information that independent observers obtained. Since then, more recent research has provided compelling evidence of temperamental stability. Measures of temperament have improved, such as the objectivity of parents' reports. The results clearly indicate that before the end of their first year, infants do indeed differ in their reactions to environmental stimuli (Bretherton, 1992; Ruff et al., 1990).

Parents usually become concerned about their infants' temperament if, in their view, it conflicts with their expectations of appropriate behavior. They sometimes ask, Do shy or overly active infants outgrow their basic disposition? The weight of the evidence to date suggests not. Highly active infants who cry often in unfamiliar situations usually become fearful children, and likewise, anxious, unhappy infants tend to become anxious, unhappy adolescents (Kagan, 1992). However, environmental factors can alter the outcome. Temperament is not necessarily fixed at the moment of conception. To answer the question of the role of heritability, studies of identical twins have been conducted. The correlation of heritability generally falls in the range between .50 and .60, suggesting a moderate influence of heredity on temperament (Plomin, 1989). The results show the malleability of children. Consistency of temperament depends on the "match" between infants' nature and parents' nurture (Saudino & Eaton, 1991).

ERIKSON'S STAGES OF PSYCHOSOCIAL DEVELOPMENT

Even after Freud founded psychoanalysis at the turn of the 20th century, serious disagreements among his followers soon surfaced. In particular, controversy centered on Freud's overemphasis on unconscious motivation and sexuality. Discontent led to a reassessment of his theory. One of the notable attempts to preserve but infuse new life in psychoanalysis was found in the pioneering work of Erikson (1950). In contrast to Freud's predominately negative view of human nature, Erikson instead examined the influential role of social and cultural factors in development. He argued that developmental crises occur as a person tries to reconcile societal expectations with personal goals (Erikson, 1968).

According to Erikson, each of his eight stages consists of a psychosocial crisis. The first major crisis in life, corresponding to the first year, involves the establishment of trust versus mistrust. Because of their helplessness at birth, infants must depend on others to meet their needs. For example, if they are fed on demand or soothed when crying, over time, they learn to trust their caregivers. Predictability fosters the development of trust. Infants learn to tolerate their parents' absence only when they develop a sense of security and certainty. At the same time, a measure of mistrust is needed to survive in the world as when children are told not to talk to strangers or cross the street alone. However, infants' failure to achieve a favorable balance in the direction of trust leads to anxiety and suspicion at others' motives later.

The next crisis in Erikson's theory occurs from 1 to 3 years of age. It is described as a crisis of autonomy versus shame and doubt. Because of increasing mobility, toddlers now want to undertake things on their own. Increasing maturation of the muscles controlling the elimination of bodily wastes focuses parents' attention on toilet training. Difficulties generally arise when parents set unreasonable limits or restrict appropriate activities. According to Erikson, a delicate balance between control and flexibility is needed. Parents must acknowledge their children's increasing assertiveness but enforce limits on dangerous behavior. However, children of overcontrolling parents who habitually ridicule their efforts or punish every little mistake might develop a sense of shame and doubt in their abilities.

DEVELOPMENT OF EMOTIONS

Emotion comes from a Latin word meaning to excite or agitate. In current usage, **emotion** concerns *an affective state that involves a physiological reaction and overt behavior.* Historically, numerous attempts have been made to classify different types of emotions. They range from positive affectivity—joy and happiness—to negative affectivity—anger and sadness. Changes in children's emotional reactions demarcate important developmental transitions during the first few years of life. Their emotional reactions offer the first glimpses of their emerging sense of self and individuality.

Emotions fulfill a number of important functions. In addition to their adaptive functions, they influence internal processes involving perception and cognition (Sroufe, 1996). People are continually forced to reevaluate their current conditions and then adjust their actions accordingly. Interpersonally, people react to the affective states of others and regulate the expression of their own emotions. Observations of anger in someone with clenched fists arouse different emotions and reactions from someone who expresses joy or fear. Infants react in similar ways as they respond to unfamiliar situations and interact with important people (Campos, Kermoian, & Whitherington, 1996).

Researchers face a daunting task in studying emotional development of infants. Because infants are not able to describe their emotions, their facial expressions are observed instead. Cross-cultural evidence shows that people associate emotions with different facial expressions. Six facial expressions—happiness, sadness, anger, surprise, disgust, and fear—have been identified in all cultures (Ekman & Friesen, 1972). Even newborns demonstrate the capacity to express emotions. At 2 hours after birth, newborns react with a contented expression to a sweet substance but respond with an expression of disgust to a bitter substance (Rosenstein & Oster, 1988). Emotional responses during the first month are clearly tied to infants' internal states. Sources of emotions relate to infants' physical discomfort that results from hunger and pain. Later, emotions reflect the recognition of infants' separateness from their environment.

Human faces typically elicit a broad grin (referred to as a social smile), appearing about 6 weeks after birth.

Infants' capacity to cope with emotionally arousing situations expands in the second half of the first year. **Emotional regulation** refers to *internal mechanisms infants use to control or modify their affective states.* At first, newborns rely on involuntary strategies such as falling asleep, although later they regulate their emotional reactions in other ways such as sucking their thumbs when they encounter unpleasant stimulation. They depend on the comfort their primary caregivers provide, especially in the presence of strangers at about 8 months of age (Bridges & Grolnick, 1995). The quality of interactions between infants and loving, caring adults facilitates the development of their emotional regulation. Infants usually rely on the words and actions of adults in interpreting unfamiliar situations. Cultural variations are found in adults' approaches to their children's distress. Japanese mothers tend to protect their children from emotionally arousing situations that provoke anger (Miyake et al., 1986). Other coping strategies emerge during the second and third years as further growth in language occurs. Infants now begin to use words intentionally in signaling distress and managing negative emotions.

Closely tied to infants' emotional regulation is their ability to recognize and respond to the emotions of others. At about 2 months, infants start to inspect the external features of human faces. They gradually recognize and discriminate the affective expressions of adults as they interact with others during the first year of life. They use both visual and auditory information to differentiate adults' facial expressions (Mume, Fernald, & Herrera, 1996). Adults serve as social references to guide infants' behavior in uncertain situations. **Social referencing** involves *infants' reliance on trusted adults' emotional reactions in their interpretation of strange or ambiguous events.* If adults express wariness or a negative emotion, infants tend to withdraw or explore the situation with caution. If, on the other hand, a positive emotion is expressed, infants are likely to approach the situation with confidence (Walker-Andrews & Dickson, 1997).

EMERGING SENSE OF SELF

Several theorists have viewed the concept of self as the central issue in the study of personality. In particular, psychoanalyst Margaret Mahler argues that infants' awareness of themselves as separate and unique entities occurs in two stages (Mahler, Pine, & Bergman, 1975):

■ **Symbiosis.** During the first 2 months, infants do not demonstrate any awareness of their immediate environment. They spend the majority of their day asleep, waking only to satisfy their basic needs. At the end of the second month, infants begin to develop an intimate sense of "oneness" with their parents. They enjoy the physical closeness of their contact with their parents and show their active interest in external stimuli and events. Their sense of self and their awareness of their surrounding world are fused together, however. Mahler believes infants do not realize that events and people exist separately. Their parents' responsiveness to their emotional cues promotes their emerging sense of self. When parents react promptly and present a positive emotional tone, infants develop the confidence they need to separate from their parents during the next stage.

■ **Separation-individuation.** Infants' inevitable sense of separateness occurs during the second half of the first year as they gain increasing mobility. Crawling infants start to venture from their parents to explore the immediate environment, but depend on the emotional support of adults. They tend to receive reassurance whenever they seek the security of their parents. As they gradually increase their physical distance, awareness of their own separateness develops. Their sense of individuation advances dramatically with the onset of walking at 1 year. Now, they begin to test their emerging capacities to do things on their own. At about 18 months, realization of their own individuation is finally developed. Although their newfound freedom sometimes results in resistance——the so-called terrible twos—the continuing support of their parents provides the reassurance they need (Mahler, 1968).

Although Mahler provides a useful theoretical framework in describing the emerging sense of self, does research support it? To get answers, researchers have examined the development of **self-awareness**, or *people's sense of themselves as distinct entities with unique characteristics*. Infants are not able to differentiate themselves from the world initially during the first several weeks. Soon, at 2 months, infants seem to be fascinated with the movements of their hands, appearing and disappearing from view (Lewis, 1991). Gradually, their awareness of their bodies and themselves increases with age as they actively explore their immediate environment. They discover that their direct actions produce interesting results and that objects continue to exist as their physical and cognitive abilities improve during the last half of the first year.

Between 12 to 18 months, infants make significant strides. Evidence of their increasing recognition of themselves comes from a classic study of infants' perceptions of their own faces in a mirror (Amsterdam, 1972). As infants played in front of a mirror, their mothers placed rouge on their infants' noses. Infants demonstrated recognition of themselves if they looked at their reflection in the mirror and then touched their own noses. During the last half of the second year, recognition of self is definitely established. Children at 2 years of age prefer to look and smile at pictures of themselves, not others, and begin to use their names in labeling their own images (Butterworth, 1992). Once self-awareness develops, it represents a major transition in their lives. The first signs of **empathy**, *the ability to sympathize with the needs of others*, start to emerge at the same time (Faude, Jones, & Robins, 1996). For example, some toddlers may give a toy to a crying child. Others may hug or offer a bandage to a child with a scraped knee.

Just as an awareness of self emerges at the end of infancy, so does an awareness of the differences between males and females. Whereas **sex** refers to *physiological differences, such as physical appearance, between males and females,* **gender** involves *nonphysiological differences that arise from a set of expectations that a culture attaches to one sex or the other.* Expectations of differences between children on the basis of gender start from the moment of birth, although in reality, the similarities between the psychological needs of both boys and girls outweigh any presumed differences. Social conventions often dictate generalizations parents and other adults make regarding expected attributes about males and females such as aggressiveness in boys or nurturance in girls (Jacklin, 1989). Social learning theory suggests that the environment molds behavioral differences between boys and girls. When boys and girls mimic or imitate stereotypic behavior in others—parents, teachers, peers, and even models on television—they receive tangible reinforcement and social praise (Maccoby, 1990).

Evidence of different cultural expectations is seen in parents' choices of clothes and toys. Differences in the way parents dress their children and the toys they buy still persist (Karraker, Vogel, & Lake, 1995). Boys are associated with blue and girls with pink. Boys are handled roughly and offered "masculine" toys such as footballs and trucks, whereas girls are encouraged to play with dolls and other stereotypic "feminine" toys (Campenni, 1999). Fathers apparently play a critical role in encouraging "masculinity" in boys and "femininity" in girls. Fathers are more likely to be concerned about culturally appropriate expectations regarding gender-specific activities (Doyle & Paludi, 1997; Fagot, 1995).

SOCIALIZATION

The family is the primary socializing agent during infancy. As infants interact with their parents, they acquire the standards and traditions of their culture. Children come into contact with others outside of the family as they enter childhood. Their peers and the media, particularly television, transmit expectations, directly and indirectly shaping their lives. Nevertheless, the family continues to play an influential role. *The acquisition of cultural values and attitudes* is referred to as **socialization**. Children are products of both nature and nurture. They become, as Neil Postman once wrote, "the living messages we send to a time we will not see (Postman, 1982, p. xi).

ROLE OF FAMILIES

The family is a microcosm of life. It brings not only joy but sometimes pain. A healthy family becomes a valuable resource during difficult times. Conversely, a dysfunctional family sometimes creates problems that sometimes persist from one generation to the next. The family has always provided physical, emotional, and economic support to its members. Even in the face of increasing industrialization and urbanization, the content of the family has not changed.

Families differ in structural composition. They include:

■ **Single-parent families.** Single-parent families consist of a parent with one or more children who reside in the same household. In 1970, about 12% of children lived in single-parent homes; today, the rate has risen to about one-third (U.S. Census Bureau, 1997).

■ **Nuclear families.** Nuclear families have traditionally included a father, a mother, and their children. As a proportion of all families, nuclear families have declined in recent years because of the high rate of divorce and unmarried parenthood.

■ **Extended families.** Extended families consist of both parents and their children and other relatives, such as grandparents. They either live in the same residence or maintain frequent contact with each other.

■ **Blended or reconstituted families.** When a divorced or widowed person with children is remarried, two families are blended or reconstituted into one. Both children and parents must adjust to new rules and expectations.

People today still associate the family with an intact unit of two parents and children. In reality, however, the structure of the family varies considerably. Nonetheless, the family remains the principal transmitter of cultural beliefs and traditions in any society. It can shape children's personality and instill modes of thought that can persist for a lifetime.

RECIPROCAL NATURE OF SOCIAL INTERACTION

From the moment of birth, infants are interested in social events. They attend and respond to the sight of the human face and sound of the human voice in addition to other social stimuli that both capture and maintain their interest and attention. Their social skills acquire increasing sophistication as they develop. Although sleep predominates the initial days and weeks, they gradually engage in social episodes with others: gazing into adults' eyes, crying to signal distress, cooing, and holding onto their parents' fingers. As periods of wakefulness increase, opportunities to interact with others grow, too. Both infants and their parents enter a new phase in their relationship. Parents begin to perceive their infants as social partners who reciprocate the attention they receive. In turn, infants learn about their physical and social world from mutual exchanges involving face-to-face interactions with their parents.

The reciprocal episodes between infants and their primary caregivers form the basis of early interactions. However, the frequency and duration of mutual exchanges differ in various cultures. European American mothers often direct their infants' attention to inanimate objects in their immediate environment. In contrast, Japanese mothers focus on the establishment of mutual intimacy in their interactions with their infants (Miyake, Chen, & Campos, 1985). In another cross-cultural comparison, European American mothers tend to rely on social overtures that stimulate and excite their infants such as tickling. The Gusii in rural Kenya engage in activities that soothe and quiet their infants

---

HISTORICALLY SPEAKING

RECIPROCAL NATURE OF SOCIAL INTERACTION
• •

Harriet Rheingold
The Social and Socializing Infant, 1969
The human infant is born into a social environment upon which he is dependent for survival. Although he is physically helpless during the first few months, he has several effective procedures for ensuring that he receives the care he requires. He is socially responsive and he invites social responses from others. By means of his cry and his smile, and to a lesser extent by means of his contended vocalizations, he modifies the caretaking behavior of his parents to suit his needs.

Source: Rheingold (1969), p. 789.

such as breast-feeding at a moment's notice. Other cultural differences exist. In non-Western cultures, older siblings tend to engage in social play and take an active role in the care of infants (Dunn, 1992; Whiting & Edwards, 1992).

Synchronized exchanges between infants and their primary caregivers emerge during the first several weeks of life. Infants modify their emotional expressiveness such as looking and smiling to match their caregivers' overtures, and adults adjust their responsiveness to match their infants' readiness to engage in social interactions (Feldman, Greenbaum, & Yirmiya, 1999). The coordinated interaction between infants and their caregivers has sometimes been described as an "intimate dance." Other terms such as *social reciprocity* and *synchrony* are also used. Dyadic episodes, however, do not always result in reciprocal interactions. Periods of dyssynchrony occur in the course of normal social interactions between infants and their caregivers (Biringen, Emde, & Pipp-Siegel, 1997). Both usually try to reestablish social contact whenever their social partner disconnects, possibly because of distractions or other reasons. Over time, infants learn to socialize with and tune in to the needs of others.

Toddlerhood provides new opportunities to extend social contacts with others. Although caregivers often notice increased negativism such as "no" or "mine," toddlers continue to make remarkable strides in social development, as shown in Table 10–1.

TABLE 10–1   MILESTONES OF SOCIAL DEVELOPMENT

Behavior	Age in Months
Regards face	0–1
Smiles in social situation	2–3
Vocalizes in response to adult's speech	3–5
Repeats enjoyable activities	4–8
Displays wariness of strangers	5–8
Responds playfully to mirror	6–9
Engages in simple imitative play	9–12
Explores environment enthusiastically	9–12
Gives toy to familiar adult on request	12–15
Likes to imitate adult's behavior	12–18
Expresses affection	18–24
Engages in parallel play	18–24
Displays negativism	18–24
Demonstrates sense of self	18–24
Attempts to comfort others in distress	22–24
Defends possessions	23–24
Uses the word *mine*	24–30
Initiates own play but requires supervision	24–36

Source: Furuno et al. (1994).

SOCIAL COMPETENCE

Infants develop social competence from interactions with their primary caregivers and later their peers. **Social competence** refers to *infants' ability to establish and maintain satisfying social interactions and relationships with others* (Premack & Premack, 1995). The overall quality of parents' relationships with their infants directly influences the development of social competence. Parents of securely attached infants enjoy physical contact with their infants and respond consistently to their needs. Gradually, infants develop internal working models of their social world, including infants' mental representations of their relationships with others and their assessment of their parents' availability and sensitivity to their needs. Parents' child-rearing styles exert a profound influence on their children's development of social competence. Two dimensions that reflect variations in disciplinary techniques involve demandingness, or parents' expectations and their attempts to control their children's development, and responsiveness, or parents' acceptance or rejection of their children (Maccoby & Martin, 1983).

As social competence develops, infants make use of environmental and personal resources to accomplish their goals. The following characteristics of socially competent infants have been identified: getting and holding the attention of adults, using adults as resources when they encounter difficult tasks, expressing affection and annoyance with adults, and taking pride in their accomplishments (White, 1985). Later, children start to interact with their peers in different contexts. Other features of social competence from the third year onward include children's ability to lead and follow their peers and to compete with their peers. In the past, children's first experiences with their peers often happened in their own backyard or neighborhood. However, because of the high percentage of working parents today, an increasing number of children begin to relate to peers in out-of-home care. Children engage in complex social skills such as taking turns and sharing toys and imitate each other in spontaneous play to the delight of the model and the imitator. Shouts of "no" and "mine" are still heard, but valuable lessons are learned about the social world (Saarni, 1999).

RELATIONS WITH PEERS

Infants are able to establish social contacts with peers during the first year. At about 3 months, they just stare at each other with only minimal physical contact (Fogel, 1979). Later, they begin to vocalize and use gestures to communicate with others as they attempt to make social contact. Toys are sometimes exchanged, but infants do not engage in reciprocal play until later (Verba, 1994). Social interaction reaches a new level of complexity during the second year. Infants demonstrate increasing interest in interacting with their peers. They gradually engage in reciprocal patterns of behavior in their spontaneous play. Further, infants like to imitate one another (Howes, 1998; La Greca & Prinstein, 1999). Each repeats the actions of the other as they show visible signs of mutual enjoyment such as increased vocalization. Interest in peers is often noticed in out-of-home care because of accessibility to other children of approximately the same age (Fagot, 1997; Sroufe, Carlson, & Shulman, 1993).

Peers play an increasingly important role, particularly in out-of-home care, in shaping development.
Photo courtesy of Tami Dawson, Photo Resource Hawaii.

Further advances in children's relations with their peers can be seen at the end of infancy. Children learn valuable lessons from each other. They slowly come to the realization that others do not always think the same way they do. Although children typically flow from one activity to another in spontaneous play, friendships begin to emerge as children start to play with certain companions. Gender differences can be found in children's play. At about the age of 2, children demonstrate stereotypic patterns reflecting cultural expectations of masculinity and femininity in their play (Fagot, Leinbach, & O'Boyle, 1992). During the preschool years, boys usually engage in rough-and-tumble play and girls in cooperative play. Genetic factors probably play an important role, but parents and other adults model and reinforce culturally acceptable behavior (Fagot & Leinbach, 1993).

FATHERS AS CAREGIVERS

Interest in the role that fathers play in their children's development has increased in recent years. With the gradual disappearance of stereotypic expectations, a large number of fathers have begun to assume child-rearing responsibilities. With changes come questions about the nature of fathers' relationship with their infants. Can fathers provide adequate cognitive stimulation and emotional nurturance? The evidence shows strong support. Fathers themselves speak in high-pitched voices with exaggerated intonation, foster the establishment of secure attachment, and synchronize their social overtures with their infants, just as mothers do. Infants generally benefit from their extended

ATTACHMENT TO FATHERS AND SIBLINGS

Infants can form affectional ties with other people. Historically, mothers have been viewed as the primary caregivers, reflecting the long-standing cultural beliefs and expectations. Cultural stereotypes have even infiltrated early theories. Freud believed that adults' intimate relationships stemmed from their first "objects" of love, their mothers. Such biases excluded fathers in studies on attachment. The generalized results often pertained only to infants and their mothers (Mintz, 1998). However, changing times have forced a reevaluation of fathers' roles. Fathers today are expected to shoulder their "significant share of nurturing responsibilities" (Poussaint, 1986, p. 9).

Does attachment to mothers differ from fathers? The answer is it depends. In one study, infants' attachment to their mothers and fathers was compared. At all ages, 6 months to 2 years, the majority of infants did not respond to their fathers' absence in the same way as they did with their mothers in a variation of the "strange situation" (Lamb, 1997). The determining factor involved the amount of time that fathers spent with their infants. Securely attached infants had fathers who participated in child-rearing responsibilities. In other studies, the results contradicted widespread misconceptions about their involvement in the lives of their infants. Fathers did respond sensitively to their infants' cues although they sometimes yielded responsibility to their wives (Parke, 1996).

In addition, infants can establish attachments with their siblings and other children of comparable age. In a number of societies, infants are cared for in multiaged groups of children at about 1 year as in the !Kung in southwestern Africa (Konner, 1976, 1977). Infants' attachment gradually shifts from their mothers to older children in multiaged groups who undertake some of the major child-rearing responsibilities. Mothers are then allowed to resume their work until the birth of the next child. Multiaged groups in many hunting and gathering societies entail numerous benefits. Children learn important lessons from observing adults in different social contexts.

In industrialized societies, about 80% of children live with at least one sibling. The arrival of a new brother or a new sister requires the adjustment of everyone in the family (Dunn, 1995). Firstborn children soon realize they need to share their parents' limited attention and affection with someone else. However, their resentment usually fades with time (Goode, 1994). New siblings are objects not only of occasional frustration but also of delight. Initially, firstborns like to imitate their new siblings. Then, the tables are turned. The new siblings now become the imitators. Differences between sexes have been found. Interactions between brothers generally involve high levels of physical aggression, whereas relationships between sisters usually reflect prosocial tendencies.

time with their fathers. Still, differences between the parenting styles of fathers and mothers exist, particularly as it relates to the amount of time each spends with their infants.

FATHERS' ROLE

Fathers and mothers do differ in the way that they interact with their infants. In particular, fathers typically engage in physical and spontaneous interaction (Lamb, 1998). They like to engage in vigorous and unpredictable games. Play between fathers and their infants seems to occur in cycles. Periods of minimal activity frequently follow periods of attention. In contrast, mothers tend to talk and sing soothingly to their infants (Rock, Trainor, & Addison, 1999). They generally like to initiate conventional games such as "pat-a-cake" or "peek-a-boo." Differences between fathers' and mothers' play are not lost

---

SUGGESTED ACTIVITIES

PSYCHOSOCIAL DEVELOPMENT

Infants are born to interact with others. Different activities can foster infants' formation of attachment to others.

Birth to 1 Year

- Respond to infants' signals of distress promptly to facilitate the establishment of trust.

- Talk about your own actions during daily routines such as feeding and diapering and imitate infants' gestures and vocalizations.

- Play simple games encouraging mutual interaction such as "peek-a-boo" and "pat-a-cake."

- Make a book with familiar photographs of the family, friends, pets, and objects and ask questions ("Can you find...?").

- Take short walks in the neighborhood and talk about the sights and sounds.

During the next 2 years, a sense of self gradually emerges. Children's successful psychosocial development depends on the quality of care they receive from their primary caregivers as they exercise increasing independence.

1 to 3 Years

- Point to your child's reflection in a mirror and name the major parts of the face and body.

- Reassure your child in an unfamiliar situation with a soothing voice and offer physical comfort.

- Use words to express your emotions such as happiness and sadness in an appropriate manner.

- Acknowledge your child's emotions without being judgmental and listen to his or her explanations.

- Encourage your child's increasing autonomy in doing things on his or her own.

on infants. Often, infants react with visible excitement when their fathers approach. The frequency of laughter increases significantly in dyadic episodes of play with fathers.

Over time, differences in the behavioral patterns between fathers and mothers widen further. Because of increasing mobility in the last half of the first year, the amount of time that fathers spend with their own infants intensifies. The incidence of physical activity is increasingly pronounced. Fathers tend to swing their infants in the air or chase them on the floor. On the other hand, mothers continue to play conventional games or read to their infants during spontaneous play. Infants usually set the pace of events with their mothers. Again, differences are reflected in infants' reactions to their parents' social overtures. At age 2, toddlers generally demonstrate increased interest in their fathers' games, judging from their smiles and laughter.

Recent research has examined the effects of fathers' involvement on children's development. Consistent results have been found (Bailey, 1994). Children of highly involved fathers exhibit increased cognitive competence later. Not surprisingly, children do benefit from the diversity of stimulation that comes from their interaction with two parents instead of one (Amato, 1998). Decreased stereotypical views of masculine and feminine roles have been noted in children of highly involved fathers. If their parents assume nonstereotypical roles, particularly their fathers, children acquire similar attitudes (Cherlin, 1998). Fathers' involvement needs to be viewed in the total context of the family because not only their own personal attributes but the quality of marital relationships with their spouses can influence the outcome. Both partners appear to complement each other as they meet their children's physical, cognitive, and psychosocial needs together (Caulfield, 1996b).

SPECIAL NEEDS

Every culture recognizes the need to protect children from harm. Yet, in the United States, the incidence of child abuse and neglect has continued to rise with an estimated 1 million confirmed cases each year (Children's Defense Fund, 1999). Child maltreatment involves not only physical injuries but also psychological abuse and emotional neglect. The accumulated effects of abuse and neglect can severely hinder children's development in all areas, particularly learning problems and difficulties in relating to others later in life (Salzinger et al., 1993).

CHANGING VIEWS OF MALTREATMENT

Conceptions of child maltreatment have changed over the years. It used to be associated only with physical abuse. However, maltreatment includes both abuse (deliberate and harmful actions) and neglect (the failure to meet children's basic needs). Abuse and neglect can be divided into five specific categories:

■ **Physical abuse.** Parents who physically abuse their children cause deliberate injury to the body. Obvious signs of physical abuse include bruises, burns, broken limbs, and battered bodies.

- **Sexual abuse.** Sexual abuse concerns deliberate involvement in or exposure to sexual exploitation. Because of their immaturity and vulnerability, children are not always able to resist sexual advances from adults.

- **Psychological abuse.** Psychologically abused children suffer from the deliberate destruction of their emotional well-being. Examples include incessant criticisms and verbal threats that degrade or belittle children's sense of self.

- **Physical neglect.** Physical neglect results from parents' failure to meet the basic needs of their children. Physically neglected children may not receive sufficient food or medical attention.

- **Psychological neglect.** Adults engaging in psychological abuse may fail to provide affection and emotional support to their children. They may either capriciously withhold or withdraw love and comfort.

ETIOLOGY AND PREVENTION OF MALTREATMENT

When child maltreatment was first studied, it was believed to be rooted in the psychological disturbance of adults. Initial studies indicated that adults who abused or neglected their children lived at one time in abusive families themselves and demonstrated poor control of impulses (Spinetta & Rigler, 1972). However, more recent studies demonstrate that a common denominator identifying abusive parents does not exist. Abused parents do not always repeat the cycle of physical violence or neglect their own children (Simons et al., 1991). Instead of pinpointing a single cause, child maltreatment is currently viewed in the broad context of both the family and culture. A multitude of interacting factors may influence parents' maltreatment of children. In particular, certain children, including premature and extremely sick infants or temperamentally difficult and overactive children, usually tend to become targets of abuse and neglect. In turn, abusive parents may resort to harsh, punitive measures because they attribute their children's unruliness to stubbornness (Belsky, 1993; Miller-Perrin & Perrin, 1999).

Other factors may provoke abusive behavior in parents. Parental stress has been linked to marital conflicts, overcrowded living conditions, low income, and unemployment. Frustrations can sometimes overwhelm parents who may then vent their anger on their children. They may even overlook basic child-rearing responsibilities. In addition, isolation from others may hinder abusive parents' ability to cope with the everyday stresses. Some may have learned to mistrust and avoid others because of their own experiences as abused children. They may lack skills that establish and maintain positive and supportive relationships with relatives and friends (Ten Bensel, Rheinberger, & Radbill, 1997). Further, abusive parents typically live in neighborhoods lacking supportive links between families and communities. Culture may also play an influential role. The beliefs and laws of a particular culture may have an impact on parents' attitudes and practices in raising children. Unfortunately, the frequency of child maltreatment increases in cultures tolerating violent behavior such as the United States. It rarely gains a foothold in countries that frown on physical punishment such as Japan, China, Luxembourg, and Sweden (Zigler & Hall, 1989).

Efforts to prevent child maltreatment must involve both families and communities in addition to society as a whole. Abusive parents need to learn effective child-rearing and disciplinary skills to meet children's basic physical and psychological needs. Examples include the use of social praise and time-out to encourage appropriate and discourage inappropriate behavior. To foster knowledge of children's development, emphasis should be placed on developing realistic expectations and constructive parenting skills. Social support is also needed to reduce possible isolation. Local chapters of Parents Anonymous, a national organization, maintain regular contact with parents and provide parenting workshops. Other preventive steps include public announcements in newspapers and television about the detrimental effects of child abuse and neglect. Although the legal system protects the rights of children, it does not always punish chronic abusers.

SUMMARY

Emotional Development

■ Harlow found in his experiments that monkeys formed an attachment with surrogates, not because of the nourishment they provided, but because of comfort. His research contradicted the prevailing theoretical orientations of attachment of the mid-20th century.

■ Bowlby believed that human attachment evolved to ensure infants' survival. He proposed a series of four stages in the formation of infants' attachment to their primary caregivers.

■ Ainsworth devised the "strange situation" to measure the quality of infants' attachment. She examined infants' reactions to the presence of an unfamiliar adult after their mothers briefly left and later returned to a room.

■ The results of Ainsworth's studies indicate that the quality of care in the first year affects attachment. Parents' sensitivity to their infants' needs seems to be highly associated with secure attachment.

■ Temperament refers to inborn dispositions affecting both the quality and intensity of a person's emotional reactions to unfamiliar situations. However, environmental factors shape its expression.

■ Erikson's work refined and expanded Freud's psychoanalytic theory. Erikson argued that development represents a continuous process, involving the resolution of potential conflicts between the self and society and progressing in stages from infancy to adulthood.

■ The first major crisis involves the establishment of trust versus mistrust in the world from birth to 1. The next crisis from 1 to 3 is described as a crisis of autonomy versus shame and doubt.

■ Researchers face a daunting task in studying emotional development of infants. Because infants are not able to describe their emotions, their facial expressions are observed in studies of affective states.

■ Mahler believes that infants' awareness of themselves as unique entities emerges in two stages. At first, they do not demonstrate any awareness of their immediate environment, but their sense of separateness occurs during the second half of the first year.

Socialization

■ The family provides physical, emotional, and economic support to its members. Even in the face of increasing demographic changes, the content of the family has not been changed.

■ Opportunities to interact with social partners increase with age. Mutual exchanges facilitate infants' understanding of their physical and social world.

■ Infants develop social competence as they interact with their primary caregivers and, later on, peers. Social competence refers to infants' ability to establish and maintain satisfying social interactions and relationships with others.

Relations with Peers

■ Interactions with peers begin with minimum physical contact at first. As toddlers begin to engage in mutual play over time, reciprocal exchanges increase in frequency.

■ Gender differences in children's play reflect cultural expectations of masculinity and femininity. Caregivers across the world tend to reinforce rough-and-tumble play in boys and cooperative play in girls.

Fathers as Caregivers

■ Fathers and mothers differ in the way they interact with their infants. Fathers generally tend to engage in vigorous spontaneous play, whereas mothers typically like to initiate structured conventional games.

Special Needs

■ Child maltreatment was historically associated only with physical abuse. However, it has now been expanded to include five separate categories of abuse and neglect.

PROJECTS

1. Observe a parent and child and comment on the reciprocity of their mutual interaction.

2. Design an informational brochure advising new parents about ways of fostering infants' sense of trust and autonomy at home.

3. Ask someone from a local chapter of PREVENT Child Abuse to talk about the harmful effects of abuse and neglect on infants and young children.

HEALTH AND NUTRITION

Life's not just living; it's living in health.
Martial, *Epigrams*

Health
    Communicable Diseases
    Common Illnesses
    Safety
Nutrition
    Feeding Practices

Sensitivity to Food
Nutritional Significance of Vitamins
    and Minerals
Summary
Projects

Part 3 examined the major areas of development during the first few years. Although there are individual and cultural variations, infants across the world generally follow the same sequence of milestones. Part 4 focuses attention on important parenting issues involving health and nutrition in Chapter 11 and guidance and early education in Chapter 12. Both chapters highlight the impact of their respective topics on infants' optimal development.

Healthy development is not a matter of luck. It reflects choices parents and professional caregivers make, such as following the recommended schedule of immunizations to protect infants from deadly diseases and childproofing the environment to prevent accidental injuries. Likewise, good nutrition sustains both body and brain during a period of rapid physical growth in the first few years. Increasing physical activity provides further opportunities to explore the world and interact with others. Therefore, good health and nutrition are vital links to optimal development. After communicable diseases and precautionary steps to ensure safety are discussed, attention is turned to the nutritional needs of infants.

HEALTH

Traditionally, the presence of disease has been used as the primary indication of health. Statistics on both **mortality**—*the frequency of death*—and **morbidity**—*the rate of illness*—in a given population can provide information on the causes of death and illness.

PARENTING ISSUES

SHAKEN BABY SYNDROME: INTENTIONAL CEREBRAL INJURIES

Violent shaking during the first year, particularly the first 6 months, can lead to serious cerebral injuries. It is often committed in response to an infant's incessant crying. The term *shaken baby syndrome* dates back to 1972 when pediatric radiologist John Caffey described a constellation of clinical results, including hemorrhage in the brain without evidence of external cranial trauma. He postulated that severe jerking motions of the head caused retinal and subdural hemorrhages in the brain (Caffey, 1972). Subsequent research has substantiated his conclusions, although recent evidence has surfaced that violent shaking alone does not necessarily cause severe trauma. The force of rapid deceleration resulting from the shaken head hitting any surface, even a bed or pillow, can result in serious intracranial injuries (Duhaime et al., 1998).

Too often, the seriousness of intentional shaking is not realized until later. Parents do not always seek immediate medical attention because of their own culpability in the matter (Conway, 1998). Shaken infants with mild ocular and cerebral trauma tend to exhibit lethargic and irritable behavior and poor appetite during the first few days and weeks after the incident. Medical help is not always sought because the incident is frequently hidden from other people. If parents do seek help, doctors may attribute the symptoms to mild viral illnesses, feeding dysfunctions, or colic (severe abdominal pain in infants). Violent shaking can cause convulsion, unconsciousness, and sadly, death in severe cases (Lancon, Haines, & Parent, 1998).

Infants surviving serious cerebral trauma usually face a bleak future. Many experience profound mental retardation, spastic quadriplegia, and severe motor dysfunction later (Wecht, 1999). Because of its severity, any suspicion of injuries resulting from child maltreatment should be reported to the proper authorities. Once reported, a doctor will try to resuscitate and stabilize the shaken infant (American Academy of Pediatrics, 1993). Then, a diagnostic team consisting of specialists in pediatric radiology, neurology, and ophthalmology will examine the extent of the injuries, treating and documenting any ocular and neurologic sequelae (conditions of the trauma). If conclusive evidence of intentional cerebral trauma can be established, criminal charges can be brought against the implicated adult. Another important factor to consider in any discussion of child maltreatment involves prevention. Announcements on radio or television may be the best way of informing the public about the detrimental effects of child abuse in general but inflicted cerebral trauma in particular.

Infant mortality has decreased dramatically in the United States and other industrialized countries over the last 100 years. At the turn of the 20th century, an estimated 200 deaths per 1,000 births occurred; in 1997, the rate dropped to 7 per 1,000 births (Guyer et al., 1998). The decrease resulted from improved control and prevention of infectious diseases, nutritional advances, and the advent of antibiotics and antibacterial agents. Furthermore, medical advances in prenatal care and childbirth have had an impact. Prior to the 20th century, only poor and unwed mothers gave birth in hospitals. In 1950, the number reached 80% (Shorter, 1982), whereas today nearly all women give birth in hospitals.

Although medical science has cut the overall infant mortality rate, congenital anomalies still continue to be the leading cause of death during the first week (an estimated 20% of all deaths at the time of birth). The incidence of congenital anomalies has not changed substantially during the last 50 years. Most congenital anomalies are directly associated with low birth weight. The prevention of congenital anomalies depends on adequate prenatal care to reduce the overall number of infants with low birth weight (Mili et al., 1991). Although the overall infant mortality rate has dropped in the United States, the disparity between African Americans and European Americans has not changed. Infant mortality among African American infants is double the rate among European Americans (Naeye, 1993).

Even in the event of a healthy childbirth, infectious diseases may still pose a threat. The next section examines communicable diseases, once deadly scourges of childhood, and scheduled immunizations to protect infants.

COMMUNICABLE DISEASES

Infants develop resistance to a number of infectious diseases because of antibodies they receive from their mothers during prenatal development. The formation of antibodies to specific antigens requires mothers' exposure to foreign agents prior to pregnancy, either from an actual illness or a previous vaccination. Immunities passed on to infants include diphtheria, measles, poliomyelitis, and mumps. However, protection only lasts about 3 months. Infants are nevertheless equipped with other lines of defense against infection. The skin and mucous membranes protect the body from invading organisms. Cellular elements of the immunological system produce cells that attach pathogens in the body. Phagocytes refer to cells that engulf and destroy foreign agents.

Since the introduction of immunizations in the 1950s, the incidence of infectious diseases has steadily declined. However, some infectious diseases can still occur. Death in infancy and childhood was accepted as part of life before the turn of 20th century. An estimated one-third of infants died before 1 year of age, and nearly half of all children died before their tenth birthday (Lofland, 1986). Today, death is thought of as a phenomenon of "old age." Because of medical advances, childhood is no longer considered a dreaded period in life (Bertman, 1991).

The identification of infectious agents is needed to prevent any exposure to susceptible individuals. Professional caregivers and public health nurses are usually the first to see any signs of communicable diseases such as a rash. A sore throat usually signifies a minor viral infection. Parents are generally notified if a recent exposure to a known case is identified.

Prevention of infectious diseases consists of two components. First is the prevention of infectious diseases; second is the control of their spread to others. Primary prevention rests on immunization. Although used interchangeably, **vaccination** involves *the administration of an immunological agent*, whereas **immunization** refers to *the development of adequate immunity*.

Recommended Schedule of Immunizations.   In the United States, two national advisory organizations govern recommendations concerning the vaccination of children. The Committee on Infectious Diseases of the American Academy of Pediatrics and the Advisory Committee on Immunization Practices (ACIP) of the U.S. Public Health Service Centers for Disease Control and Prevention provide detailed guidelines (see Table 11–1). Although ACIP is involved with health issues, both are concerned with the promotion of infants' optimal development. To obtain the maximum level of immunity, scheduled immunizations are recommended from birth:

■ **Hepatitis B virus (HBV).**   A potentially fatal viral infection, HBV eventually causes cirrhosis, or cancer of the liver, without immunization. Although a safe, effective vaccine, the incidence of HBV has doubled in certain groups, particularly children of immigrants from countries with widespread HBV.

■ **Diphtheria, tetanus, and pertussis (DTaP).**   A combined vaccine is recommended with children from 2 months to 6 years of age. All three infectious diseases enter the body from an outside source: discharges from the mucous membranes of the nose

TABLE 11–1 IMMUNIZATION OF HEALTHY INFANTS AND CHILDREN: RECOMMENDED SCHEDULE	
Age	**Vaccination**
Birth–2 months	HBV
1–4 months	HBV
2 months	DTaP, Hib, IPV
4 months	DTaP, Hib, IPV
6 months	DTaP, Hib
6–18 months	HBV, OPV
12–15 months	Hib, MMR
12–18 months	Var
15–18 months	DTaP
4–6 years	DTaP, OPV, MMR

Abbreviations: HBV=hepatitis B virus vaccine; DTaP=diphtheria, tetanus, and pertussis vaccine; Hib=H. influenzae-type B vaccine; IPV=inactivated poliovirus vaccine; OPV=oral poliovirus vaccine; MMR=measles, mumps, and rubella viruses vaccine; Var=varicella vaccine (chicken pox)
Source: American Academy of Pediatrics (1999).

and nasopharynx or respiratory tract of infected persons for diphtheria and pertussis and wounds for tetanus.

■ **Polio (OPV).**   During the first 6 years of life, a trivalent form of oral poliovirus (OPV) is administered in recommended doses. Acute forms of poliomyelitis attack the body's central nervous system and may result in paralysis, muscular atrophy, and sometimes deformity.

■ **Measles, mumps, and rubella (MMR).**   MMR is given in a combined dosage at 12 to 15 months. Pediatricians do not administer MMR prior to age 1 because residual maternal antibodies may interfere with the body's immunological response.

SOCIOCULTURAL INFLUENCES

CULTURE AND HEALTH

Cultural beliefs and practices can influence the extent and quality of medical care infants receive. Professional caregivers working with infants should take into account the values and traditions of their parents in promoting cultural diversity. Further, they should examine any possible personal biases and cultural stereotypes that may interfere with their work. Wide individual differences exist, but the following generalizations highlight the important contributions cultures make in the context of health:

BELIEFS

Asians

Chinese

■ A healthy body is viewed as a gift from parents and ancestors.

■ Health results from the balance between the *yin* (cold) and *yang* (hot)—forces of energy that rule the world.

■ The imbalance of forces causes illness.

■ Deficiencies in blood, the source of life, is believed to produce fatigue and prolonged illness.

Japanese

■ The Chinese influence is seen in the belief that good health is achieved through the balance between self and society.

■ Disharmony with society causes diseased conditions.

■ Indigenous religious beliefs (the veneration of ancestors and spirits) exert a strong influence.

■ Outside spirits can cause poor health.

Vietnamese

■ Good health involves the balance between yin and yang.

■ Cosmic forces influence people's health.

■ Harmony with the existing universal order (pleasing good spirits and avoiding bad ones) is valued.

■ Some believe in *am duc*, the good deeds of a person's ancestors.

Filipinos

■ God's will and supernatural forces govern the universe.

(continued)

SOCIOCULTURAL INFLUENCES

■ Illness, accidents, or other misfortunes occur because of God's punishment of people who violate His will.

Hispanics

Mexicans

■ Imbalance of the body, *caliente* (hot) and *frio* (cold), causes illnesses.

■ Some maintain that good health results from good luck or good behavior.

■ Illnesses are prevented when proper food is eaten and when religious artifacts are worn.

■ Health parallels religious beliefs (poor health reflects God's punishment because of wrongdoing).

Puerto Ricans

■ Belief in the theory of hot and cold causation of illness is held.

■ Some believe that evil spirits and forces can cause illness.

African Americans

■ Serious illness is seen as God's punishment.

■ Some believe in the influence of evil forces.

Native Americans

■ Theology and medicine are strongly intertwined.

■ Good health depends on personal harmony with nature and the universe.

■ Proper care begins with respect of the body.

■ Violation of a restriction or prohibition is thought to cause illness.

PRACTICES

Chinese

■ The goal of therapy is to restore the balance of yin and yang.

■ Acupuncturists apply needles to appropriate meridians identified in terms of yin and yang.

■ In certain areas of the body, acupressure and *tai chi* can be used in place of acupuncture.

■ Medicinal herbs are applied in prescribed ways.

Japanese

■ Purification removes evil spirits.

■ Acupuncture, acupressure, and massage restore energy in affected meridians.

■ The use of natural herbs is practiced.

■ Both Eastern and Western healing methods are followed.

Vietnamese

■ The family employs all possible means before it seeks outside medical care.

■ Astrologers are consulted to calculate cyclical changes and forces.

■ Temples are visited to procure divine intervention.

■ Special diets are followed to prevent illness and promote health.

Filipinos

■ Some use amulets as protection from witchcraft or as good luck.

■ Catholics may substitute religious artifacts and other items.

(continued)

SOCIOCULTURAL INFLUENCES

Mexicans

■ Prescriptions and prohibitions of food are followed in the treatment and prevention of illnesses.

■ Treatment involves the use of herbs, religious artifacts, and rituals—visiting shrines, offering prayers, and making promises.

Puerto Ricans

■ Medical care is sought infrequently.

■ The use of herbs and rituals is practiced.

African Americans

■ Prayer is used as a common means of treatment and prevention.

■ Personal remedies are tried first before medical attention is sought.

Native Americans

■ The expertise of native American medicinal and spiritual specialists is sought.

■ Herbs and rituals may be used to restore health.

Possible Reactions. Vaccines provide a safe, effective way of developing immunities against communicable diseases. Although children may experience minor secondary effects after the administration of certain vaccines, rarely do any serious reactions result. In the case of inactivated antigens, such as DTaP, secondary effects may occur in a matter of a few hours. Reactions include tenderness and swollenness at the site of the injection, accompanied by mild fever. Parents may notice behavioral changes in their children shortly after the vaccination such as prolonged or unusual cries, drowsiness, fretfulness, or loss of appetite. The severity of reactions to DTaP may worsen if children had problems with a previous administration.

Important considerations in working with young children in out-of-home care are the prevention of common illnesses and injuries.
Photo courtesy of Tami Dawson, Photo Resource Hawaii

COMMON ILLNESSES

Immunizations can protect children from infectious diseases, but a host of other illnesses still exist, some disappearing on their own without treatment and others requiring the medical attention of pediatricians. Sometimes, the seriousness of a particular illness may warrant medication to alleviate its symptoms. However, parents and other caregivers should remember not to diagnose or medicate children in their care without appropriate consultation. Common illnesses can be categorized in one of six general areas of the body: eyes; ears, nose, and throat; lungs; digestive tract; urinary tract; and skin, as shown in Table 11–2. Symptoms of the common cold are listed in Table 11–3.

SAFETY

As infants make significant strides in locomotor and manipulative skills, the likelihood of accidents increases. The leading cause of death during the first few years is preventable injuries. Because of their natural curiosity, infants are interested in actively

---

TABLE 11–2   COMMON ILLNESSES

Eyes

- Conjunctivitis ("pink eye")

A common but highly contagious condition in children, conjunctivitis involves the inflammation of the conjunctiva, the mucous membrane that lines the inner surface of the eyelids.

Cause: virus, bacteria, or dirt

Treatment: antibacterial drops during the day and ointment at bedtime

Ears, Nose, and Throat

- Otitis externa (earaches)

Inflammation of the external canal of the ear results in earaches, which may lead to temporary hearing loss because of excessive accumulation of fluid and debris.

Cause: excessive wetness from contract with water such as swimming or bathing or increased dryness

Treatment: relief of pain with analgesics in addition to the restoration of cerumen, the waxy secretion of the external ear

- Otitis media (inflammation of the middle ear)

A prevalent disease that affects the middle ear, 70% of children had at least one episode and 33% had three or more episodes before the age of 2 (Williams et al., 1993).

Cause: two bacteria, either *Streptococcus pneumoniae* or *Haemophilus influenzae,* or blocked eustachian tubes

Treatment: administration of antibiotics and prevention of recurrence such as inserting tiny, plastic tubes to aid draining and avoid hearing loss, although not routinely done

- Allergic rhinitis (seasonal allergy)

A common allergic disorder in children as well as adults, allergic rhinitis occurs during certain times of the year.

Cause: exposure to microscopic, airborne foreign particles, principally pollens and environmental dusts

Treatment: avoidance of offending allergens and use of medication and immunotherapy (hypersensitization or desensitization)

(continued)

TABLE 11–2 CONTINUED

■ Acute viral nasopharyngitis (common cold)

Common symptoms include runny nose, fever, sore throat, and cough.

Cause: a number of different viruses, usually rhinoviruses, respiratory syncytial virus, adenovirus, influenza virus, or parainfluenza virus

Treatment: relief of fever and sore throat with acetaminophen

■ Pharyngitis and sore throat

Inflammation of the pharynx (the section of the digestive tract extending from the nasal cavities to the larynx) is involved.

Cause: bacterial infection, streptococcus, that may result in strep throat

Treatment: oral penicillin to control acute streptococcal sore throat

■ Laryngitis and croup

Laryngitis refers to an inflammation of the larynx resulting in the loss of voice; croup, a common respiratory illness, involves an infection of the tissues surrounding the larynx causing a barklike cough, fever, and noisy respiration.

Cause: viruses

Treatment: consumption of fluids and use of humidified air

Lungs

■ Asthma

Asthma involves the restriction of bronchioles (the small breathing tubes of the lungs) resulting in shortness of breath.

Cause: hypersensitivity to environmental agents such as pollens and viral infections

Treatment: reduction in exposure to airborne allergens and irritants and medication to dilate the bronchioles

■ Bronchitis

Sometimes referred to as tracheobronchitis, bronchitis involves the inflammation of the trachea and bronchi, large airways of the body.

Cause: viral infection of the breathing tubes

Treatment: antibiotics, high humidity, adequate intake of fluids, and rest

Digestive Tract

■ Diarrhea

A leading cause of illness in children, diarrhea causes dehydration that may result in death, an incidence affecting roughly 400 children in the United States each year (Rhoads, 1999).

Cause: bacterial or viral infection of the bowels or allergic reaction to certain food

Treatment: restoration of fluids and reintroduction of food with acute dehydration

Urinary Tract

■ Urinary infection

Urinary infections involve the uretha, bladder, ureters, or kidneys with symptoms such as painful or frequent urination, abdominal pain, blood in the urine, and the loss of appetite.

Cause: microorganisms in the urinary tract

Treatment: elimination of the infection with anti-infective agents and identification of contributing factors to reduce the risk of recurrence

(continued)

TABLE 11–2 CONTINUED

Skin

■ Eczema

An inflammation of the skin, eczema results in a red rash, primarily on on the face, elbows, and knees.

Cause: repeated exposure to irritants such as rough fabrics, woolen clothes, detergents, and powders

Treatment: administration of medication to alleviate pruritus, or severe itchiness, and reduction of exposure to irritants

---

engaging with the world such as putting small objects into their mouths and opening drawers. The key is to strike a balance between maximizing opportunities to explore and minimizing accidents. The first step is to get on one's hands and knees and inspect each area of the home or child-care facility from an infant's perspective. Hazards such as electrical cords and dangerous bottled cleaning solutions are often overlooked (Marotz, Rush, & Cross, 1998).

Causes of Accidents.   Preventable accidents take an extremely high toll in infancy. Each year, an estimated 1 million children seek medical care in the United States because of accidental injuries that occur at home (Shelov, 1991). Of the total, about 40 to 50% may suffer permanent disability, and 4,000 children may die each year. Table 11–4 provides a list of numerous potential hazards in eight areas: asphyxiation of foreign objects, suffocation, vehicular injuries, falls, poisoning, burns, drowning, and bodily damage.

Furniture and Equipment.   In addition to childproofing areas of the home or child-care facility, parents and professional caregivers need to select furniture and equipment with safety in mind. Accidental injuries and sometimes even death can result from the inappropriate use of commercial products. Although they can save money, secondhand

---

TABLE 11–3 EARLY WARNING SIGNS OF RESPIRATORY COMPLICATIONS

Any number of different viruses can cause acute nasopharyngitis (the common cold). Parents should notify their doctor if any of the following symptoms are noted:

· Fever over 101°F
· Evidence of earaches
· Respirations that exceed 50 to 60 per minute
· Listlessness
· Increased irritability with or without fever
· Persistent cough
· Wheezing
· Refusal to eat
· Restlessness and poor sleeping patterns

Source: D. L. Wong (1998).

HISTORICALLY SPEAKING

SAFETY

Harold Stuart
The Healthy Child, 1960
Accidents differ in the prevailing types and causes and in the incidence of each type by age, because many of the reasons for their occurrence are highly related to the developmental status of the child: mental, emotional, physical, and educational. For these reasons several approaches to their prevention must be adapted, each differing with age and environment, and consistently pursued to keep their incidence to a minimum.

Source: Stuart (1960), p. 16.

TABLE 11–4 POTENTIAL HAZARDS

Asphyxiation of Foreign Objects

Asphyxiation occurs when children put small foreign objects into their respiratory tract and suffocate. Spherical or cylindrical objects 1 1/4 inches or less can obstruct the airway completely.

■ Steps to take:

Inspect toys with small removable parts such as rattles with beads or stuffed animals with plastic eyes or buttons.

Avoid certain kinds of food such as nuts, hard candies, hot dogs, and fruits with pits or seeds.

Suffocation

Pressure on the throat or chest or cutoff of oxygen such as entrapment in refrigerators can cause suffocation. Most deaths result from nonfood items.

■ Steps to take:

Dispose of balloons, the leading cause of choking deaths (Holida, 1993), and large plastic bags.

Never purchase pillows that can mold to the face and block airways (Rollins, 1990) or place cribs next to blinds with hanging cords.

Vehicular Injuries

During the second year, vehicular injuries represent the leading cause of death in children. Each year, many children are injured or die from improper restraint in vehicles.

■ Steps to take:

Always use a federally approved car seat facing rearward in the middle of the back seat.

Never carry the baby or put the car seat in the front seat of a vehicle with a passenger-side airbag.

Falls

Falls increase in frequency after 4 months when children typically learn to roll over. However, falls can occur at any age, resulting in serious injuries.

TABLE 11–4 CONTINUED

■ Steps to take:

Never leave children unattended on a changing table or infant seat, even when restrained with a strap.

Use gates to block access to stairs at the top and bottom.

Poisoning

Accidental poisoning occurs at an alarming rate among 1- to 3-year-olds because of increased mobility. About one-third of all poisonings happen in the kitchen because of improper storage, but even the leaves of certain toxic plants provide another source.

■ Steps to take:

Store toxic agents, including medication and cleaning solutions, on high shelves, preferably in locked cabinets.

Post the number of the local Poison Center in a convenient location near the phone in the event of an emergency.

Burns

Serious burns occur not only from heating elements such as stoves and furnaces but also from excessive exposure to hot water and direct sunlight. Infants' sensitive skin poses a danger.

■ Steps to take:

Be sure to manually lower the water heater temperature at home to 120° F and install smoke detectors in central locations, such as the kitchen.

Avoid prolonged exposure to direct sunlight and apply sunscreen on exposed skin.

Drowning

Because of their disproportionate head size, children can drown in only an inch of water. Constant supervision in the bathtub or wading pool or even the toilet or bucket of water is required.

■ Steps to take:

Never leave children unattended in water.

Place nonskid strips on the floor of the bathtub's surface to prevent falls.

Bodily Damage

Accidental injuries can occur in other lethal ways. Sharp, jagged objects such as toothpicks or forks can cause serious damage as can prolonged exposure to excessive noise.

■ Steps to take:

Store dangerous articles in secured drawers or cabinets.

Protect children from attacks by animals, particularly dogs.

furniture and equipment do not always meet current federally approved standards. To increase awareness of the proper use of commercial furniture and equipment, suggested recommendations from the Consumer Product Safety Commission can be found in Table 11–5.

In sum, prevention is the key to ensure infants' safety. As infants begin to expand their horizons, parents and professional caregivers should take steps to prevent accidental injuries and accidents.

TABLE 11–5 FURNITURE OR EQUIPMENT SAFETY

Cribs

Slats are not cracked or missing or spaced more than 2 3/8 inches apart to prevent entrapment of the head.

Mattress fits snugly.

Decorative posts or cutouts in head and footboards pose hazards such as entanglement of the head or clothes.

Latches securely hold the sides of the crib in raised position.

■ Recommendation:

Replace crib with a bed when children reach 35 inches or begin to climb over the sides.

Changing Tables

Straps should be used to prevent accidental falls.

Buy tables with built-in drawers or shelves to increase accessibility to diapers.

■ Recommendation:

Never leave children unattended on the table.

High Chairs

Straps are needed to fasten and secure the waist and crotch.

Tray locks securely.

The four legs of the high chair should provide a wide, stable base.

A folding high chair needs a secure locking device.

■ Recommendation:

Keep the high chair away from tables and counters to prevent children from pushing off with their feet and falling.

Gates and Enclosures

Small openings in the mesh should not entrap children's head.

Gates can be securely locked in place and resist pressure from children.

■ Recommendation:

Never use accordion-style gates having large v-shaped openings on top to avoid entrapment of the head.

Playpens

One side of the playpen should never be left in a down position to avoid possible entrapment and suffocation.

The mesh should contain small weaves with openings less than 1/4 inch.

■ Recommendation:

Do not leave children in playpens without securely locking the sides.

Strollers

The stroller should be constructed with a wide base and have brakes.

Straps should be securely attached to the frame.

■ Recommendation:

Never leave children unattended in strollers.

The next section discusses the nutritional needs of infants. In particular, feeding practices such as the pros and cons of breast- and bottle-feeding are examined.

NUTRITION

Heredity plays a critical role in determining the rate that healthy infants grow. Proper nutrition can maximize optimal development of the body and brain. Conversely, undernutrition and in severe cases malnutrition can have a negative impact. Children need to consume sufficient quantities of food to sustain adequate health and physical growth. The metabolism of fats, carbohydrates, and proteins maintain bodily functions and energy. Vitamins perform a variety of metabolic functions. Their contributions depend on the intake of other nutrients. Also, minerals regulate metabolic processes although they only contribute to about 3 to 4% of the body's weight.

Feeding practices have undergone dramatic changes in the United States and other countries since the turn of the 20th century. A reliance on human milk shifted to modified cow's milk. Two observations illustrate the gradual transformation. The author of one book advised, "Every mother ought to nurse her own child, if she is fit to do it" (Nichols, 1855, p. 455). He went on to say that "no woman is fit to have a child who is not fit to nurse it," a widely held view in the 19th century. Another author remarked 70 years later that "[a] bottle mother may still be a perfect mother" (Holt, 1957, p. 65). The shift in attitudes reflected the increasing dominance of doctors and other experts as dispensers of child-rearing information. They now started to advocate the use of artificial milk as a modern convenience in infants' diet.

The high infant mortality rate of the late 19th century stimulated interest in artificial milk. Many of the deaths were blamed on poor diet. The "frightful" infant mortality rate spurred public concern. A doctor wrote that "nine-tenths [of the deaths] are from preventable causes" (Wood, 1888, p. 38). Inadequate nutrition was pinpointed as the primary cause of mortality in the first year. As Rotch (1893) argued, "The preventive medicine of early life is pre-eminently the intelligent management of the nutriment" (p. 505).

After the turn of the 20th century, artificial milk increasingly gained in popularity. Doctors sought to reduce the high infant mortality rate with scientific feeding methods. Mothers were now encouraged to bottle-feed their infants. The percentage of mothers breast-feeding their infants consequently dropped during the first half of the 20th century. Although statistics varied from one geographic region to another in the United States, they all showed a downward trend in breast-feeding practices. At the turn of the 20th century, practically all mothers breast-fed their infants compared to only 23% of mothers in 1948 (Apple, 1987).

Dramatic changes in feeding practices corresponded with major shifts in attitudes about childbirth. Prior to the turn of the 20th century, almost all childbirths occurred at home. As doctors expressed serious concerns about the unsanitary conditions at home, childbirth gradually shifted to hospitals. Medical intervention reached its apex in the mid-20th century, resulting in the exclusion of fathers and reliance on anesthesia during childbirth. However, as studies in subsequent decades revealed the importance of fa-

HISTORICALLY SPEAKING

FEEDING PRACTICES

Jessie Fenton
A Practical Psychology of Babyhood, 1925

Regularity is the first essential in establishing good habits in feeding, and this regularity should be established from the beginning. This is an essential for health, and no less important on psychological grounds.

Adherence to schedule must be tempered with common sense. If a baby is wailing from hunger fifteen minutes before the clock decrees that dinner-time has arrived, there is no point in letting him spend that time screaming himself into a state of exhaustion.

Source: Fenton (1925), p. 259.

thers' involvement and possible negative effects of anesthesia, the pendulum changed direction. Today, hospitals are not only creating a homelike atmosphere, but also encouraging fathers' participation during childbirth; in addition, mothers are increasingly breast-feeding their infants again. In 1970, only 25% of infants were breast-fed during the first few months of life. At the end of the 20th century, the figure stood at about 60% (National Center for Health Statistics, 1994).

FEEDING PRACTICES

Infants' feeding habits and nutritional requirements vary according to age. The following section is divided into three parts: the first 6 months, 6 to 12 months, and 1 to 3 years.

First 6 Months. Infants depend primarily on a diet of human milk or commercial formula during the first several months. Built-in rooting, sucking, and swallowing reflexes facilitate the intake of liquids. When a finger or nipple touches infants' cheeks, they turn their heads, latch on with their mouths, and begin to suck. Reflexes begin to disappear within the first 3 to 4 months as infants gain voluntary control of the mouth, tongue, and swallowing actions.

If infants are breast-fed, a yellowish fluid known as colustrum is ingested. It contains high concentrations of proteins and antibodies providing protection from infections and diseases during the first few weeks and months. Between the third and sixth day after birth, it changes to transitional milk. Sometime before the end of the tenth day, mature milk is produced. Although a personal decision, mothers are usually encouraged to breast-feed their infants within the first few hours or days after birth because of human milk's nutritional and immunological benefits. Prolonged **lactation**, or *the production of human milk,* is associated with successful nursing soon after delivery. However, the decision to breast- or bottle-feed must be made prior to birth. Each method has its own distinct advantages and disadvantages.

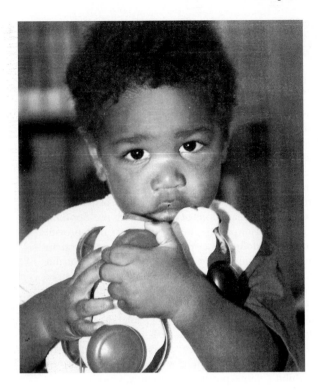

To maximize optimal physical growth and development, a well-balanced diet is a must.
Photo courtesy of Tami Dawson, Photo Resource Hawaii.

Cow's milk is not advised for the first year. There are significant nutritional differences between human milk and cow's milk (Lawrence, 1998). Cow's milk contains high concentrations of protein. Compared to 3.5 g/dl in cow's milk, human milk consists only of 0.7 g/dl in protein. The type of protein in each differs, too. Human milk is comprised of a reduced ratio of casein to whey. The large amount of casein in cow's milk results in the formation of large, hard curds. In contrast, human milk is easily digested because of the presence of soft, flocculent curds. Further, the type of fat in both varies. Human milk contains monosaturated fatty acids, whereas cow's milk consists of polysaturated fatty acids. The small fat globules in human milk increases infants' ability to absorb human milk. Therefore, breast-fed infants tend to feed more frequently than their bottle-fed counterparts (Kitzinger, 1998).

Commercial formulas have tried over the years to match the nutritional content of human milk. However, they do not entirely duplicate human milk (Fomon, 1993). In particular, human milk contains high quantities of cholesterol and saturated fatty acids in comparison to commercial formulas. The total cholesterol in breast-fed infants exceeds that of bottle-fed infants although it decreases once parents introduce solid foods. Without a doubt, human milk provides the optimal level of nutrition that infants need. Some question the imbalance of low cholesterol and high polyunsaturated fats in artificial milk (Kallio et al., 1992). Artificial milk is prepared in one of three ways. Although it comes in ready-to-use cans or bottles, concentrated liquid, or powdered form, an important consideration involves cost.

PARENTING ISSUES

COLIC

In medical terms, **colic** refers to paroxysmal abdominal pain. It is defined as *severe abdominal pain that results in loud, protracted cries and muscular spasms of legs.* Research shows that symptoms such as frequent fussiness and crying increases during the evening. However, other studies indicate that onset can occur at other times (St. James-Roberts, 1999). Colic usually affects very young babies. Still, despite obvious indications of pain, colicky infants do gain weight and thrive (Carey, 1992).

Different theories have been proposed to pinpoint the etiology of colic. Causes range from ingesting milk too fast, overeating, swallowing excessive air, or utilizing improper feeding positions. Bottle-feeding has often been faulted as the probable cause, but breast-fed infants also exhibit colic. Some discount biological causes of colic, attributing the problem instead to parents' ineffective responses to infants' cries (Barr, 1998). In addition, infants with a difficult temperament usually show a higher incidence of colic. Perhaps some parents of colicky infants are not able to tolerate excessive crying (Lester et al., 1992).

Both the biological and psychological explanations of colic present two opposing viewpoints. Research does not provide definitive evidence supporting the conclusions of one or the other. In all probability, colic has multiple causes. Prolonged crying that starts with abdominal discomfort usually elicits negative reactivity in parents exhibiting low tolerance. Parents should consult with their pediatricians about the best course of action to take. Suggested steps may include changing infants' positions frequently, swaddling them in a soft blanket, going on soothing rides in car seats, and using a pacifier.

Human milk involves numerous benefits. In addition to nutritional content, it provides:

■ **Immunological protection.** Human milk contains mothers' immunities. Mothers' antibodies provide the initial protection after birth.

■ **Psychological involvement.** Compared to other species, human milk is not concentrated but diluted. Because breast-fed infants need to nurse a lot, they benefit from their extended contact and mutual interaction with their caregivers.

■ **Low Cost.** Another benefit of breast-feeding involves cost. Although half of mothers typically switch to bottle-feeding before the end of the first 6 months, mothers who breast-feed do not need to purchase bottles or formulas.

■ **Easy Availability.** Lactation in human breasts operates on supply and demand. Lactating mothers produce just the right quantity of milk at the right temperature.

Many mothers who breast-feed may experience the loss of independence. In particular, some may feel overwhelmed with the time-consuming task of breast-feeding every 2 to 3 hours for the first few weeks. A few may even decide to discontinue shortly after they return to work. However, many decide to breast-feed before and after work, supplemented with either expressed milk or commercial formula during the day. Success depends on the physical and emotional support breast-feeding mothers receive from others, particularly fathers who, in increasing numbers, choose to participate in feeding and other child-rearing responsibilities. Mothers need constant support and assistance both during their postpartum stay in hospitals and at home (Pugh & Milligan, 1998). Encouragement of early and frequent breast-feeding immediately after birth improves its likelihood of continuation at home. Above all, breast-feeding is not something that comes naturally but must be learned (Scott & Binns, 1999). Sources of support include La Leche League, an organization providing breast-feeding information. In addition, parenting books have been published to help lactating mothers.

As with breast-feeding, bottle-feeding also provides numerous benefits. It refers to the use of a commercial formula in bottles but does include mothers' expressed milk. It is either poured directly from the can into a bottle or, in powdered form, mixed with water. Some parents may choose to heat the bottle in warm water or in a specially designed heating unit (microwaves should never be used). Afterwards, bottles and nipples should be boiled in water or placed in the dishwasher after each use to prevent contamination. Persons who prepare the formula should wash their hands properly. Any leftover milk in the bottles should be discarded after each use because of bacterial growth. Opened cans should be covered and refrigerated until used again.

Although not completely the same as human milk, artificial milk does contain the essential nutrients infants need. Other benefits include:

- **Flexibility.**   Bottle-feeding frees mothers as the only source of nourishment. Others, including fathers, can participate in feeding responsibilities.

- **Convenience.**   Parents can determine how much milk their infants took in. In addition, mothers do not have to worry about any personal embarrassment in bottle-feeding their infants in public places as with breast-feeding.

In selecting one feeding method (or both), parents should weigh the pros and cons of each. Sick or extremely ill mothers do not always have the energy and stamina to breast-feed their infants. Any medication they take will enter their breast milk and pose potential dangers to their infants. Breast-fed infants may initially nurse every 2 to 3 hours because of breast milk's easy digestibility. On the other hand, parents who bottle-feed face the added cost and preparation of commercial formulas. Further, if a bottle is routinely given to infants lying on their backs in the crib, they are deprived of human contact. Also, middle-ear infections (otitis media) and caries may arise because of bacterial growth. Given the advantages and disadvantages of each method, some parents may simply decide to combine both.

Six to 12 Months.   During the next 6 months, milk should continue to be the primary source of nourishment for both breast- and bottle-fed infants. If breast-feeding is to be discontinued, an iron-fortified commercial formula is recommended. The major transition

SOCIOCULTURAL INFLUENCES

ABORIGINAL FEEDING PRACTICES IN AUSTRALIA

The introduction of other cultural beliefs has had an influential impact on the child-rearing practices of indigenous populations. The Aborigines of Australia provide an excellent example. Prior to the arrival of Europeans in the late 18th century, Aboriginal mothers traditionally breast-fed on demand and carried their infants during their daily routines, an arrangement that allowed continuous nourishment. Other lactating mothers served as substitutes in emergencies, maintaining the availability of milk. Infants were not typically weaned until their second year. The arrival of European settlers restricted the Aborigines' hunting and gathering lifestyles. Over time, Aborigines increasingly migrated into urban areas. As both contact with Europeans and urbanization continued, traditional breast-feeding practices declined significantly (Harrison, 1991).

Changes in feeding practices did not occur overnight. During the early 20th century, Aboriginal mothers continued to breast-feed their infants despite the availability of artificial milk. Since then, Aboriginal feeding patterns followed the same course as Australian mothers. Only 50% of Aboriginal and Australian mothers breast-fed their infants at 3 months in 1940. The trend declined to about 20% in 1970. As with other industrialized countries, prospective parents began to take an active role in childbirth. Prepared childbirth staged the return of natural feeding. At the same time, positive attitudes developed as doctors stressed the physiological and psychological benefits of breast-feeding. Still, in remote areas, traditional practices are followed. Ninety-six percent of rural Aboriginal mothers breast-feed. In contrast, only half in urban areas do. Perhaps the connotation between artificial milk and affluence may account for the differences (Lund-Adams & Heywood, 1995).

will involve the gradual introduction of solid food to infants' diet. It occurs roughly between 4 to 6 months of age at the convergence of several important milestones. The gastrointestinal system is now able to handle complex nutrients and tolerate potentially allergenic food. Teeth begin to erupt, facilitating biting and chewing. Control of the head and trunk increases infants' ability to sit and shake their head in disapproval of certain kinds of food. Increased eye–hand coordination encourages independence. They can grasp food with their fingers and eventually hold a spoon to feed themselves.

The choice of foods to introduce should be based on nutritional content. Parents are usually advised to start with dry cereal because of its high concentration of iron. Commercially produced dry cereals include rice, barley, and oatmeal. Rice cereal is typically introduced to infants' diet first because of easy digestibility. With breast-fed infants, cereal is either mixed with mothers' expressed milk or water. With bottle-fed infants, cereal is combined with commercial formula until whole milk is introduced. At 6 months, parents can mix juices with dry cereal. A rich source of vitamin C, juices increase the absorption of iron in the cereal.

Thereafter, addition of other kinds of food will vary considerably according to individual families' preferences. The sequence typically starts with strained fruits and vegetables and then meat. Commercially prepared baby food in jars is often used because of convenience. However, because of the high cost, some parents may choose to prepare homemade food. Fresh fruits and vegetables can be steamed in water and pureed in a blender. Other considerations in the selection of food may include:

■ Introduce one new food at a time.

■ Wait 1 week before introducing another.

■ After each new food, watch the child's possible allergic reactions.

■ If the child show signs such as diarrhea or rash, call the doctor.

When parents decide to encourage independent use of a spoon, some infants may react with dissatisfaction. Parents should try to avoid punitive measures, following their infants' lead instead. A small-bowled, long-handled spoon allows easy placement of a small portion of food on the back of the tongue. If placed on the front, it will usually be rejected. Attempts to use the spoon tend to work better after infants' ingestion of their mothers' milk or commercial formula. Then, the experience of using a spoon is associated with pleasurable sensations. After repeated successes with a spoon, infants' meals generally begin to coincide with their families' schedule. Although parents should introduce a variety of new food, they must be accepting their infants' preferences.

One to 3 Years.   Physical growth slows down considerably over the next 2 years. Compared to the typical gain of 10 inches in the first year, toddlers usually grow only about 5 inches in the second and 3 inches in the third. Toddlers' appetite generally decreases after their first birthday. Some now become picky eaters (in severe cases, it is referred to as physiologic anorexia). They sometimes eat everything at one meal, perhaps nothing at the next. Parents should remember not to turn mealtimes into sparring matches but offer a selection of nutritious foods. Toddlers require 1,000 calories each day to meet their bodies' nutritional demands. Food should come from the four basic nutritional groups of food:

■ Meat, fish, poultry, and eggs

■ Dairy products

■ Fruits and vegetables

■ Cereal grains, potatoes, rice, and bread

Doctors generally recommend discontinuing breast- or bottle-feeding at the end of the first year. Referred to as weaning, it is sometimes regarded as a potentially traumatic experience in many industrialized countries, because after all, infants are being asked to relinquish a source of oral pleasure and gratification. Parents' patience is particularly needed during the transition from one source of nourishment to another. During the second half of the first year, children begin to show a few definite signs of readiness, including infants' increased eye–hand coordination and willingness to hold and drink from cups and eat with a spoon.

Generally speaking, when children are being weaned they are still being breast- or bottle-fed four times a day. They either take a full breast or drink about 6 to 8 ounces from a bottle at each feeding. A gradual weaning schedule usually eases the transition. Children may abandon the fourth feeding, either early in the morning or late at night, and begin to settle into a regular pattern of three feedings per day. Over time, each subsequent breast- or bottle-feeding is replaced with a meal. Some mothers continue to breast-feed into the second year, but now the bulk of children's nutrition comes from the table.

As children assume more responsibility for feeding themselves, parents need to accept occasional refusals to eat or accidental spills. As children gain increased motor coordination, their "messiness" eventually disappears. Children will better able to master needed skills at mealtimes successfully when parents develop realistic expectations. Other important reminders include:

■ **Never force children to eat.** Parents' insistence despite their children's unwillingness to eat can result in unavoidable tug-of-wars. Even picky eaters can still receive a balanced diet from a wide selection of nutritious foods.

■ **Do not use food as punishment.** Meals should never be used to discipline children's misbehavior. Food is required to meet the nutritional requirements of children's growing bodies and minds.

SENSITIVITY TO FOOD

Some children may develop an adverse reaction to certain kinds of food. Sensitivities to food can be classified in two broad groups: hypersensitivity and intolerance. Hypersensitivity refers to adverse reactions involving immunological mechanisms, particularly immunoglobulin E (or IgE). Exposure to allergens in food, usually proteins, induces the formation of IgE antibody. Subsequent exposure after the first ingestion of allergens can trigger allergic reactions. Common allergens in children's diet include cow's milk, eggs, peanuts, soy, corn, and fish. Allergies often occur during the first year because of children's immature intestinal tract, which increases the likelihood of an immunological response. In general, allergies are genetically linked (one parent with an allergy increases the risk 50%; both parents with allergies, 100%).

In contrast, intolerance refers to reactions to certain foods involving nonimmunological mechanisms. Lactose intolerance is a good example. Although resembling an allergic reaction, it results from a deficiency of lactase, an enzyme, in the digestive system. Lactase is needed to digest lactose in human milk and commercial formulas. Although rare, lactose intolerance appears soon after birth. Causes are attributed to gastrointestinal infections or disorders such as AIDS. Treatment consists of eliminating offending dairy products. Soy-based formulas are substituted instead of human milk and modified cow's milk. Pretreated milk with microbial deprived lactase has been shown to improve the absorption of lactose in the digestive system. Because calcium and vitamin D are obtained from dairy products, supplementation is required to prevent the deficiency of essential nutrients.

NUTRITIONAL SIGNIFICANCE OF VITAMINS AND MINERALS

Vitamins and minerals play a vital role in maintaining good health. The vitamins and minerals shown in Table 11–6 perform a number of physiological functions.

In sum, feeding practices have changed dramatically over the last 100 years. Knowledge of the pros and cons of breast- and bottle-feeding as well as the nutritional value of vitamins and minerals provides parents and professional caregivers with the tools to maximize infants' optimal development.

TABLE 11–6. ESSENTIAL VITAMINS AND MINERALS

Vitamins

A (retinol)

Functions: normal growth of bones and teeth
Sources: milk and vegetables (carrots, sweet potatoes, and spinach)
Deficiencies: retarded growth and impaired formation of bones

B2 (riboflavin)

Functions: normal maintenance of healthy skin
Sources: milk and its products, eggs, green leafy vegetables such as spinach and broccoli, and legumes
Deficiencies: seborrheic dermatitis (inflammatory reaction of the skin that occurs commonly on the scalp) and delayed healing of wounds

Niacin

Functions: maintenance of healthy nervous system, skin, and normal digestion
Sources: meat, poultry, fish, whole or enriched gains, peanuts, beans, and peas
Deficiencies: loss of weight, diarrhea, apathy, and fatigue

B6 (pyridoxine)

Functions: formation of antibodies and hemoglobin
Sources: meat, poultry, fish, cereal grains, yeast, and soybeans
Deficiencies: retarded growth, anemia, scaly skin, and irritability

Folic Acid

Functions: formation of red blood cells
Sources: green leafy vegetables, cabbage, asparagus, liver, eggs, nuts, whole grain cereals, and bananas
Deficiencies: intestinal malabsorption and abnormally large red blood cells (macrocytic anemia)

B12 (cobalamin)

Functions: normal maintenance of nervous tissue
Sources: meat, liver, poultry, fish, milk, cheese, eggs, and nutritional yeast
Deficiencies: delayed growth of brain and degeneration of spinal cord

(continued)

TABLE 11–6. CONTINUED

C (absorbic acid)

Functions: absorption of iron in formation of hemoglobin

Sources: fruits and vegetables such as cabbage and broccoli

Deficiencies: dry, rough skin and bleeding muscles and joints

D (calciferol)

Functions: absorption of calcium and phosphorus in skeletal formation

Sources: direct sunlight, salmon, tuna, and sardines

Deficiencies: rickets (defective growth of bones)

E (tocopherol)

Functions: production of red blood cells

Sources: milk, eggs, fish, whole grains, nuts, legumes, and vegetables such as spinach and broccoli

Deficiencies: hemolytic anemia from hemolysis (shortened life of red blood cells)

Minerals

Calcium

Functions: development of bones and teeth and coagulation of blood in wounds

Sources: dairy products, eggs, green leafy vegetables, soybeans, dried beans, and peas

Deficiencies: impaired growth of bones and teeth and tetany (painful muscular spasms)

Iodine

Functions: production of thyroid hormone

Sources: seafood, iodized salt, enriched bread, and milk

Deficiencies: goiter (enlargement of thyroid gland)

Iron

Functions: formation of hemoglobin and myoglobin

Sources: meat, poultry, fish, nuts, fortified cereal products, and green vegetables

Deficiencies: anemia

Magnesium

Functions: neural conduction to muscles

Sources: meat, nuts, raisins, soybeans, whole and enriched bread, and uncooked leafy vegetables

Deficiencies: irregular heartbeat and muscular weakness

Phosphorus

Functions: healthy development and maintenance of bones and teeth in combination with calcium

Sources: dairy products, eggs, meat, poultry, legumes, and carbonated beverages

Deficiencies: weakness, anorexia, depression, and pain in bones

(continued)

TABLE 11–6. CONTINUED

Potassium

Functions: neural conduction and muscular contraction, particularly heart

Sources: bananas, citrus fruits, meat, fish, bran, and legumes

Deficiencies: cardiac arrhythmias (irregular heartbeats) and muscular weakness

Sodium

Functions: permeability of cells and contraction of muscles

Sources: seafood, meat, poultry, and prepared food with salt

Deficiencies: dehydration and hypotension

Zinc

Functions: synthesis of nucleic acids and proteins in immune system and coagulation of blood

Sources: seafood, particularly oysters, meat, poultry, and legumes

Deficiencies: loss of appetite and diminished sensation of gustation

SUMMARY

Health

- The presence of disease is often used as the prime indicator of health. However, the goal of good health is not only reducing illness but maximizing physical, mental, and social well-being.

- The infant mortality rate in the United States took a nosedive over the last 100 years. Contributing factors include the control and prevention of infectious diseases and the advent of antibiotics.

- Infectious diseases still pose a threat to infants' health today. Regularly scheduled immunizations are therefore recommended.

- Common illnesses sometimes require immediate medical attention. They can be grouped into six areas of the body: eyes; ears, nose, and throat; lungs; digestive tract; urinary tract; and skin.

- Factors contributing to accidental injuries and sometimes deaths include asphyxiation, suffocation, vehicular injuries, falls, poisoning, burns, drowning, and bodily damage. Parents and other caregivers should supervise children carefully.

Nutrition

- Dramatic shifts in feeding practices occurred over the last 100 years in the United States and other industrialized countries. Bottle-feeding gained in popularity at one time because of its "modern" convenience, but today many mothers choose to breast-feed or supplement breast milk with a commercial formula.

■ During the first 6 months, milk is the primary source of nutrition. Solid food is gradually introduced into the diet during the last half of the first year.

■ Some young children may develop adverse reactions to certain types of food. Sensitivity to food can be divided into one of two types: hypersensitivity and intolerance.

■ Hypersensitivity and intolerance separately involve immunological and nonimmunological mechanisms. In either case, the offending food should be avoided or substituted.

■ Vitamins and minerals play an important role in the maintenance of the body. During the second half of the first year and thereafter, a well-balanced, varied diet provides the necessary nutrients.

PROJECTS

1. Make a list of dos and don'ts in childproofing four areas of the home: kitchen, living room, bathroom, and bedroom.

2. Invite a speaker from the local Poison Center to discuss steps to take in preventing accidental poisoning.

3. Design a brochure for prospective parents explaining the advantages and disadvantages of breast- and bottle-feeding.

GUIDANCE
AND EARLY EDUCATION

Just as the Twig is bent, the Tree's inclin'd.
Alexander Pope, *Epistles to Several Persons*

As children gain mobility and exercise their newfound sense of independence, parents and professional caregivers start to impose limits. Because of their natural curiosity, children *should be supervised closely to prevent accidental injuries to themselves or others. Further, given the increasing number of working parents in recent years, child care has become an important issue. Chapter 12 examines ways of guiding and managing children's behavior and choosing developmentally appropriate child care during the first few years of life.*

Children's natural curiosity will at some point come into conflict with their environment. As "little scientists," their unbounded exploration of the world taxes the patience of both parents and professional caregivers alike. The challenge is striking a balance between providing maximum opportunities to explore and enforcing limits to protect children from harm. The first half of the chapter addresses various parenting strategies in guiding and managing children's appropriate and inappropriate behavior. Because professional caregivers use the same principles of guidance in their work with children, the remainder of the chapter focuses on issues involving child care. In particular, characteristics of child care, including arrangement of space and interactions between professional caregivers and children, are examined.

GUIDANCE

Two terms refer to adults' imposition of limitations on children's behavior. **Discipline**, a word meaning "instruction" in Latin, describes *child-rearing methods that adults institute to correct and control the behavior of children.* However, it has acquired a negative connotation because of its association with coercive punishment in the past. On the other hand, **guidance** involves *realistic expectations of children's behavior that combine both empathy and firmness.*

Historical accounts have painted a harsh picture of discipline. In the 17th century, for example, William Gouge published *Of Domesticall Duties* regarding parents' responsibilities in raising children (Gouge, 1622/1976). He warned about children's "vices" such as lack of respect. On the topic of children's stubbornness, he wrote in all too familiar terms:

> . . . children pout . . . , swell, and give no answer at all to their parents. This is too common a fault in children, and many parents are much offended. . . . (p. 435)

Gouge recognized, as most parents do today, that children require sustenance. Parents are expected, in his words, "to *nourish* children, namely with food, apparrell. . . ." However, he also advocated harshness in disciplining children. His advice was echoed in other written accounts. Susanna Wesley, the mother of Methodist founders John and Charles Wesley, enforced strict discipline at home at an early age. In an oft-quoted statement, she said:

> When turned a year old (and some before) they were taught to fear the rod and to cry softly. . . . (Greven, 1977, p. 36)

References to the "rod" were repeatedly made. To some, the biblical interpretation of the Book of Proverbs justified corporal punishment. One commonly heard aphorism, "Spare the rod and spoil the child," does not come from the Bible at all. It is found in Samuel Butler's poem "Hudibras," written in 1664 (Gibson, 1978). Other aphorisms from the Bible are cited in the language of the King James' translation. They include "He that spareth his rod hateth his son: but he that loveth him chastenth him betimes" (Proverbs 13:24) and "Withhold not correction from the child: for if thou beatest him with the rod, he shall not die" (Proverbs 23:13).

Not all resorted to harsh discipline. Some used persuasion to instill moral discipline as in the case of 19th-century minister Lyman Abbott, recalling his father's method:

I do not remember that he ever punished me. Yet I not only do not recall that I ever thought of disobeying him, but I do not remember ever to have seen a child refuse him obedience. . . . (Abbott, 1915, p. 143)

Harsh discipline is still practiced today. However, accumulated research suggests it often backfires (Marion, 1998). Coercive physical punishment may correct a misbehavior, but it may result in unintended consequences such as producing fear in children and legitimizing violence. Many experts voice their opposition to any corporal punishment (Eberlein, 1993). In their view, it is unjustified on psychological and moral grounds. They believe there are other more effective methods of managing children's misbehavior.

PURPOSES OF DISCIPLINE

Discipline involves two main purposes. The first, the one that is usually associated with discipline, is to control socially undesired behavior. Children do not enter the world with a built-in sense of right and wrong; instead, they learn from experience. The second purpose is to teach. As adults discipline children, they impart lessons reflecting cultural standards of appropriate and inappropriate behavior. Therefore, discipline cannot be separated from socialization, the process of acquiring cultural values and attitudes.

Both purposes of discipline have short- and long-term implications. Control is the short-term outcome. Adults usually take steps to protect children from harm. For example, crossing the street alone is a serious concern. A stern voice is usually enough to stop most young children from crossing a street alone, but tied to a reason, it becomes a learning experience. "We need to hold hands and look before we cross so we don't get hurt." Eventually, right and wrong are internalized. Therefore, self-control is the long-term outcome, the ability to resist the impulse to engage in socially inappropriate or dangerous behavior.

Even prior to their first birthday, infants are capable of complying with simple requests. They usually understand the immediate command of "no," often using the same word themselves. Compliance to adults' immediate requests will evolve into self-control later. Self-control starts to appear sometime during the first half of the second year (Kaler & Kopp, 1990). In Erikson's second stage of psychosocial development, children's resistance to adults' commands reflects an emerging sense of autonomy. So, a healthy dose of independence is to be expected. Children who establish secure attachment with trusted adults usually show higher levels of compliance and cooperation. For example, children have been found to vocalize morally relevant utterances such as "no, can't" before touching an electric socket or jumping on a couch (Kochanska, 1993).

During the second half of the second year, self-control definitely appears in toddlers. Its appearance coincides with the fact that parents tend to increase the number of rules or routines they expect their children to follow at home (Gralinski & Kopp, 1993). In one study, parents were asked to respond to their toddlers' constant interruptions with consistent or inconsistent reprimands. Toddlers' inappropriate demands increased when parents reprimanded misbehavior only some of the time (Acker & O'Leary, 1996). Toddlers benefit from reminders about limits as they internalize external controls.

SOCIOCULTURAL INFLUENCES

THEORETICAL APPROACHES TO DISCIPLINE

Many disciplinary techniques have their roots in theories. The following three theories can offer useful suggestions in successfully managing misbehavior.

- **Behavioral theory.** Skinner's theory, or behaviorism, is based on the belief that all human behavior is learned. The consequences of behavior determine the likelihood of its recurrence in the future. If a certain behavior is reinforced, it is likely to be repeated later. On the other hand, punishment, whether imposing something unpleasant or removing something pleasant, discourages the repetition of behavior.

Theoretical application: ignoring behavior.

Some children misbehave to get inappropriate attention. Adults should therefore ignore certain kinds of misbehavior such as whining to get their way. In Skinnerian terms, a behavior is said to be extinguished if it fails to achieve its objective. Of course, not all undesired behavior can be ignored.

- **Rogerian theory.** American psychotherapist Carl Rogers focused on the concept of the self. In his view, a person possesses the ability to control his or her own actions (Rogers, 1961). The goal is to become a fully functioning individual in tune with his or her emotions. Therefore, nonjudgmental communication of acceptance is desired in interacting with children.

Theoretical application: developing active listening skills.

One of the major concepts in Rogerian theory concerns the ownership of problems. Children do not learn to solve their own problems if adults interfere. Adults should listen to their children's concerns nonjudgmentally instead without taking ownership of the problem. The challenge is not to offer advice but to trust children's ability to learn from their mistakes.

- **Adlerian theory.** Austrian psychoanalyst Alfred Adler trained with Freud. However, both held divergent views of the personality. While Freud focused on unconscious forces, Adler believed that people actively direct and affect their own course of development. Further, in Adler's view, children do not misbehave because of unconscious urges but because of faulty perceptions in seeking membership in a particular group (Adler, 1964).

Theoretical application: using natural and logical consequences.

Natural and logical consequences can encourage children's ability to take responsibility of their own actions. To illustrate, when children do not put on their jacket in cold weather, they will learn about the natural consequences of their own actions; when children clean up their own mess such as drawing on the wall or spilling food on the floor, they will recognize the logical consequences of their behavior.

Parents using gentle insistence instead of coercive punishment and adhering to consistent rules limiting behavior tend to produce favorable outcomes in children.

PARENTING STYLES

Discipline varies from parent to parent. Child-rearing styles reflect personal differences in values and expectations. Some parents value conformity in children; others prize independence. Researchers have been interested in studying the long-term effects of different parenting styles on children's behavior. Diana Baumrind was the first to systematically observe parents' interactions with their children. In a series of studies, two broad dimensions emerged (Baumrind, 1967). The first involves demandingness. Some parents establish high standards and expect their children to conform to their expectations; others rarely inhibit their children's behavior. The second concerns responsiveness. Some parents respond sensitively to their children's needs; others reject their children's social overtures.

Based on the two dimensions, parenting styles have been classified into one of four major types (see Table 12–1). Baumrind focused on three: authoritative, authoritarian, and permissive. However, since her initial research, a fourth type, the uninvolved parent, has been identified. Each type has a definite outcome.

■ **Authoritative style.** Parents using an authoritative style attempt to direct children's actions responsibly in a demanding but responsive manner. They exert firm control, enforcing reasonable rules, whenever disobedience occurs. Words, not punitive measures, are used to explain parents' intentions. At the same time, authoritative parents exhibit high levels of warmth and affection. They listen sensitively to children's points of view and encourage input into decisions. The authoritative style has been found to be associated with high esteem, internalized moral standards, social maturity, and superior academic performance in childhood (Gray & Steinberg, 1999).

■ **Authoritarian style.** Authoritarian parents demand obedience from children. Because they value conformity, they tend to reject children's opposing opinions and beliefs. Children are expected to accept parents' words unquestioningly. Otherwise, punitive actions may be used to curb children's will. Children's verbal input is not sought or allowed. The authoritarian style has been shown to be linked to anxious and insecure, yet hostile and aggressive, children in childhood (Scarr & Deater-Deckard, 1997).

■ **Permissive style.** Permissive parents neither assert their authority nor impose controls of any kind. They simply accept their children's impulses and actions. Children are al-

TABLE 12–1 CLASSIFICATION OF BAUMRIND'S PARENTING STYLES

Demandingness	Responsiveness	
	Responsive	Unresponsive
Demanding	Authoritative	Authoritarian
Undemanding	Permissive	Uninvolved

lowed to make virtually all their own decisions. Some permissive parents believe that children benefit from lax discipline. Others just lack confidence in their ability. The permissive style has been associated with poor impulse control, rebelliousness, aggressiveness, and social immaturity in childhood (Robinson et al., 1995).

■ **Uninvolved style.** Uninvolved parents usually neglect their responsibility as caregivers. The daily pressures and stresses of life seem to overwhelm such parents. They exert only minimum efforts to meet their children's basic needs. Actions may be taken to establish and enforce rules. However, attempts to fulfill parenting obligations are fleeting. The uninvolved style is associated with noncompliant, demanding behavior in childhood.

Cultural factors can play a mediating role. When children from different ethnic groups are compared, the effects of culture can be seen. For example, adolescent achievement is apparently linked to the predominant parenting style of some ethnic groups. High-achieving Chinese American (Steinberg, Dornbusch, & Brown, 1992; Steinberg et al., 1991) and African American adolescents (Bradley, 1998) generally come from authoritarian homes. Clearly, cultural interpretations of parenting styles should be considered in making judgments about parents' behavior. Parental strictness in one culture may be associated with support, whereas in another, it may be interpreted as rejection (Lamborn, Dornbusch, & Steinberg, 1996).

In sum, although there are many ways of parenting, effective parents are able to adjust their level of involvement to meet their children's changing developmental needs. Overbearing or detached emotional involvement is associated with behavioral and emotional difficulties later in childhood. Arbitrariness and inconsistency produce unstable and unpredictable living conditions. Research has confirmed the existence of the relationship between parents' empathy and children's capacity to respond sympathetically to others (Eisenber et al., 1991; Eisenberg et al., 1992).

STRATEGIES IN GUIDING INFANTS' BEHAVIOR

Parents can influence children's development both directly and indirectly. Their words and actions matter greatly. Although people may differ in terms of discipline, they typically share the same goals of protecting children from harm and instilling values that over time develop into self-control. The following strategies focus on positive discipline, a method of treating all children with dignity and respect.

Anticipating Problems.   An important component of discipline involves prevention. Parents and professional caregivers should take preventive steps to short-circuit potential problems before they occur. Instead of saying "no, don't touch" all the time, adults should simply childproof the environment, securing breakable or dangerous items in locked cabinets or closets. Other preventive steps may include communicating expectations beforehand (e.g., staying together in a crowded setting) and planning age-appropriate schedules (e.g., interspersing active and quiet activities during a long day).

Modeling.   Children learn from direct observations of others. When adults model socially desired behavior, children will typically follow in the same footsteps. Lots of examples can be found in everyday situations. Parents who show empathy when someone falls,

The starting point in guiding and managing behavior is the quality of a child's relationship with trusted caregivers.
Photo courtesy of Tami Dawson, Photo Resource Hawaii.

scraping a knee, will often see the same behavior in their children. Likewise, parents who severely punish misbehavior may unknowingly encourage aggressive and confrontational styles of resolving conflicts and problems. Therefore, children can benefit from positive models in their environment.

Setting Limits. Adults who state their expectations of desired behavior often achieve good results. Reasonable limits of unacceptable behavior should be explained and consistently enforced to protect children's safety and teach self-control. Examples include washing hands before eating and using words instead of fists in venting anger or frustration. Appropriate limits should be based on knowledge of children's developmental needs. Authoritarian parents may enforce arbitrary rules, whereas permissive parents may not set enough limits. In contrast, authoritative parents generally select and communicate fair limits.

Modifying Environment. Parents and professional caregivers can modify the physical environment to encourage or restrict children's behavior. In most cases, preventive steps would lessen the need to intervene. Examples include the insertion of plastic covers in electrical outlets and putting gates at the top and bottom of stairways at home. In out-of-home care, organization of the physical setting, both indoors and outdoors, requires careful, thoughtful preparation such as using low bookshelves to control the flow of traffic.

Providing Reinforcement. According to behavioral theory, the recurrence of a behavior increases after immediate reinforcement. With children, almost anything serves as reinforcement. Examples include a toy, a cookie, a smile, or a pat on the back. The last two are referred to as social reinforcers. They generally contribute to children's sense of worth. The following guidelines are recommended to improve the effectiveness of social reinforcement:

■ **Specificity.** Specific aspects of the behavior should be praised.

Example: Instead of saying "You're a good boy (or girl)," say "I like the way you washed your hands before eating."

■ **Sincerity.** Praise should be given enthusiastically, not perfunctorily.

Example: Instead of saying "Good job," say "Wow, you worked on the puzzle until you finished all the pieces!"

Other tips focus on behavior, not children's self-worth. They include commenting on the action, not the person, and breaking difficult tasks into small, manageable steps to maximize children's success (see Table 12–2).

Using Reflective Language. Another effective tool is acknowledging children's feelings and reflecting on the effect of their behavior on someone. Children may not be able to communicate their feelings with words. Listening nonjudgmentally to them acknowledges their self-worth and willingness to solve problems with words. Likewise, because children do not always realize the effect of their behavior on another person, "I-messages" can convey adults' reactions to children's specific actions (Gordon, 1970, 1989). Elements of "I-messages" include adults' reaction, the event that caused the reac-

---

TABLE 12–2 DOS AND DON'TS IN GUIDING INFANTS' BEHAVIOR

Do

Praise a child's efforts.

Use words that recognize each child's uniqueness.

Share a child's accomplishments with other people.

Encourage the use of words in resolving conflicts.

Provide a reason in making a request or prohibiting an unacceptable action.

Don't

Constantly scold or nag.

Use judgmental or derogatory words such as *good, bad, stupid*, or *slow*.

Talk to other adults about a particular child in his or her presence.

Correct a child's speech.

Force a child to do something with coercive actions.

Withhold food as punishment.

HISTORICALLY SPEAKING

STRATEGIES IN GUIDING INFANTS' BEHAVIOR

Sidonie Gruenberg
Your Child, 1920
The proper punishment, administered in the right spirit, may cure or correct a fault; *but punishment does not make children good.* If children are punished frequently, it may even make them bad.

Source: Gruenberg (1920), p. 29.

tion, and the reason (e.g., "I felt upset when you climbed on the table because you might have gotten hurt if you fell"). "I-messages" differ from "you-messages," which shift the blame of adults' response onto children (e.g., "You are always getting into trouble").

Redirecting Behavior.   Instead of prohibiting an undesired activity, other alternatives such as diverting children's attention and providing an acceptable substitution often work. For example, if a child repeatedly plays with the water in the dog's dish at home, one way of resolving the situation would be to redirect attention to something else or substitute the activity with another. Instead of reprimanding the child, he or she would be allowed to pour water into containers at bath time. Often, a simple explanation or reminder about an existing rule may be all that is needed (e.g., "Remember we said yesterday that the dog won't have any water left if it's spilled all over the floor?").

PARENTING ISSUES

TIME-OUT

Time-out is often used to discipline toddlers. It refers to the brief cessation of an activity because of an unacceptable infraction of an established rule. Disruptive children are usually removed from the situation and are asked to sit on a chair in a quiet area of another room. Removal provides an opportunity to regain composure and exercise self-control. The length of time-out depends on the chronological age of the child. As a rule of thumb, it corresponds to 1 minute for each year in the child's age (e.g., 2 minutes for a 2-year-old).

Time-out should be used judiciously. Other methods should be tried first. Misuse of time-out can defeat its purpose. A child constantly receiving time-out does not benefit from frequent removal in the long run if adults fail to talk to the child and use other disciplinary techniques in resolving the problem.

Giving Limited Choices. Limited choices between two alternatives may be an effective way to resolve a potential problem. Bedtime is a good example. If a parent asks, "Do you want to go to bed?" children will almost always say, "No!" The question can be framed differently: "Before you go to bed, do you want to take a bath first or brush your teeth?" Limited choices can avoid time-consuming confrontations and recognize children's increasing ability to make their own decisions. However, sometimes there are no choices. Children should never be allowed to cross the street alone or play with matches.

TYPICAL CONCERNS

Toddlers may not always express negative emotions in constructive ways. Two common concerns that many parents and professional caregivers working with children encounter involve biting and throwing tantrums.

Biting. Biting is a common occurrence. One reason some children may bite is because of their inability to communicate frustration. Others may bite to get adults' attention. If adults themselves nibble or playfully bite to display affection, children may want to imitate the same behavior. Regardless of the cause, biting can cause serious injuries to another person. If the flesh is punctured, there is a chance of bacterial infection.

Adults should take immediate steps to prevent the recurrence of biting. After taking care of and comforting the bitten person, the biter should be firmly reprimanded:

SOCIOCULTURAL INFLUENCES

DISCIPLINE IN HISPANIC AMERICAN FAMILIES

Hispanic American families consist of a diverse group sharing common ancestral and cultural ties. Shared Hispanic American beliefs include familial obligation, respectfulness of authority, and deferential behavior in children (Fracasso & Busch-Rossnagel, 1994). The family's unity, welfare, and honor have traditionally occupied a central place in the social fabric of many Hispanic American families and communities. The importance of children's socialization is recognized as an integral responsibility of families.

Discipline is aimed at the preservation of traditional cultural values in Hispanic American families. Familism describes a sense of commitment to the family. The family is the focal point of the individual's identity. In times of trouble, the family represents the bedrock of strength. The value that is placed on deference to authority is initially learned at home but later expanded. Respect fosters obedience of children to their parents and other adults. Both boys and girls are punished if disobedience or rudeness is noted. In particular, fathers generally follow an authoritarian style in their undisputed role as disciplinarians. Children learn to use titles in the presence of an adult or authority. Such forms of address are used to teach respect (Garcia-Coll, Meyer, & Brillon, 1995).

"Biting is not allowed, ever!" If biting is likely to occur again, the child should be supervised closely. The child should be reminded again not to bite but use words instead. Never bite children back. The same action only serves to legitimize biting as a way of resolving problems.

Throwing Tantrums.   Almost all children engage in occasional tantrums resulting from disappointments in not getting their way. Each child handles frustration differently. Some willingly move on to another interesting activity. Others may cry, scream, hit, or kick to express anger when adults limit their activity because of legitimate concerns.

As children learn to express emotions, tantrums generally disappear on their own. Some points to remember in dealing with tantrums are to:

- Ignore tantrums as long as children do not harm themselves or others or destroy property.

- Model and praise age-appropriate behavior in achieving desired goals.

In sum, adults perform an important task in guiding children's behavior. Parents and professional caregivers need to find effective ways of encouraging appropriate behavior as children actively engage with their physical and social world.

EARLY EDUCATION

The last half of the 20th century witnessed dramatic social changes in the structure of families. Most American children today live in families with two employed parents or a single working parent (Hoffreth et al., 1991). Parents in the United States face the difficult challenge of finding affordable and accessible child care. The type of child care varies considerably in cost and quality. On the surface, the decision in selecting appropriate child care seems to be a wholly personal decision. However, some experts believe the quality of child care invariably touches everyone (Galinsky & Friedman, 1993). In their view, child care is seen as an investment in the future. The economic health of the nation, they argue, depends on the quality of child care its children receive.

Historically, considerations of early education rested solely with parents and families. Although families usually received economic and social support from their communities, parents provided sustenance and nurturance to their children. Philosophers sought to provide specific child-rearing advice. For example, Plutarch, living in the last half of the first century, advocated that parents manipulate infants' limbs to facilitate optimal physical growth (Ulrich, 1954). Later, other philosophers such as Locke and Rousseau introduced their own child-rearing ideas. Locke viewed the human mind at birth as a blank tablet, or tabula rasa, recognizing the value of formal education, whereas Rousseau argued that society unnecessarily impeded the natural progression of children's development.

In the United States, society's role in early education took its first steps during the early 19th century. The following time line illustrates some of the historical and demographic shifts in the introduction of nonmaternal care (Spring, 1997):

■ 1820s

The first center-based care opened in Boston in 1828. A center was established to take care of infants and children of poor mothers seeking employment. The philosophy of the program focused on religious and moral education in the lives of disadvantaged children.

■ 1850s

The first American "creche" or foundling hospital at the Children's Hospital started in New York City in 1854. The hospital provided extended daytime care and medical treatment of children 3 months to 3 years of age. The center, as with many other programs at the time, catered to the needs of European immigrants and rural Americans who sought better opportunities in the industrial centers of the nation.

■ 1890s

National Federation of Day Nurseries was founded. The first national association concerned with early education attempted to promote high standards of child care. Even then, the demand exceeded the existing supply of 175 programs at the time.

■ 1900s

Theodore Roosevelt convened the first Conference on Children. Concerned citizens and experts met to discuss the state of the nation's children. Recommendations led to the establishment of the Children's Bureau, a counterpart to the Agricultural Bureau, focusing on the needs of children and families.

■ 1920s

Experimental preschool programs were established to study children's development at selected universities. Arnold Gesell of Yale recorded observations of children's development on film. His pioneering work increased dissemination of caregiving practices fostering children's optimal development.

HISTORICALLY SPEAKING

EARLY EDUCATION

Abigail Eliot
Report of the Ruggles Street Nursery School and Nursery Training Center of Boston, 1924
Education begins at birth. Much that many people think of as inherited is learned in the earliest years. These years are the most fruitful time for teaching, since a little child learns at a greater speed than he ever will again, and the early associations have a permanence which none formed in later life can rival. Psychologists say the fundamental bases of character and personality are established during this period when the brain is growing.

Source: Braun and Edwards (1972), p. 153.

■ 1930s

Franklin Roosevelt's Federal Emergency Relief Act and Works Progress Administration (WPA) allocated federal funds to create jobs. The effort focused on jump-starting the economy during the Depression. However, it led to the employment of hundreds of preschool teachers to provide child care for working parents, marking the federal government's first efforts in early education.

■ 1940s

The Landham Act provided federal funds to institute child care in factories employing women during World War II. The allocated funds established 3,102 centers across the country, serving about 600,000 children. However, only an estimated 40% of the eligible children received child care at the time.

■ 1960s

Project Head Start was initiated in 1965 with Lyndon Johnson's effort to break the cycle of poverty. The project was designed to serve economically disadvantaged preschool children. Its eventual success led to increasing acceptance of early education and provided one model of high-quality child care.

■ 1990s

Early Head Start was launched to include the first 3 years of life. Research found that the beneficial effects of Head Start declined as time passed. Efforts concentrated on reaching economically disadvantaged children before preschool to sustain the positive effects of Head Start.

Today, although the demand for high-quality child care still outpaces the supply, a variety of options do exist. Parents consider many things in making their choice, but two in particular—affordability and accessibility—often top the list (Galinsky & Friedman, 1993). Cost depends on numerous factors such as the ratio of adults to children and the educational level of the caregivers. Relatives of families take care of about 20% of children, birth to 5 years of age (Hoffreth et al., 1991). Over half of children are placed in the care of nonrelatives (neighbors, friends, or professional caregivers). The remainder of children stay at home with one parent. Different terms are used to refer to various types of child care. To eliminate ambiguity, two broad types of child care are distinguished here: home- and center-based programs.

HOME- AND CENTER-BASED CARE

The distinction between home- and center-based care lies in the location of the program and number of children served. Home-based programs provide care in the homes of private providers, whereas center-based programs operate in centers such as churches or preschools. Local state licensing standards are required in every type of child care. However, not all home-based providers may be licensed. In selecting home-based care, parents are basically choosing someone operating a business in his or her home. Typically, one provider takes care of unrelated children of different ages. In selecting center-based care, parents are not just selecting a caregiver but an organization, usually consisting of a staff of caregivers taking care of children of similar ages along with a director or lead teacher overseeing the day-to-day operations of the center. Each type of care has its distinct advantages and disadvantages, as shown in Table 12–3.

SELECTION OF CARE

Selecting one type of child care can be a difficult task. Two things can be done to facilitate the decision-making process:

TABLE 12–3 HOME- AND CENTER-BASED CARE: ADVANTAGES AND DISADVANTAGES

Home-Based Care

Potential Advantages

- Individualization and continuity of care are more likely to occur.
- The physical setting looks more homelike.
- Children and their parents may benefit from a sense of "extended family."
- A heterogeneous group provides interactions with others of different ages.
- Providers may be willing to accommodate parents' unusual work hours.

Potential Disadvantages

- Providers often work alone unsupervised.
- Long hours and isolation may lead to caregiver fatigue and stress.
- Caregivers' illness or emergency may create disruptive hardships.
- Providers may lack resources to meet the needs of multiaged children.
- Inexperienced caregivers tend to quit without warning.

Center-Based Care

Potential Advantages

- Teamwork can create an atmosphere of cooperation.
- A similar philosophy can provide consistency from one age to the next.
- Indoor and outdoor space is designed for a specific age group.
- Written records of each child can be kept and shared with parents.
- Caregivers' illness or emergency usually does not interfere with the center's operations.

Potential Disadvantages

- Children's exposure to a large group setting may increase health risks.
- An institutional or impersonal atmosphere may be experienced.
- Conformity to, instead of flexibility of, routines may be seen.
- High staff turnover may affect the formation of secure attachment with the children's primary caregivers.
- Breakdowns in communication between the staff and parents may occur.

CHARACTERISTICS OF HIGH-QUALITY
HOME- AND CENTER-BASED CARE

A high-quality caregiver . . .

■ Encourages children's active exploration of the world.

■ Talks with children during routine caregiving activities.

■ Fosters children's sense of pride in their accomplishments.

■ Affirms a commitment to continual professional development.

■ Develops productive relationships of mutual trust with families.

■ Acknowledges and builds on strengths and competence of each child.

■ Respects the dignity of each family's cultural traditions and beliefs.

■ Reports and interprets each child's progress to parents.

A high-quality physical environment . . .

■ Protects children's safety.

■ Offers appropriate materials to promote children's development.

■ Values child-, not adult-, directed play.

■ Adheres to a flexible but consistent daily schedule.

■ Alternates quiet and noisy activities during the day.

■ Encourages the use of small and large muscles.

■ Follows sanitary procedures to ensure children's health.

■ Maintains an adequate ratio of adults to children at all times.

Sources: Gestwicki, 1998; NAEYC, 1996.

■ **Interviewing provider or director.** An interview with the provider or director is suggested to obtain specific information about the program. Examples of questions to ask include:

What kinds of experiences do you have in working with babies?

How do you respond to babies' crying?

How do you deal with discipline?

How do you handle unexpected emergencies?

How do you wean a baby from a bottle or toilet train a toddler?

What does a typical day look like?

■ **Observing program.** Nothing replaces direct observation of any program. Parents should feel that a program provides the same kind of emotional contact and same level of optimal stimulation their children would receive at home. Parents should also take the time to examine both the indoor and the outdoor environment. Valuable firsthand information on such matters as the variety of available toys in the program and sanitary conditions of eating and sleeping areas can be obtained.

Table 12–4 provides some warnings to be aware of when interviewing the director and observing the program.

CHARACTERISTICS OF HIGH-QUALITY CARE

High-quality care means different things to different people, but common ingredients include recognition of children's active involvement in the learning process and the provision of varied experiences facilitating children's physical, cognitive, and psychosocial development. The remainder of the chapter focuses on the caregivers' role, learning environment, and partnership with families.

Caregivers' Role.   Professional caregivers directly influence the success of home- and center-based programs. They not only plan stimulating activities but also strive to protect, comfort, and nurture children in their care. A demanding job, caregivers need an abundance of patience in working with young children. Low wages do not equate with the sacrifices caregivers make day in and day out on behalf of children and their families. Neither do stereotypic attitudes help in recruiting and retaining highly qualified staff. Even today, caregivers may be mistakenly referred to as "babysitters."

TABLE 12–4 WARNING SIGNS OF POOR-QUALITY CHILD CARE

Parents should take the time to interview the director or provider and observe the program. Possible warning signs of poor-quality child care include

- The staff does not allow unannounced visits during the day.
- Parents are not allowed to stay in the caregiving areas at any time.
- Children do not want to stay or dislike certain caregivers.
- The caregivers' voice and manner convey harshness and indifference.
- Children's artwork is displayed at the adults' level.
- The program is not equipped with a sufficient number and variety of toys.
- Parents are not allowed to express their concerns in constructive ways.
- There is a high turnover of caregivers.

Source: Katzez and Bragdon (1990).

The educational preparation of professional caregivers ranges from high school to college. Some decide to earn a Child Development Associate (CDA) or an associate or baccalaureate degree in early education after gaining experience in the field, whereas others start with a certificate or degree first (Willer, 1994). At the moment, licensing standardization in the United States is sorely lacking in comparison to other industrialized countries. However, continuing efforts are being made to improve the overall quality of child care with minimum standards (Bradekamp, 1996). Work with children necessitates mastery of competencies in several areas. Some minimum competencies include:

■ **Knowledge of children's development.** Developmentally appropriate activities should be planned on the basis of professional caregivers' knowledge of early development. It takes into account each child's individuality and cultural heritage.

■ **Curricula.** Although structured activities may be planned, freely chosen play should be valued above all else. Professional caregivers know that children learn from direct involvement and engagement with actual objects and people.

■ **Observation and assessment.** Observation and assessment of children provide information about their developmental progress and special needs. In practice, input from parents should be sought on an ongoing basis.

■ **Professionalism.** Professionalism involves not only attendance at workshops to improve overall level of expertise but also adherence to a code of ethical standards. Its observance encourages appropriate professional conduct and raises the quality of caregiving practices (Caulfield, 1997).

PARENTING ISSUES

DEVELOPMENTAL APPROPRIATENESS

High-quality child care incorporates developmentally appropriate practices into their programs. Developmental appropriateness involves two dimensions: age and uniqueness of each child (Bradekamp & Copple, 1997).

■ **Age of child.** Caregivers who maintain high standards attempt to provide activities that facilitate children's development in challenging ways. They realize that infants learn primarily from their sensory exploration of objects and direct interaction with people.

■ **Uniqueness of each child.** Although development proceeds in a sequential fashion, children do develop at their own rate. Their individual patterns of development reflect their unique temperament and learning style.

Characteristics of developmentally appropriate out-of-home care include a low adult–child ratio and hands-on opportunities to engage with the world.
Photo courtesy of Tami Dawson, Photo Resource Hawaii.

Learning Environment.   Contact between caregivers and children occurs in the context of the physical environment, indoor and outdoor. Its organization requires thoughtful consideration of children's developmental needs. Infants and toddlers need different kinds of arrangement because of differences in locomotion and independence. Nevertheless, in both cases, the room should be divided into functionally separate areas. Each area should be designed and equipped to increase the management and efficiency of caregiving routines. The available physical space determines the overall density (or the maximum number of children). Licensing requirements vary from state to state but generally require 20 to 50 square feet per child. The average requirement is about 35 square feet per child.

Appropriate adult–child ratios ensure that every infant receives sufficient one-to-one attention which encourages the formation of secure attachment. Table 12–5 summarizes the recommended adult–child ratios.

TABLE 12–5 RECOMMENDED ADULT–CHILD RATIO					
Size of Group					
Age	6	8	10	12	14
Birth to 12 months	1:3	1:4			
12 to 24 months	1:3	1:4	1:5	1:4	
24 to 30 months		1:4	1:5	1:6	
30 to 36 months				1:6	1:7

Source: Goodwin and Schrag (1996).

Home- and center-based programs differ in physical arrangement, but they typically share some common traits. Because organization of physical space can influence the quality of interactions between caregivers and children, several factors should be taken into consideration, as shown in Table 12–6.

The outdoor environment should complement the indoor area. Realistically, the outdoor playground depends on the facilities' availability of space, licensing requirements, financial resources, and the creativity of the caregivers. As with the indoor areas, safety is of the utmost concern. In addition to padded and soft surfaces, other recommendations include a secured, fenced-in area; supervised opportunities to play with water in large, shallow containers; hard surfaces to ride trikes; and large climbing equipment.

TABLE 12–6 ORGANIZATION OF PHYSICAL SPACE: CENTER-BASED PROGRAMS

Main Area

- **Low shelves.** Sturdy shelves serve not only to store materials but also to divide noisy and quiet areas of the room. Sharp corners should be padded to prevent accidental injuries.
- **Storage.** Toys and other materials should be rotated on an ongoing basis. Either locked cabinets or mounted shelves can be used to facilitate caregivers' accessibility to materials.
- **Large equipment.** Low climbing equipment adds diversity to the main area. It encourages children's use of large muscles.
- **Mirrors and pictures.** Unbreakable mirrors can stimulate children's self-concept. Pictures of familiar objects (people, animals, etc.) in addition to children's artwork can encourage visual exploration and brighten the room.

Feeding Area

- **Schedules and records.** Infants' individual schedules should be recorded on a mounted board in the room. The board should list not just infants' feeding but also diapering and sleeping information to ensure efficient management of the staff's time.
- **Furniture.** The arrangement of furniture should be based on the age of the children. For example, infants require high chairs, but toddlers can eat in child-sized chairs at a low table.

Diapering Area

- **Equipment.** A changing table with straps to prevent accidental falls is a necessity. A sink to wash hands and a covered wastebasket is needed to protect the health of both children and caregivers.
- **Supplies.** Shelves provide easy accessibility to diapers and other essential supplies. An unbreakable mirror on the side or overhanging mobile can provide entertainment during routine changes, but nothing replaces caregivers' mutual interaction.

Sleeping Area

- **Furniture.** Sufficient cribs are needed to accommodate different sleeping patterns of infants, although toddlers should be able to take a regular nap on a sleeping mat. A playpen should never be used as a sleeping area because of concerns with possible entrapment.
- **Supplies.** Waterproof pads to protect the mattresses from accidental leakage from diapers are a must. Individual blankets can provide adequate warmth.

Partnership with Families.   The work of professional caregivers is not limited only to the care of children. It also involves collaboration with families. Because of children's vulnerability, continuity of care between the program and home becomes an important factor. Mutual cooperation can strengthen the overall quality of home- and center-based care in two ways (Caulfield, 1996c):

■ **Shared commitment.** Parents can share anecdotal information with caregivers. Together, they can both work on mutual goals to meet the unique needs of children.

■ **Positive outcomes.** Although concerns have been raised about the possible negative effects of nonmaternal care on infants, positive outcomes have been well documented in studies. When developmentally appropriate care is provided, infants' secure attachment with their parents is not weakened but in fact strengthened (Clarke-Stewart, 1989; Phillips et al., 1987).

A collaborative partnership with parents involves hard work. Successful caregivers make an effort to communicate with parents and encourage their involvement at every opportunity in a variety of ways:

PARENTING ISSUES

PARENTAL EMPLOYMENT AND SICK CHILDREN

Today, an increasing number of mothers in industrialized countries are employed. In the United States, the traditional family with fathers as breadwinners and mothers as homemakers comprises only a small percentage of all families (Littman, 1998). Most mothers work because of financial necessity, but others choose to seek personal fulfillment. One of the major issues many working mothers face involve child care. At the moment, the demand far exceeds the supply of affordable, accessible child care. Only a few large companies can offer on-site child care for their employees.

For many working mothers, one problem consistently ranks at the top of any survey of work-related concerns. It concerns sick children. Both home- and center-based programs exclude ill children.

Mothers are usually forced to find substitute care on short notice. Although fathers are shouldering a larger share of child-rearing responsibilities today, their involvement in child care is restricted because of societal stereotypes. In fact, only 30% of single-parent fathers stay at home to take care of their sick children in comparison to 65% of single-parent mothers (Googins, 1991).

Currently, there are few available options. Only a handful of workplaces are designed to handle the needs of sick children (Landis & Earp, 1987). Employers often worry about lost productivity, and parents lost wages. Sadly, the shortage of sick care affects primarily single parents working on an hourly basis, struggling to balance the competing demands of work and home (Benin & Chong, 1993).

- **Newsletters.** In large centers, newsletters provide opportunities to announce upcoming events, suggest simple activities to do at home, emphasize the importance of nutritious snacks, and share other tidbits of information. Parents' confidence in their children's child care receives a shot in the arm whenever caregivers take the time to keep in touch with parents.

- **Transitional contacts.** Nothing takes the place of personal exchanges between caregivers and parents during daily transitions at the start and end of each day. Although a sense of hurriedness is sometimes felt, efforts to make personal contact, as in a brief summary of the child's day, are always appreciated.

- **Written messages.** Periodic short written messages in notebooks provides further individual contact with parents. Any relevant concerns (eating, sleeping, or toileting) or a short anecdote of the day can be shared.

- **Scheduled or unscheduled conferences.** Whether planned or unplanned, conferences can be a vehicle to exchange information about a child's progress in a relaxed, informal atmosphere. The focus should be placed on the child's strengths, not just weaknesses.

In sum, caregivers can ensure high standards in early care and education when they work cooperatively with parents. Children become the beneficiaries of their joint efforts.

SUMMARY

Guidance

- Historically, discipline had been associated with corporal punishment, or coercive means of correcting misbehavior. However, today, discipline refers to child-rearing methods adults use to guide and manage children's behavior.

- Discipline involves two purposes with short- and long-term implications. The control parents provide now will develop into self-control later.

- The child-rearing practices of parents differ in terms of demandingness and responsiveness. There are four possible combinations of disciplinary styles: authoritative, authoritarian, permissive, and uninvolved.

- Research confirms the effectiveness of the authoritative style. It is associated with high levels of internalized moral standards and superior academic performance later in childhood.

- Parents can influence children's development both directly and indirectly. Their words and actions matter greatly.

- Knowledge of children's age and stage can increase parents' effectiveness in guiding and managing behavior. Anticipating possible problems or conflicts and modeling socially acceptable behavior are two effective techniques.

Early Education

■ Historically in the United States, child care rested in the hands of families. The increasing percentage of working parents today requires out-of-home care.

■ Home- and center-based care differ on the location of the program and number of children it serves. Home-based programs provide care in the homes of private providers, whereas center-based programs operate in facilities.

■ Children are either taken care of in the homes of private providers or in centers. Each has its distinct advantages and disadvantages.

■ Several factors affect the overall quality of home- and center-based care. Exemplary programs establish standards in regard to caregivers' role, learning environment, and partnership with families.

PROJECTS

1. Think of reflective, nonjudgmental statements to use in the following situations involving a child who:

   Constantly runs indoors after repeated reminders not to.

   Orders other children to do things his way only.

   Forcibly takes a toy from another child.

2. Make a list of important considerations in selecting home- or center-based care.

3. Review the licensing standards of your state, particularly the level of the staff's education and experience and adult–child ratio for infants and toddlers.

DEVELOPMENTAL CHECKLIST

At 6 months, does the child...?

Area of Development

Physical

- Large muscles
    - ( ) control head?
    - ( ) turn from back to stomach and stomach to back?
    - ( ) creep forward or backward?

- Small muscles
    - ( ) reach with one arm and grasp objects?
    - ( ) hold and manipulate objects?
    - ( ) change objects from one hand to another?

Cognitive
- ( ) recognize familiar objects?
- ( ) look for dropped objects?
- ( ) use senses in exploring and manipulating objects?

Language
- ( ) respond to different intonations and inflections?
- ( ) use variety of sounds to express emotions?
- ( ) imitate adults' intonations and inflections?

Psychosocial
- ( ) respond to name?
- ( ) enjoy simple games with adults such as peek-a-boo?
- ( ) react with fear to strangers?

At 12 months, does the child...?

Area of Development

Physical

■ Large muscles
- ( ) stand without support?
- ( ) walk with assistance?
- ( ) climb stairs?

■ Small muscles
- ( ) use two hands at same time to manipulate objects?
- ( ) show preference for one hand?
- ( ) undress self or untie shoes?

Cognitive
- ( ) show increased memory?
- ( ) explore new ways of solving problems?
- ( ) imitate adults' actions at later time?

Language
- ( ) say two to eight words?
- ( ) understand simple directions?
- ( ) use gestures to express self?

Psychosocial
- ( ) show affection?
- ( ) feed self?
- ( ) obey simple commands?

At 18 months, does the child...?

Area of Development

Physical

■ Large muscles
- ( ) walk quickly?
- ( ) run with confidence?
- ( ) hold rail or hand in climbing stairs?

■ Small muscles
- ( ) use crayon to scribble and imitate marks?
- ( ) feed self?
- ( ) enjoy pouring and filling activities?

Cognitive
- ( ) follow simple commands?
- ( ) work on simple puzzles?
- ( ) engage in dramatic play?

Language
- ( )   combine two words together in talking?
- ( )   use words to gain attention?
- ( )   like to look at books?

Psychosocial
- ( )   imitate adults in dramatic play?
- ( )   show interest in helping with chores?
- ( )   demonstrate beginning control of bladder and bowel?

At 24 months, does the child...?

Area of Development

Physical

■ Large muscles
- ( )   run headlong and experience trouble in turning and stopping?
- ( )   throw and kick ball?
- ( )   balance momentarily on one foot?

■ Small muscles
- ( )   put on some clothes?
- ( )   hold fork, spoon, and cup but still spill?
- ( )   turn pages in book?

Cognitive
- ( )   identify parts of body?
- ( )   fit shapes into formboard?
- ( )   solve simple problems in head?

Language
- ( )   use personal pronouns (I, me, or you)?
- ( )   utter two- to three-word sentences?
- ( )   know at least 50 words?

Psychosocial
- ( )   assert independence?
- ( )   take pride in accomplishments?
- ( )   say "no" even to things he or she wants?

At 36 months, does the child...?

Area of Development

Physical

■ Large muscles
- ( )   walk and run with control, climb, and throw ball with aim?
- ( )   jump in place?
- ( )   balance on one foot?

■ Small muscles
( )   feed self alone?
( )   draw or copy circle?
( )   exercise control of bladder and bowel?

Cognitive
( )   count to two or three?
( )   draw face or simple figure?
( )   point to major parts of body?

Language
( )   converse in short sentences and answer questions?
( )   articulate clearly?
( )   name pictures and label actions?

Psychosocial
( )   play with sustained interest?
( )   interact with another child?
( )   conform to group for short periods?

Sources: Allen and Marotz (1989); Gonzalez-Mena and Eyer (1993).

CAREERS WITH INFANTS

A wide range of options exists for those wanting to pursue a career with infants and toddlers. The possible points of entry into the field are shown below. At the preparaprofessional level, you can start a career as a teacher's aide after high school. However, opportunities, not to mention income, expand considerably when you obtain a more advanced degree. At the paraprofessional level, you can enroll in a 2-year college and receive an associate degree in early education or a related field. A baccalaureate degree from a 4-year university provides additional opportunities at the professional level in diverse fields such as early education, medicine, psychology, or social work. A PhD is needed to teach in an area of specialization at universities and conduct research. In the medical field, pediatricians can earn their MD after 4 years of medical school and an extended period of internship and residency. A psychiatrist follows a similar course with internship and residency in psychiatry instead of pediatrics.

CAREERS IN EARLY EDUCATION AND RELATED FIELDS

		Careers in	
Level	Minimum Education	Early Education	Related Fields
1	High School	Caregiver's Aide	
		Paraprofessional	
2	Associate Degree	Caregiver	
		Professional	
3	Bachelor's Degree	Master Caregiver	Social Worker
		Special Educator	Registered Nurse
		Director	Occupational Therapist
		Trainer	Physical Therapist
4	Master's and Doctorate Degrees	College Teacher	Psychologist
	Medical Degree		Pediatrician
			Psychiatrist

GLOSSARY

Accommodation. The process of altering existing schemes to fit reality.

Adaptation. The process of adjusting to the external world.

Age of viability. The likelihood of sustained life.

Allele. Each member of a pair of genes.

Amniocentesis. A medical procedure of removing fluid with a hollow needle from the amniotic sac to analyze the chromosomes of the fetus.

Analgesics. Drugs that relieve pain.

Anesthesia. An artificially induced painkiller that blocks sensation to the affected area of the body.

Anoxia. The temporary absence of fetal oxygen during labor.

Apgar scale. A rating system of five vital signs.

Aphasia. A generalized communicative disorder.

Arcuate fasciculus. A bundle of subcortical fibers that connects the Wernicke's and Broca's areas.

Assimilation. The process of incorporating new information from the world into existing schemes.

Attachment. The affectional bonds that infants establish with special people in their lives and that persist over time.

Autosomes. Matching pairs of chromosomes.

Avoidant attachment. A relationship between infants and their parents based on the active avoidance of parents after a brief separation.

Axons. Branchlike structures that transmit information to other neurons.

Babbling. The repetition of consonants and vowels in alternating sequences that increasingly resemble adults' speech.

Blastocyst. A mass of cells that forms a ball of fluid.

Broca's area. The front left region of the brain that controls expressive language.

Canalization. The tendency of physical growth to return to its normal pattern after prolonged illness or dietary deficiency.

Categorization. The ability to organize information into meaningful groups mentally.

Cephalocaudal. Development proceeds from "head to tail" or top to bottom.

Cesarean delivery. The removal of the baby from the uterus through a surgical incision on the mother's abdomen.

Chorionic villus sampling. A prenatal diagnostic test that analyzes cells taken from the hairlike villi on the membrane of the placenta.

Chromosomes. Threadlike structures that store and transmit genetic information.

Circular reactions. The use of familiar actions to achieve the same results.

Cognition. The mental process involved in making sense of the world.

Colic. Severe abdominal pain that results in loud, protracted cries and muscular spasms of legs.

Colostrum. The milk secreted during the first few days after birth.

Comprehension. The ability to understand the speech of others.

Conditioning. An association between two events after repeated trials.

Continuity of development. The belief that development involves gradual, continuous changes.

Cooing. Vowel-like utterances that infants make.

Correlational study. A method of collecting information on existing groups without altering their experience in any way.

Critical period. A time of vulnerability with long-lasting, irreversible consequences.

Cross-cultural studies. The comparison of a culture with one or more other cultures.

Crossing over. The exchange of genes between a pair of chromosomes.

Cross-sectional design. The collection of data from two or more groups of subjects of different ages at the same time.

Culture. A set of attitudes and beliefs transmitted from one generation to another within a particular group of people.

Deciduous teeth. The first set of teeth.

Deep structure. The basic grammatical relationship between the subject and object in a sentence.

Deferred imitation. The ability to retain and copy a representation of an observed behavior.

Dendrites. Branchlike structures that receive information from other neurons.

Deoxyribonucleic acid (DNA). Long strands of molecules that contain the genetic code of the cell.

Dependent variables. The changes caused by the independent variables.

Dilate. To widen.

Discipline. Child-rearing methods that adults institute to correct and control the behavior of children.

Discontinuity of development. The belief that development consists of a series of distinct stages.

Dishabituation. Increased attention to a different set of stimuli.

Disorganized attachment. A relationship between infants and their parents based on inconsistent patterns of behavior after a brief separation.

Dizygotic twins. Two individuals who come from different fertilized eggs.

Dominant allele. An allele that is expressed when it is paired with an identical or recessive allele.

Ectoderm. The outer layer of cells of the embryoblast.

Efface. To thin.

Ego. The conscious, rational part of the personality in psychoanalytic theory.

Embryoblast. The inner mass of cells of the blastocyst.

Emotion. An affective state that involves a physiological reaction and overt behavior.

Emotional regulation. Internal mechanisms infants use to control or modify their affective states.

Empathy. The ability to sympathize with the needs of others.

Endoderm. The inner layer of the embryoblast.

Epiphyses. Areas of the bone that manufacture new cells.

Episiotomy. A surgical incision in the perineum that widens the vaginal cavity in order to expedite the delivery of a baby.

Epistemology. A branch of philosophy that is concerned with the nature of knowledge.

Equilibration. A balanced state of cognitive structures.

Exosystem. Social units that indirectly influence the infant.

Experimental approach. Controlled procedures that introduce a change in subjects' experience and then measure its effect on their behavior.

Extinction. The elimination of a learned behavior.

Fetal monitor. An electronic device that tracks the fetal heart rate and measures the frequency and duration of the mother's contractions.

Fetoscopy. A procedure that photographs the fetus and samples its tissue and blood.

Fine motor skills. Movements that require complex coordination between the eyes and hands.

Fixation. In psychoanalytic theory, an obsessive or unhealthy preoccupation because of insufficient or excessive gratification in a particular stage.

Fontanels. The space between the cranial bones of the newborn.

Forceps. An instrument that resembles a pair of pincers and that assists the expulsion of a child at birth.

Gametes. The sperm and ovum.

Gender. Nonphysiological differences that arise from a set of expectations that a culture attaches to one sex or the other.

Generalizability. The applicability of a study's conclusions to the entire population of subjects.

Genes. Units of hereditary information.

Genotype. The underlying genetic pattern of a person.

Gestation. The elapsed time between conception and birth.

Goodness of fit. The quality of the match between temperament and the demands of the environment.

Gross motor skills. Movements that involve the entire body.

Guidance. Realistic expectations of children's behavior that combine both empathy and firmness.

Habituation. The gradual decline in attention that results from prolonged exposure to a particular stimulus.

Holophrastic speech. The use of single words to convey complex ideas in full sentences.

Hypothesis. A tentative statement about the relationship between variables.

Id. In psychoanalytic theory, the source of instinctual urges and needs that a person seeks to satisfy.

Immunization. The development of adequate immunity.

Imprinting. A biological ability to establish an attachment with an object or person during a limited period of time.

Independent variables. The variables that the researcher manipulates.

Induced labor. An obstetric procedure of rupturing the amnion or administering oxytocin, a hormone that hastens contractions.

Isolette. A modified crib that is designed to provide a regulated environment.

Karyotype. A pictorial arrangement of chromosomes.

Kwashiorkor. A form of severe malnutrition that results from a deficiency of protein in children's diet.

Lactation. The production of human milk.

Language. A complex system of arbitrary symbols that are used to express and understand ideas and emotions.

Lanugo. The newborn's prenatal hair that disappears within a few days of birth.

Lateralization. The specialization of functions in the two hemispheres of the cerebral cortex.

Linguistics. The science of language.

Locomotion. Movement from one place to another.

Longitudinal design. The repeated collection of data on the same group of subjects over a long period of time.

Long-term memory. The permanent storage of sensory input.

Low birth weight. A birth weight of 2,500 grams, or 5.5 pounds, or less.

Macrosystem. The influence of culture, particularly its beliefs and traditions.

Marasmus. An extreme form of malnutrition that leads to a wasted condition of the body.

Maturation. The orderly sequence of changes that occur during infancy as a result of genetic factors.

Mean length of utterance. The average length of children's sentences.

Meiosis. The division of cells that reduces the number of chromosomes.

Memory. The capacity to retain and retrieve past experience.

Mesoderm. The middle layer of the embryoblast.

Mesosystem. The interrelationship between microsystems.

Microsystem. The interaction between a developing infant and his or her immediate environment.

Mitosis. The division of a cell into two identical cells.

Monozygotic twins. Two individuals who come from one fertilized egg.

Morbidity. The rate of illness.

Morphemes. The smallest units of meaning in a language.

Morphology. The rules that govern the construction of words in a language.

Mortality. The frequency of death.

Myelin. A white, fatty substance that improves the efficiency of neural transmission.

Myelinization. A process that coats the axons of neurons with an insulating sheath of myelin.

Natural or **prepared childbirth**. A method of childbirth that tries to reduce medical intervention.

Naturalistic observation. The description of behavior in unstructured situations.

Nature. The biological and genetic factors that influence development.

Neonate. The newborn.

Neural tube. A primitive spinal cord.

Neurons. Cells that receive and transmit information in the brain.

Neurotransmitters. The chemical substance that is involved in the transmission of neural information.

Norms. The average ages that typical skills are achieved based on a large sample of infants.

Nucleus. A spherical body that contains the hereditary material of the cell, controlling its growth and reproduction.

Nurture. The influence of environment and experience on development.

Objectivity. The investigator's suspension of judgment about the outcome of his or her research.

Obstetrics. A branch of medicine that deals with the care of women before and after childbirth.

Organogenesis. A period during the embryonic stage that marks the formation of the major organs.

Orthogenetic prinicple. The progression from global to specific movements of the body.

Ossification. The formation of bones.

Overextension. The application of a word to a variety of objects that share a common characteristic.

Overregularization. The application of regular grammatical rules in exceptional cases.

Parentese. A pattern of speech that consists of a high-pitched voice and exaggerated intonation.

Perception. The brain's capacity to make sense of information that it receives from the body's sensory modalities.

Personality. Enduring personal qualities and behavioral patterns that define a person's own individuality.

Phenotype. The observable physical and behavioral traits of a person.

Phonemes. The basic sounds of a language.

Phonology. The rules that control the combination of sounds in a language.

Pincer grasp. A highly refined grasp that involves the thumb's opposition to the forefinger.

Placenta. The organ that separates the mother's bloodstream from the fetus but permits the exchange of nutrients and wastes.

Plasticity. The ability of other areas of the brain to assume the functions of the damaged regions.

Postmature. After the 42nd week of pregnancy.

Postpartum depression. A prolonged state of depression during the period after birth.

Pragmatics. The rules that govern the practical use of language to communicate with others in a variety of conversational and social situations.

Prehension. The ability to grasp objects.

Premature. Before the 37th week of gestation.

Primary circular reactions. Repetitive actions that center on the body.

Production. The spoken communication of children.

Proximodistal. Development proceeds from "near to far" or center of the body outward.

Psycholinguistics. The study of the psychological processes that underlie language.

Punishment. The presentation of an unpleasant stimulus or the withdrawal of a pleasant stimulus as a consequence of a particular behavior.

Recessive allele. An allele that is expressed only when it is paired with a matching recessive allele.

Reciprocity. The mutual accommodation, or continual adjustment, between infants and their caregivers.

Reflexes. Inborn, involuntary responses to specific stimuli.

Rehearsal. Repetition of information.

Reinforcement. A consequence that increases the repetition of a particular behavior.

Reliability. The consistency of a measurement an investigator uses in collecting information.

Replicability. The likelihood of obtaining the same results as the original study.

Resistant attachment. A relationship between infants and their parents based on reluctance at separation but ambivalence at reunion.

Sample. A group of subjects who are asked to participate in a study.

Scheme. An organized pattern of behavior.

Scientific method. The collection of information that either supports or refutes a hypothesis.

Secondary circular reactions. Repetitive actions that produce interesting results on the environment.

Secure attachment. A warm, positive relationship between infants and their parents based on infants' trust in their parents' physical and emotional availability.

Self-awareness. People's sense of themselves as distinct entities with unique characteristics.

Semantics. The study of the meaning of words.

Sensation. The body's ability to detect a particular stimulus.

Sensitive period. A time of vulnerability with long-lasting but not necessarily irreversible consequences.

Sensorimotor play. The intrinsically satisfying repetition of simple motor skills.

Sex. Physiological differences between males and females.

Short-term memory. Sensory information that is stored temporarily.

Social competence. Infants' ability to establish and maintain satisfying social interactions and relationships with others.

Social referencing. Infants' reliance on trusted adults' emotional reactions in their interpretation of strange or ambiguous events.

Socialization. The acquisition of cultural values and attitudes.

Species-specific innate behavior. Behavioral patterns that occur only in one particular species and that result from natural selection.

Speech. The production of spoken words and other meaningful sounds.

Stage. A period of development with distinct qualitative changes.

States. Newborns' different levels of sleep and wakefulness.

Structured observation. A method of observing and recording a behavior of interest in a laboratory.

Superego. In psychoanalytic theory, the component of the personality that contains parental and societal expectations and prohibitions.

Surface structure. The linear arrangements of words.

Symbolic play. Imaginative activities that are intended to represent reality.

Symbolic representation. The internalization of reality.

Synapses. The spaces between neurons.

Syntax. The combination of words into meaningful sentences.

Systems. A set of interdependent components.

Tabula rasa. Locke's conception of the human mind as a blank tablet at birth.

Telegraphic speech. Children's two-word utterances that convey an idea with a minimal number of words.

Temperament. Stable, inherited dispositions that determine the quality and intensity of a person's emotional reaction to different situations.

Teratogens. Environmental agents that result in congenital abnormalities.

Tertiary circular reactions. Actions that are deliberately repeated to discover new variations of established schemes.

Theory. A set of interrelated statements used to describe and explain unobservable mechanisms or processes.

Transition. The end of the first stage of labor.

Triadic reciprocality. Learning that results from the mutual interaction between cognitive factors as well as enviromental contexts.

Ulnar grasp. A clumsy motion that involves the closure of the fingers on the palm.

Ultrasonography. Computerized visual images of the fetus and its internal organs in the amniotic sac.

Umbilical cord. A long cord that delivers nutrients and removes wastes.

Underextension. The use of words to refer to a narrow category.

Vaccination. The administration of an immunological agent.

Validity. The accuracy of the conclusions researchers make.

Vernix caseosa. An oily substance that covers the newborn's skin.

Vicarious reinforcement. The repetition of another person's behavior in an observed event.

Visual accommodation. The ability of the eyes to bring objects into focus.

Visual acuity. Sharpness of vision.

Wariness of strangers. The distressed reactions that infants display to the presence of new adults.

Wernicke's area. The posterior left temporal lobe of the brain that governs receptive language.

Zygote. The union of the sperm and ovum at conception.

REFERENCES

Abbott, L. (1915). *Reminiscences*. Boston: Houghton Mifflin.

Abel, E. L. (1998). *Fetal alcohol abuse syndrome*. New York: Plenum.

Abrams, R. M., Griffiths, S. K., Huang, X., Sain, J., Langford, G., & Gerhardt, K. J. (1998). Fetal music perception: The role of sound transmission. *Music Perception, 15*, 307–317.

Achenbach, T. M., Howell, C. T., Aoki, M. F., & Rauh, V. A. (1993). Nine-year outcome of the Vermont intervention program for low-birthweight infants. *Pediatrics, 91*, 45–55.

Acker, M. M., & O'Leary, S. G. (1996). Inconsistency of mothers' feedback and toddlers' misbehavior and negative affect. *Journal of Abnormal Child Psychology, 24*, 703–714.

Adams, A. (1961). Abigail Adams to Mercy Otis Warren. In L. H. Butterfield (Ed.), *Adams family correspondence* (Vol. 2, pp. 84–85). Cambridge, MA: Belknap.

Adams, G., & Davidson, M. (1987). Present concepts of infant colic. *Pediatric Annals, 16*, 817–820.

Adams, R. J., & Courage, M. L. (1998). Human newborn color vision: Measurement with chromatic stimuli varying in excitation purity. *Journal of Experimental Child Psychology, 68*, 22–34.

Adams, R. J., Courage, M. L., & Mercer, M. E. (1994). Systematic measurement of human neonatal color vision. *Vision Research, 34*, 1691–1701.

Adler, A. (1964). *Social interest: A challenge to mankind*. New York: Capricorn Books.

Adler, S. M. (1998). *Mothering, education, and ethnicity: The transformation of Japanese American culture*. New York: Garland.

Adolph, K. E. (1997). Learning in the development of infant locomotion. *Monographs of the Society for Research in Child Development, 62*(3, Serial No. 251).

Adolph, K. E., Vereijken, B., & Denny, M. A. (1998). *Child Development, 69*, 1299–1312.

Ainsworth, M. D. S. (1973). The development of infant–mother attachment. In B. M. Caldwell & H. N. Ricciuti (Eds.), *Review of child development research* (Vol. 3, pp. 1–94). Chicago: University of Chicago Press.

Ainsworth, M. D. S. (1982). Attachment: Retrospect and prospect. In C. M. Parkes & J. Stevenson-Hinde (Eds.), *The place of attachment in human behavior* (pp. 3–30). New York: Basic Books.

Ainsworth, M. D. S., & Bell, S. M. (1970). Attachment, exploration, and separation: Illustrated by the behavior of one-year-olds in a strange situation. *Child Development, 41*, 49–67.

Ainsworth, M. D. S., Blehar, M. C., Waters, E., & Wall, S. (1978). *Patterns of attachment: A psychological study of the strange situation*. Hillsdale, NJ: Erlbaum.

Ainsworth, M. D. S., & Wittig, B. A. (1969). Attachment and exploratory behavior of one-year-olds in a strange situation. In B. M. Foss (Ed.), *Determinants of infant behaviour* (Vol. 4, pp. 111–136). London: Methuen.

Aitken, R. J. (1995). The complexities of conception. *Science, 269*, 39–40.

Al-Azzawi, F. (1998). *Childbirth and obstetric practices* (2nd ed.). St. Louis: Mosby.

Alcott, A. B. (1882). Letter to Mrs. Talbot with notes from his diary. *Journal of Social Science*.

Alcott, B. (1938). *The journals of Bronson Alcott*. Boston: Little, Brown.

Allen, K. E., & Marotz, L. (1989). *Developmental profiles: Birth to six*. Albany, NY: Delmar.

American Academy of Pediatrics, Committee on Child Abuse and Neglect. (1993). Shaken baby syndrome: Inflicted cerebral trauma. *Pediatrics, 92*, 872–875.

American Academy of Pediatrics, Committee on Infectious Diseases. (1999). *Report of the Committee on Infectious Diseases*. Elk Grove Village, IL: Author.

American Association on Mental Retardation. (1992). *Mental retardation: Definition, classification, and systems of support*. Washington, DC: Author.

Amsterdam, B. (1972). Mirror self-image reactions before age two. *Developmental Psychobiology, 5,* 297–305.

Amato, P. R. (1998). More than money? Men's contributions to their children's lives. In A. Booth & A. C. Crouter (Eds.), *Men in families: When do they get involved? What difference does it make?* (pp. 241–278). Mahwah, NJ: Erlbaum.

Anastasiow, N., & Nucci, C. (1994). Social, historical, and theoretical foundations of early childhood special education and early intervention. In P. L. Safford, B. Spodek, & O. N. Saracho (Eds.), *Early childhood special education* (pp. 7–25). New York: Teachers College Press.

Anglin, J. M. (1993). Vocabulary development: A morphological analysis. *Monographs of the Society for Research in Child Development, 58*(10, Serial No. 238).

Apgar, V. A. (1953). A proposal for a new method of evaluation in the newborn infant. *Current Research in Anesthesia and Analgesia, 32,* 260–267.

Apple, R. D. (1987). *Mothers and medicine: A social history of infant feeding, 1890–1950.* Madison: University of Wisconsin Press.

Aries, P. (1962). *Centuries of childhood: A social history of family life.* New York: Vintage. (Original work published in 1960)

Axtell, J. L. (1981). *The European and the Indian: Essays in the ethnohistory of colonial North America.* New York: Oxford University Press.

Bahrick, L. E., Moss, L., & Fadil, C. (1996). Development of visual self-recognition in infancy. *Ecological Psychology, 8,* 189–208.

Bahrick, L. E., Netto, D., & Hernandez-Reif, M. (1998). Intermodal perception of adult and child faces and voices by infants. *Child Development, 69,* 1263–1275.

Bailey, D. B., & Wolery, M. (1992). *Teaching infants and preschoolers with disabilities* (2nd ed.). New York: Macmillan.

Bailey, W. T. (1994). A longitudinal study of fathers' involvement with young children: Infancy to age 5. *Journal of Genetic Psychology, 155,* 331–339.

Bailey, W. T. (1995). Comparison of infants' reunion with fathers and mothers. *Psychological Reports, 75,* 1227–1234.

Baillargeon, R. (1987). Object permanence in 3 1/2- and 4 1/2-month-old infants. *Developmental Psychology, 23,* 655–664.

Baillargeon, R. (1993). The object concept revisited: New directions in the investigation of infants' physical knowledge. In C. Granrud (Ed.), *Visual perception and cognition in infancy* (pp. 265–315). Hillsdale, NJ: Erlbaum.

Baillargeon, R. (1998). Infants' understanding of the physical world. In M. Sabourin, F. Craik, & M. Robert (Eds.), *Advances in psychological science: Biological and cognitive aspects* (Vol. 2, pp. 503–529). Hove, England: Psychology Press.

Baillargeon, R., Graber, M., DeVos, J., & Black, J. (1990). Why do young infants fail to search for hidden objects? *Cognition, 36,* 255–284.

Bakeman, R., Adamson, L. B., Konner, M., & Barr, R. G. (1990). !Kung infancy: The social context of object exploration. *Child Development, 61,* 794–809.

Baker, D. L., Schuette, J. L., & Uhlmann, W. R. (1998). *A guide to genetic counseling.* New York: Wiley.

Bandura, A. (1977). *Social learning theory.* Englewood Cliffs, NJ: Prentice-Hall.

Bandura, A. (1986). *Social foundations of thought and action: A social cognitive theory.* Englewood Cliffs, NJ: Prentice-Hall.

Bandura, A., & Walters, R. H. (1959). *Adolescent aggression: A study of the influence of child-training practices and family interrelationships.* New York: Ronald Press.

Bandura, A., & Walters, R. H. (1963). *Social learning and personality development.* New York: Holt, Rinehart and Winston.

Banks, M. S., & Shannon, E. (1993). Spatial and chromatic visual efficiency in human neonates. In C. Granrud (Ed.), *Visual perception and cognition in infancy* (pp. 1–46). Hillsdale, NJ: Erlbaum.

Barnat, S. B., Klein, P. J., & Meltzoff, A. N. (1996). Deferred imitation across changes in context and object: Memory and generalization in 14-month-old infants. *Infant Behavior and Development, 19,* 241–251.

Baron, N. S. (1992). *Growing up with language: How children learn to talk.* Reading, MA: Addison-Wesley.

Barr, R., Dowden, A., & Hayne, H. (1996). Developmental changes in deferred imitation by 6- to 24-month-old infants. *Infant Behavior and Development, 19*, 159–170.

Barr, R. G. (1998). Crying in the first year of life: Good news in the midst of distress. *Child: Care, Health and Development, 24*, 425–439.

Barrera, M. E., & Maurer, D. (1981). Discrimination of strangers by the three-month-old. *Child Development, 52*, 558–563.

Barros, F. C., Victora, C. G., & Weiderpass, E. (1995). Use of pacifiers is associated with decreased breast-feeding duration. *Pediatrics, 95*, 497–499.

Bartholomew. (1924). *Mediaeval lore from Bartholomaeus Anglicus*. London: Chatto & Windus. (Original work published 13th Century)

Bates, E., Thal, D., & Janowsky, J. S. (1992). Early language development and its neural correlates. In S. J. Segalowitz & I. Rapin (Eds.), *Handbook of neuropsychology* (Vol. 7, pp. 69–110). Amsterdam: Elsevier.

Bates, J. E. (1989). Concepts and measures of temperament. In G. A. Kohnstamm, J. E. Bates, & M. K. Rothbart (Eds.), *Temperament in childhood* (pp. 3–26). Chichester: Wiley.

Bateson, P., & Hinde, R. A. (1987). Developmental changes in sensitivity of experience. In M. H. Bornstein (Ed.), *Sensitive periods in development: Interdisciplinary perspectives* (pp. 19–34). Hillsdale, NJ: Erlbaum.

Bauer, P. J. (1996). What do infants recall of their lives? Memory for specific events by one- to two-year-olds. *American Psychologist, 51*, 29–41.

Baum, S. R., & Boyczuk, J. P. (1999). Speech timing subsequent to brain damage: Effects of utterance length and complexity. *Brain and Language, 67*, 30–45.

Baumrind, D. (1967). Child care practices anteceding three patterns of preschool behavior. *Genetic Psychology Monographs, 75*, 43–88.

Baumrind, D. (1971). Current patterns of parental authority. *Developmental Psychology, 4*, 1–103.

Bayley, N. (1935). The development of motor abilities during the first three years. *Monographs of the Society for Research on Child Development, 1*(1, Serial No. 231).

Bayley, N. (1969). *Bayley scales of infant development*. New York: Psychological Corporation.

Bean, C. A. (1990). *Methods of childbirth* (rev. ed.). New York: Morrow.

Becerra, R. M. (1998). The Mexican-American family. In C. H. Mindel, R. W. Habenstein, & R. Wright (Eds.), *Ethnic families in America: Patterns and variations* (4th ed., pp. 153–171). Upper Saddle River, NJ: Prentice-Hall.

Begley, S. (1995, September 4). The baby myth. *Newsweek, 126*, 38–45, 47.

Begley, S. (1996, February 19). Your child's brain. *Newsweek, 127*, 55–58.

Begley, S. (1998, September 7). The parent trap. *Newsweek, 132*, 53–59.

Behrman, R. E. (1999). *Nelson textbook of pediatrics* (16th ed.). Philadelphia: Saunders.

Bell, M. A., & Fox, N. A. (1994). Brain development over the first year of life: Relations between electroencephalographic frequency and coherence and cognitive and affective behaviors. In G. Dawson & K. W. Fischer (Eds.), *Human behavior and the developing brain* (pp. 314–345). New York: Guilford.

Belsky, J. (1980). Mother–infant interaction at home and in the laboratory: A comparative study. *Journal of Genetic Psychology, 137*, 37–47.

Belsky, J. (1986). Infant day care: A cause for concern? *Zero to Three, 6*(5), 1–7.

Belsky, J. (1987). Risks remain. *Zero to Three, 7*(3), 22–24.

Belsky, J. (1990). Infant day care, child development, and family policy. *Society, 27*(5), 10–12.

Belsky, J. (1993). Etiology of child maltreatment: A developmental-ecological analysis. *Psychological Bulletin, 114*, 413–434.

Benbow, C. P. (1986). Physiological correlates of extreme intellectual precocity. *Neuropsychologia, 24*, 719–725.

Benedict, R. (1934). *Patterns of culture*. Boston: Houghton Mifflin.

Benin, M., & Chong, Y. (1993). Child care concerns of employed mothers. In J. Frankel (Ed.), *The employed mother and the family context* (pp. 229–244). New York: Springer.

Bernard, J. (1946). Human fetal reactivity to tonal stimulation. *American Psychologist, 1,* 256.

Bersoff, D. N. (Ed.). (1999). *Ethical conflicts in psychology* (2nd ed.). Washington, DC: American Psychological Association.

Bertenthal, B. I. (1996). Origins and early development of perception, action, and representation. *Annual Review of Psychology, 47,* 431–459.

Bertenthal, B. I., & Boker, S. M. (1997). New paradigms and new issues: A comment on emerging themes in the study of motor development. *Monographs of the Society for Research in Child Development, 62*(3, Serial No. 251).

Bertenthal, B. I., & Campos, J. J. (1990). A systems approach to the organizing effects of self-produced locomotion during infancy. In C. Rovee-Collier & L. P. Lipsitt (Eds.), *Advances in infancy research* (Vol. 6, pp. 1–60). Norwood, NJ: Ablex.

Bertenthal, B. I., Campos, J. J., & Barrett, K. C. (1984). Self-produced locomotion: An organizer of emotional, cognitive, and social development in infancy. In R. N. Emde & R. J. Harmon (Eds.), *Continuities and discontinuities in development* (pp. 175–210). New York: Plenum.

Bertenthal, B., & Hofsten, C. von (1998). Eye, head and trunk control: The foundation for manual development. *Neuroscience and Biobehavioral Reviews, 22,* 515–520.

Bertman, S. L. (1991). *Facing death: Images, insights, and interventions.* New York: Hemisphere.

Bhatia, T. K., & Ritchie, W. C. (1999). The bilingual child: Some issues and perspectives. In W. C. Ritchie & T. K. Bhatia (Eds.), *Handbook of child language acquisition* (pp. 569–643). San Diego: Academic Press.

Bialystok, E. (1997). Effects of bilingualism and biliteracy on children's emerging concepts of print. *Developmental Psychology, 33,* 429–440.

Bialystok, E., & Majumder, S. (1998). The relationship between bilingualism and the development of cognitive processes in problem solving. *Applied Psycholinguistics, 19,* 69–85.

Biller, H. B., & Trotter, R. J. (1994). *The father factor: What you need to know to make a difference.* New York: Pocket.

Biringen, Z., Emde, R. N., & Pipp-Siegel, S. (1997). Dyssynchrony, conflict, and resolution: Positive contributions in infant development. *American Journal of Orthopsychiatry, 67,* 4–19.

Birnholz, J. C., & Benacerraf, B. R. (1983). The development of human fetal hearing. *Science, 22,* 516–518.

Bjork, D. W. (1993). *B. F. Skinner: A life.* New York: Basic Books.

Blass, E. M., & Hoffmeyer, L. B. (1991). Sucrose as an analgesic for newborn infants. *Pediatrics, 87,* 215–218.

Blechman, E. A., & Brownell, K. D. (Eds.). (1998). *Behavioral medicine and women: A comprehensive handbook.* New York: Guilford.

Bloom, L. (1993). *The transition from infancy to language: Acquiring the power of expression.* New York: Cambridge University Press.

Blundell, J. (1834). *The principles and practice of obstetricy.* Washington, DC: Green.

Boero, D. L., Volpe, C., Marcello, A., Bianchi, C., & Lenti, C. (1998). Newborns crying in different contexts: Discrete or graded signals. *Perceptual and Motor Skills, 86,* 1123–1140.

Bohannon, J. N., & Bonvillian, J. D. (1997). Theoretical approaches to language acquisition. In J. B. Gleason (Ed.), *The development of language* (4th ed., pp. 259–316). Boston: Allyn & Bacon.

Bomba, P. C., & Siqueland, E. R. (1983). The nature and structure of infant form categories. *Journal of Experimental Child Psychology, 35,* 294–328.

Bornstein, M. H. (1989). Sensitive periods in development: Structural characteristics and causal interpretations. *Psychological Bulletin, 105,* 179–197.

Bornstein, M. H., Azuma, H., Tamis-LeMonda, C., & Ogino, M. (1990). Mother and infant activity and interaction in Japan and in the United States: I. A comparative macroanalysis of naturalistic exchanges. *International Journal of Behavioral Development, 13,* 267–287.

Bornstein, M. H., Toda, S., Azuma, H., Tamis-LeMonda, C., & Ogino, M. (1990). Mother and infant activity and interaction in Japan and in the United States: II. A comparative microanalysis of naturalistic exchanges focused on the organisation of infant attention. *International Journal of Behavioral Development, 13,* 289–308.

Borst, C. G. (1996). *Catching babies: The professionalization of childbirth, 1870–1920.* Cambridge, MA: Harvard University Press.

Boukydis, C. F. Z. (1985). Perception of infant crying as an interpersonal event. In B. M. Lester & C. F. Z. Boukydis (Eds.), *Infant crying: Theoretical and research perspectives* (pp. 187–215). New York: Plenum.

Bowerman, M. (1982). Reorganizational processes in lexical and syntactic development. In E. Wanner & L. R. Gleitman (Eds.), *Language acquisition: The state of the art* (pp. 319–346). Cambridge: Cambridge University Press.

Bowes, W. A. (1994). Clinical aspects of normal and abnormal labor. In R. K. Creasy & R. Resnik (Eds.), *Maternal–fetal medicine: Principles and practice* (3rd ed., pp. 527–557). Philadelphia: Saunders.

Bowlby, J. (1940). The influence of early environment in the development of neurosis and neurotic behavior. *International Journal of Psycho-Analysis, 21,* 154–178.

Bowlby, J. (1958). The nature of the child's ties to his mother. *International Journal of Psycho-Analysis, 39,* 350–373.

Bowlby, J. (1967). Foreword. In M. D. S. Ainsworth (Ed.), *Infancy in Uganda: Infant care and the growh of love* (pp. v–vi). Baltimore: Johns Hopkins University Press.

Bowlby, J. (1969). *Attachment and loss: Vol. 1. Attachment.* London: Hogarth Press.

Boysen, S. T., & Himes, G. T. (1999). Current issues and emerging theories in animal cognition. *Annual Review of Psychology, 50,* 683.

Boysson-Bardies, B. de, & Vihman, M. M. (1991). Adaptation to language: Evidence from babbling and first words in four languages. *Language, 67,* 297–319.

Brackbill, Y. (1970). Acoustic variation and arousal level in infants. *Psychophysiology, 6,* 517–526.

Brackbill, Y. (1975). Continuous stimulation and arousal level in infancy: Effects of stimulus intensity and stress. *Child Development, 46,* 364–369.

Brackbill, Y., McManus, K., & Woodward, L. (1985). *Medication in maternity: Infant exposure and maternal information.* Ann Arbor: University of Michigan Press.

Bradekamp, S. (1996). Early childhood education. In J. P. Sikula (Ed.), *Handbook of research on teacher education* (2nd ed., pp. 323–347). New York: Macmillan.

Bradekamp, S., & Copple, C. (Eds.). (1997). *Developmentally appropriate practice in early childhood programs* (rev. ed.). Washington, DC: NAEYC.

Bradley, C. R. (1998). Child rearing in African American families: A study of the disciplinary practices of African American parents. *Journal of Multicultural Counseling and Development, 26,* 273–281.

Bradstreet, A. (1981). In J. R. McElrath & A. P. Robb (Eds.), *The complete works of Anne Bradstreet.* Boston: Twayne.

Brambati, B., & Tului, L. (1998). Prenatal genetic diagnosis through chorionic villus sampling. In A. Milunsky (Ed.), *Genetic disorders and the fetus* (4th ed., pp. 150–178). Baltimore: Johns Hopkins University Press.

Braun, S. (1996). New experiments underscore warnings on maternal drinking. *Science, 273,* 738–739.

Braun, S. J., & Edwards, E. P. (1972). *History and theory of early childhood education.* Worthington, OH: Jones.

Brazelton, T. B., & Cramer, B. G. (1990). *The earliest relationship: Parents, infants, and the drama of early attachment.* Reading, MA: Addison-Wesley.

Brazelton, T. B., Koslowski, B., & Tronick, E. (1976). Neonatal behavior among urban Zambians and Americans. *Journal of the American Academy of Child Psychiatry, 15,* 97–107.

Brazelton, T. B., & Nugent, J. K. (1995). *Neonatal behavioral assessment scale.* London: Mac-Keith.

Brazelton, T. B., Tronick, E., Lechtig, A., Lasky, R. E., & Klein, R. E. (1977). The behavior of nutritionally deprived Guatemalan infants.

Developmental Medicine and Child Neurology, 19, 364–372.

Bretherton, I. (1992). Attachment and bonding. In V. B. Van Hasselt & M. Hersen (Eds.), *Handbook of social development* (pp. 133–155). New York: Plenum.

Breuer, J., & Freud, S. (1957). *Studies on hysteria.* New York: Basic Books. (Original work published 1895)

Bridges, L. J., & Grolnick, W. S. (1995). The development of self-regulation in infancy and early childhood. In N. Eisenberg (Ed.), *Social development* (pp. 185–211). Thousand Oaks, CA: Sage.

Brislin, R. (1997). *Understanding culture's influence on behavior.* Ft. Worth, TX: Harcourt Brace.

Britton, G. A. (1998). A review of women and tobacco: Have we come such a long way? *Journal of Obstetric, Gynecologic, and Neonatal Nursing, 27*, 241–249.

Bronfenbrenner, U. (1977). Toward an experimental ecology of human development. *American Psychologist, 32*, 513–531.

Bronfenbrenner, U. (1979). *The ecology of human development: Experiments by nature and design.* Cambridge, MA: Harvard University Press.

Bronfenbrenner, U. (1995). Developmental ecology through space and time: A future perspective. In P. Moen, G. H. Elder, & K. Luscher (Eds.), *Examining lives in context: Perspectives on the ecology of human development* (pp. 619–647). Washington, DC: American Psychological Association.

Bronson, G. W. (1994). Infants' transitions toward adult-like scanning. *Child Development, 65*, 1243–1261.

Brott, A. A., & Ash, J. (1998). *The expectant father: Facts, tips, and advice for dads-to-be.* New York: Abbeville.

Brown, A. M. (1990). Development of visual sensitivity to light and color vision in human infants: A critical review. *Vision Research, 30*, 1159–1188.

Brown, R., & Fraser, C. (1963). The acquisition of syntax. In C. N. Cofer & B. S. Musgrave (Eds.), *Verbal behavior and learning: Problems and processes* (pp. 158–209). New York: McGraw-Hill.

Brush, S. G. (1976). Fact and fantasy in the history of science. In M. H. Marx & F. E. Goodson (Eds.), *Theories in contemporary psychology* (2nd ed.). New York: Macmillan.

Burack, J. A., Zigler, E. F., & Hodapp, R. M. (Eds.). (1998). *Handbook of mental retardation and development.* Cambridge: Cambridge University Press.

Burchinal, M. R., Follmer, A., & Bryant, D. M. (1996). The relations of maternal social support and family structure with maternal responsiveness and child outcomes among African American families. *Developmental Psychology, 32*, 1073–1083.

Burk, M. E., Wieser, P. C., & Keegan, L. (1995). Cultural beliefs and health behaviors of Mexican-American women: Implications for primary care. *Advances in Nursing Science, 14*(4), 37–52.

Bushnell, I. W. R. (1998). The origins of face perception. In F. Simion & G. Butterworth (Eds.), *The development of sensory, motor and cognitive capacities in early infancy: From perception to cognition* (pp. 69–86). Hove, England: Psychology Press.

Butler, D. (1998). *Babies need books: Sharing the joys of books with your child from birth to six.* Oxford: Heinemann.

Butterworth, G. (1992). Origins of self-perception in infancy. *Psychological Inquiry, 3*, 103–111.

Byrne, J. M., & Horowitz, F. D. (1981). Rocking as a soothing intervention: The influence of direction and type of movement. *Infant Behavior and Development, 4*, 207–218.

Caffey, J. (1972). On the theory and practice of shaking infants: Its potential residual effects of permanent brain damage and mental retardation. *American Journal of Diseases of Children, 124*, 161–169.

Caine, J. (1991). The effects of music on the selected stress behaviors, weight, caloric and formula intake, and length of hospital stay of premature and low birth weight neonates in a newborn intensive care unit. *Journal of Music Therapy, 28*, 180–192.

Campbell, D. (1997). *The Mozart Effect: Tapping the power of music to heal the body, strengthen the mind, and unlock the creative spirit.* New York: Avon.

Campenni, C. E. (1999). Gender stereotyping of children's toys: A comparison of parents and nonparents. *Sex Roles, 40,* 121–138.

Campos, J. J., Kermoian, R., & Whitherington, D. (1996). An epigenetic perspective on emotional development. In R. D. Kavanaugh & B. Zimmerberg (Eds.), *Emotion: Interdisciplinary perspectives* (pp. 119–138). Mahwah, NJ: Erlbaum.

Campos, R. G. (1989). Soothing pain-elicited distress in infants with swaddling and pacifiers. *Child Development, 60,* 781–792.

Campos, R. G. (1994). Rocking and pacifiers: Two comforting interventions for heelstick pain. *Research in Nursing and Health, 17,* 321–331.

Canfield, R. L., Smith, E. G., Brezsnyak, M. P., & Snow, K. L. (1997). Information processing through the first year of life. *Monographs of the Society for Research in Child Development, 62*(2, Serial No. 250).

Caplan, T. (1993). *The first twelve months of life* (rev. ed.). New York: Perigee.

Cappa, S. F. (1999). The neurological foundations of language. In G. Denes & L. Pizzamiglio (Eds.), *Handbook of psychology and experimental neuropsychology* (pp. 155–179). Hove, England: Psychology Press.

Carey, W. B. (1992). "Colic" or primary excessive crying in young infants. In M. D. Levine, W. B. Carey, & A. C. Crocker (Eds.), *Developmental-behavioral pediatrics* (2nd ed., pp. 350–353). Philadelphia: Saunders.

Carlson, B. M. (1998). *Human embryology and developmental biology* (2nd ed.). St. Louis: Mosby.

Carroll, D. W. (1999). *Psychology of language* (3rd ed.). Belmont, CA: Wadsworth.

Caruso, D. A. (1996). Maternal employment status, mother–infant interaction, and infant development in day care and non-day care groups. *Child and Youth Care Forum, 25,* 125–134.

Carver, L. J., & Bauer, P. J. (1999). When the event is more than the sum of its parts: 9-month-olds' long-term ordered recall. *Memory, 7,* 147–174.

Cassidy, J., & Shaver, P. R. (Eds.). (1999). *Handbook of attachment: Theory, research, and clinical applications.* New York: Guilford.

Caulfield, R. (1994). Infants' sensory abilities: Caregiving implications and recommendations. *Day Care & Early Education, 21*(4), 31–35.

Caulfield, R. (1995). Reciprocity between infants and caregivers during the first year of life. *Early Childhood Education Journal, 23,* 3–8.

Caulfield, R. (1996a). Physical and cognitive development in the first 2 years. *Early Childhood Education Journal, 23,* 239–242.

Caulfield, R. (1996b). Social and emotional development in the first 2 years. *Early Childhood Education Journal, 24,* 55–58.

Caulfield, R. (1996c). Partnership with families. *Early Childhood Education Journal, 24,* 125–128.

Caulfield, R. (1997). Professionalism in early care and education. *Early Childhood Education Journal, 24,* 261–263.

Cernoch, J. M., & Porter, R. H. (1985). Recognition of maternal axillary odors by infants. *Child Development, 56,* 1593–1598.

Chabon, I. (1966). *Awake and aware.* New York: Delacorte.

Chapman, M. (1988). *Constructive evolution: Origins and development of Piaget's thought.* New York: Cambridge University Press.

Charlesworth, W. R. (1992). Darwin and developmental psychology: Past and present. *Developmental Psychology, 28,* 5–16.

Chase-Lansdale, P. L., Brooks-Gunn, J., & Zamsky, E. S. (1994). Young African-American multigenerational families in poverty: Quality of mothering and grandmothering. *Child Development, 65,* 373–393.

Chase-Lansdale, P. L., & Owen, M. T. (1987). Maternal employment in a family context: Effect on infant–mother and infant–father attachments. *Child Development, 58,* 1505–1512.

Cheal, D. (1993). Unity and difference in postmodern families. *Journal of Family Issues, 14,* 5–19.

Cherlin, A. J. (1998). On the flexibility of fatherhood. In A. Booth & A. C. Crouter (Eds.), *Men in families: When do they get involved? What difference does it make?* (pp. 41–46). Mahwah, NJ: Erlbaum.

Chess, S., Thomas, A., & Birch, H. (1959). Characteristics of the individual child's behavioral responses to the environment. *American Journal of Orthopsychiatry, 29,* 791–802.

Chez, B. F. (1997). Electronic fetal monitoring then and now. *Journal of Perinatal and Neonatal Nursing, 10,* 1–4.

Children's Defense Fund. (1999). *The state of America's children.* Washington, DC: Author.

Chiron, C., Jambaque, I., Nabbout, R., Lounes, R., Syrota, A., & Dulac, O. (1997). The right brain hemisphere is dominant in human infants. *Brain, 120,* 1057–1065.

Chomsky, N. (1957). *Syntactic structures.* The Hague: Mouton.

Chomsky, N. (1965). *Aspects of the theory of syntax.* Cambridge, MA: MIT Press.

Chomsky, N. (1968). *Language and mind.* New York: Harcourt Brace & World.

Chomsky, N. (1999). On the nature, use, and acquisition of language. In W. C. Ritchie & T. K. Bhatia (Eds.), *Handbook of child language acquisition* (pp. 33–54). San Diego: Academic Press.

Clarke-Stewart, K. A. (1989). Infant day care: Maligned or malignant? *American Psychologist, 44,* 266–273.

Clarke-Stewart, K. A., Gruber, C. P., & Fitzgerald, L. M. (1994). *Children at home and in day care.* Hillsdale, NJ: Erlbaum.

Clarkson, M. G., Clifton, R. K., Swain, I. U., & Perris, E. E. (1989). Stimulus duration and repetition rate influence newborns' head orientation toward sound. *Developmental Psychobiology, 22,* 683–705.

Clayman, C. B. (Ed.). (1989). *The American Medical Association encyclopedia of medicine.* New York: Random House.

Cohen, M. R., & Nagel, E. (1934). *An introduction to logic and scientific method.* New York: Harcourt, Brace.

Cohen, S. (Ed.). (1974). *Education in the United States: A documentary history* (Vol. 4). New York: Random House.

Cohn, J. F., Campbell, S. B., Matias, R., & Hopkins, J. (1990). Face-to-face interactions of postpartum depressed and nondepressed mother-infant pairs at 2 months. *Developmental Psychology, 26,* 15–23.

Cole, M. (1999). Culture in development. In M. H. Bornstein & M. E. Lamb (Eds.), *Developmental psychology: An advanced textbook* (4th ed., pp. 73–123). Mahwah, NJ: Erlbaum.

Coles, C. D., Platzman, K. A., Smith, I., James, M. E., & Falek, A. (1992). Effects of cocaine and alcohol use in pregnancy on neonatal growth and neurobehavioral status. *Neurotoxicology and Teratology, 14,* 23–33.

Colin, V. L. (1996). *Human attachment.* New York: McGraw-Hill.

Cone-Wesson, B., & Ramirez, G. M. (1997). Hearing sensitivity in newborns estimated from ABRS to bone-conducted sounds. *Journal of the American Academy of Audiology, 8,* 299–307.

Conel, J. L. (1939–1967). *The postnatal development of the human cerebral cortex* (Vols. 1–8). Cambridge, MA: Harvard University Press.

Consumer Product Safety Commission. (1999, April 8). *News from CPSC.* Washington, DC: Author.

Conway, E. E. (1998). Nonaccidental head injury in infants: "The shaken baby syndrome revisited." *Pediatric Annals, 27,* 677–690.

Coolbear, J., & Benoit, D. (1999). Failure to thrive: Risk for clinical disturbance of attachment? *Infant Mental Health Journal, 20,* 87–104.

Coontz, S. (1988). *The social origins of private life: A history of American families 1600–1900.* London: Verso.

Cooper, R. P. (1993). The effects of prosody in young infants' speech perception. In C. Rovee-Collier & L. P. Lipsitt (Eds.), *Advances in infancy research* (Vol. 8, pp. 137–167). Norwood, NJ: Ablex.

Cooper, R. P., Abraham, J., Berman, S., & Staska, M. (1997). The development of infants' preference for motherese. *Infant Behavior and Development, 20,* 477–488.

Cooper, R. P., & Aslin, R. N. (1990). Preference for infant-directed speech in the first month after birth. *Child Development, 61,* 1584–1595.

Cooper, R. P., & Aslin, R. N. (1994). Developmental differences in infant attention to the spectral properties of infant-directed speech. *Child Development, 65,* 1163–1677.

Cornell, E. H., & McDonnell, P. M. (1986). Infants' acuity at twenty feet. *Investigative Opthalmalogy and Visual Science, 27,* 1417–1420.

Cosminsky, S., Mhloyi, M., & Ewbank, D. (1993). Child feeding practices in a rural area of Zimbabwe. *Social Science and Medicine, 36,* 937–947.

Cotton, P. (1990). Sudden infant death syndrome: Another hypothesis offered but doubts remain. *Journal of the American Medical Association, 263,* 2865, 2869.

Courage, M. L., & Adams, R. J. (1997). Visual acuity in extremely low birth weight infants. *Journal of Developmental and Behavioral Pediatrics, 18,* 4–12.

Courage, M. L., Adams, R. J., Reyno, S., & Kwa, P. (1994). Visual acuity in infants and children with Down syndrome. *Developmental Medicine and Child Neurology, 36,* 586–593.

Crain, W. C. (1999). *Theories of development: Concepts and applications* (4th ed.). Upper Saddle River, NJ: Prentice-Hall.

Crook, C. K. (1978). Taste perception in the newborn infant. *Infant Behavior and Development, 1,* 52–69.

Cuisinier, M., Janssen, H., de Graauw, K., & Hoogduin, K. (1998). Predictors of maternal reactions to excessive crying of newborns. *Early Development and Parenting, 7,* 41–50.

Cunningham, F. G., MacDonald, P. C., Gant, N. F., Leveno, K. J., & Gilstrap, L. C. (1993). *Williams obstetrics* (19th ed.). Norwalk, CT: Appleton & Lange.

Curtis, G. B. (1997). *Your pregnancy: Questions & answers* (rev. ed.). Tucson, AZ: Fisher.

Darwin, C. (1859). *On the origins of species.* Cambridge, MA: Harvard University Press.

Darwin, C. (1971). *A biographical sketch of an infant.* London: Spastics International Medical Publications. (Original work published 1877)

Davis-Floyd, R. E. (1992). *Birth as an American rite of passage.* Berkeley: University of California Press.

Dawson, W. R. (1929). *The custom of couvade.* Manchester: Manchester University Press.

DeCasper, A. J., & Fifer, W. P. (1980). Of human bonding: Newborns prefer their mothers' voices. *Science, 208,* 1174–1176.

DeCasper, A. J., & Prescott, P. A. (1984). Human newborns' perception of male voices: Preference, discrimination, and reinforcing value. *Developmental Psychobiology, 17,* 481–491.

DeCasper, A. J., & Sigafoos, A. D. (1983). The intrauterine heatbeat: A potent reinforcer for newborns. *Infant Behavior and Development, 6,* 19–25.

DeCasper, A. J., & Spence, M. J. (1986). Prenatal maternal speech influences newborns' perception of speech sounds. *Infant Behavior and Development, 9,* 133–150.

Dejin-Karlsson, E., Hanson, B. S., Ostergen, P. O., Sjoberg, N. O., & Marsal, K. (1998). Does passive smoking in early pregnancy increase risk for small-for-gestational age infants? *American Journal of Public Health, 88,* 1523–1527.

de Michelena, M. I., Burstein, E., Lama, J. R., & Vasquez, J. C. (1993). Paternal age as a risk factor for Down syndrome. *American Journal of Medical Genetics, 45,* 679–682.

Demos, J. (1970). *A little commonwealth: Family life in Plymouth colony.* New York: Oxford University Press.

Demos, J. (1986). *Past, present, and personal: The family and the life course in American history.* New York: Oxford University Press.

Dennis, W. (1973). *Children of the Creche.* New York: Appleton-Century-Crofts.

Dennis, W., & Dennis, M. G. (1940). The effect of cradling practices upon the onset of walking in Hopi children. *Journal of Genetic Psychology, 56,* 77–86.

deMause, L. (1974). The evolution of childhood. In L. deMause (Ed.), *The history of childhood* (pp. 1–73). New York: Harper & Row.

de Villiers, P. A., & de Villiers, J. G. (1992). Language development. In M. H. Bornstein & M. E. Lamb (Eds.), *Developmental psychology: An advanced textbook* (3rd ed., pp. 337–418). Hillsdale, NJ: Erlbaum.

deVries, M. W. (1984). Temperament and infant mortality among the Masai of east

Africa. *American Journal of Psychiatry, 141,* 1189–1194.

Diamond, A. (1988). Abilities and neural mechanisms underlying AB performance. *Child Development, 59,* 523–527.

Dick-Read, G. (1953). *Childbirth without fear: The principles and practices of natural childbirth* (rev. ed.). New York: Harper. (Original work published 1944)

DiPietro, J. A., & Porges, S. W. (1991). Relations between neonatal states and 8-month developmental outcome in preterm infants. *Infant Behavior and Development, 14,* 441–450.

Dixon, S. (1992). *The Roman family.* Baltimore: Johns Hopkins University Press.

Doi, T. (1973). *The anatomy of dependence.* Tokyo: Kodansha.

Dollaghan, C. (1985). Child meets word: "Fast mapping" in preschool children. *Journal of Speech and Hearing Research, 28,* 449–454.

Dore, F. Y., & Dumas, C. (1987). Psychology of animal cognition: Piagetian studies. *Psychological Bulletin, 102,* 219–233.

Doyle, J. A., & Paludi, M. A. (1997). *Sex and gender: The human experience* (4th ed.). New York: McGraw-Hill.

Dubofsky, M. (1996). *Industrialism and the American worker, 1865–1920* (3rd ed.). Arlington Heights, IL: Davidson.

Duhaime, A. C., Christian, C. W., Rorke, L. B., & Zimmerman, R. A. (1998). Nonaccidental head injury in infants—The "shaken baby syndrome." *New England Journal of Medicine, 338,* 872–875.

Dunham, P., & Dunham, F. (1992). Lexical development during middle infancy: A mutually driven infant-caregiver process. *Developmental Psychology, 28,* 414–420.

Dunham, P. J., Dunham, F., & Curwin, A. (1993). Joint-attentional states and lexical acquisition at 18 months. *Developmental Psychology, 29,* 827–831.

Dunn, J. (1977). *Distress and comfort.* Cambridge, MA: Harvard University Press.

Dunn, J. (1992). Sisters and brothers: Current issues in developmental research. In F. Boer & J. Dunn (Eds.), *Children's sibling relationships: Developmental and clinical issues* (pp. 1–17). Hillsdale, NJ: Erlbaum.

Dunn, J. (1995). *From one child to two: What to expect, how to cope, and how to enjoy your growing family.* New York: Fawcett.

Dwyer, T., Ponsonby, A., & Couper, D. (1999). Tobacco smoke exposure at one month of age and subsequent risk of SIDS—A prospective study. *American Journal of Epidemiology, 149,* 593–602.

Eberlein, T. (1993, June). The 10 worst discipline mistakes parents make (and how to avoid them). *Redbook,* p. 172.

Edelson, E. (1999). *Gregor Mendel, and the roots of genetics.* Oxford: Oxford University Press.

Eden, A. N. (1992). Let's potty. *American Baby, 54*(1), 52.

Egeland, B., & Hiester, M. (1995). The long-term consequences of infant day-care and mother-infant attachment. *Child Development, 66,* 474–485.

Eimas, P. D. (1994). Categorization in early infancy and the continuity of development. *Cognition, 50,* 83–93.

Eimas, P. D., Sigueland, E. R., Jusczyk, P., & Vigorito, J. (1971). Speech perception in infants. *Science, 171,* 303–306.

Eisenberg, A., Murkoff, H. E., & Hathaway, S. E. (1996a). *What to expect the first year.* New York: Workman.

Eisenberg, A., Murkoff, H. E., & Hathaway, S. E. (1996b). *What to expect the toddler years.* New York: Workman.

Eisenberg, N., Fabes, R. A., Carlo, G., Troyer, D., Speer, A. L., Karbon, M., & Switzer, G. (1992). The relations of maternal practices and characteristics to children's vicarious emotional responsiveness. *Child Development, 63,* 583–602.

Eisenberg, N., Fabes, R. A., Schaller, M., Carlo, G., & Miller, P. A. (1991). The relations of parental characteristics and practices to children's vicarious emotional responding. *Child Development, 62,* 1393–1408.

Eitzen, D. S., & Zinn, M. B. (1989). *The reshaping of America: Social consequences of the changing economy.* Englewood Cliffs, NJ: Prentice-Hall.

Ekman, P., & Friesen, W. V. (1972). Constants across cultures in the face and emotion. *Journal of Personality and Social Psychology, 17,* 124–129.

Elias, M. (1995, May 16). More older moms likely to have healthy babies. *USA Today*, p. D1.

Elicker, J., Englund, M., & Sroufe, L. A. (1992). Predicting peer competence and peer relationships in children from early parent–child relationships. In R. D. Parke & G. W. Ladd (Eds.), *Family–peer relationships: Modes of linkage* (pp. 77–106). Hillsdale, NJ: Erlbaum.

Elkind, D. (1988). *The hurried child: Growing up too fast too soon* (rev. ed.). Reading, MA: Addison-Wesley.

Elkind, D. (1998). *Reinventing childhood: Raising and educating children in a changing world.* Rosemont, NJ: Modern Learning Press.

Elwood, R. W., & Mason, C. (1994). The couvade and the onset of paternal care: A biological perspective. *Ethology and Sociobiology, 15*, 145–156.

Emde, R. N., & Robinson, J. (1979). The first two months: Recent research in developmental psychobiology and the changing views of the newborn. In J. Noshpitz (Ed.), *Basic handbook of child psychiatry* (Vol. 1, pp. 72–105). New York: Basic Books.

Emerson, C. N. (1999). Postpartum major depression: Detection and treatment. *American Family Physician, 59*, 2247–2254.

Erikson, E. H. (1950). *Childhood and society.* New York: Norton.

Erikson, E. H. (1968). *Identity: Youth and crisis.* New York: Norton.

Erneling, C. E. (1993). *Understanding language acquisition: The framework of learning.* Albany: State University of New York Press.

Eyer, D. E. (1993). *Maternal–infant bonding: A scientific fiction.* New Haven: Yale University Press.

Fagot, B. I. (1995). Psychosocial and cognitive determinants of early gender-role development. *Annual Review of Sex Research, 6*, 1–31.

Fagot, B. I. (1997). Attachment, parenting, and peer interactions of toddler children. *Developmental Psychology, 33*, 489–499.

Fagot, B. I., & Leinbach, M. D. (1993). Gender-role development in young children: From discrimination to labeling. *Developmental Review, 13*, 205–224.

Fagot, B. I., Leinbach, M. D., & O'Boyle, C. (1992). Gender labeling, gender stereotyping, and parenting behaviors. *Developmental Psychology, 28*, 225–230.

Fantz, R. L. (1963). Pattern vision in newborn infants. *Science, 140*, 296–297.

Fantz, R. L., Fagan, J. F., & Miranda, S. B. (1975). Early visual selectivity. In L. B. Cohen & P. Salapatek (Eds.), *Infant perception: From sensation to cognition* (Vol. 1, pp. 249–345). New York: Academic Press.

Farley, R., & Bianchi, S. (1991). The growing racial differences in marriage and family patterns. In R. Staples (Ed.), *The black family* (pp. 5–22). Belmont, CA: Wadsworth.

Faude, J. A., Jones, C. W., & Robins, M. (1996). The affective life of infants: Empirical and theoretical foundations. In D. L. Nathanson (Ed.), *Knowing feeling: Affect, script, and psychotherapy* (pp. 219–256). New York: Norton.

Feldman, R., Greenbaum, C. W., & Yirmiya, N. (1999). Mother–infant affect synchrony as an antecedent of the emergence of self-control. *Developmental Psychology, 35*, 223–231.

Fenton, J. C. (1925). *A practical psychology of babyhood: The mental development and mental hygiene of the first year of life.* Boston: Houghton Mifflin.

Fergusson, D. M., Horwood, L. J., & Lynskey, M. T. (1993). Maternal smoking before and after pregnancy: Effects on behavioral outcomes in middle childhood. *Pediatrics, 92*, 815–822.

Fernald, A. (1989). Intonation and communicative intent in mothers' speech to infants: Is melody the message? *Child Development, 60*, 1497–1510.

Fernald, A. (1993). Approval and disapproval: Infant responsiveness to vocal affect in familiar and unfamiliar languages. *Child Development, 64*, 657–674.

Fernald, A., & Kuhl, P. (1987). Acoustic determinants of infant preference for motherese speech. *Infant Behavior and Development, 10*, 279–293.

Fernald, A., & Mazzie, C. (1991). Prosody and focus in speech to infants and adults. *Developmental Psychology, 27*, 209–221.

Fernald, A., & McRoberts, G. (1996). Prosodic bootstrapping: A critical analysis of the argument and the evidence. In J. L. Morgan & K. Demuth (Eds.), *Signal to syntax: Bootstrapping from speech to grammar in early acquisition* (pp. 365–388). Mahwah, NJ: Erlbaum.

Fernald, A., & Morikawa, H. (1993). Common themes and cultural variations in Japanese and American mothers' speech to infants. *Child Development, 64,* 637–656.

Field, T. (Ed.). (1995). *Touch in early development.* Hillsdale, NJ: Erlbaum.

Field, T., Gerwitz, J. L., Cohen, D., Garcia, R., Greenberg, R., & Collins, K. (1984). Leavetaking and reunions of infants, toddlers, preschoolers, and their parents. *Child Development, 55,* 628–635.

Field, T. M., Schanberg, S. M., Scafidi, F., Bauer, C. R., Vega-Lahr, N., Garcia, R., Nystrom, J., & Kuhn, C. M. (1986). Tactile/ kinesthetic stimulation effects on preterm neonates. *Pediatrics, 77,* 654–658.

Fischer, K. W., & Bidell, T. R. (1998). Dynamic development of psychological structures in action and thought. In R. M. Lerner (Ed.), *Handbook of child psychology: Theoretical models of human development* (Vol. 1, 5th ed., pp. 467–562). New York: Wiley.

Fischer, K. W., & Rose, S. P. (1996). Dynamic growth cycles of brain and cognitive development. In R. W. Thatcher & G. R. Lyon (Eds.), *Developmental neuroimaging: Mapping the development of brain and behavior* (pp. 263–279). New York: Academic Press.

Flavell, J. H., Miller, P. H., & Miller, S. A. (1993). *Cognitive development* (3rd ed.). Englewood Cliffs, NJ: Prentice-Hall.

Flavell, J. H. (1963). *The developmental psychology of Jean Piaget.* Princeton, NJ: Van Nostrand.

Fletcher, J., Page, M., & Jeffrey, H. E. (1998). Sleep states and neonatal pulse oximetry. *Sleep, 21,* 305.

Fogel, A. (1979). Peer vs. mother directed behavior in 1- to 3-month-old infants. *Infant Behavior and Development, 2,* 215–226.

Fomon, S. J. (1993). *Nutrition of normal infants.* St. Louis: Mosby.

Fox, N. A., Kimmerly, N. L., & Schafer, W. D. (1991). Attachment to mother/attachment to father: A meta-analysis. *Child Development, 62,* 210–225.

Fracasso, M. P., & Busch-Rossnagel, N. A. (1994). Parents and children of Hispanic origin. In M. E. Procidano & C. B. Fisher (Eds.), *Contemporary families: A handbook for school professionals* (pp. 83–98). New York: Teachers College Press.

Francis, P. L., Self, P. A., & Horowitz, F. D. (1987). The behavioral assessment of the neonate: An overview. In J. D. Osofsky (Ed.), *Handbook of infant development* (2nd ed., pp. 723–779). New York: Wiley.

Franco, V. H. M., Hotta, J. K. S., Jorge, S. M., & dos Santos, J. E. (1999). Plasma fatty acids in children with grade III protein-energy malnutrition in its different clinical forms: Marasmus, marasmic kwashiorkor, and kwashiokor. *Journal of Tropical Pediatrics, 45,* 71–75.

Frankel, K. A., & Bates, J. E. (1990). Mother–toddler problem-solving: Antecedents in attachment, home behavior, and temperament. *Child Development, 61,* 810–819.

Frazer, J. G. (1910). *Totemism and exogamy: A treatise on certain forms of superstition and society* (Vol. 1). London: Macmillan.

Freeseman, L. J., Colombo, J., & Coldren, J. T. (1993). Individual differences in infant visual attention. *Child Development, 64,* 1191–1203.

Freud, S. (1920). *A general introduction to psychoanalysis.* New York: Boni & Liveright.

Freud, S. (1950). *The interpretation of dreams.* New York: Random House. (Original work published 1900)

Freud, S. (1953). Three essays on the theory of sexuality. In J. Strachey (Ed.), *The standard edition of the complete psychological works of Sigmund Freud* (Vol. 7, pp. 135–243). London: Hogarth Press. (Original work published 1905)

Freud, S. (1957). Five lectures on psycho-analysis. In J. Strachey (Ed.), *The standard edition of the complete psychological works of Sigmund Freud* (Vol. 11, pp. 7–55). London: Hogarth Press. (Original work published 1910)

Freud, S. (1957). Thoughts for the times on war and death. In J. Strachey (Ed.), *The standard edition of the complete psychological works of Sigmund Freud* (Vol. 14, pp. 275–300).

London: Hogarth Press. (Original work published 1915)

Freud, S. (1959). An autobiographical study. In J. Strachey (Ed.), *The standard edition of the complete psychological works of Sigmund Freud* (Vol. 20, pp. 7–70). London: Hogarth Press. (Original work published 1925)

Freud, S. (1961). The ego and the id. In J. Strachey (Ed.), *The standard edition of the complete psychological works of Sigmund Freud* (Vol. 19, pp. 13–66). London: Hogarth Press. (Original work published 1923)

Freud, S. (1964). New introductory lectures on psycho-analysis. In J. Strachey (Ed.), *The standard edition of the complete psychological works of Sigmund Freud* (Vol. 22, pp. 7–182). London: Hogarth Press. (Original work published 1933)

Fried, P. A., Watkinson, B., & Siegel, L. S. (1997). Reading and language in 9- to 12-year olds prenatally exposed to cigarettes and marijuana. *Neurotoxicology and Teratology, 19,* 171–183.

Friedman, E. A. (1987). *Labor and delivery: Impact on offspring.* St. Louis: Mosby.

Friedman, L. J. (1999). *Identity's architect: An authorized biography of Erik Erikson.* New York: Simon & Schuster.

Furuno, S., O'Reilly, K. A., Hosaka, C. M., Inatsuka, T. T., Allman, T. L., & Zeisloft, B. (1994). *Hawaii early learning profile* (rev. ed.). Palo Alto, CA: VORT.

Galinsky, E., & Friedman, D. F. (1993). *Education before school: Investing in quality child care.* New York: Scholastic.

Galler, J. R. (1984). Behavioral consequences of malnutrition in early life. In J. R. Galler (Ed.), *Nutrition and behavior* (Vol. 5, pp. 63–117). New York: Plenum.

Galler, J. R., & Ramsey, F. (1989). A follow-up study of the influence of early malnutrition on development: Behavior at home and at school. *Journal of the American Academy of Child and Adolescent Psychiatry, 28,* 254–261.

Garcia-Coll, C. T. (1990). Developmental outcome of minority infants: A process-oriented look into our beginnings. *Child Development, 61,* 270–289.

Garcia-Coll, C. T., Meyer, E. C., & Brillon, L. (1995). Ethnic and minority parenting. In

M. H. Bornstein (Ed.), *Handbook of parenting* (Vol. 2, pp. 189–209). Mahwah, NJ: Erlbaum.

Gardiner, H. W., Mutter, J. D., Kosmitzki, C. (1998). *Lives across cultures: Cross-cultural human development.* Boston: Allyn & Bacon.

Gardner, H. (1995). The development of competence in culturally defined domains: A preliminary framework. In N. R. Goldberger & J. Bennet (Eds.), *The culture and psychology reader* (pp. 222–244). New York: New York University Press.

Gardner, R. J. M., & Sutherland, G. R. (1996). *Chromosomal abnormalities and genetic counseling* (2nd ed.). New York: Oxford University Press.

Garvey, C. (1990). *Play* (2nd ed.). Cambridge, MA: Harvard University Press.

Gesell, A. (1925). *The mental growth of the preschool child: A psychological outline of normal development from birth to the sixth year.* New York: Macmillan.

Gesell, A. (1934). *An atlas of infant behavior: A systematic delineation of the forms and early growth of human behavior patterns* (Vols. 1–2). New Haven, CT: Yale University Press.

Gesell, A. (1940). *The first five years of life: A guide to the study of the preschool child.* New York: Harper & Row.

Gesell, A., & Thompson, H. (1938). *The psychology of early growth.* New York: Macmillan.

Gestwicki, C. (1998). *Developmentally appropriate practice: Curriculum and development in early education.* Albany, NY: Delmar.

Gibson, E. J., & Walk, R. D. (1960). The "visual cliff." *Scientific American, 202,* 64–71.

Gibson, I. (1978). *The English vice: Beating, sex, and shame in Victorian England and after.* London: Duckworth.

Gies, F., & Gies, J. (1987). *Marriage and the family in the Middle Ages.* New York: Harper & Row.

Gies, F., & Gies, J. (1990). *Life in a medieval village.* New York: Harper & Row.

Gill, M. (1959). The present state of psychoanalytic theory. *Journal of Abnormal and Social Psychology, 58,* 1–8.

Gleason, H. A. (1955). *An introduction to descriptive linguistics.* New York: Holt.

Glenn, E. N., & Yap, S. G. H. (1994). Chinese American families. In R. L. Taylor (Eds.), *Minority families in the United States: A multi-cultural perspective* (pp. 115–145). Belmont, CA: Wadsworth.

Glover, V. (1997). Maternal stress or anxiety in pregnancy and emotional development of the child. *British Journal of Psychiatry, 17,* 105–106.

Godwin, A., & Schrag, L. (1996). *Setting up for infant/toddler care: Guidelines for centers and family child care homes* (rev. ed.). Washington, DC: NAEYC.

Golab, C. (1977). The impact of the industrial experience on the immigrant family: The huddled masses reconsidered. In R. L. Ehrlich (Ed.), *Immigrants in industrial America, 1850–1920* (pp. 1–32). Charlottesville: University of Virginia Press.

Goldberg, S. (1983). Parent–infant bonding: Another look. *Child Development, 54,* 1355–1382.

Goldberg, W. A., & Easterbrooks, M. A. (1984). Role of marital quality in toddler development. *Developmental Psychology, 20,* 504–514.

Goldfarb, W. (1945). Effects of psychological deprivation in infancy and subsequent stimulation. *American Journal of Psychiatry, 102,* 18–33.

Goldfield, B. A., & Reznick, J. S. (1990). Early lexical acquisition: Rate, content, and the vocabulary spurt. *Journal of Child Language, 17,* 171–183.

Golinkoff, R. M. (1983). The preverbal negotiation of failed messages: Insights into the transition period. In R. M. Golinkoff (Ed.), *The transition from prelinguistic to linguistic communication* (pp. 57–78). Hillsdale, NJ: Erlbaum.

Golinkoff, R. M. (1986). "I beg your pardon?": The preverbal negotiation of failed messages. *Journal of Child Language, 13,* 455–476.

Golinkoff, R. M., Hirsh-Pasek, K., Bailey, L. M., & Wenger, N. R. (1992). Young children and adults use lexical principles to learn new nouns. *Developmental Psychology, 28,* 99–108.

Golinkoff, R. M., Hirsh-Pasek, K., Cauley, K. M., & Gordon, L. (1987). The eyes have it: Lexical and syntactic comprehension in a new paradigm. *Journal of Child Language, 14,* 23–45.

Gonzalez-Mena, J., & Eyer, D. W. (1993). *Infants, toddlers, and caregivers* (3rd ed.). Mountain View, CA: Mayfield.

Goode, E. E. (1994, January 10). The secret world of siblings. *U.S. News & World Report, 116,* 45–50.

Googins, B. K. (1991). *Work/family conflicts: Private lives, public responses.* New York: Auburn House.

Goossens, F. A., & van Ijzendoorn, M. H. (1990). Quality of infants' attachment to professional caregivers: Relation to infant–parent attachment and day-care characteristics. *Child Development, 61,* 832–837.

Gopnik, A. (1996). The post-Piaget era. *Psychological Science, 7,* 221–225.

Gordon, T. (1970). *Parent effectiveness training: The "no-lose" program for raising responsible children.* New York: Wyden.

Gordon, T. (1989). *Teaching children self-discipline.* New York: Times Books.

Gottlieb, B. (1993). *The family in the western world from the Black Death to the Industrial Age.* New York: Oxford University Press.

Gouge, W. (1976) *Of domesticall duties.* Amsterdam: Theatrum Orbis Terrarum. (Original work published 1622)

Gould, J. L., & Keeton, W. T. (1996). *Biological science* (6th ed.). New York: Norton.

Gralinski, J. H., & Kopp, C. B. (1993). Everyday rules for behavior: Mothers' requests to young children. *Developmental Psychology, 29,* 573–584.

Grantham-McGregor, S. M., & Back, E. H. (1971). Gross motor development in Jamaican infants. *Developmental Medicine and Child Neurology, 13,* 79–87.

Gray, M. R., & Steinberg, L. (1999). Unpacking authoritative parenting: Reassessing a multi-dimensional construct. *Journal of Marriage and the Family, 61,* 574–587.

Green, J. A., & Gustafson, G. E. (1997). Perspectives on an ecological approach to social communicative development in infancy. In C. Dent-Reed & P. Zukow-Goldring (Eds.), *Evolving explanations of development: Ecological approaches to organism-environment systems* (pp. 515–546). Washington, DC: American Psychological Association.

Green, M. (1989). *Theories of human development: A comparative approach.* Englewood Cliffs, NJ: Prentice-Hall.

Greenspan, S. I. (1997). *The growth of the mind.* Reading, MA: Addison-Wesley.

Greenspan, S. I., & Wieder, S. (1998). *The child with special needs: Encouraging intellectual and emotional growth.* Reading, MA: Addison Wesley Longman.

Greeno, J. G. (1989). A perspective on thinking. *American Psychologist, 44,* 134–141.

Greenough, W. T. (1991). Experience as a component of normal development: Evolutionary considerations. *Developmental Psychology, 27,* 14–17.

Greven, P. J. (1977). *The Protestant temperament: Patterns of child-rearing, religious experience, and the self in early America.* New York: Knopf.

Grieser, D. L., & Kuhl, P. K. (1988). Maternal speech to infants in a tonal language: Support for universal prosodic features in motherese. *Developmental Psychology, 24,* 14–20.

Groos, K. (1901). *The play of man.* New York:

Gruenberg, S. M. (1920). *Your child: Today and tomorrow.* Philadelphia: Lippincott.

Grusec, J. E. (1992). Social learning theory and developmental psychology: The legacies of Robert Sears and Albert Bandura. *Developmental Psychology, 28,* 776–786.

Guntheroth, W., & Spiers, P. (1997). The apnea/SIDS debate. *Pediatrics, 99,* 924.

Gustafson, G. E., & Harris, K. L. (1990). Women's responses to young infants' cries. *Developmental Psychology, 26,* 144–152.

Gutman, H. B. (1976). *The black family in slavery and freedom, 1750–1925.* New York: Pantheon.

Guyer, B., MacDormant, M. F., Martin, J. A., Peters, K. D., & Strobino, D. M. (1998). Annual summary of vital statistics—1997. *Pediatrics, 102,* 1333–1349.

Haight, W., & Miller, P. J. (1992). The development of everyday pretend play: A longitudinal study of mothers' participation. *Merrill-Palmer Quarterly, 38,* 331–349.

Haines, D. (1999). *Neuroanatomy: An atlas of structures, sections, and systems* (5th ed.). Philadelphia: Lippincott Williams & Wilkins.

Hainline, L., & Abramov, I. (1992). Assessing visual development: Is infant vision good enough. In C. Rovee-Collier & L. P. Lipsitt (Eds.), *Advances in infancy research* (Vol. 7, pp. 39–102). Norwood, NJ: Ablex.

Haith, M. M. (1993). The formation of expectations in early infancy. *Advances in Infancy Research, 8,* 251–297.

Haith, M. M., & Benson, J. B. (1998). Infant cognition. In D. Kuhn & Siegler, R. S. (Eds.), *Handbook of child psychology: Cognition, perception, and language* (Vol. 2, 5th ed., pp. 199–254). New York: Wiley.

Haith, M. M., Bergman, T., & Moore, M. J. (1977). Eye contact and face scanning in early infancy. *Science, 198,* 853–855.

Hale, C. B. (1990, April). *Infant mortality: An American tradegy* (No. 18). Washington, DC: Population Reference Bureau.

Hale, J. (1994). *The civilization of Europe in the Renaissance.* New York: Atheneum.

Hall, G. S. (1891). Notes on the study of infants. *Pedagogical Seminary, 1,* 127–138.

Halliday, J. L., Watson, L. F., Lumley, J., Danks, D. M., & Sheffield, L. S. (1995). New estimates of Down syndrome risks at chorionic villus sampling, amniocentesis, and live birth in women of advanced maternal age from a uniquely defined population. *Prenatal Diagnosis, 15,* 455–465.

Hanawalt, B. A. (1988). *The ties that bound: Peasant families in medieval England.* New York: Oxford University Press.

Hanlon, R. E., Lux, W. E., & Dromerick, A. W. (1999). Global aphasia without hemiparesis: Language profiles and lesion distribution. *Journal of Neurology, Neurosurgery and Psychiatry, 66,* 365–369.

Harding, C. (1984). Acting with intention: A framework for examining the development of the intention to communicate. In L. Feagans, C. Garvey, & R. Golinkoff (Eds.), *The origins and growth of communication* (pp. 123–135). Norwood, NJ: Ablex.

Harkness, S., & Super, C. M. (1985). Child–environment interactions in the socialization of affect. In M. Lewis & C. Saarni

(Eds.), *The socialization of emotions* (pp. 21–36). New York: Plenum.

Harlow, H. F. (1958). The nature of love. *American Psychologist, 13,* 673–685.

Harlow, H. F. (1959). Love in infant monkeys. *Scientific American, 200*(6), 68–74.

Harlow, H. F., & Harlow, M. K. (1962). Social deprivation in monkeys. *Scientific American, 207*(5), 136–146.

Harlow, H. F., & Harlow, M. K. (1965). The affectional systems. In A. M. Schrier, H. F. Harlow, & F. Stollnitz (Eds.), *Behavior of nonhuman primates: Modern research trends* (Vol. 2, pp. 287–334). New York: Academic Press.

Harlow, H. F., & Harlow, M. K. (1966). Learning to love. *American Scientist, 54,* 244–272.

Harlow, H. F., & Zimmerman, R. R. (1959). Affectional responses in the infant monkey. *Science, 130,* 421–432.

Harris, J. R. (1998). *The nurture assumption: Why children turn out the way they do.* New York: Free Press.

Harrison, L. (1991). Food, nutrition and growth in Aboriginal communities. In J. Reid & P. Trompf (Eds.), *The health of Aboriginal Australia* (pp. 151–172). Sydney: Harcourt Brace Jovanovich.

Harrison, M. R. (1996). Fetal surgery. *American Journal of Obstetrics and Gynecology, 174,* 1255–1264.

Hartl, D. L., & Jones, E. W. (1998). *Essential genetics* (2nd ed.). Boston: Jones & Bartlett.

Hartmann, D. P., & George, T. P. (1999). Design, measurement, and analysis in developmental research. In M. H. Bornstein & M. E. Lamb (Eds.), *Developmental psychology: An advanced textbook* (4th ed., pp. 125–195). Mahwah, NJ: Erlbaum.

Hartshorn, K., Rovee-Collier, C., Gerhardstein, P., Bhatt, R. S., Wondoloski, T. L., Klein, P., Gilch, J., Wurtzel, N., & Carvalho, M. C. de. (1998). The ontogeny of long-term memory over the first year-and-a-half of life. *Developmental Psychobiology, 32,* 69–89.

Harwood, R. L., Miller, J. G., & Irizarry, N. L. (1994). *Culture and attachment: Perceptions of the child in context.* New York: Guilford.

Harwood, R. L., Schoelmerich, A., Schulze, P. A., & Gonzales, Z. (1999). Cultural differences in maternal beliefs and behaviors: A study of middle-class Anglo and Puerto Rican mother-infant pairs in four everyday situations. *Child Development, 70,* 1005–1016.

Hassold, T., Sherman, S., & Hunt, P. A. (1995). The origin of trisomy in humans. In C. J. Epstein, T. Hassold, I. T. Lott, L. Nadel, & D. Patterson (Eds.), *Etiology and pathogenesis of Down syndrome* (pp. 1–12). New York: Wiley.

Haustein, K. O. (1999). Cigarette smoking, nicotine, and pregnancy. *International Journal of Clinial Pharmacology and Therapeutics, 37,* 417–427.

Hayne, H., Rovee-Collier, C., & Perris, E. E. (1987). Categorization and memory retrieval by three-month-olds. *Child Development, 58,* 750–767.

Hebb, D. O. (1960). The American revolution. *American Psychologist, 15,* 735–745.

Heinowitz, J. (1995). *Pregnant fathers: Entering parenthood together.* San Diego: Parents as Partners Press.

Heller, S. (1997). *The vital touch: How intimate contact with your baby leads to happier, healthier development.* New York: Holt.

Hetherington, S. E. (1990). A controlled study of the effect of prepared childbirth classes on obstetric outcomes. *Birth, 17,* 86–90.

Hoffreth, S. L., Brayfield, A., Deich, S., & Holcomb, P. (1991). *National child care survey, 1990.* Washington, DC: Urban Institute Press.

Hofsten, C. von. (1989). Motor development as the development of systems: Comments on the special section. *Developmental Psychology, 25,* 950–953.

Holbrook, M. C. (Ed.). (1996). *Children with visual impairments: A parent's guide.* Bethesda, MD: Woodbine House.

Holida, D. L. (1993). Latex balloons: They can take your breath away. *Pediatric Nursing, 19,* 39–43, 68.

Holt, L. E. (1957). *The Good Housekeeping book of baby and child care.* New York: Popular Library.

Hopkins, B. (1991). Facilitating early motor development: An intracultural study of West Indian mothers and their infants living in Britain. In J. K. Nugent, B. M. Lester, & T. B. Brazelton (Eds.), *The cultural context of infancy* (Vol. 2, pp. 93–143). Norwood, NJ: Ablex.

Hopkins, B., & Ronnqvist, L. (1998). Human handedness: Developmental and evolutionary perspectives. In F. Simion & G. Butterworth (Eds.), *The development of sensory, motor and cognitive capacities in early infancy: From perception to cognition* (pp. 191–236). Hove, England: Psychology Press.

Hopkins, B., & Westra, T. (1988). Maternal handling and motor development: An intracultural study. *Genetic, Social, and General Psychology Monographs, 114,* 377–408.

Hopkins, B., & Westra, T. (1990). Motor development, maternal expectations, and the role of handling. *Infant Behavior and Development, 13,* 117–122.

Horchler, J. N., & Morris, R. R. (1997). *The SIDS survival guide: Information and comfort for grieving family and friends and professionals who seek to help them.* Cheverly, OH: SIDS Educational Services.

Howes, C. (1998). The earliest friendships. In W. M. Bukowshi, A. F. Newcomb, & W. W. Hartup (Eds.), *The company they keep: Friendship in childhood and adolescence* (pp. 66–86). New York: Cambridge University Press.

Howes, C., Hamilton, C. E., & Matheson, C. C. (1994). Children's relationships with peers: Differential associations with aspects of the teacher–child relationship. *Child Development, 65,* 253–263.

Hsu, L. Y. F. (1998). Prenatal diagnosis of chromosomal abnormalities through amniocentesis. In A. Milunsky (Ed.), *Genetic disorders and the fetus* (4th ed., pp. 179–248). Baltimore: Johns Hopkins University Press.

Hughes, F. P. (1995). *Children, play, and development* (2nd ed.). Boston: Allyn & Bacon.

Hutt, S. J., Hutt, C., Lenard, H. G., Bernuth, H. V., & Muntjewerff, W. J. (1968). Auditory responsivity in the human neonate. *Nature, 218,* 888–890.

Huttenlocher, P. R. (1994). Synaptogenesis in human cerebral cortex. In G. Dawson & K. W. Fischer (Eds.), *Human behavior and the developing brain* (pp. 137–152). New York: Guilford.

Infante-Rivard, C., Gautrin, D., Malo, J. L., & Suissa, S. (1999). Maternal smoking and childhood asthma. *American Journal of Epidemiology, 150,* 528–531.

Isabella, R. A. (1993). Origins of attachment: Maternal interactive behavior across the first year. *Child Development, 64,* 605–621.

Jacklin, C. N. (1989). Female and male: Issues of gender. *American Psychologist, 44,* 127–133.

Jackson, J. F. (1993). Multiple caregiving among African Americans and infant attachment: The need for an emic approach. *Human Development, 36,* 87–102.

Jacobsen, T., Edelstein, W., & Hofmann, W. (1994). A longitudinal study of the relation between representations of attachment in childhood and cognitive functioning in childhood and adolescence. *Developmental Psychology, 30,* 112–124.

Jacobson, J. W., & Mulick, J. A. (Eds.). (1996). *Manual of diagnosis and professional practice in mental retardation.* Washington, DC: American Psychological Association.

Jacobson, T., Huss, M., Fendrich, M., Kruesi, M. J. P., & Ziegenhain, U. (1997). Children's ability to delay gratification: Longitudinal relations to mother–child attachment. *Journal of Genetic Psychology, 158,* 411–426.

James, W. (1950). *The principles of psychology* (Vol. 1). New York: Dover. (Original work published 1890)

Jankowiak, W. (1992). Father–child relations in urban China. In B. S. Hewlett (Ed.), *Father–child relations: Cultural and biosocial contexts* (pp. 345–363). New York: Gruyter.

Jenkins, M. R., & Culbertson, J. L. (1996). Prenatal exposure to alcohol. In R. L. Adams, O. A. Parsons, J. L. Culbertson, & S. J. Nixon (Eds.), *Neuropsychology for clinical practice: Etiology, assessment, and treatment* (pp. 409–452). Washington, DC: American Psychological Association.

Jones, S. S. (1996). Imitation or exploration? Young infants matching of adults' oral gestures. *Child Development, 67,* 1952–1969.

Jordan, B. (1993). *Birth in four cultures* (4th ed.). Prospect Heights, IL: Waveland.

Jordan, H. E., & Kindred, J. E. (1932). *A textbook of embryology.* New York: Appleton.

Jusczyk, P. W. (1995). Language acquisition: Speech sounds and the beginning of phonology. In J. L. Miller & P. D. Eimas (Eds.),

Speech, language, and communication (pp. 263–301). San Diego: Academic Press.

Kagan, J. (1989). Temperamental contributions to social behavior. *American Psychologist, 44,* 668–674.

Kagan, J. (1992). Behavior, biology, and the meanings of temperamental constructs. *Pediatrics, 90,* 510–513.

Kagan, J., Kearsley, R. B., & Zelazo, P. R. (1978). *Infancy: Its place in development.* Cambridge, MA: Harvard University Press.

Kagan, J., & Klein, R. E. (1973). Cross-cultural perspectives on early development. *American Psychologist, 28,* 947–961.

Kagan, J., & Moss, H. A. (1962). *Birth to maturity: A study of psychological development.* New York: Wiley.

Kagan, J., Reznick, J. S., & Snidman, N. (1999). Biological basis of shyness. In A. Slater & D. Muir (Eds.), *The Blackwell reader in developmental psychology* (pp. 65–78). Malden, MA: Blackwell.

Kagan, J., & Snidman, N. (1991). Temperamental factors in human development. *American Psychologist, 46,* 856–862.

Kaitz, M., Lapidot, P., Bronner, R., & Eidelman, A. I. (1992). Parturient woman can recognize their infants by touch. *Developmental Psychology, 28,* 35–39.

Kaler, S. R., & Kopp, C. B. (1990). Compliance and comprehension in very young toddlers. *Child Development, 61,* 1997–2003.

Kallio, M. J. T., Salmenpera, L., Siimes, M. A., Perheentupa, J., & Miettinen, T. A. (1992). Exclusive breast-feeding and weaning: Effect on serum cholesterol and lipoprotein concentrations in infants during the first year of life. *Pediatrics, 89,* 663–666.

Kantrowitz, B., Wingert, P., & Hager, M. (1988, May 16). Preemies. *Newsweek, 111,* 62–70.

Kaplan, H., & Dove, H. (1987). Infant development among the Ache of eastern Paraguay. *Developmental Psychology, 23,* 190–198.

Kaplan, P. S., Goldstein, M. H., Huckeby, E. R., & Cooper, R. P. (1995). Habituation, sensitization, and infants' responses to motherese speech. *Developmental Psychology, 28,* 45–57.

Karen, R. (1998). *Becoming attached.* New York: Oxford University Press.

Karmel, M. (1959). *Thank you, Dr. Lamaze: A mother's experience in painless childbirth.* Philadelphia: Lippincott.

Karmiloff-Smith, A. (1992). *Beyond modularity: A developmental perspective on cognitive science.* Cambridge, MA: MIT Press.

Karraker, K. H., Vogel, D. A., & Lake, M. A. (1995). Parents' gender-stereotyped perceptions of newborns: The eye of the beholder revisited. *Sex Roles, 33,* 687–701.

Kataria, S., Frutiger, A. D., Lanford, B., & Swanson, M. S. (1988). Anterior fontanel closure in healthy term infants. *Infant Behavior and Development, 11,* 229–333.

Katzez, A. R., & Bragdon, N. H. (1990). *Childcare solutions: A guide for parents.* New York: Avon.

Kaye, K. (1982). *The mental and social life of babies: How parents create persons.* Chicago: University of Chicago Press.

Kaye, K., & Wells, A. J. (1980). Mothers' jiggling and the burst-pause pattern in neonatal feeding. *Infant Behavior and Development, 3,* 29–46.

Keesing, R. M. (1981). Theories of culture. In R. W. Casson (Ed.), *Language, culture, and cognition: Anthropological perspectives* (pp. 42–66). New York: Macmillan.

Kelsey, K. (1993). Failure to thrive. In S. W. Ekvall (Ed.), *Pediatric nutrition in chronic diseases and developmental disorders: Prevention, assessment, and treatment* (pp. 183–188). New York: Oxford University Press.

Kennell, J., Klaus, M., McGrath, S., Robertson, S., & Hinkley, C. (1991). Continuous emotional support during labor in a US hospital: A randomized controlled trial. *Journal of the American Medical Association, 265,* 2197–2201.

Kessler, D. B., & Dawson, P. (Eds.). (1999). *Failure to thrive and pediatric undernutrition: A transdisciplinary approach.* Baltimore: Brookes.

Kiernan, L. (1995, July 16). Fertility advances give birth to dilemmas. *Chicago Tribune,* pp. C1.

Kitano, K. J., & Kitano, H. H. L. (1998). The Japanese-American family. In C. H. Mindel, R. W. Habenstein, & R. Wright (Eds.), *Ethnic families in America: Patterns and variations* (4th ed., pp. 311–330). Upper Saddle River, NJ: Prentice-Hall.

Kitzinger, S. (1996). *The complete book of pregnancy and childbirth* (2nd ed.). New York: Knopf.

Kitzinger, S. (1998). *Breastfeeding your baby*. New York: Knopf.

Klahr, D. (1992). Information-processing approaches to cognitive development. In M. H. Bornstein & M. E. Lamb (Eds.), *Developmental psychology: An advanced textbook* (3rd ed., pp. 273–335). Hillsdale, NJ: Erlbaum.

Klahr, D., & MacWhinney, B. (1998). Information processing. In D. Kuhn & R. S. Siegler (Eds.), *Handbook of child psychology: Cognition, perception, and language* (Vol. 2, 5th ed., pp. 631–678). New York: Wiley.

Klaus, M. H., & Kennell, J. H. (1976). *Maternal–infant bonding: The impact of early separation or loss on family development*. St. Louis: Mosby.

Klaus, M. H., & Kennell, J. H., Plumb, N., & Zuehlke, S. (1970). Human maternal behavior at the first contact with her young. *Pediatrics, 46*, 187–192.

Klein, H. (1991). Couvade syndrome: Male counterpart to pregnancy. *International Journal of Psychiatry in Medicine, 21*, 57–69.

Klein, A. H., & Ganon, J. A. (1998). *Caring for your premature baby: A complete resource for parents*. New York: HarperCollins.

Kliewer, C. (1998). *Schooling children with Down syndrome: Toward an understanding of possibility*. New York: Teachers College Press.

Klopfer, P. H. (1971). Mother love: What turns it on? *American Scientist, 59*, 404–407.

Knox, D., & Schacht, C. (1997). *Choices in relationships: An introduction to marriage and the family* (5th ed.). Belmont, CA: Wadsworth.

Koch, R. K. (1999). Issues in newborn screening for phenylketonuria. *American Family Physician, 60*, 1462–1466.

Kochanska, G. (1993). Toward a synthesis of parental socialization and child temperament in early development of conscience. *Child Development, 64*, 325–347.

Kolb, B., & Winshaw, I. Q. (1995). *Fundamentals of human neuropsychology* (4th ed.). New York: Freeman.

Konner, M. (1976). Maternal care, infant behavior and development among the !Kung. In R. B. Lee & I. DeVore (Eds.), *Kalahari hunters-gatherers: Studies of the !Kung San and their neighbors* (pp. 218–245). Cambridge, MA: Harvard University Press.

Konner, M. (1977). Infancy among the Kalahari Desert San. In P. H. Leiderman, S. R. Tulkin, & A. Rosenfeld (Eds.), *Culture and infancy: Variations in the human experience* (pp. 287–328). New York: Academic Press.

Koop, C. E. (1997, Spring/Summer). The tiniest patients: Fetal and pediatric surgery can save babies who once didn't have a chance. *Newsweek, 129*, 51.

Kopera-Frye, K., Olson, H. C., & Streissguth, A. P. (1997). Teratogenic effects of alcohol on attention. In J. A. Burack (Ed.), *Attention, development, and psychopathology* (pp. 171–204). New York: Guilford.

Kopp, C. B. (1982). Antecedents of self-regulation: A developmental perspective. *Developmental Psychology, 18*, 199–214.

Kopp, C. B. (1989). Regulation of distress and negative emotions: A developmental view. *Developmental Psychology, 25*, 343–354.

Korbin, J. E. (1994). Sociocultural factors in child maltreatment. In G. B. Melton & F. D. Barry (Eds.), *Protecting children from abuse and neglect: Foundations for a new strategy* (pp. 182–223). New York: Guilford.

Korner, A. F. (1974). The effect of the infant's state, level of arousal, sex, and ontogenetic stage of the caregiver. In M. Lewis & L. A. Rosenblum (Eds.), *The effect of the infant on its caregiver* (pp. 105–121). New York: Wiley.

Kotelchuck, M. (1995). Reducing infant mortality and improving birth outcomes for families of poverty. In H. E. Fitzgerald, B. M. Lester, & B. Zuckerman (Eds.), *Children of poverty: Research, health, and policy issues* (pp. 151–166). New York: Garland.

Kozma, C., & Stock, J. S. (1993). What is mental retardation? In R. Smith (Ed.), *Children with mental retardation: A parent's guide* (pp. 1–49). Rockville, MD: Woodbine House.

LaFuente, M. J., Grifol, R., Segarra, J., Soriano, J., Gorba, M. A., & Montesinos, A. (1997). Effects of the Firstart method of prenatal stimulation on psychomotor development: The first six months. *Pre- and Peri-Natal Psychology Journal, 11*, 151–162.

La Greca, A. M., & Prinstein, M. J. (1999). Peer group. In W. K. Silverman & T. H. Ollendick (Eds.), *Developmental issues in the clinical treatment of children* (pp. 171–198). Boston: Allyn & Bacon.

Lamaze, F. (1970). *Painless birth: Psychoprophylactic method.* Chicago: Contemporary Books. (Original work published 1956)

Lamb, M. E. (1997). The development of father–infant relationships. In M. E. Lamb (Ed.), *The role of the father in child development* (3rd ed., pp. 104–120). New York: Wiley.

Lamb, M. E. (1998). Fatherhood then and now. In A. Booth & A. C. Crouter (Eds.), *Men in families: When do they get involved? What difference does it make?* (pp. 47–52). Mahwah, NJ: Erlbaum.

Lamb, M. E., Leyendecker, B., Scholmerich, A., & Francasso, M. P. (1998). Everyday experiences of infants in Euro-American and Central American immigrant families. In M. Lewis & C. Feiring (Eds.), *Families, risk, and competence* (pp. 113–131). Mahwah, NJ: Erlbaum.

Lamb, M. E., & Malkin, C. M. (1986). The development of social expectations in distress-relief sequences: A longitudinal study. *International Journal of Behavioral Development, 9,* 235–249.

Lamb, M. E., Morrison, D. C., & Malkin, C. M. (1987). The development of infant social expectations in face-to-face interaction: A longitudinal study. *Merrill-Palmer Quarterly, 33,* 241–254.

Lamborn, S. D., Dornbusch, S. M., & Steinberg, L. (1996). Ethnicity and community context as moderators of the relations between family decision making and adolescent adjustment. *Child Development, 67,* 283–301.

Lampl, M., Veldhuis, J. D., & Johnson, M. L. (1992). Saltation and stasis: A model of human growth. *Science, 258,* 801–803.

Lancon, J. A., Haines, D. E., & Parent, A. D. (1998). Anatomy of the shaken baby syndrome. *Anatomical Record, 253,* 13–18.

Landis, S. E., & Earp, J. A. (1987). Sick care options: What do working mothers prefer? *Women and Health, 12*(1), 61–77.

Landry, S. H., Chapieski, M. L., Richardson, M. A., Palmer, J., & Hall, S. (1990). The so-cial competence of children born prematurely: Effects of medical complications and parent behaviors. *Child Development, 61,* 1605–1616.

Lash, J. P. (1980). *Helen and teacher: The story of Helen Keller and Anne Sullivan Macy.* New York: Delacorte.

Lawrence, R. A. (1998). *Breastfeeding: A guide for the medical profession* (5th ed.). St. Louis: Mosby.

Leach, P. (1997). *Your baby & child from birth to age five* (3rd ed.). New York: Knopf.

Leboyer, F. (1975). *Birth without violence.* New York: Knopf.

Lee, K. (1994). The crying pattern of Korean infants and related factors. *Developmental Medicine and Child Neurology, 36,* 601–607.

Lee, Y. T. (1993). Perceived homogeneity and familial loyalty between Chinese and Americans. *Current Psychology, 12,* 260–267.

Lenneberg, E. H. (1964). *New directions in the study of language.* Cambridge, MA: MIT Press.

Lenneberg, E. H. (1969). On explaining language. *Science, 164,* 635–643.

Lester, B. M., Boukydis, C. F. Z., Garcia-Coll, C. T., Hole, W. T., & Peucker, M. (1992). Infantile colic: Acoustic cry characteristics, maternal perception of cry, and temperament. *Infant Behavior and Development, 15,* 15–26.

Lester, B. M., & Zeskind, P. S. (1982). A biobehavioral perspective on crying in early infancy. In H. E. Fitzgerald, B. M. Lester, & M. W. Yogman (Eds.), *Theory and research in behavioral pediatrics* (Vol. 1, pp. 133–180). New York: Plenum.

LeVine, R. A. (1988). Human parental care: Universal goals, cultural strategies, individual behavior. In R. A. LeVine, P. M. Miller, & M. M. West (Eds.), *Parental behavior in diverse societies* (pp. 3–11). San Francisco: Jossey-Bass.

LeVine, R. A., Dixon, S., LeVine, S., Richman, A., Leiderman, P. H., Keefer, C. H., & Brazelton, T. B. (1994). *Child care and culture: Lessons from Africa.* Cambridge: Cambridge University Press.

LeVine, R. A., & LeVine, S. (1988). Parental strategies among the Gusii of Kenya. In R. A. LeVine, P. M. Miller, & M. M. West (Eds.),

Parental behavior in diverse societies (pp. 27–35). San Francisco: Jossey-Bass.

Levitt, A. G. (1993). The acquisition of prosody: Evidence from French- and English-learning infants. In B. de Boysson-Bardies & S. de Schonene (Eds.), *Developmental neurocognition: Speech and face processing in the first year of life* (pp. 385–398). Dordrecht, Netherlands: Kluwer.

Lewis, M. (1977). The busy, purposeful world of a baby. *Psychology Today, 10*(9), 53–56.

Lewis, M. (1991). Self-knowledge and social influence. In M. Lewis & S. Feinman (Eds.), *Social influence and socialization* in infancy (pp. 111–134). New York: Plenum.

Lewkowicz, D. J. (1994). Development of intersensory perception in human infants. In D. J. Lewkowicz & R. Lickliter (Eds.), *The development of intersensory perception: Comparative perspectives* (pp. 165–203). Hillsdale, NJ: Erlbaum.

Li, L., & Ballweg, J. A. (1995). Unsanctioned births in China. *Sociological Focus, 28,* 129–146.

Lieven, E. V., Pine, J. M., & Baldwin, G. (1997). Lexically-based learning and early grammatical development. *Journal of Child Language,* 24, 187–219.

Lipsitt, L. P. (1990). Learning and memory in infants. *Merrill-Palmer Quarterly, 36,* 53–66.

Litt, I. F. (1997). *Taking our pulse: The health of America's women.* Stanford, CA: Stanford University Press.

Littman, M. S. (Ed.). (1998). *A statistical portrait of the United States.* Lanham, SD: Bernan.

Locke, J. (1894). *An essay concerning human understanding.* Oxford: Clarendon. (Original work published 1690)

Locke, J. (1958). *Essays on the law of nature* (2nd ed.). Oxford: Clarendon.

Loesch, D. Z., Hopper, J. L., Rogucka, E., & Huggins, R. M. (1995). Timing and genetic rapport between growth in skeletal maturity and height around puberty: Similarities and differences between girls and boys. *American Journal of Human Genetics, 56,* 753–759.

Lofland, L. H. (1986). When others die. *Generations, 10*(4), 59–61.

Longfellow, H. W. (1886). In S. Longfellow (Ed.), *Life of Henry Wadsworth Longfellow: With extracts from his journals and correspondence* (Vol. 2). Boston: Ticknor.

Longstreth, L. E. (1981). Revisiting Skeels' final study: A critique. *Developmental Psychology, 17,* 620–625.

Lonner, W. J., & Malpass, R. (Eds.). (1994). *Psychology and culture.* Boston: Allyn & Bacon.

Lorenz, K. (1965). *Evolution and modification of behavior.* Chicago: University of Chicago Press.

Lorenz, K. Z. (1981). *The foundations of ethology.* New York: Springer-Verlag.

Lowenbraun, S., & Thompson, M. D. (1990). Hearing impairments. In N. G. Haring & L. McCormick (Eds.), *Exceptional children and youth: An introduction to special education* (5th ed., pp. 365–401). Columbus, OH: Merrill.

Lowrey, G. H. (1986). *Growth and development of children* (8th ed.). Chicago: Year Book Medical Publishers.

Luke, B., & Keith, L. G. (1992). *Principles and practice of maternal nutrition.* New York: Parthenon.

Lund-Adams, M., & Heywood, P. (1995). Breastfeeding in Australia. In A. P. Simopoulos, J. E. Dutra de Oliveira, & I. D. Desai (Eds.), *Behavioral and metabolic aspects of breastfeeding: International trends* (pp. 74–113). Basel: Karger.

Maccoby, E. E. (1990). Gender and relationships: A developmental account. *American Psychologist, 45,* 513–520.

Maccoby, E. E., & Martin, J. A. (1983). Socialization in the context of the family: Parent-child interaction. In P. H. Mussen (Ed.), *Handbook of child psychology* (Vol. 4, pp. 1–101). New York: Wiley.

MacDonald, K. (1992). Warmth as a developmental construct: An evolutionary analysis. *Child Development, 63,* 753–773.

Mackner, L. M., Starr, R. H., & Black, M. M. (1997). The cumulative effect of neglect and failure to thrive on cognitive functioning. *Child Abuse and Neglect, 21,* 691–700.

Mahler, M. S. (1968). *On human symbiosis and the vicissitudes of individuation.* New York: International Universities Press.

Mahler, M. S., Pine, F., & Bergman, A. (1975). *The psychological birth of the human infant.* New York: Basic Books.

Main, M., & Heese, E. (1990). Parents' unresolved traumatic experiences are related to infant disorganized attachment status: Is frightened and/or frightening parental behavior the linking mechanism? In M. T. Greenberg, D. Ciccetti, & E. M. Cummings (Eds.), *Attachment in the preschool years: Theory, research, and intervention* (pp. 161–182). Chicago: University of Chicago Press.

Makin, J., Fried, P. A., & Watkinson, B. (1991). A comparison of active and passive smoking during pregnancy: Long-term effects. *Neurotoxicology and Teratology, 13,* 5–12.

Makin, J. W., & Porter, R. H. (1989). Attractiveness of lactating females' breast odors to neonates. *Child Development, 60,* 803–810.

Malnory, M. (1993). Electronic fetal monitoring. In B. K. Rothman (Ed.), *Encyclopedia of childbearing: Critical perspectives* (pp. 120–121). Phoenix, AZ: Oryx.

Manary, M. J., Broadhead, R. L., & Yarasheski, K. E. (1998). Whole-body protein kinetics in marasmus and kwashiorkor during acute infection. *American Journal of Clinical Nutrition, 67,* 1205–1209.

Mander, R. (1998). *Pain in childbearing and its control.* Oxford: Blackwell.

Mandler, J. M. (1998). Representation. In D. Kuhn & R. S. Siegler (Eds.), *Handbook of child psychology: Cognition, perception, and language* (Vol. 2, 5th ed., pp. 255–308). New York: Wiley.

Mange, E. J., & Mange, A. P. (1998). *Basic human genetics* (2nd ed.). Sunderland, MA: Sinauer.

Manginello, F. P., & DiGeronimo, T. F. (1998). *Your premature baby: Everything you need to know about childbirth, treatment, and parenting* (2nd ed.). New York: Wiley.

Marcus, G. F. (1995). Children's overregularization of English plurals: A quantitative analysis. *Journal of Child Language, 22,* 447–459.

Marcus, G. F., Pinker, S., Ullman, M., Hollander, M., Rosen, T. J., & Xu, F. (1992). Overregularization in language acquisition.

Monographs of the Society for Research in Child Development, 57(4, Serial No. 228).

Marion, M. (1998). *Guidance of young children* (5th ed.). Upper Saddle River, NJ: Prentice-Hall.

Marotz, L. R., Rush, J. M., & Cross, M. Z. (1998). Health, safety, and nutrition for the young child (4th ed.). Albany, NY: Delmar.

Marsh, D. T. (1992). *Families and mental retardation: New directions in professional practice.* Westport, CT: Greenwood.

Martin, A. (1881). *Atlas of obstetrics and gynaecology* (2nd ed.). Philadelphia: Presley Blakiston.

Martin, G. B., & Clark, R. D. (1982). Distress crying in neonates: Species and peer specificity. *Developmental Psychology, 18,* 3–9.

Masur, E. F. (1997). Maternal labelling of novel and familiar objects: Implications for children's development of lexical constraints. *Journal of Child Language, 24,* 127–139.

Matas, L., Arend, R. A., & Sroufe, L. A. (1978). Continuity of adaptation in the second year: The relationship between quality of attachment and later competence. *Child Development, 49,* 547–556.

Mather, C. (1911/1957). In W. C. Ford (Ed.), *Diary of Cotton Mather* (Vol. 1). New York: Ungar.

Mayseless, O. (1998). Maternal caregiving strategy: A distinction between the ambivalent and the disorganized profile. *Infant Mental Health Journal, 19,* 20–33.

Maziade, M., Cote, R., Boutin, P., Bernier, H., & Thivierge, J. (1988). Temperament and intellectual development: A longitudinal study from infancy to four years. In S. Chess, A. Thomas, & M. E. Hertzig (Eds.), *Annual progress in child psychiatry and child development* (pp. 335–349). New York: Brunner/Mazel.

McAdoo, H. P. (1998). African-American families. In C. H. Mindel, R. W. Habenstein, & R. Wright (Eds.), *Ethnic families in America: Patterns and variations* (4th ed., pp. 361–381). Upper Saddle River, NJ: Prentice-Hall.

McCarthy, L. F. (1999, December/January). What babies really know inside the womb. *Parenting,* pp. 120–125.

McGraw, M. B. (1935). *Growth: A study of Johnny and Jimmy.* New York: Appleton-Century.

McLaughlin, S. (1998). *Introduction to language development.* San Diego: Singular.

McLean, M. E., Bailey, D. B., & Wolery, M. (1996). *Assessing infants and preschoolers with special needs* (2nd ed.). Upper Saddle River, NJ: Prentice-Hall.

McLeod, P., Plunkett, K., & Rolls, E. T. (1998). *Introduction to connectionist modelling of cognitive processes.* New York: Oxford University Press.

McNeil, D. (1970). *The acquisition of language: The study of developmental psycholinguistics.* New York: Harper & Row.

Mead, M. (1930). *Growing up in New Guinea: A comparative study of primitive education.* New York: Blue Ribbon Books.

Mead, M. (1935). *Sex and temperament in three primitive cultures.* New York: Morrow.

Meltzoff, A. N. (1988a). Infant imitation and memory: Nine-month-olds in immediate and deferred tests. *Child Development, 59,* 217–225.

Meltzoff, A. N. (1988b). Infant imitation after a 1-week delay: Long-term memory for novel acts and multiple stimuli. *Developmental Psychology, 24,* 470–476.

Meltzoff, A. N., & Kuhl, P. K. (1994). Faces and speech: Intermodal processing of biologically relevant signals in infants and adults. In D. J. Lewkowicz & R. Lickliter (Eds.), *The development of intersensory perception: Comparative perspectives* (pp. 335–369). Hillsdale, NJ: Erlbaum.

Meltzoff, A. N., & Moore, M. K. (1977). Imitation of facial and manual gestures by human neonates. *Science, 198,* 75–78.

Meltzoff, A. N., & Moore, M. K. (1979). Interpreting "imitative" responses in early infancy. *Science, 205,* 217–219.

Meltzoff, A. N., & Moore, M. K. (1989). Imitation in newborn infants: Explaining the range of gestures imitated and underlying mechanisms. *Developmental Psychology, 25,* 954–962.

Meltzoff, A. N., & Moore, M. K. (1997). Explaining facial imitation: A theoretical model. *Early Development and Parenting, 6,* 179–192.

Meltzoff, J. (1998). *Critical thinking about research: Psychology and related fields.* Washington, DC: American Psychological Association.

Meyer, E. C., Lester, B. M., Boukydis, C. F. Z., & Bigsby, R. (1998). Family-based intervention with high-risk infants and their families. *Journal of Clinical Psychology in Medical Settings, 5,* 49–69.

Mili, F., Edmonds, L. D., Khoury, M. J., & McClearn, A. B. (1991). Prevalence of birth defects among low-birth-weight infants. *American Journal of Diseases of Children, 145,* 1313–1318.

Miller, F., & Bachrach, S. J. (1998). *Cerebral palsy: A complete guide for caregiving.* Baltimore: Johns Hopkins University Press.

Miller, N. E., & Dollard, J. (1941). *Social learning and imitation.* New Haven, CT: Yale University Press.

Miller, P. H. (1993). *Theories of developmental psychology* (3rd ed.). New York: Freeman.

Miller, S. A. (1998). *Developmental research methods* (2nd ed.). Upper Saddle, NJ: Prentice-Hall.

Miller-Loncar, C. L., Erwin, L. J., Landry, S. H., Smith, K. E., & Swank, P. R. (1998). Characteristics of social support networks of low socioeconomic status African American, Anglo American, and Mexican American mothers of full term and preterm infants. *Journal of Community Psychology, 26,* 131–143.

Miller-Perrin, C. L., & Perrin, R. D. (1999). *Child maltreatment: An introduction.* Thousand Oaks, CA: Sage.

Mintz, S. (1998). From patriarchy to androgyny and other myths: Placing men's family roles in historical perspective. In A. Booth & A. C. Crouter (Eds.), *Men in families: When do they get involved? What difference does it make?* (pp. 3–30). Mahwah, NJ: Erlbaum.

Mintz, S., & Kellogg, S. (1988). *Domestic revolutions: A social history of American family life.* New York: Free Press.

Mitchell, S. A., & Black, M. J. (1995). *Freud and beyond: A history of modern psychoanalytic thought.* New York: Basic Books.

Miyake, K., Campos, J. J., Kagan, J., & Bradshaw, D. L. (1986). Issues on socioemotional development. In H. Stevenson, H. Azuma, &

K. Hakuta (Eds.), *Child development and education in Japan* (pp. 239–261). New York: Freeman.

Miyake, K., Chen, S., & Campos, J. J. (1985). Infant temperament, mother's mode of interaction, and attachment in Japan: An interim report. *Monographs of the Society for Research in Child Development, 50*(1–2, Serial No. 209).

Moen, P., Elder, G. H., & Luscher, K. (Eds.). (1995). *Examining lives in context: Perspectives on the ecology of human development.* Washington, DC: American Psychological Association.

Monk, H. (1996). Obstetric anesthesia abuse: Delivering us from evil. *Pre- and Pari-Natal Pscyhology Journal, 11*, 31–53.

Montessori, M. (1967). *The absorbent mind.* New York: Holt, Rinehart and Winston. (Original work published 1949)

Morelli, G. A., Oppenheim, D., Rogoff, B., & Goldsmith, D. (1992). Cultural variation in infants' sleeping arrangements: Questions of independence. *Developmental Psychology, 28*, 604–613.

Morelli, G. A., & Tronick, E. Z. (1991). Parenting and child development in the Efe foragers and Lese farmers of Zaire. In M. H. Bornstein (Ed.), *Cultural approaches to parenting* (pp. 91–113). Hillsdale, NJ: Erlbaum.

Morelli, G. A., & Tronick, E. Z. (1992). Male care among Efe-foragers and Lese farmers. In B. S. Hewlett (Ed.), *Father–child relations: Cultural and biosocial contexts* (pp. 231–261). New York: Gruyter.

Morgan, B. L. (1990). Nutritional requirements for normative development of the brain and behavior. *Annals of the New York Academy of Sciences, 602*, 127–132.

Morgan, E. S. (1966). *The Puritan family: Religion and domestic relations in seventeenth-century New England* (rev. ed.). New York: Harper & Row.

Morgan, L. H. (1965). *Houses and house-life of the American aborigines.* Chicago: University of Chicago Press. (Original work published 1881)

Morikawa, H., Shand, N., & Kosawa, Y. (1988). Maternal speech to prelingual infants in Japan and the United States: Relationships among functions, forms, and referents. *Journal of Child Language, 15,* 237–256.

Morse, M. B. (1995). What your baby sees, hears, smells, tastes, and feels. *Parents, 70*(6), 60.

Mothander, P. R. (1992). Maternal adjustment during pregnancy and the infant's first year. *Scandinavian Journal of Psychology, 33,* 20–28.

Mowrer, O. H. (1960). *Learning theory and the symbolic processes.* New York: Wiley.

Muckenhoupt, M. (1999). *Sigmund Freud: Explorer of the unconscious.* Oxford: Oxford University Press.

Mume, D. L., Fernald, A., & Herrera, C. (1996). Infants' responses to facial and vocal emotional signals in a social referencing paradigm. *Child Development, 67,* 3219–3237.

Munakata, Y. (1997). Perseverative reaching in infancy: The roles of hidden toys and motor history in the AB task. *Infant Behavior and Development, 20,* 405–416.

Muret-Wagstaff, S., & Moore, S. G. (1989). The Hmong in America: Infant behavior and rearing practices. In J. K. Nugent, B. M. Lester, & T. B. Brazelton (Eds.), *The cultural context of infancy* (Vol. 1, pp. 319–339). Norwood, NJ: Ablex.

Murray, A. D., Dolby, R. M., Nation, R. L., & Thomas, D. B. (1981). Effects of epidural anesthesia on newborns and their mothers. *Child Development, 52,* 71–82.

Naeye, R. L. (1993). Race and infant mortality. *American Journal of Diseases of Children, 147,* 1030–1031.

NAEYC. (1996). NAEYC's code of ethical conduct: Guidelines for responsible behavior in early childhood education. *Young Children, 51*(3), 57–60.

Nakagawa, M., Lamb, M. E., & Miyake, K. (1992). Antecedents and correlates of the Strange Situation behavior in Japanese infants. *Journal of Cross-Cultural Psychology, 23,* 300–310.

Nash, J. M. (1997, February 3). Fertile minds. *Time, 149,* 48–56.

National Center for Health Statistics. (1994). *Advance report of final natality statistics* (Vol. 42). Hyattsville, MD: Author.

National Center for Health Statistics. (1999). *Health people 2000 review, 1998–99.* Hyattsville, MD: Author.

Nelson, K. (1973). Structure and strategy in learning to talk. *Monographs of the Society for Research in Child Development, 38*(1–2, Serial No. 149).

Nelson, K., Rescorla, L., Gruendel, J., & Benedict, H. (1978). Early lexicons: What do they mean? *Child Development, 49,* 960–968.

Newman, J., Rosenbach, J. H., Burns, K. L., Latimer, B. C., Matocha, H. R., & Vogt, E. R. (1995). An experiment test of "The Mozart Effect": Does listening to his music improve spatial ability? *Perceptual and Motor Skills, 81,* 1379–1387.

Nichols, T. L. (1855). *Esoteric anthropology.* New York:

Nielson, L. (1991). Spatial relations in congenitally blind infants: A study. *Journal of Visual Impairment and Blindness, 85,* 11–16.

Nilsson, L., & Hamberger, L. (1990). *A child is born.* New York: Dell.

Ninio, A., & Snow, C. E. (1999). *The development of pragmatics: Learning to use language appropriately.* In W. C. Ritchie & T. K. Bhatia (Eds.), Handbook of child language acquisition (pp. 347–383). San Diego: Academic Press.

Oakley, A., Hickey, D., Rajan, L., & Rigby, A. S. (1996). Social support in pregnancy: Does it have long-term effects? *Journal of Reproductive and Infant Psychology, 14,* 7–22.

Ochs, E., & Schieffelin, B. B. (1984). Language acquisition and socialization: Three developmental stories and their implications. In R. A. Schweder & R. A. LeVine (Eds.), *Culture theory: Essays on mind, self, and emotion* (pp. 276–320). Cambridge: Cambridge University Press.

Ogawa, D. M., & Grant, G. (1978). *Kodomo no tame ni—for the sake of the children: The Japanese American experience in Hawaii.* Honolulu: University of Hawaii Press.

O'Grady, W. (1999). The acquisition of syntactic representations: A general nativist approach. In W. C. Ritchie & T. K. Bhatia (Eds.), *Handbook of child language acquisition* (pp. 157–193). San Diego: Academic Press.

O'Hara, M. W. (1997). The nature of postpartum depressive disorders. In L. Murray, & P. J. Cooper (Eds.), *Postpartum depression and child development* (pp. 3–31). New York: Guilford.

O'Rahilly, R., & Muller, F. (1996). *Human embryology and teratology* (2nd ed.). New York: Wiley.

Out, L., van Soest, A. J., Savelsbergh, G. J. P., & Hopkins, B. (1998). The effect of posture on early reaching movements. *Journal of Motor Behavior, 30,* 260–272.

Owen, M. T., & Cox, M. J. (1997). Marital conflict and the development of infant–parent attachment relationships. *Journal of Family Psychology, 11,* 152–164.

Owst, G. R. (1961). *Literature and pulpit in medieval England.* New York: Barnes & Noble.

Owst, G. R. (1965). *Preaching in medieval England.* New York: Russell & Russell. (Original work published 1926)

Palmer, R. R., & Colton, J. (1995). *A history of the modern world* (8th ed.). New York: Knopf.

Panneton, R. K., & DeCasper, A. J. (1986, April). *Newborn's postnatal preferences for a prenatally experienced melody.* Paper presented at the International Conference on Infant Studies, Los Angeles, CA.

Papousek, M., & Papousek, H. (1996). Infantile persistent crying, state regulation, and interaction with parents: A systems view. In M. H. Borstein & J. L. Genevro (Eds.), *Child development and behavioral pediatrics: Crosscurrents in contemporary psychology* (pp. 11–33). Hillsdale, NJ: Erlbaum.

Park, K. A., & Waters, E. (1989). Security of attachment and preschool friendships. *Child Development, 60,* 1076–1081.

Parke, R. D. (1996). *Fatherhood.* Cambridge, MA: Harvard University Press.

Parkman, E. (1961). The diary of Ebenezer Parkman. *Proceedings of the American Antiquarian Society, 71,* 361–448.

Pegg, J. E., Werker, J. F., & McLeod, P. J. (1992). Preference for infant-directed over adult-directed speech: Evidence from 7-week-old infants. *Infant Behavior and Development, 15,* 325–345.

Phillips, D., McCartney, K., Scarr, S., & Howes, C. (1987). Selective review of infant day care research: A cause for concern! *Zero to Three,* *7*(3), 18–21.

Piaget, J. (1926). *The language and thought of the child.* New York: Harcourt, Brace. (Original work published 1923)

Piaget, J. (1952). *The origins of intelligence in children.* New York: International Universities Press. (Original work published 1936)

Piaget, J. (1952). Jean Piaget. In E. G. Boring, H. S. Langfeld, H. Werner, & R. M. Yerkes (Eds.), *A history of psychology in autobiography* (Vol. 4, pp. 237–256). New York: Russell & Russell.

Piaget, J. (1954). *The construction of reality in the child.* New York: Basic Books. (Original work published 1937)

Piaget, J. (1962). *Play, dreams and imitation in childhood.* New York: Norton. (Original work published 1951)

Piaget, J. (1970). Piaget's theory. In P. H. Mussen (Ed.), *Carmichael's manual of child psychology* (Vol. 1, 3rd ed., pp. 703–732). New York: Wiley.

Piaget, J. (1977). The first year of life of the child. In H. E. Gruber & J. J. Voneche (Eds.), *The essential Piaget* (pp. 198–214). New York: Basic Books. (Original work published in 1927)

Piaget, J., & Inhelder, B. (1969). *The psychology of the child.* New York: Basic Books.

Pierce, G. R., Sarason, B. R., Joseph, H. J., & Henderson, C. A. (1996). Conceptualizing and assessing social support in the context of the family. In G. R. Pierce, B. R. Sarason, & I. G. Sarason (Eds.), *Handbook of social support and the family* (pp. 3–23). New York: Plenum.

Pinker, S. (1999). *How the mind works.* New York: Norton.

Pipes, P. L., & Trahms, C. M. (1993). Nutrient needs of infants and children. In P. L. Pipes & C. M. Trahms (Eds.), *Nutrition in infancy and early childhood* (5th ed., pp. 30–58). St. Louis: Mosby.

Plomin, R. (1989). Environment and genes: Determinants of behavior. *American Psychologist, 44,* 105–111.

Plomin, R. (1995). *Genetics and experience.* Thousand Oaks, CA: Sage.

Plomin, R., & DeFries, J. C. (1985). *Origins of individual differences in infancy.* New York: Academic Press.

Plomin, R., DeFries, J. C., McClearn, G. E., & Rutter, M. (1997). *Behavioral genetics: A primer* (3rd ed.). New York: St. Martin's Press.

Poets, C. F., & Southall, D. P. (1993). Prone sleeping position and sudden infant death. *New England Journal of Medicine, 329,* 425–426.

Poincare, H. (1913). *The foundations of science.* New York: Science Press.

Ponsonby, A., Dwyer, T., Gibbons, L. E., Cochrane, J. A., & Wang, Y. (1993). Factors potentiating the risk of sudden infant death syndrome associated with the prone position. *New England Journal of Medicine, 329,* 377–382.

Porter, R. H., Balogh, R. D., & Makin, J. W. (1988). Olfactory influences on mother–infant interactions. In C. Rovee-Collier & L. P. Lipsitt (Eds.), *Advances in infancy research* (Vol. 5, pp. 39–68). Norwood, NJ: Ablex.

Porter, R. H., Makin, J. W., Davis, L. B., & Christensen, K. M. (1992). Breast-fed infants respond to olfactory cues from their own mothers and unfamiliar lactating females. *Infant Behavior and Development, 15,* 85–93.

Postman, N. (1982). *The disappearance of childhood.* New York: Delacorte.

Poti, P., & Spinozzi, G. (1994). Early sensorimotor development in chimpanzees (Pan troglodytes). *Journal of Comparative Psychology, 108,* 93–103.

Poussaint, A. F. (1986). Introduction. In B. Cosby, *Fatherhood* (pp. 1–11). Garden City, NY: Doubleday.

Premack, D., & Premack, A. J. (1995). Origins of human social competence. In M. S. Gazzaniga (Ed.), *The cognitive neurosciences* (pp. 205–218). Cambridge, MA: MIT Press.

Preyer, W. (1897). *Mental development in the child.* New York: Appleton. (Original work published 1893)

Pueschel, S. M., Scola, P. S., & Weiderman, L. E. (1995). *The special child: A source book for parents of children with developmental disabilities.* Baltimore: Brookes.

Pugh, L. C., & Milligan, R. A. (1998). Nursing intervention to increase the duration of breastfeeding. *Applied Nursing Research, 11,* 190–194.

Quinn, P. C., & Eimas, P. D. (1996). Perceptual organization and categorization in young infants. In C. Rovee-Collier & P. P. Lipsitt (Eds.), *Advances in infancy research* (Vol. 10, pp. 1–36). Norwood, NJ: Ablex.

Rand, W., Sweeney, M. E., & Vincent, E. L. (1930). *Growth and development of the young child.* Philadelphia: Saunders.

Rapaport, D. (1960). The structure of psychoanalytic theory: A systematizing attempt. *Psychological Issues, 2*(2, Monograph No. 6). New York: International Universities Press.

Ratner, N. B. (1996). From "signal to syntax": But what is the nature of the signal? In J. L. Morgan & K. Demuth (Eds.), *Signal to syntax: Bootstrapping from speech to grammar in early acquisition* (pp. 135–150). Mahwah, NJ: Erlbaum.

Rauscher, F. H., Shaw, G. L., & Ky, K. N. (1993). Music and spatial task performance. *Nature, 365,* 611.

Rauscher, F. H., Shaw, G. L., & Ky, K. N. (1995). Listening to Mozart enhances spatial-temporal reasoning: Towards a neurophysiological basis. *Neuroscience Letters, 185,* 44–47.

Rawson, B. (1991). Adult–child relationships in Roman society. In B. Rawson (Ed.), *Marriage, divorce, and children in ancient Rome* (pp. 7–30). Oxford: Oxford University Press.

Read, M. (1959). *Children of their fathers: Growing up among the Ngoni of Nyasaland.* London: Methuen.

Reznick, J. S., & Goldfield, B. A. (1992). Rapid change in lexical development in comprehension and production. *Developmental Psychology, 28,* 406–413.

Rheingold, H. L. (1968). Infancy: Infant development. In D . L. Sills (Ed.), *International encyclopedia of the social sciences* (Vol. 7, pp. 274–285). New York: Macmillan.

Rheingold, H. L. (1969). The social and socializing infant. In D. A. Goslin (Ed.), *Handbook of socialization theory and research* (pp. 779–790). Chicago: Rand McNally.

Rhoads, M. (1999). Management of acute diarrhea in infants. *Journal of Parenteral and Enteral Nutrition, 23,* S18-S19.

Ricciuti, H. N. (1993). Nutrition and mental development. *Current Directions in Psychological Science, 2*(2), 43–46.

Rice, F. P. (1998). *Intimate relationships, marriages, and families* (4th ed.). Mountain View, CA: Mayfield.

Richards, J. E., & Casey, B. J. (1992). Development of sustained visual attention in the human infant. In B. A. Campbell, H. Hayne, & R. Richardson (Eds.), *Attention and information processing in infants and adults* (pp. 30–60). Hillsdale, NJ: Erlbaum.

Rieber, R. W. (Ed.). (1987–1999). *The collected works of L. S. Vygotsky* (Vols. 1–6). New York: Plenum.

Righard, L. (1998). Are breastfeeding problems related to incorrect breastfeeding technique and the use of pacifiers and bottles? *Birth, 25,* 40–44.

Ritter, J. M., Casey, R. J., & Langlois, J. H. (1991). Adults' responses to infants varying in appearance of age and attractiveness. *Child Development, 62,* 68–82.

Robinson, C. C., Mandelco, B., Olsen, S. F., & Hart, C. H. (1995). Authoritative, authoritarian, and permissive parenting practices: Development of a new measure. *Psychological Reports, 77,* 819–830.

Robinson, J. L., Kagan, J., Reznick, J. S., & Corley, R. (1992). The inheritability of inhibited and uninhibited behavior: A twin study. *Developmental Psychology, 28,* 1030–1037.

Rochat, P. (1997). Early development of the ecological self. In C. Dent-Read & P. Zukow-Goldring, (Eds.), *Evolving explanations of development: Ecological approaches to organism-environment systems* (pp. 91–121). Washington, DC: American Psychological Association.

Rochat, P., & Goubet, N. (1995). Development of sitting and reaching in 5- to 6-month-old infants. *Infant Behavior and Development, 18,* 53–68.

Rock, A. M. L., Trainor, L. J., & Addison, T. L. (1999). Distinctive messages in infant-directed lullabies and play songs. *Developmental Psychology, 35,* 527–534.

Roffwarg, H. P., Muzio, J. N., & Dement, W. C. (1966). Ontogenetic development of the human sleep-dream cycle. *Science, 152,* 604–619.

Rogers, C. R. (1961). *On becoming a person: A therapist's view of psychotheraphy.* Boston: Houghton Mifflin.

Roggman, L. A., Langlois, J. H., Hubbs-Tait, L., & Rieser-Danner, L. A. (1994). Infant daycare, attachment, and the "filedrawer problem." *Child Development, 65,* 1429–1443.

Rogoff, B. (1990). *Apprenticeship in thinking: Cognitive development in social context.* New York: Oxford University Press.

Rogoff, B. (1991). The joint socialization of development by young children and adults. In M. Lewis & S. Feinman (Eds.), *Social influences and socialization in infancy* (pp. 253–280). New York: Plenum.

Rogoff, B. (1993). Children's guided participation and participatory appropriation in sociocultural activity. In R. H. Wozniak & K. W. Fischer (Eds.), *Development in context: Acting and thinking in specific contexts* (pp. 121–153). Hillsdale, NJ: Erlbaum.

Rogoff, B. (1998). Cognition as a collaborative process. In D. Kuhn & R. S. Siegler (Eds.), *Handbook of child psychology: Theoretical models of human development* (Vol. 1, 5th ed., pp. 679–744). New York: Wiley.

Rollins, J. (1990). Recall of baby pillows likely. *Pediatric Nursing, 16*(3), 282.

Romaine, S. (1995). *Bilingualism.* Oxford: Blackwell.

Rooks, J. P. (1999). *Midwifery and childbirth in America.* Philadelphia: Temple University Press.

Rosenstein, D., & Oster, H. (1988). Differential facial responses to four basic tastes in newborns. *Child Development, 59,* 1555–1568.

Rosser, R. (1994). *Cognitive development: Psychological and biological perspectives.* Boston: Allyn & Bacon.

Rotch, T. M. (1893). The general principles underlying all good methods of infant feeding. *Boston Medical and Surgical Journal, 129,* 505.

Roush, J., & McWilliam, R. A. (1994). Family-centered early intervention: Historical, philosophical, and legislative issues. In J. Roush & N. Matkin (Eds.), *Infants and toddlers with hearing loss: Family-centered assessment and intervention* (pp. 3–21). Timonium, MD: York.

Rousseau, J. J. (1911). *Emile.* London: Everyman's Library. (Original work published 1762).

Rovee-Collier, C. (1984). The ontogeny of learning and memory in human infancy. In R. Kail & N. E. Spear (Eds.), *Comparative perspectives on the development of memory* (pp. 103–134). Hillsdale, NJ: Erlbaum.

Rovee-Collier, C. (1987). Learning and memory in infancy. In J. D. Osofsky (Ed.), *Handbook of infant development* (2nd ed., pp. 98–148). New York: Wiley.

Rovee-Collier, C. K., & Bhatt, R. S. (1993). Evidence of long-term memory in infancy. In R. Vasta (Ed.), *Annals of child development,* (Vol. 9, pp. 1–45). London: Kingsley.

Rovee-Collier, C. K., & Shyi, G. (1992). A functional and cognitive analysis of infant long-term retention. In M. L. Howe, C. J. Brainerd, & V. I. Reyna (Eds.), *Development of long-term retention* (pp. 3–55). New York: Springer-Verlag.

Ruff, H. A., Lawson, K. R., Parrinello, R., & Weissberg, R. (1990). Long-term stability of individual differences in sustained attention in the early years. *Child Development, 61,* 60–75.

Russell, M. J., Mendelson, T., & Peeke, H. V. S. (1983). Mothers' identification of their infants' odors. *Ethology and Sociobiology, 4,* 29–31.

Rylko-Bauer, B. (1996). Abortion from a cross-cultural perspective: An introduction. *Social Science and Medicine, 42,* 479–482.

Saarni, C. (1999). *The development of emotional competence.* New York: Guilford.

Sadler, L., Belanger, K., Saftlas, A., Leaderer, J. E., Hellenbrand, K., MacSharry, J. E., & Bracken, M. B. (1999). Environmental tobacco smoke exposure and small-for-gestational age birth. *American Journal of Epidemiology, 150,* 695–705.

Sadler, T. (2000). *Langman's medical embryology* (8th ed.). Philadelphia: Lippincott-Raven.

Sagi, A. (1990). Attachment theory and research from a cross-cultural perspective. *Human Development, 33,* 10–22.

Sagi, A., & Hoffman, M. L. (1976). Empathic distress in the newborn. *Developmental Psychology, 12,* 175–176.

Sagi, A., van Ijzendoorn, M. H., & Koren-Karie, N. (1991). Primary appraisal of the Strange Situation: A cross-cultural analysis of preseparation episodes. *Developmental Psychology, 27,* 587–596.

St. James-Roberts, I. (1999). What is distinct about infants' "colic" cries? *Archives of Disease in Childhood, 80,* 56–61.

Salk, L. (1973). The role of the heartbeat in the relations between mother and infant. *Scientific American, 228*(5), 24–29.

Salzinger, S., Feldman, R. S., Hammer, M., & Rosario, M. (1993). The effects of physical abuse on children's social relationships. *Child Development, 64,* 169–187.

Salzman, Z. (1993). *Language, culture, & society: An introduction to linguistic anthropology.* Boulder, CO: Westview.

Sameroff, A. J. (Ed.). (1978). Organization and stability of newborn behavior: A commentary on the Brazelton Neonatal Behavior Assessment Scale. *Monographs of the Society for Research in Child Development, 43*(5–6, Serial No. 177).

Sarnat, H. B. (1978). Olfactory reflexes in the newborn infant. *Journal of Pediatrics, 92,* 624–626.

Saudino, K. J., & Eaton, W. O. (1991). Infant temperament and genetics: An objective twin study of motor activity level. *Child Development, 62,* 1167–1174.

Scafidi, F. A., Field, T., & Schanberg, S. M. (1993). Factors that predict which preterm infants benefit most from massage therapy. *Journal of Developmental and Behavioral Pediatrics, 14,* 176–180.

Scarr, S. (1985). Constructing psychology: Making facts and fables for our times. *American Psychologist, 40,* 499–512.

Scarr, S. (1992). Developmental theories for the 1990s: Development and individual differences. *Child Development, 63,* 1–19.

Scarr, S., & Deater-Deckard, K. (1997). Family effects on individual differences in development. In S. S. Luthar & J. A. Burack (Eds.), *Developmental psychopathology: Perspectives on adjustment, risk, and disorder* (pp. 115–136). New York: Cambridge University Press.

Scarr, S., & Eisenberg, M. (1993). Child care research: Issues, perspectives, and results. *Annual Review of Psychology, 44,* 613–644.

Schmuckler, M. A. (1996). Visual-propioceptive intermodal perception in infancy. *Infant Behavior and Development, 19,* 221–232.

Schneider-Rosen, K., & Wenz-Gross, M. (1990). Patterns of compliance from eighteen to thirty months of age. *Child Development, 61,* 104–112.

Schoendorf, K. C., & Kiely, J. L. (1992). Relationship of sudden infant death syndrome to smoking during and after pregnancy. *Pediatrics, 90,* 905–908.

Scholmerich, A., Lamb, M. E., Leyendecker, B., & Francasso, M. P. (1997). Mother–infant teaching interactions and attachment security in Euro-American and Central-American immigrant families. *Infant Behavior and Development, 20,* 165–174.

Scholten, C. M. (1985). *Childbearing in American society: 1650–1850.* New York: New York University Press.

Schultz, D. P., & Schultz, S. E. (1999). *A history of modern psychology* (7th ed.). Fort Worth, TX: Harcourt Brace.

Scott, J. A., & Binns, C. W. (1999). Factors associated with the initiation and duration of breastfeeding: A review of the literature. *Breastfeeding Review, 7,* 5–16.

Scott, J. R., Di Saia, P. J., Hammond, C. B., & Spellacy, W. N. (1999). *Danforth's obstetrics and gynecology* (8th ed.). Philadelphia: Lippincott Williams & Wilkins.

Sears, R. R. (1943). *Survey of objective studies of psychoanalytic concepts: A report prepared for the Committee on Social Adjustment.* New York: Social Sciences Research Council.

Sears, R. R., Maccoby, E. E., & Levin, H. (1957). *Patterns of child rearing.* Evanston, IL: Row, Peterson.

Segall, M. H., Berry, J. W., Dasen, P. R., & Poortinga, Y. H. (1992). *Human behavior in global perspective: An introduction to cross-cultural psychology.* Boston: Allyn & Bacon.

Seifer, R., Schiller, M., Sameroff, A. J., Resnick, S., & Riordan, K. (1996). Attachment, maternal sensitivity, and infant temperament during the first year of life. *Developmental Psychology, 32,* 12–25.

Self, P. A., Horowitz, F. D., & Paden, L. Y. (1972). Olfaction in newborn infants. *Developmental Psychology, 7,* 349–363.

Shapiro, J. L. (1987). The expectant father. *Psychology Today, 21*(1), 36–39, 42.

Shatz, M. (1991). Using cross-cultural research to inform us about the role of language in development. In M. H. Bornstein (Ed.), *Cultural approaches to parenting* (pp. 139–153). Hillsdale, NJ: Erlbaum.

Shelov, S. P. (Ed.). (1991). *Caring for your baby and young child: Birth to age 5.* New York: Bantam.

Sherman, T. (1985). Categorization skills in infants. *Child Development, 56,* 1561–1573.

Shirley, M. M. (1931–1933). *The first two years: A study of twenty-five babies* (Vols. 1–3). Minneapolis: University of Minnesota Press.

Shorter, E. (1982). *A history of women's bodies.* New York: Basic Books.

Shostak, M. (1976). A !Kung woman's memories of childhood. In R. B. Lee & I. DeVore (Eds.), *Kalahari hunters-gatherers: Studies of the !Kung San and their neighbors* (pp. 246–278). Cambridge, MA: Harvard University Press.

Shostak, M. (1981). *Nisa: The life and words of a !Kung woman.* Cambridge, MA: Harvard University Press.

Shyrock, R. H. (1960). *Medicine and society in America, 1660–1860.* New York: New York University Press.

Siegler, R. S. (1997). *Children's thinking* (3rd ed.). Upper Saddle River, NJ: Prentice-Hall.

Simion, F., Valenza, E., & Umilta, C. (1998). Mechanisms underlying face perception at birth. In F. Simion & G. Butterworth (Eds.), *The development of sensory, motor and cognitive capacities in early infancy: From perception to cognition* (pp. 87–101). Hove, England: Psychology Press.

Simon, S. (1997). *The brain: Our nervous system.* New York: Morrow.

Simons, R. L., Whitbeck, L. B., Conger, R. D., & Chyi-In, W. (1991). Intergenerational transmission of harsh parenting. *Developmental Psychology, 27,* 159–171.

Skinner, B. F. (1938). *The behavior of organisms: An experimental analysis.* New York: Appleton-Century-Crofts.

Skinner, B. F. (1969). *Contingencies of reinforcement: A theoretical analysis.* New York: Appleton-Century-Crofts.

Skinner, B. F. (1971). *Beyond freedom and dignity.* New York: Knopf.

Skodak, M., & Skeels, H. M. (1945). A follow-up study of children in adoptive homes. *Journal of Genetic Psychology, 66,* 21–58.

Skodak, M., & Skeels, H. M. (1949). A final follow-up study of one hundred adopted children. *Journal of Genetic Psychology, 75,* 85–125.

Slater, A., & Johnson, S. P. (1998). Visual sensory and perceptual abilities of the newborn: Beyond the blooming, buzzing confusion. In F. Simion & G. Butterworth (Eds.), *The development of sensory, motor and cognitive capacities in early infancy: From perception to cognition* (pp. 121–141). Hove, England: Psychology Press.

Small, M. F. (1999). *Our babies, ourselves: How biology and culture shape the way we parent.* New York: Doubleday.

Smith, B. A., & Blass, E. M. (1996). Taste-mediated claming in premature, preterm, and full-term human infants. *Developmental Psychology, 32,* 1084–1089.

Smith, D. B. (1982). The study of the family in early America: Trends, problems, and prospects. *William and Mary Quarterly, 39,* 2–28.

Snyder, L. H. (1935). *The principles of heredity.* Boston: Heath.

Solomon, J., George, C., & Ivins, B. (1987, April). *Mother—child interactions in the home and security of attachment at age 6.* Paper presented at the meeting of the Society for Research in Child Development, Baltimore.

Somer, E. (1995). *Nutrition for a healthy pregnancy: The complete guide to eating before, during, and after your pregnancy.* New York: Holt.

Sommer, B. B., & Sommer, R. (1997). *A practical guide to behavioral research: Tools and techniques.* Washington, DC: American Psychological Association.

Sorce, J. F., Emde, R. N., Campos, J., & Klinnert, M. D. (1985). Maternal emotional signaling: Its effect on the visual cliff behavior of 1-year-olds. *Developmental Psychology, 21,* 195–200.

Sosa, R., Kennell, J., Klaus, M., Robertson, S., & Urrutin, J. (1980). The effect of a supportive companion on perinatal problems, length of labor, and mother-infant interaction. *New England Journal of Medicine, 303,* 597–600.

Sparling, J., Lewis, I., Ramey, C. T., Wasik, B. H., Bryant, D. M., & LaVange, L. M. (1991). Partners: A curriculum to help premature, low birthweight infants get off to a good start. *Topics in Early Childhood Special Education, 11*(1), 36–55.

Spears, W. C., & Hohle, R. H. (1967). Sensory and perceptual processes in infants. In Y. Brackbill (Ed.), *Infancy and early childhood: A handbook and guide to human development* (pp. 51–121). New York: Free Press.

Spelke, E. S., & Newport, E. L. (1998). Nativism, empiricism, and the development of knowledge. In R. M. Lerner (Ed.), *Handbook of child psychology: Theoretical models of human development* (Vol. 1, 5th ed., pp. 199–254). New York: Wiley.

Spencer, H. (1897). *The principles of psychology* (Vols. 1–3). New York: Appleton.

Spencer, P. (1998). *Parenting guide to pregnancy & childbirth.* New York: Ballentine.

Spinetta, J. J., & Rigler, D. (1972). The child-abusing parent: A psychological review. *Psychological Bulletin, 77,* 296–304.

Spitz, R. A. (1945). Hospitalism. *Psychoanalytic Study of the Child, 1,* 53–74.

Spitz, R. A. (1946). Hospitalism: A follow-up report. *Psychoanalytic Study of the Child, 2,* 113–118.

Spitz, S. I. (1993). Your child's behavior: Questions about toilet-training issues. *American Baby, 55*(1), 24.

Spock, B. (1995, April). Dear Dr. Spock. *Parenting,* pp. 74–79.

Spock, B., & Parker, S. J. (1998). *Dr. Spock's baby and child care* (7th ed.). New York: Pocket Books.

Spring, J. H. (1997). *The American school, 1642–1996* (4th ed.). New York: McGraw-Hill.

Springen, K. (1998, June 1). The bountiful breast. *Newsweek, 131,* 71.

Sroufe, L. A. (1996). *Emotional development: The organization of emotional life in the early years.* Cambridge: Cambridge University Press.

Sroufe, L. A., Carlson, E., & Shulman, S. (1993). Individuals in relationships: Development from infancy through adolescence. In D. C. Funder, R. D. Parke, C. Tomlinson-Keasey, & K. Widaman (Eds.), *Studying lives through time: Personality and development* (pp. 315–342). Washington, DC: American Psychological Association.

Steele, H., Steele, M., & Fonagy, P. (1996). Associations among attachment classifications of mothers, fathers, and their infants. *Child Development, 67,* 541–555.

Steinberg, L., Dornbusch, S. M., & Brown, B. B. (1992). Ethnic differences in adolescent achievement: An ecological perspective. *American Psychologist, 47,* 723–729.

Steinberg, L., Mounts, N. S., Lamborn, S. D., & Dornbusch, S. M. (1991). Authoritative parenting and adolescent adjustment across various ecological niches. *Journal of Research on Adolsecents, 1,* 19–36.

Steiner, J. E. (1979). Human facial expressions in response to taste and smell stimuation. In H. W. Reese & L. P. Lipsitt (Eds.), *Advances in child development and behavior* (Vol. 13, pp. 257–295). New York: Academic Press.

Stern, D. N., Spieker, S., & MacKain, K. (1982). Intonation contours as signals in maternal speech to prelinguistic infants. *Developmental Psychology, 18,* 727–735.

Stevens, R. (1983). *Erik Erikson: An introduction.* New York: St. Martin's Press.

Stine, G. J. (1998a). *Acquired immune deficiency syndrome: Biological, medical, social, and legal issues* (3rd ed.). Upper Saddle River, NJ: Prentice-Hall.

Stine, G. J. (1998b). *AIDS update 1999: An annual overview of acquired immune deficiency syndrome.* New York: Simon & Schuster.

Stough, C., Kerkin, B., Bates, T., & Mangan, G. (1994). Music and spatial IQ. *Personality and Individual Differences, 17,* 695.

Strang, R. (1938). *An introduction to child study* (rev. ed.). New York: Macmillan.

Strathern, P. (1999). *The big idea: Crick, Watson, and DNA.* Garden City, NY: Doubleday.

Streissguth, A. P. (1997). *Fetal alcohol syndrome: A guide for families and communities.* Baltimore: Brookes.

Strelau, J. (1998). *Temperament: A psychological perspective.* New York: Plenum.

Stuart, H. C. (1960). *The healthy child: His physical, psychological, and social development.* Cambridge, MA: Harvard University Press.

Super, C. M. (1976). Environmental effects on motor development: The case of 'African infant precocity.' *Developmental Medicine and Child Neurology, 18,* 561–567.

Super, C. M. (1981). Behavioral developmental in infancy. In R. H. Munroe, R. L. Munroe, & B. B. Whiting (Eds.), *Handbook of cross-cultural human development* (pp. 181–270). New York: Garland.

Super, C. M., & Harkness, S. (1986). The developmental niche: A conceptualization of the interface of child and culture. *International Journal of Behavioral Development, 9,* 545–569.

Tabors, P. O. (1997). *One child, two languages: A guide for preschool educators of children learning English as a second language.* Baltimore: Brookes.

Takagi, D. Y. (1994). Japanese American families. In R. L. Taylor (Ed.), *Minority families in the United States: A multicultural perspective* (pp. 146–163). Belmont, CA: Wadsworth.

Takahashi, K. (1986). Examining the strange situation procedure with Japanese mothers and 12-month-old infants. *Developmental Psychology, 22,* 265–270.

Takahashi, K. (1990). Are the key assumptions of the "Strange Situation" procedure universal? A view from Japanese research. *Human Development, 33,* 23–30.

Talbot, E. (1882). Papers on infant development. *Journal of Social Science, 15.*

Tanner, J. M. (1990). *Foetus into man: Physical growth from conception to maturity* (rev. ed.). Cambridge, MA: Harvard University Press.

Taylor, R. L. (1994). Black American families. In R. L. Taylor (Ed.), *Minority families in the United States: A multicultural perspective* (pp. 19–46). Englewood Cliffs: Prentice-Hall.

Ten Bensel, R. W., Rheinberger, M. M., & Radbill, S. X. (1997). Children in a world of violence: The roots of child maltreatment. In M. E. Helfer, R. S. Kempe, & R. D. Krugman

(Eds.), *The battered child* (pp. 3–28). Chicago: University of Chicago Press.

Thelen, E. (1987). The role of motor development in developmental psychology: A view of the past and an agenda for the future. In N. Eisenberg (Ed.), *Contemporary topics in developmental psychology* (pp. 3–33). New York: Wiley.

Thelen, E. (1989). The (re)discovery of motor development: Learning new things from an old field. *Developmental Psychology, 25,* 946–949.

Thelen, E. (1990). Dynamical systems and the generation of individual differences. In J. Colombo & J. Fagen (Eds.), *Individual differences in infancy: Reliability, stability, prediction* (pp. 19–43). Hillsdale, NJ: Erlbaum.

Thelen, E., & Spencer, J. P. (1998). Postural control during reaching in young infants: A dynamic systems approach. *Neuroscience and Biobehavioral Reviews, 22,* 507–514.

Thelen, E., & Ulrich, B. D. (1991). Hidden skills: A dynamic systems analysis of treadmill stepping during the first year. *Monographs of the Society for Research in Child Development, 56*(1, Serial No. 223).

Thoman, E. B., & Whitney, M. P. (1990). Behavioral states in infants: Individual differences and individual analyses. In J. Colombo & J. Fagen (Eds.), *Individual differences in infancy: Reliability, stability, prediction* (pp. 113–135). Hillsdale, NJ: Erlbaum.

Thomas, A., & Chess, S. (1977). *Temperament and development.* New York: Brunner/Mazel.

Thomas, A., & Chess, S. (1980). *The dynamics of psychological development.* New York: Brunner/Mazel.

Thomas, A., Chess, S., & Birch, H. (1970). The origin of personality. *Scientific American, 223*(2), 102–109.

Thomas, A., Chess, S., Birch, H., Hertzig, M. E., & Korn, S. (1963). *Behavioral individuality in early childhood.* New York: New York University Press.

Thompson, R. A. (1990). Vulnerability in research: A developmental perspective on research risk. *Child Development, 61,* 1–16.

Thompson, R. A. (1991a). Attachment theory and research. In M. Lewis (Ed.), *Child and adolescent psychiatry: A comprehensive text-*

book (pp. 100–108). Baltimore: Williams & Wilkins.

Thompson, R. A. (1991b). Infant day care: Concerns, controversies, choices. In J. V. Lerner & N. L. Galambos (Eds.), *Employed mothers and their children* (pp. 9–36). New York: Garland.

Thompson, R. A. (1993). Socioemotional development: Enduring issues and new challenges. *Developmental Review, 13,* 372–402.

Thorp, J. M., & Bowes, W. A. (1989). Episiotomy: Can its routine use be defended? *American Journal of Obstetrics and Gynecology, 160,* 1027–1033.

Tiedemann, D. (1927). Tiedemann's observations on the development of the mental faculties of children. *Pedagogical Seminary and Journal of Genetic Psychology, 34,* 205–230. (Original work published 1787)

Toda, S., Fogel, A., & Kawai, M. (1990). Maternal speech to three-month-old infants in the United States and Japan. *Journal of Child Language, 17,* 657–674.

Tomasello, M. (1996). The cultural roots of language. In B. M. Velichkovsky & D. M. Rumbaugh (Eds.), *Communicating meaning: The evolution and development of language* (pp. 275–307). Mahwah, NJ: Erlbaum.

Trelease, J. (1995). *The read-aloud handbook* (4th ed.). New York: Penguin.

Triebenbacher, S. L. (1997). Children's use of transitional objects: Parental attitudes and perceptions. *Child Psychiatry and Human Development, 27,* 221–230.

Tronick, E. Z. (1989). Emotions and emotional communication in infants. *American Psychologist, 44,* 112–119.

Tronick, E. Z., & Winn, S. A. (1992). The neurobehavioral organization of Efe (pygmy) infants. *Journal of Developmental and Behavioral Pediatrics, 13,* 421–424.

Tulloch, J. D., Brown, B. S., Jacobs, H. L., Prugh, D. G., & Greene, W. A. (1964). Normal heartbeat sound and the behavior of newborn infants: A replication study. *Psychosomatic Medicine, 26,* 661–670.

Ulich, R. (1954). *Three thousand years of educational wisdom: Selections from great documents* (2nd ed.). Cambridge, MA: Harvard University Press.

Ullstadius, E. (1998). Neonatal imitation in a mother–infant setting. *Early Development and Parenting, 7,* 1–8.

UNICEF. (1998). *The state of the world's children 1999.* New York: Author.

U.S. Census Bureau. (1997). *How we are changing: The demographic state of the nation, 1997.* Washington, DC: Author.

Valenza, E., Simion, F., Cassia, V. M., & Umilta, C. (1996). Face perception at birth. *Journal of Experimental Psychology: Human Perception and Performance, 22,* 892–903.

Van den Bergh, B. R. (1990). The influence of maternal emotions during pregnancy on fetal and neonatal behavior. *Pre- and Peri-Natal Psychology Journal, 5,* 119–130.

Van der Fits, I. B. M., & Hadders-Algra, M. (1998). *Neuroscience and Biobehavioral Reviews, 22,* 521–526.

Vauclair, J. (1996). *Animal cognition: An introduction to modern comparative psychology.* Cambridge, MA: Harvard University Press.

Vaughn, B. E., Stevenson-Hinde, J., Waters, E., Kotsaftis, A., Lefever, G. B., Shouldice, A., Trudel, M., & Belsky, J. (1992). Attachment security and temperament in infancy and early childhood: Some conceptual clarifications. *Developmental Psychology, 28,* 463–473.

Verba, M. (1994). The beginnings of collaboration in peer interaction. *Human Development, 37,* 123–139.

Vidal, F. (1994). *Piaget before Piaget.* Cambridge, MA: Harvard University Press.

Vihman, M. M. (1996). *Phonological development: The origins of language in the child.* London: Blackwell.

Vohr, B. R., & Garcia-Coll, C. T. (1988). Follow-up studies of high-risk low-birthweight infants: Changing trends. In H. E. Fitzgerald, B. M. Lester, & M. W. Yogman (Eds.), *Theory and research in behavioral pediatrics* (Vol. 4, pp. 1–65). New York: Plenum.

Vygotsky, L. S. (1962). *Thought and language.* Cambridge, MA: MIT Press.

Vygotsky, L. S. (1978). Interaction between learning and development. In M. Cole, V. John-Steiner, S. Scribner, & E. Souberman (Eds.), *Mind in society: The development of higher psychological processes* (pp. 79–91). Cambridge, MA: Harvard University Press.

Vygotsky, L. S. (1987). Thinking and speech. In R. W. Rieber & A. S. Carton (Eds.), *The collected works of L. S. Vygotsky* (Vol. 1, pp. 37–285). New York: Plenum.

Wachs, T. D., Sigman, M., Bishry, Z., Moussa, W., Jerome, N., Neumann, C., Bwibo, N., & McDonald, M. A. (1992). Caregiver child interaction patterns in two cultures in relation to nutritional intake. *International Journal of Behavioral Development, 15,* 1–18.

Waddington, C. H. (1957). *The strategy of the genes: A discussion of some aspects of theoretical biology.* London: Allen & Unwin.

Wakschlag, L. S., Chase-Lansdale, P. L., & Brooks-Gunn, J. (1996). Not just "ghosts in the nursery": Contemporaneous intergenerational relationships and parenting in young African-American families. *Child Development, 67,* 2131–2147.

Walden, T. A., & Baxter, A. (1989). The effect of context and age on social referencing. *Child Development, 60,* 1511–1518.

Walker-Andrews, A. S., & Dickson, L. R. (1997). Infants' understanding of affect. In S. Hala (Ed.), *The development of social cognition* (pp. 161–186). Hove, England: Psychology Press.

Walton, G. E., Armstrong, E. S., & Bower, T. G. R. (1997). Faces as forms in the world of the newborn. *Infant Behavior and Development, 20,* 537–543.

Warren, D. H. (1991). *Blindness and early childhood development.* New York: American Foundation for the Blind Press.

Watson, J. B. (1914). *Behavior: An introduction to comparative psychology.* New York: Holt.

Watson, J. B. (1924). *Behaviorism.* New York: Norton.

Watson, J. B. (1928). *Psychological care of infant and child.* New York: Norton.

Watson, J. D., & Crick, F. H. C. (1953). Molecular structure of nucleic acids. *Nature, 171,* 737–738.

Watson, J. B., & Rayner, R. (1920). Conditioned emotion reactions. *Journal of Experimental Psychology, 3,* 1–14.

Wecht, C. H. (1999). Shaken baby syndrome. *American Journal of Forensic Medicine and Pathology, 20,* 301–302.

Wegman, M. E. (1996). Infant mortality: Some international comparisons. *Pediatrics, 98,* 1020–1027.

Wells, R. V. (1982). *Revolutions in Americans' lives: A demographic perspective on the history of Americans, their families, and their society.* Westport, CT: Greenwood Press.

Weiner, L., & Morse, B. A. (1990). Alcohol, pregnancy, and fetal development. In R. C. Engs (Ed.), *Women: Alcohol and other drugs* (pp. 61–68). Dubuque, IA: Kendall/Hunt.

Werner, E. E. (1995). Resilience in development. *Current Directions in Psychological Science, 4,* 81–85.

Werner, E. E., & Smith, R. S. (1982). *Vulnerable but invincible: A longitudinal study of resilient children and youth.* New York: McGraw-Hill.

Werner, H. (1957). The concept of development from a comparative and organismic view. In D. B. Harris (Ed.), *The concept of development: An issue in the study of human behavior* (pp. 125–148). Minneapolis: University of Minnesota Press.

Wertsch, J. V. (1985). *Vygotsky and the social formation of the mind.* Cambridge, MA: Harvard University Press.

Wertsch, J. V. (1991). *Voices of the mind: A sociocultural approach to mediated action.* Cambridge, MA: Harvard University Press.

Wertsch, J. V., & Tulviste, P. (1992). L. S. Vygotsky and contemporary developmental psychology. *Developmental Psychology, 28,* 548–557.

Wertz, R. W., & Wertz, D. C. (1977). *Lying-in: A history of childbirth in America.* New York: Free Press.

Wexler, K. (1999). Maturation and growth of grammar. In W. C. Ritchie & T. K. Bhatia (Eds.), *Handbook of child language acquisition* (pp. 55–109). San Diego: Academic Press.

Whiffen, V. E., & Gotlib, I. H. (1989). Infants of postpartum depressed mothers: Temperament and cognitive status. *Journal of Abnormal Psychology, 98,* 274–279.

White, B. L. (1985). *The first three years of life* (rev. ed.). Englewood Cliffs, NJ: Prentice-Hall.

Whiting, B. B., & Edwards, C. P. (1992). *Children of different worlds: The formation of social behavior.* Cambridge, MA: Harvard University Press.

Wiener, D. N. (1996). *B. F. Skinner: Benign anarchist.* Boston: Allyn & Bacon.

Wille, D. E. (1991). Relation of preterm birth with quality of infant-mother attachment at one year. *Infant Behavioral and Development, 14,* 227–240.

Willer, B. (1994). A conceptual framework for early childhood professional development. In J. Johnson & J. McCracken (Eds.), *The early childhood career lattice: Perspectives on professional development.* (pp. 4–23). Washington, DC: NAEYC.

Williams, R. L., Chalmers, T. C., Stange, K. C., Chalmers, F. T., & Bowlin, S. J. (1993). Use of antibiotics in preventing recurrent acute otitis media and in treating otitis media with effusion. *Journal of the American Medical Association, 270,* 1344–1351.

Wilson, J. D., George, F. W., & Griffin, J. E. (1981). The hormonal control of sexual development. *Science, 211,* 1278–1284.

Winzer, M. A. (1993). *The history of special education.* Washington, DC: Gallaudet University Press.

Wolff, P. H. (1959). Observations of newborn infants. *Psychosomatic Medicine, 21,* 110–118.

Wolff, P. H. (1966). The causes, controls, and organization of behavior in the neonate. *Psychological Issues, 5*(1, Serial No. 17).

Wolff, P. H. (1969). The natural history of crying and other vocalization in early infancy. In B. M. Foss (Ed.), *Determinants of infant behaviour* (Vol. 4, pp. 81–109). London: Methuen.

Wong, D. L. (Ed.). (1998). *Whaley and Wong's nursing care of infants and children* (6th ed.). St. Louis: Mosby.

Wong, M. G. (1998). The Chinese-American family. In C. H. Mindel, R. W. Habenstein, & R. Wright (Eds.), *Ethnic families in America: Patterns and variations* (4th ed., pp. 284–310). Upper Saddle River, NJ: Prentice-Hall.

Wood, E. A. (1888). Address on dietetics. *Journal of the American Medical Association, 11,* 38–39.

Wynn, K. (1992). Addition and subtraction by human infants. *Nature, 358,* 749–750.

Wynn, K. (1995). Infants possess a system of numerical knowledge. *Current Directions in Psychological Science, 4,* 172–177.

Yavas, M. (1995). Phonological selectivity in the first fifty words of a bilingual child. *Language and Speech, 38,* 189–202.

Young, D. (1997). A new push to reduce cesareans in the United States. *Birth, 24,* 1–3.

Younger, B. (1990). Infants' detection of correlations among feature categories. *Child Development, 61,* 614–620.

Younger, B., & Gotlieb, S. (1988). Development of categorization skills: Changes in the nature or structure of infant form categories? *Developmental Psychology, 24,* 611–619.

Yu, K. H., & Kim, L. I. (1983). The growth and development of Korean-American children. In G. J. Powell (Ed.), T*he psychosocial development of minority group children* (pp. 147–158). New York: Brunner/Mazel.

Zeskind, P. S., & Lester, B. M. (1978). Acoustic features and auditory perceptions of the cries of newborns with prenatal and perinatal complications. *Child Development, 49,* 580–589.

Zeskind, P. S., & Marshall, T. R. (1988). The relation between variations in pitch and maternal perceptions of infant crying. *Child Development, 59,* 193–196.

Zeskind, P. S., & Shingler, E. A. (1991). Child abusers' perceptual responses to newborn infant cries varying in pitch. *Infant Behavior and Development, 14,* 335–347.

Zigler, E., & Hall, N. W. (1989). Physical child abuse in America: Past, present, and future. In D. Cicchetti & V. Carlson (Eds.), *Child maltreatment: Theory and research on the causes and consequences of child abuse and neglect* (pp. 38–75). Cambridge: Cambridge University Press.

Zinn, M. B. (1994). Adaptation and continuity in Mexican-origin families. In R. L. Taylor (Ed.), *Minority families in the United States: Amulticultural perspective* (pp. 64–81). Belmont, CA: Wadsworth.

Name Index

SUBJECT INDEX